Hike AMERICA™

OREGON

Contact

Dear Readers:

Every effort was made to make this the most accurate, informative, and easy-to-use guidebook on the planet. Any comments, suggestions, and corrections regarding this guide are welcome and should be sent to:

Outside America™
c/o Editorial Dept.
300 West Main St., Ste. A
Charlottesville, VA 22903
editorial@outside-america.com
www.outside-america.com

We'd love to hear from you so we can make future editions and future guides even better.

Thanks and happy trails!

Hike AMERICA™

OREGON

An Atlas of Oregon's Greatest
Hiking Adventures

by Lizann Dunegan

The Globe Pequot Press

Guilford, Connecticut

Published by
The Globe Pequot Press
P.O. Box 480
Guilford, CT 06437
www.globe-pequot.com

Produced by
Beachway Press Publishing, Inc.
300 West Main St., Ste A
Charlottesville, VA 22903
www.beachway.com

Cover Design Beachway Press

Photographer Lizann Dunegan

Maps designed and produced by Beachway Press

Find Outside America™ at **www.outside-america.com**

*Cover Photo: An autumn hike along Deep Creek Trail near
Telluride, Colorado. Wilson Peaks in the background. Photo by
Amanda Williams*

Library of Congress Cataloging-in-Publication Data
is available

ISBN 0-7627-0762-3

Printed in the United States of America
First Edition/First Printing

Acknowledgments

I've been very fortunate to be able to work on a second guidebook for the Outside America™ guidebook series. *Hike America: Oregon* has been a labor of love from the start. For the past 10 years, I've been hiking trails all throughout Oregon. When the opportunity arose to write about some of these places, I jumped at the chance. Working on this guidebook has consumed my life for the past year—just ask my friends who haven't seen much of me. I've spent countless hours hiking trails, driving to remote regions of Oregon, and even more time sitting in front of my computer trying to capture what I think are some of the best trails this state has to offer.

This book wouldn't have been possible without Ken Skeen, who was my hiking partner on most of the hikes in this book as well as chauffeur, photographer, and in-house editor. Ken has legs of iron and the longest steps you can imagine—especially going up hills, where he always seems to go even faster. He set a good pace for me on many trails and was always a source of inspiration when we put in long hours driving to remote locations and had over 40 miles worth of hikes to complete in a two- or three-day period. My other two constant companions over the past year were my two Border collies, Levi and Sage. They always make our outings more fun with their sense of play and natural curiosity—you'll find these two in pictures scattered throughout this book. I think more and more hikers want to take their canine pals on trails with them, and you'll find most of the trails in this book allow dogs. Other hiking partners I'd like to thank are Rahul Ravel, Sheila Blacstone, Mike Paholsky, and Fred Siebenmann for having the patience to wait for me while I took notes on hikes and shot pictures. I'd also like to thank my parents and friends—who are very supportive of all of my writing endeavors—and Heather Sharfeddin for her great illustrations.

Also, thanks to Ryan Croxton and to the other folks at Beachway Press who were very patient with me as I was trying to finish up the manuscript for this book. Without their help, this book would not be possible.

Lizann Dunegan
October 2000

Table of

Contents

Central Oregon

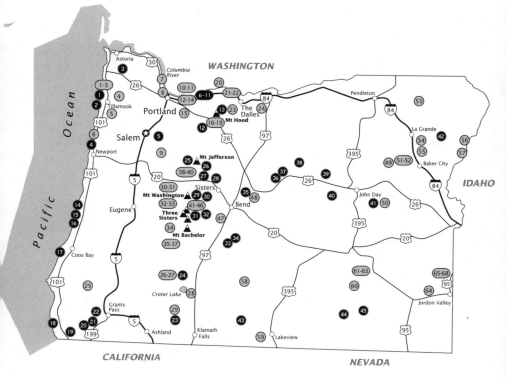

HIKES AT A GLANCE

1. Cape Meares State Park

Multiple Route Options

Length: Multiple trail lengths
Difficulty Rating: Easy
Time: 15–30 minutes each
Nearby: Tillamook, OR

2. Cape Lookout

Length: 5.4-mile out-and-back
Difficulty Rating: Easy
Time: 2–3 hours
Nearby: Tillamook, OR

3. Saddle Mountain

Length: 5.2-mile out-and-back
Difficulty Rating: Difficult
Time: 2–3 hours
Nearby: Cannon Beach, OR

4. Yaquina Head Outstanding Natural Area

Multiple Route Options

Length: 4.2-mile out-and-back
Difficulty Rating: Easy to Moderate
Time: 15 min.–1 hour
Nearby: Newport, OR

5. Silver Falls State Park

Length: 6.9-mile loop
Difficulty Rating: Moderate
Time: 4–5 hours
Nearby: Silver Falls, OR

6. Angels Rest

Length: 4.4-mile out-and-back
Difficulty Rating: Moderate
Time: 2–3 hours
Nearby: Portland, OR

7. Larch Mountain

Length: 13.6-mile out-and-back
Difficulty Rating: Difficult
Time: 6–8 hours
Nearby: Portland, OR

8. Horsetail, Oneonta, and Triple Falls

Length: 5.4-mile out-and-back
Difficulty Rating: Moderate
Time: 2–3 hours
Nearby: Portland, OR

9. Munra Point

Length: 2.0-mile out-and-back
Difficulty Rating: Difficult
Time: 4–5 hours
Nearby: Portland, OR

10. Wahclella Falls

Length: 2.2-mile out-and-back
Difficulty Rating: Easy
Time: 1 hour
Nearby: Portland, OR

11. Eagle Creek to High Bridge

Length: 7.0-mile out-and-back
Difficulty Rating: Moderate
Time: 3–4 hours
Nearby: Portland, OR

12. Salmon River

Length: 7.6-mile out-and-back
Difficulty Rating: Easy to Moderate
Time: 4–6 hours
Nearby: Zigzag, OR

13. Cooper Spur Trail

Length: 7.6-mile out-and-back
Difficulty Rating: Difficult
Time: 4–6 hours
Nearby: Hood River, OR

14. Cape Perpetua Scenic Area

Multiple Route Options

Length: 26+-miles
Difficulty Rating: Easy to Difficult
Time: 1–6 hours
Nearby: Yachats, OR

15. Heceta Head Lighthouse

Length: 1.0-mile out-and-back
Difficulty Rating: Easy
Time: 1 hour
Nearby: Florence, OR

16. Sutton Creek Sand Dunes

Multiple Route Options

Length: Varies
Difficulty Rating: Easy to Moderate
Time: 1–4 hours
Nearby: Florence, OR

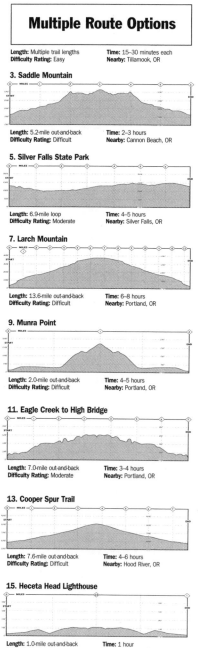

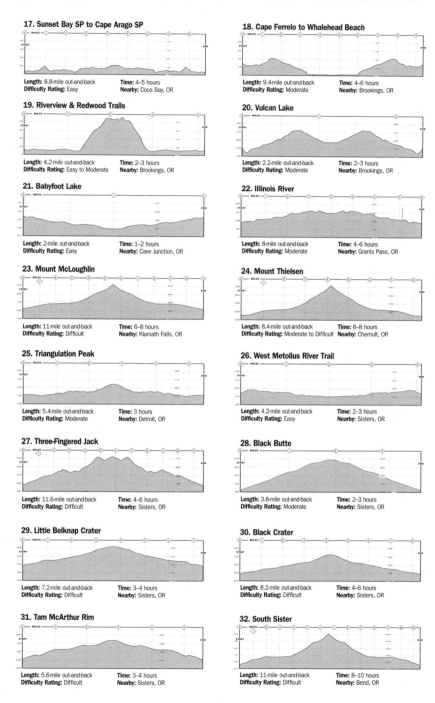

17. Sunset Bay SP to Cape Arago SP

Length: 8.8-mile out-and-back
Difficulty Rating: Easy
Time: 4–5 hours
Nearby: Coos Bay, OR

18. Cape Ferrelo to Whalehead Beach

Length: 9.4-mile out-and-back
Difficulty Rating: Moderate
Time: 4–6 hours
Nearby: Brookings, OR

19. Riverview & Redwood Trails

Length: 4.2-mile out-and-back
Difficulty Rating: Easy to Moderate
Time: 2–3 hours
Nearby: Brookings, OR

20. Vulcan Lake

Length: 2.2-mile out-and-back
Difficulty Rating: Moderate
Time: 2–3 hours
Nearby: Brookings, OR

21. Babyfoot Lake

Length: 2-mile out-and-back
Difficulty Rating: Easy
Time: 1–2 hours
Nearby: Cave Junction, OR

22. Illinois River

Length: 8-mile out-and-back
Difficulty Rating: Moderate
Time: 4–6 hours
Nearby: Grants Pass, OR

23. Mount McLoughlin

Length: 11-mile out-and-back
Difficulty Rating: Difficult
Time: 6–8 hours
Nearby: Klamath Falls, OR

24. Mount Thielsen

Length: 8.4-mile out-and-back
Difficulty Rating: Moderate to Difficult
Time: 6–8 hours
Nearby: Chemult, OR

25. Triangulation Peak

Length: 5.4-mile out-and-back
Difficulty Rating: Moderate
Time: 3 hours
Nearby: Detroit, OR

26. West Metolius River Trail

Length: 4.2-mile out-and-back
Difficulty Rating: Easy
Time: 2–3 hours
Nearby: Sisters, OR

27. Three-Fingered Jack

Length: 11.6-mile out-and-back
Difficulty Rating: Difficult
Time: 4–6 hours
Nearby: Sisters, OR

28. Black Butte

Length: 3.8-mile out-and-back
Difficulty Rating: Moderate
Time: 2–3 hours
Nearby: Sisters, OR

29. Little Belknap Crater

Length: 7.2-mile out-and-back
Difficulty Rating: Difficult
Time: 3–4 hours
Nearby: Sisters, OR

30. Black Crater

Length: 8.2-mile out-and-back
Difficulty Rating: Difficult
Time: 4–6 hours
Nearby: Sisters, OR

31. Tam McArthur Rim

Length: 5.6-mile out-and-back
Difficulty Rating: Difficult
Time: 3–4 hours
Nearby: Sisters, OR

32. South Sister

Length: 11-mile out-and-back
Difficulty Rating: Difficult
Time: 8–10 hours
Nearby: Bend, OR

HIKES AT A GLANCE

33. Paulina Peak

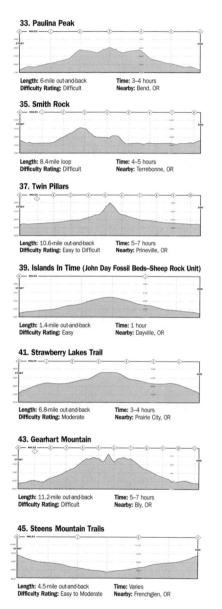

Length: 6-mile out-and-back
Difficulty Rating: Difficult
Time: 3–4 hours
Nearby: Bend, OR

34. Big Obsidian Flow Trail

Length: 0.7-mile loop
Difficulty Rating: Easy
Time: 1 hour
Nearby: Bend, OR

35. Smith Rock

Length: 8.4-mile loop
Difficulty Rating: Difficult
Time: 4–5 hours
Nearby: Terrebonne, OR

36. Steins Pillar

Length: 5.2-mile out-and-back
Difficulty Rating: Moderate
Time: 2 hours
Nearby: Prineville, OR

37. Twin Pillars

Length: 10.6-mile out-and-back
Difficulty Rating: Easy to Difficult
Time: 5–7 hours
Nearby: Prineville, OR

38. Painted Hills Unit (John Day Fossil Beds N.M)

Multiple Route Options

Length: 3.0-mile
Difficulty Rating: Easy to Moderate
Time: 30–90 minutes
Nearby: Mitchell, OR

39. Islands In Time (John Day Fossil Beds–Sheep Rock Unit)

Length: 1.4-mile out-and-back
Difficulty Rating: Easy
Time: 1 hour
Nearby: Dayville, OR

40. Black Canyon Trail

Length: 5.2-mile out-and-back
Difficulty Rating: Difficult
Time: 3–4 hours
Nearby: Dayville, OR

41. Strawberry Lakes Trail

Length: 6.8-mile out-and-back
Difficulty Rating: Moderate
Time: 3–4 hours
Nearby: Prairie City, OR

42. Lakes Basin

Length: 20.2-mile out-and-back
Difficulty Rating: Difficult
Time: 10–12 hours
Nearby: Lostine, OR

43. Gearhart Mountain

Length: 11.2-mile out-and-back
Difficulty Rating: Difficult
Time: 5–7 hours
Nearby: Bly, OR

44. Poker Jim Ridge

Length: 4-mile out-and-back
Difficulty Rating: Moderate
Time: 2 hours
Nearby: Plush, OR

45. Steens Mountain Trails

Length: 4.5-mile out-and-back
Difficulty Rating: Easy to Moderate
Time: Varies
Nearby: Frenchglen, OR

Hikes for Backpackers

Hike 11: Eagle Creek to High Bridge
Hike 17: Sunset Bay State Park to Cape Arago State Park
Hike 18: Cape Ferrelo to Whalehead Beach
Hike 27: Three-Fingered Jack
Hike 29: Little Belknap Crater
Hike 31: Tam McArthur Rim
Hike 32: South Sister
Hike 37: Twin Pillars
Hike 40: Black Canyon
Hike 41: Strawberry Lakes Trail
Hike 42: Lakes Basin
Hike 44: Poker Jim Ridge
Hike 45: Steens Mountain Trails

Hikes for Beach/Coast Lovers

Hike 1: Cape Meares State Park
Hike 2: Cape Lookout
Hike 4: Yaquina Head Outstanding Natural Area
Hike 14: Cape Perpetua Scenic Area
Hike 16: Sutton Creek Recreational Area
Hike 17: Sunset Bay State Park to Cape Arago State Park
Hike 18: Cape Ferrelo to Whalehead Beach

Hikes for Children and Beginning Hikers

Hike 1: Cape Meares State Park
Hike 4: Yaquina Head Outstanding Natural Area
Hike 10: Wahclella Falls
Hike 12: Salmon River Trail
Hike 14: Cape Perpetua Scenic Area
Hike 15: Heceta Head Lighthouse
Hike 16: Sutton Creek Recreational Area
Hike 19: Riverview and Redwood Nature Trails
Hike 21: Babyfoot Lake
Hike 26: West Metolius River Trail
Hike 28: Black Butte
Hike 34: Big Obsidian Flow Trail
Hike 35: Smith Rock State Park
Hike 38: Painted Hills Unit Trails – John Day Fossil Beds National Monument
Hike 39: Island in Time Trail (John Day Fossils Beds – Sheep Rock Unit)
Hike 45: Steens Mountain Trails

HIKES AT A GLANCE

Hikes for Geology Lovers

Hike 3: Saddle Mountain
Hike 9: Munra Point
Hike 13: Cooper Spur Trail
Hike 17: Sunset Bay State Park to Cape Arago State Park
Hike 22: Illinois River
Hike 23: Mount McLoughlin
Hike 24: Mount Thielsen
Hike 27: Three-Fingered Jack
Hike 29: Little Belknap Crater
Hike 30: Black Crater
Hike 31: Tam McArthur Rim
Hike 32: South Sister
Hike 34: Big Obsidian Flow Trail
Hike 35: Smith Rock State Park
Hike 36: Steins Pillar
Hike 37: Twin Pillars
Hike 38: Painted Hills Unit Trails – John Day Fossil Beds National Monument
Hike 39: Island in Time Trail (John Day Fossils Beds – Sheep Rock Unit)
Hike 42: Lakes Basin
Hike 43: Gearhart Mountain
Hike 45: Steens Mountain Trails

Hikes for Creek/River Lovers

Hike 5: Silver Falls State Park
Hike 7: Larch Mountain
Hike 10: Wahclella Falls
Hike 11: Eagle Creek to High Bridge
Hike 12: Salmon River Trail
Hike 19: Riverview and Redwood Nature Trails
Hike 22: Illinois River
Hike 26: West Metolius River Trail
Hike 35: Smith Rock State Park
Hike 37: Twin Pillars
Hike 40: Black Canyon Trail
Hike 41: Strawberry Lakes Trail
Hike 42: Lakes Basin

Hikes for Lake Lovers

Hike 20: Vulcan Lake
Hike 21: Babyfoot Lake
Hike 33: Paulina Peak
Hike 41: Strawberry Lakes Trail
Hike 42: Lakes Basin
Hike 45: Steens Mountain Trails

Hikes for Lighthouse Lovers

Hike 4: Yaquina Head Outstanding Natural Area
Hike 15: Heceta Head Lighthouse
Hike 17: Sunset Bay State Park to Cape Arago State Park

Hikes for Peak Baggers

Hike 3: Saddle Mountain
Hike 7: Larch Mountain
Hike 9: Munra Point
Hike 13: Cooper Spur Trail
Hike 23: Mount McLoughlin
Hike 24: Mount Thielsen
Hike 25: Triangulation Peak
Hike 27: Three-Fingered Jack
Hike 28: Black Butte
Hike 30: Black Crater
Hike 31: Tam McArthur Rim
Hike 32: South Sister
Hike 33: Paulina Peak
Hike 37: Twin Pillars
Hike 43: Gearhart Mountain
Hike 45: Steens Mountain Trails

Hikes for Waterfall Lovers

Hike 5: Silver Falls State Park
Hike 6: Angels Rest
Hike 7: Larch Mountain
Hike 8: Horsetail, Oneonta, and Triple Falls
Hike 10: Wahclella Falls
Hike 11: Eagle Creek to High Bridge
Hike 41: Strawberry Lakes Trail
Hike 42: Lakes Basin

Hikes for Hot Spring Lovers

Hike 44: Poker Jim Ridge
Hon. Men. 9: Bagby Hot Springs
Hon. Men. 26: Umpqua Hot Springs
Hon. Men. 35: Wall Creek Warm Springs
Hon. Men. 37: McCredie Hot Springs

HOW TO USE THIS BOOK

Take a close enough look and you'll find that this little guide contains just about everything you'll ever need to choose, plan for, enjoy, and survive a hike in the state of Oregon. We've done everything but load your pack and tie up your bootlaces. Stuffed with 384 pages of useful Oregon-specific information, *Hike America: Oregon*™ features 45 mapped and cued hikes and 68 honorable mentions, as well as everything from advice on getting into shape to tips on getting the most out of hiking with your children or your dog. And as you'd expect with any Outside America™ guide, you get the best maps man and technology can render. With so much information, the only question you may have is: How do I sift through it all? Well, we answer that, too.

We've designed our Hike America™ series to be highly visual, for quick reference and ease-of-use. What this means is that the most pertinent information rises quickly to the top, so you don't have to waste time poring through bulky hike descriptions to get mileage cues or elevation stats. They're set aside for you. And yet, an Outside America™ guide doesn't read like a laundry list. Take the time to dive into a hike description and you'll realize that this guide is not just a good source of information; it's a good read. And so, in the end, you get the best of both worlds: a quick-reference guide and an engaging look at a region. Here's an outline of the guide's major components.

WHAT YOU'LL FIND IN A *HIKE AMERICA*™ GUIDE. Let's start with the individual chapter. To aid in quick decision-making, we start each chapter with a **Hike Summary**. This short overview gives you a taste of the hiking adventure at hand. You'll learn about the trail terrain and what surprises the route has to offer. If your interest is peaked, you can read more. If not, skip to the next Hike Summary. The **Hike Specs** are fairly self-explanatory. Here you'll find the quick, nitty-gritty details of the hike: where the trailhead is located, the nearest town, hike length, approximate hiking time, difficulty rating, type of trail terrain, and what other trail users you may encounter. Our **Getting There** section gives you dependable directions from a nearby city right down to where you'll want to park. The **Hike Description** is the meat of the chapter. Detailed and honest, it's the author's carefully researched impression of the trail. While it's impossible to cover everything, you can rest assured that we won't miss what's important. In our **Miles/Directions** section we provide mileage cues to identify all turns and trail name changes, as well as points of interest. Between this and our Route Map, you simply can't get lost. The **Hike Information** box is a hodgepodge of information. In it you'll find trail hotlines (for updates on trail conditions), park schedules and fees, local outdoor retailers (for emergency trail supplies), and a list of maps available to the area. We'll also tell you where to stay, what to eat, and what else to see while you're hiking in the area. Lastly, the **Honorable Mentions** section details all of the hikes that didn't make the cut, for whatever reason—in many cases it's not because they aren't great hikes, instead it's because they're over-crowded or environmentally sensitive to heavy traffic. Be sure to read through these. A jewel might be lurking among them.

Map Legend

We don't want anyone, by any means, to feel restricted to just the routes and trails that are mapped here. We hope you will have an adventurous spirit and use this guide as a platform to dive into Oregon's backcountry and discover new routes for yourself. One of the simplest ways to begin this is to just turn the map upside down and hike the course in reverse. The change in perspective is fantastic and the hike should feel quite different. With this in mind, it will be like getting two distinctly different hikes on each map.

For your own purposes, you may wish to copy the directions for the course onto a small sheet to help you while hiking, or photocopy the map and cue sheet to take with you. Otherwise, just slip the whole book in your backpack and take it all with you. Enjoy your time in the outdoors and remember to pack out what you pack in.

Symbol	Description
5	Interstate Highway
8	U.S. Highway
3	State Road
CR 23	County Road
T 145	Township Road
FS 45	Forest Road
	Paved Road
	Paved Bike Lane
	Maintained Dirt Road
	Unmaintained Jeep Trail
	Singletrack Trail
	Highlighted Route
	Ntl Forest/County Boundaries
	State Boundaries
	Railroad Tracks
	Power Lines
	Special Trail
	Rivers or Streams
	Water and Lakes
	Marsh

✝	Airfield	⚑	Golf Course
✈	Airport	🏃🏃	Hiking Trail
🚲	Bike Trail	⛏	Mine
🚳	No Bikes	✕	Overlook
⛴	Boat Launch	⛩	Picnic
)(	Bridge	P	Parking
🚌	Bus Stop	✕	Quarry
▲	Campground	((A))	Radio Tower
⚲	Campsite	⚐	Rock Climbing
⚓	Canoe Access	▮	School
⊟	Cattle Guard	▰	Shelter
†	Cemetery	⚲	Spring
✝	Church	🏊	Swimming
⌂	Covered Bridge	⚑	Train Station
⌒→	Direction Arrows	⚑	Wildlife Refuge
⛷	Downhill Skiing	🍇	Vineyard
⛫	Fire Tower	◆◆	Most Difficult
⚑	Forest HQ	◆	Difficult
🛺	4WD Trail	☐	Moderate
⛲	Gate	●	Easy

HOW TO USE THESE MAPS   Map Descriptions

1 Area Locator Map

This thumbnail relief map at the beginning of each hike shows you where the hike is within the state. The hike area is indicated by the white star.

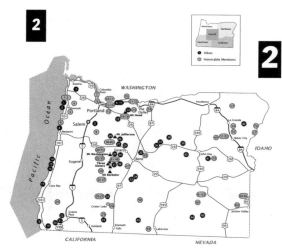

2 Regional Location Map

This map helps you find your way to the start of each hike from the nearest sizeable town or city. Coupled with the detailed directions at the beginning of the cue, this map should visually lead you to where you need to be for each hike.

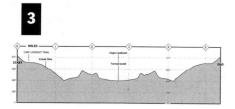

3 Profile Map

This helpful profile gives you a cross-sectional look at the hike's ups and downs. Elevation is labeled on the left, mileage is indicated on the top. Road and trail names are shown along the route with towns and points of interest labeled in bold.

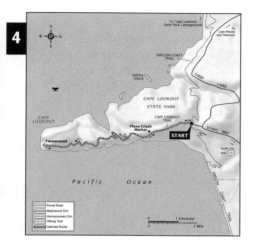

4
Route Map

This is your primary guide to each hike. It shows all of the accessible roads and trails, points of interest, water, towns, landmarks, and geographical features. It also distinguishes trails from roads, and paved roads from unpaved roads. The selected route is highlighted, and directional arrows point the way. Shaded topographic relief in the background gives you an accurate representation of the terrain and landscape in the hike area.

Hike Information *(Included in each hike section)*

☎ Trail Contacts:
This is the direct number for the local land managers in charge of all the trails within the selected hike. Use this hotline to call ahead for trail access information, or after your visit if you see problems with trail erosion, damage, or misuse.

◷ Schedule:
This tells you at what times trails open and close, if on private or park land.

$ Fees/Permits:
What money, if any, you may need to carry with you for park entrance fees or tolls.

Ⓝ Maps:
This is a list of other maps to supplement the maps in this book. They are listed in order from most detailed to most general.

Any other important or useful information will also be listed here such as local attractions, outdoor shops, nearby accommodations, etc.

A note from the folks behind this endeavor...

We at Outside America look at guidebook publishing a little differently. There's just no reason that a guidebook has to look like it was published out of your Uncle Ernie's woodshed. We feel that guidebooks need to be both easy to use and nice to look at, and that takes an innovative approach to design. You see, we want you to spend less time fumbling through your guidebook and more time enjoying the adventure at hand. We hope you like what you see here and enjoy the places we lead you. And most of all, we'd like to thank you for taking an adventure with us.

Happy Trails!

Introdu

Introduction

Welcome to the adventure of hiking in Oregon! Like no other activity, hiking allows people of all ages and ability levels to experience the outdoors. For hundreds of years, explorers, naturalists, and the average outdoorsman have been deeply impacted by the beauty and diversity of the Western wilderness. John Muir, writer and naturalist, eloquently captured nature's rejuvenating effects when he said: "Climb the mountains and get their good tidings. Nature's peace will flow into you as sunshine flows into trees. The winds will blow their own freshness into you, and the storms their energy, while cares will drop off like autumn leaves." Muir's writings have inspired generations to take a walk in the woods and further explore their natural surroundings.

This guidebook is designed to let you take your own walk into Oregon's wild places. The trails found here will take you to some of the state's most scenic locales, including rugged, rocky coast; high alpine forests, lakes, and volcanic peaks; high desert sagebrush plains; and rivers and waterfalls. You'll find trails in this guidebook for hikers of all levels, and, in addition, most of the hikes listed are canine-friendly. To get you started, I've categorized many of my favorite hikes to help you quickly find the type of hike you're most interested in. Please see page xiii in the **Hikes at a Glance** section to view this list.

Oregon Weather

Oregon's climate is as diverse as its landscapes. The cool, moist, marine air that rises off the Pacific Ocean on the west side of the Cascade Mountains contributes to a very wet, seasonal weather pattern. While rainfall averages about 40 inches per year in Portland and other parts of the Willamette Valley, the coastal regions can receive up to 100 inches. Fog and drizzle are common in the winter, spring, and late fall, and trails above 3,000 feet are generally snowed-in during the winter. Temperatures are fairly mild in the west, usually hovering between 30 and 50 degrees Fahrenheit in the winter—freezing temperatures don't generally occur except at higher elevations. Summer temperatures usually fall in the range of 65 to 85 degrees Fahrenheit during the day, but things can cool off significantly at night. Fall can often be dry and sunny whereas spring can be unpredictable and rainy.

The Cascade Mountains create a rain shadow in the eastern half of the state, halting the moist Pacific air and making the climate on the east side of the mountains much drier and sunnier than on the west. The rainfall on the east side of the mountains varies widely: as little as four inches of rain per year can fall in some sections of southeastern Oregon's high desert, whereas the mountain regions receive heavy annual rainfall. In addition, heavy snowfall blankets most mountain ranges in the winter—high mountain trails are often snowed-in until mid July. Since the climate of the east isn't tempered by the Pacific Ocean, it's more extreme than in the west. Temperatures can range from lows of 0 degrees Fahrenheit in the winter to 100-plus in the summer.

Flora and Fauna

Drastically different precipitation patterns yield dramatically different ecosystems. Naturally, the eastern and western halves of Oregon support very different vegetation and wildlife.

The forests on the west side of Oregon are primarily dense stands of Douglas fir. In the coastal regions, expect to find Sitka spruce, red cedar, Western hemlock, maple, and oak trees mixed in as well. In the southwest portion of the state, madrone and white oak trees dominate the landscape. Other distinctive forest-floor plants include the purple-fruited Oregon grape, brightly flowered rhododendrons, the vine maple, salmonberries, and a variety of mosses and ferns. When you're on the trail, keep an eye out for juicy marionberries, thorny blackberries, and bright-red huckleberries; they make a tasty treat while hiking. However, *be sure you are familiar with a type of berry before you decide to pop one in your mouth*—don't mistake a poisonous berry for a harmless snack. In the spring and summer months, go wildflower hunting for the likes of trillium, bleeding hearts, white bunchberry, phlox, columbine, Indian paintbrush, and purple lupine.

If wildlife is more your thing, western Oregon offers a distinct blend of birds, small mammals, and aquatic life. Look up to catch glimpses of some of the birds native to the Oregon coast, including gulls, cormorants, pelicans, and puffins. In coastal tide pools, it's common to see mussels, barnacles, sea anemones, starfish, and hermit crabs. Sea lions and seals also frequent the rocky headlands and mouths of the coastal rivers where they feast on salmon and steelhead. Majestic gray whales can be seen during their semi-annual migration from December through June. Along streams and marshes blue herons, mallard ducks, belted kingfishers, and black-necked loons can be seen feeding. Mammals roaming the coastal forests include the mule deer and black bears.

On the dryer, eastern side of the Cascade Mountains, the forests are mainly filled with ponderosa pine, lodgepole pine, and Douglas fir. The stately ponderosa pine forms park-like stands on the sunny mountain slopes and plateaus. The first written accounts of these trees occurred during the Lewis and Clark expedition in 1804–1806. David Douglas, a botanical explorer, named the trees *ponderosa* due to their magnificent size—they average three feet in diameter and can grow to heights of more than 120 feet. Moreover, the trees can live to be 400 to 500 years old. Their yellowish bark and large, cylindrical cones are easily distinguishable features. In contrast, the lodgepole pine is a tall, slender tree that grows in crowded clusters.

On the savannas and plateaus of eastern Oregon, the dominant tree species is the Western juniper. (The central part of the state is home to the second largest juniper forest in the world.) The hardy tree grows well in the hot sun and can thrive on less than eight inches of rain per year. Stands of Western juniper are interspersed throughout the mixed landscape of sagebrush, rabbitbrush, and native grasses. Poplars and cottonwoods flourish along the rivers and streams. These fast-growing trees are a common sight on farms and ranches where they provide shade and serve as windbreakers. Wildflowers like purple

> Have you ever wanted to rent a fire lookout or rustic Forest Service Cabin? If so, visit *www.naturenw.org/cabins/cabins-ore.html* to find out descriptions and rental prices for fire lookouts and cabins throughout Oregon.

lupine, Indian paintbrush, yarrow, and yellow balsamroot add splashes of color to the landscape.

Many species of raptors can be seen soaring in the skies in the eastern part of the state. Red-tail hawks are common, and you may see osprey and bald eagles along streams and near lakes. Coyotes thrive on the eastern side of the mountains and their distinct, haunting calls can often be heard in the late evenings. Mule deer, black bears, jackrabbits, chipmunks, and squirrels are also abundant in this region. In the Blue Mountains you can find the majestic Rocky Mountain elk—listen for its bugling call in the fall mating season. A small population of about 200 mountain goats lives on the windswept ridges of the Wallowa Mountains in the Eagle Cap Wilderness and in some parts of the Elkhorn Mountains in the northeastern part of the state. These tough characters were re-introduced into the area in the 1950s and are currently thriving. Bighorn sheep have also been re-introduced to some of the remote mountain areas. Pronghorn antelope—the fastest land mammals in North America—roam the hills and valleys in the central and southeastern parts of the state. Be on the lookout for rattlesnakes as they're common in the area. They can often be seen sunning themselves on ledges and rock outcroppings.

Wilderness Restrictions/Regulations

Oregon's 12 national forests and 38 wilderness areas provide a magical retreat for hikers wanting to visit unadulterated nature. The Bureau of Land Management and the U.S. Forest Service manage most of the public lands in Oregon. These organizations have the difficult responsibility of trying to balance the public urge to get outdoors and the need to keep these areas wild. With more and more people heading into the Oregon wilds each year, many of our popular national forests and wilderness areas are finding it necessary to issue wilderness permits and charge usage fees at trailheads.

In the year 2000, Oregon and Washington national forests and scenic areas teamed up in an effort to make trailhead passes easier to obtain. Trailhead fees are now $5 per day, or you can buy an annual **Northwest Forest Pass** for $30—good at all participating national forests and scenic areas in Oregon and Washington. National forests in Oregon participating in this program include Deschutes, Mount Hood, Rogue River, Siskiyou, Siuslaw, Umatilla, Umpqua, Wallowa-Whitman, Willamette, Winema, and the Columbia River Gorge National Scenic Area. You can find out about participating national forests and locations for purchasing a Northwest Forest Pass by visiting *www.fs.fed.us/r6/feedemo* or by calling 1–800–270–7504.

Before you head into the backcountry, find out what type of permits and restrictions are in place for the area you're going to visit. Trail park passes can be purchased at local ranger stations, at participating outdoor outlets, and at some trailheads. Most permits for day hikers are self-issued at wilderness trailheads. If you're planning an overnight trip into a wilderness area, call ahead to the local ranger station to see if a permit is required.

Thanks for purchasing *Hike America: Oregon!*
Happy Hiking!

Lizann Dunegan
October 2000

Getting Around Oregon

⦿ AREA CODES
The area code 503 covers Portland, Salem, and Northwestern Oregon, and is now overlaid with the recently added 971 area code. The area code 541 serves the remainder of Oregon.

⦿ ROADS
For winter road conditions, call 1–800–977–6368. To contact the Oregon Department of Transportation, call (503) 986–4000 or visit *www.odot.state.or.us* for current road closings and openings, traffic updates, and road construction plans and timetables.

⦿ BY AIR
Portland International Airport (PDX) is Oregon's main airport. A number of smaller airports throughout the state have connections through Portland International. The resort/ski area or a travel agent can best advise you on the cheapest and/or most direct way to connect from wherever you're departing. They can also arrange transportation from the airport to the ski area.

To book reservations on-line, check out your favorite airline's website or search one of the following travel sites for the best price: *www.cheaptickets.com*, *www.expedia.com*, *www.previewtravel.com*, *www.priceline.com*, *http://travel.yahoo.com*, *www.travelocity.com*, *www.trip.com*—just to name a few. Many of these sites can connect you with a shuttle or rental service to get you from the airport to the ski area.

⦿ BY BUS
Greyhound services Portland, Eugene, Bend, Sisters, and Ashland. Schedules and fares are available online at *www.greyhound.com* or by phone at 1–800–231–2222. The RAZ Trax Airporter connects Amtrak, Greyhound, and downtown Portland with the Portland International Airport. Call (503) 684–3322 for schedules and pick-up info. Pierce Pacific Stage services Portland, Cannon Beach, Seaside, and Astoria. Call 1–888–483–1111 for information and fares. Pacific Trailways connects Portland with Lincoln City. Call (503) 692–4437.

⦿ BY TRAIN
Amtrak's Cascade Corridor trains service Portland and Eugene four times a day from Seattle, WA. The Empire Builder train runs daily to Portland from Chicago, IL; Minneapolis, MN; and Spokane, WA. The Coast Starlight train services Portland and Eugene every day from Los Angeles, CA; San Francisco, CA; and Klamath Falls, OR. Amtrak offers connecting bus service to Bend, Ashland, and Boise, ID. Amtrak information and reservations are available online at *www.amtrak.com* or by phone at 1–800–872–7245.

⦿ VISITOR INFORMATION
For visitor information or a travel brochure, call the Oregon Tourism Commission at 1–800–547–7842 or visit their website at *www.traveloregon.com*. The state's official site is *www.state.or.us*.

Northwest

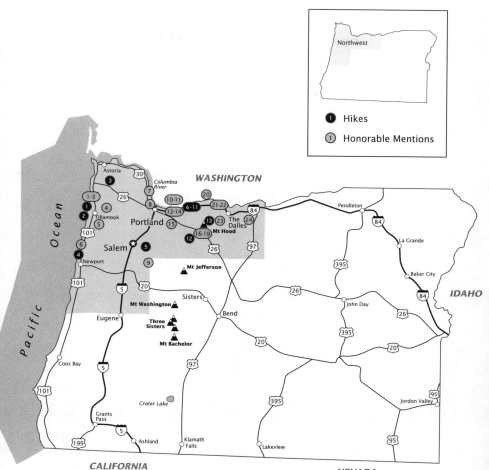

Northwest

● Hikes

◉ Honorable Mentions

WASHINGTON

Astoria
Columbia River
Pacific Ocean
Tillamook
Portland
The Dalles
Mt Hood
Salem
Newport
Mt Jefferson
Sisters
Mt Washington
Eugene
Three Sisters
Bend
Mt Bachelor
Coos Bay
Crater Lake
Grants Pass
Ashland
Klamath Falls
Lakeview
Pendleton
La Grande
Baker City
John Day
Jordon Valley
IDAHO
CALIFORNIA
NEVADA

Oregon

Northwest Oregon

Northwest Oregon is host to some of the most scenic and varied landscapes in the state. Starting in the west with the scenic, rocky coastline, the eastbound traveler can progress through the cascading waterfalls and magnificent scenery of the Columbia River Gorge, and before long arrive at the high alpine landscapes of 11,235-foot Mount Hood—all in a matter of hours.

The center of activity for this region is Portland. The largest city in Oregon, Portland has been called an *urban nirvana*. Forest Park, one of the world's largest city parks, rests right in the heart of city limits. This hiking and biking friendly city has miles of scenic trails that wind through the cool, big-leaf maple and Douglas fir forest, including Wildwood Trail, which runs for 26 miles through the heart of Forest Park.

Just 90 minutes west of Portland you can explore the rocky coast and view pounding surf on trails accessible off U.S. Route 101, the main north-south artery along Oregon's coastline. For those who settled the northern Oregon coast in the late 1800s and early 1900s, fishing, logging, and agriculture dominated the region, but by 1910 the state government had set aside the entire coastline as public land. Today, forests, rivers, and beaches are publicly accessible.

As you travel south along U.S. Route 101, your first stop should be the artsy seaside town of Cannon Beach, which swells with tourists during the summer months. Here, the nearby beach boasts prominent rocky sea stacks—including the 235-foot Haystack Rock. Take a walk along the beach and view tide pools at the base of this rock. Located about two miles north of Cannon Beach, Ecola State Park has hiking trails leading to both scenic viewpoints on rocky headlands and to secluded beaches. Be sure to check out the four-mile out-and-back hike to Indian Beach; this trail takes you through an old-growth forest along a rocky headland to Indian Beach, providing many a fantastic viewpoint along the way.

Located about 10 miles south of Cannon Beach is Oswald West State Park. Within it you'll have access to Arch Cape, Cape Falcon, Neahkahnie Mountain, Smugglers Cove, and Short Sands Beach. Get a bird's eye view of the area: hike to the top of Neahkahnie Mountain. To explore more coastal mountains, head just east of Cannon Beach on U.S. Route 26 to the Saddle Mountain trailhead. Here you can begin a strenuous five-mile expedition to the top of Saddle Mountain, the highest point in the northern Coastal Mountains.

As you continue south on U.S. Route 101, be sure to tour some of the scenic, rocky capes by driving on the Three Capes Scenic Route, which heads west from U.S. Route 101 at Tillamook. Your first stop should be Cape Meares State Park, which features a scenic lighthouse and many cliff-side viewpoints where you can watch for migrating gray whales and observe large colonies of nesting sea birds. As you continue south on the Three Capes Scenic Route, your next destination should be Cape Lookout. This spectacular headland takes you through an ancient old-growth Sitka spruce forest to a spectacular viewpoint where you'll have the opportunity to view gray whales on their semi-annual migration.

A quick 30-minute drive east from Portland takes you into the scenic Columbia River Gorge. This magnificent gorge is carved by the mile-wide Columbia River: the dividing line between Oregon and Washington. Thanks to legislation passed in 1986, the Columbia Gorge is a designated National Scenic Area. It will remain undeveloped for all to enjoy. Filled with over 75 cascading waterfalls, wind-swept forests and ridges, wildflower meadows, and bubbling creeks, this special destination has hundreds of miles of hiking trails. If you're a waterfall lover you'll enjoy the Eagle Creek, Wahclella Falls, Horsetail/Oneonta/Triple Falls, and Larch Mountain hikes. If you're into vistas, check out the Munra Point hike and Angel's Rest hike.

Drive another hour east on Interstate 84 to reach the community of Hood River, gateway to the Hood River Valley, Mount Hood, and the Mount Hood National Forest. At the center of this national forest is 11,235-foot Mount Hood—Oregon's tallest peak. This expansive forest boasts 189,200 acres of designated wilderness and countless miles of trails. To get a close up view of Mount Hood's impressive glaciers and snow-capped peak, try the Cooper Spur Trail. For a pristine river hike, check out the Salmon River Trail as it traipses along the Salmon River through the Salmon-Huckleberry Wilderness. Take note: trails up to 4,000 feet are usually snow-free by June 1st; trails at 7,000 feet are usually open by mid July. Remember, there's a chance for snow at any time—always be prepared for cold weather when you are hiking at higher elevations.

And don't miss Silver Falls State Park—Oregon's largest—found 21 miles east of Salem off Oregon 214. The park features a classic seven-mile loop trail that takes you on a one-of-a-kind tour of 10 cascading waterfalls. We recommend that you try this hike during September and October when the leaves are turning golden-yellow and burnt-orange and the summer crowds have thinned.

Cape Meares State Park

Hike Summary

Cape Meares, located in Cape Meares State Park, is one of three scenic capes along the Three Capes Scenic Highway—the other two capes are Cape Lookout *[see Hike 28]* and Cape Kiwanda. A hike here includes numerous opportunities to view seabirds and migrating gray whales. Other attractions include the Cape Meares Lighthouse, which was built in 1890; old-growth Sitka spruce trees; spectacular ocean views; and abundant wildlife and coastal forestland. Plan on spending the better part of a day here and be sure to bring your binoculars.

Hike Specs

Start: From the state park parking area approximately 11 miles west of Tillamook off the Three Capes Scenic Loop Highway
Length: 0.2–0.4 miles
Approximate Hiking Time: 15–30 minutes
Difficulty Rating: Easy due to the flat terrain and well-maintained trails
Trail Surface: The Cape Meares Lighthouse and Octopus Tree Trails are paved; the Big Spruce Tree Trail is a level, forested path. The Cape Meares Lighthouse and Octopus Tree Trails are wheelchair-accessible out-and-backs; the Big Spruce Tree Trail is a loop.
Lay of the Land: Trails lead to an historic lighthouse and scenic viewpoints on the tip of a magnificent headland. You will also find spectacular ocean views, abundant wildlife, and a coastal forest.
Land Status: State park
Nearest Town: Tillamook, OR
Other Trail Users: Hikers only
Canine Compatibility: Dogs permitted

Getting There

From U.S. 101 in Tillamook: Follow the signs to Cape Lookout Loop Road (the Three Capes Scenic Highway). Drive approximately 10 miles west on the Three Capes Scenic Highway to the Cape Meares State Park sign. If you want to view the Big Spruce Tree, turn right into a pullout right before the Cape Meares State Park turnoff. A short loop trail will take you by the Big Spruce Tree. To proceed to the main parking area in the park, turn right (west) on the Park Road and drive 0.6 miles to a parking area.
From Pacific City: Drive 26 miles north on Cape Lookout Road (the Three Capes Scenic Highway) to the Cape Meares State Park sign. Turn west (left) and drive 0.6 miles on the Park Road to the parking area. *DeLorme: Oregon Atlas & Gazetteer:* Page 58 A1

The 233-acre Cape Meares State Park is a must-see stop for anyone traveling along the North Oregon Coast. This scenic cape is well known for its large concentration of nesting seabirds and for its historic lighthouse. You can start your exploration by walking down the 0.4-mile out-and-back paved *Cape Meares Lighthouse Trail* to the 40-foot-tall Cape Meares Lighthouse. Along the way, you'll pass seabird colonies nesting on the sheer, 200-foot rocky cliffs. Bring binoculars for close-up views of these feathered Cape residents, which include double-crested cormorants,

Cape Meares Lighthouse.

11

Brandt's cormorants, pelagic cormorants, pigeon guillemots, common murres, and tufted puffins. Bald eagles and peregrine falcons have also been spotted in the area.

In 1886 the U.S. Army Corp of Engineers sent a representative to survey the Cape Meares site and the Cape Lookout site, located south of Cape Meares, to see which would be more suitable for a lighthouse. After several days of surveying, the engineers determined that the Cape Meares site was more suitable for a lighthouse because of its lower elevation, which would allow light to travel farther in foggy weather. Additionally, it had a spring nearby that could provide fresh water, and it was more accessible than the Cape Lookout site. In 1887 Congress passed a bill that provided funding to begin construction on the lighthouse. A road was built to the site and con-

MilesDirections

0.0 START The *Cape Meares Lighthouse Trail* and the *Octopus Tree Trail* start from the main parking area. The *Big Spruce Tree Trail* begins in a dirt pullout on the north side of the park road just before the entrance to the park.

Bird Identification 101

There are many different bird species living along the cliffs and offshore islands of this scenic cape. Following are descriptions of just a few.
- Pelagic cormorants are solid black with a white patch on their flank during breeding season. These birds nest predominantly on the south side of the cape.
- Brandt's cormorants have a buff-colored patch adjacent to a blue throat patch and solid black coloring with a sprinkling of fine white feathers on the back and neck.
- Double-crested cormorants have bright-yellow and orange markings on their throat and face and have a crooked neck in flight.
- Tufted puffins have a stocky black body, white facial mask, yellow feather tufts on their head, and bright-orange feet.
- Common murres are dark brown on the head, back, and wings. They also have a white breast patch and dark-yellow feet. They nest on the cliff faces on the north side of the cape.

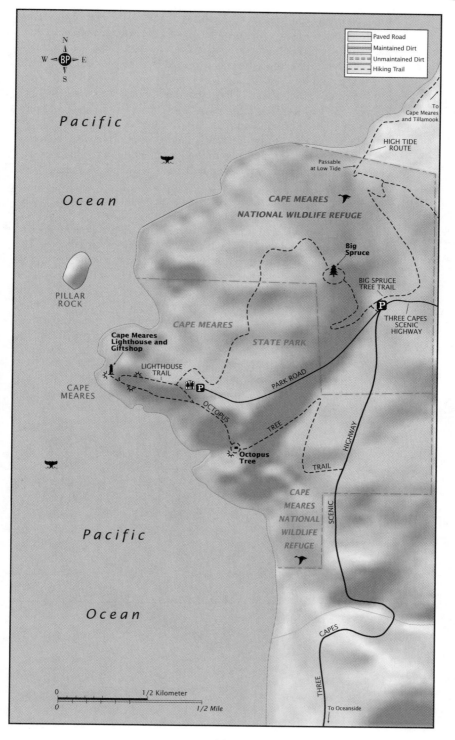

struction finally commenced in the spring of 1889. The interior walls were built with bricks made at the construction site; the exterior walls made from sheet iron shipped in from Portland. In November of 1889, the lighthouse was complete. At the time, the light consisted of a five-wick oil lamp turned by a 200-pound lead weight. The lens is a first-order Fresnel lens that was shipped from Paris via Cape Horn and then up the west coast to Cape Meares. The lens itself has eight sides: four primary lenses, and four bull's-eye lenses covered with red panels.

To view the intricate Fresnel lens, climb a series of steps to the top of the lighthouse tower. A gift shop in the lower section of the lighthouse is open daily May through September and on the weekends in March, April, and October.

If visiting the lighthouse isn't enough, check out another amazing attraction at this park called the Octopus Tree. A short, 0.2-mile, out-and-back, wheelchair-accessible trail leads from the main parking area to an ancient Sitka spruce whose low-slung branches truly resemble an octopus. The spruce was used as a burial tree in Native American ceremonies and its octopus-shaped arms held the canoes in which were placed the bodies of the tribe's dead. It is speculated that Native Americans, who lived along the North Oregon Coast for nearly 30,000 years, bent the younger tree's more pliable branches outward into a horizontal position. Eventually, the tree's branches would take shape and continue to grow. The Octopus Tree is one such specimen that is thought to have endured this ritual when it was very young, surviving to grow old, while maintaining its odd shape.

To view another old-growth Sitka spruce drive 0.6 miles to the park entrance and park in a dirt pullout on the north side of the road. A 0.4-mile

The Octopus Tree.

out-and-back loop trail leads to a magnificent 400-year-old tree. As you walk the path be on the lookout for odd-looking banana slugs. These interesting, slow-moving creatures eat plant matter and recycle the material back to the soil. They also secrete a thin coat of mucus that helps them travel over the forest floor.

Hike Information

❶ Trail Contacts:
Oregon State Parks and Recreation Department, Salem, OR 1–800–551–6949 or *www.prd.state.or.us*

◷ Schedule:
Open year round

❸ Fees/Permits:
None

❷ Local Information:
Tillamook Chamber of Commerce, Tillamook, OR (503) 842–7525 or *www.tillamookchamber.org* · Tillamook County Online: *www.tillamoo.com*

❾ Local Events/Attractions:
Tillamook Cheese Factory, Tillamook, OR (503) 842–4481 or *www.tillamookcheese.com* · Tillamook Pioneer Museum, Tillamook, OR (503) 842–4553 or *www.oregoncoast.com/Pionrmus.htm* · Tillamook County Rodeo, in June, Tillamook, OR (503) 842–7525

⊜ Accommodations:
Shilo Inn, Tillamook, OR 1–800–222–2244 or *www.shiloinns.com/*

Oregon/tillamook.html · Cape Lookout State Park and Campground, Netarts, OR, General Information: (503) 842–4981, Reservations: 1–800–551–6949

⑪ Restaurants:
McClaskeys, Tillamook, OR (503) 842–5674 · Roseanna's Cafe, Oceanside, OR (503) 842–7351 · Pelican Pub and Brewery, Pacific City, OR (503) 965–7007 · La Mexicana Restaurant, Tillamook, OR (503) 842–2101

❻ Other Resources:
Oregon Coast Magazine, Florence, OR (541) 997–8401 or *www.ocmag.com*

⊕ Local Outdoor Retailers:
Body & Sole Sport Shop, Tillamook, OR (503) 842–5378 · Kimmels Sporting Goods & Gifts, Tillamook, OR (503) 842–4281

❿ Maps:
USGS maps: Netarts, OR

Cape Lookout

Hike Summary

This easy ramble through a lush coastal forest of rare old-growth Sitka spruce leads to the end of scenic Cape Lookout in Cape Lookout State Park. Along the way there are magnificent views of Cape Meares to the north and Cape Kiwanda to the south. Gray whales can be seen in December, January, March, and April as they near the cape on their semiannual migrations.

Hike Specs

Start: From the trailhead off Cape Lookout Road (the Three Capes Scenic Highway)

Length: 5.4-mile out-and-back

Approximate Hiking Time: 2–3 hours

Difficulty Rating: Easy due to a well-maintained path over fairly flat terrain

Trail Surface: Well-maintained dirt path with occasional roots and rocks and intermittent wooden walkways over muddy sections

Lay of the Land: Hike a forested dirt path through a thick spruce forest and along some exposed cliffs to the tip of Cape Lookout.

Elevation Gain: 1,423 feet

Land Status: State park

Nearest Town: Tillamook, OR

Other Trail Users: Hikers only

Canine Compatibility: Dogs are permitted, but should be leashed due to the many steep cliffs and drop-offs.

Getting There

From Tillamook: Take Cape Lookout Road (the Three Capes Scenic Highway) 13 miles southwest to the Cape Lookout trailhead on the right side of the road.

From Beaver: Take U.S. 101 north for 3.5 miles to the Sand Lake/Cape Lookout turnoff. Turn left on Sand Lake Road and drive 4.2 miles to a stop sign. Go straight on Cape Lookout Road (the Three Capes Scenic Highway) 3.2 miles to the Cape Lookout trailhead on the left side of the road. *DeLorme: Oregon Atlas & Gazetteer:* Page 58 B1

> *Bring binoculars to help you spot migrating gray whales.*

C ape Lookout, part of the 2,000-acre Cape Lookout State Park (host to a campground, scenic Netarts Spit, and a variety of plants and animals), is a spectacular headland made up of a series of lava flows 15 to 20 million years old. Jutting into the ocean like an arrowhead, its 400-foot cliffs are regularly pounded and carved by rhythmic waves and currents. The scenic cape is popular among whale-watchers who come to observe gray whales during their semiannual migrations—epic 10,000-mile

roundtrip journeys from breeding lagoons in Baja California, Mexico, to the Arctic Ocean and back again. The whales migrate south during the months of December and January and north March through April. Mature gray whales are 35 to 45 feet long and weigh anywhere from 22 to 35 tons. Females are larger than males and can live for 50 years—some males reach the ripe old age of 60. The gentle giants feed on shrimp-like amphipods by scraping up mud from the ocean bottom and then filtering unwanted material through their baleen.

To reach the tip of the cape, take the trail that travels left just past the trailhead sign. The path begins by descending a series of switchbacks through a thick grove of Sitka spruce. These tough, stout trees are often referred to as "tideland spruce," and they thrive in the moist, cool temperatures that are characteristic of their coastal home. The Sitka spruce ranks with the Douglas fir and Western red cedar as one of the largest tree species in the Northwest—only redwoods and sequoias are bigger.

About half a mile from the trailhead the path arrives at a commemorative marker honoring an Air Force crew that perished in a nearby plane crash in August of 1943. From here there are also views of Cape Kiwanda and Cascade Head to the south.

Continuing on, the trail includes several convenient wooden boardwalks over the seemingly endless mire of mud. Up to 90 inches of rain falls annually along this stretch of the coast! The resulting foliage is striking—notice the bright green leaves of salal and salmonberry and the feathery fans of sword and maidenhair fern that cover the forest floor.

After a while the trail reveals views of Netarts Bay, Three Arch Rocks, and Cape Meares. The sandy, flat bottom of Netarts Bay makes it a perfect environment for shellfish such as oysters, razor clams, butter clams, and crabs.

MilesDirections

0.0 START at the trailhead in the southwest corner of the Cape Lookout parking area. Take the trail that goes left. *[FYI. The trail to the right heads north to Cape Lookout Campground.]* Bear right at the first junction, just a few yards up the trail. *[FYI. A left here will lead you along the Oregon Coast Trail to Sand Lake.]* Descend through a thick grove of statuesque spruce trees.

0.5 The trail forks. Go right.

0.6 A commemorative marker honors the crew of an Air Force plane that crashed 500 feet west of this site on August 1, 1943.

1.4 Enjoy a good view of the northern coastline and Cape Meares.

2.7 Arrive at the end of the official trail and your turnaround point. Look over the edge (where there's another trail) and soak in the views of Cape Kiwanda to the south.

5.4 Reach the parking area and your vehicle.

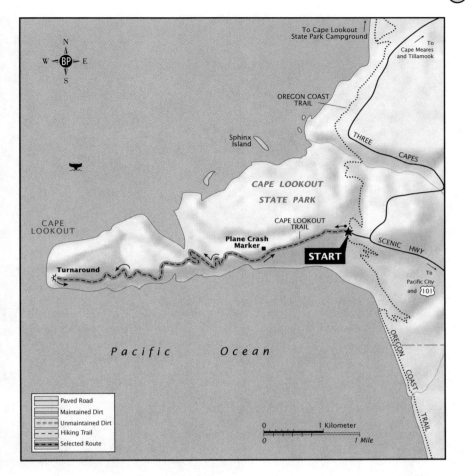

N
W ⊕BP⊕ E
S

To Cape Lookout
State Park Campground

To
Cape Meares
and Tillamook

OREGON COAST
TRAIL

Sphinx
Island

THREE

CAPES

CAPE LOOKOUT
STATE PARK

CAPE LOOKOUT
TRAIL

CAPE
LOOKOUT

Plane Crash
Marker

START

SCENIC HWY

To
Pacific City
and 101

Turnaround

Pacific   Ocean

OREGON COAST TRAIL

Paved Road
Maintained Dirt
Unmaintained Dirt
Hiking Trail
Selected Route

0   1 Kilometer
0   1 Mile

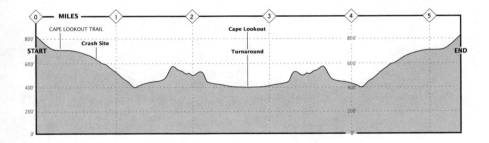

MILES   0   1   2   3   4   5

CAPE LOOKOUT TRAIL   Cape Lookout

800'   Crash Site   Turnaround   800'

START   END

600'   600'

400'   400'

200'   200'

0'   0'

19

The last half mile of the path is lined with Indian paintbrush, delicate wild iris, white yarrow, and bushy thimbleberry. The trail ends at a sharp point; if you look off the edge you'll see the frothy Pacific pounding its huge swells against the rocky cliffs below. A convenient wooden bench has been placed at this classic viewpoint. Stay a while and admire the view before turning back to your car.

Hike Information

Trail Contacts:
Oregon State Parks and Recreation Department, Salem, OR 1–800–551–6949 or *www.prd.state.or.us*

Schedule:
Open year round

Fees/Permits:
A $3 day pass can be purchased at the self-pay machine at **Cape Lookout State Park Campground** (north of the trailhead off Three Capes Scenic Highway).

Local Information:
Tillamook Chamber of Commerce, Tillamook, OR (503) 842–7525 or *www.tillamookchamber.org* · **Tillamook County Online:** *www.tillamoo.com*

Local Events/Attractions:
Tillamook Cheese Factory, Tillamook, OR (503) 842–4481 or *www.tillamookcheese.com* · **Tillamook Pioneer Museum,** Tillamook, OR (503) 842–4553 or *www.oregoncoast.com/ Pionrmus.htm*

Accommodations:
Shilo Inn, Tillamook, OR 1–800–222–2244 or *www.shiloinns.com/ Oregon/tillamook.html* · **Cape Lookout State Park and Campground,** Netarts, OR, General Information: (503) 842–4981, Reservations: 1–800–551–6949

Restaurants:
La Mexicana Restaurant, Tillamook, OR (503) 842–2101 · **McClaskey's,** Tillamook, OR (503) 842–5674

Other Resources:
Oregon Coast Magazine, Florence, OR (541) 997–8401 or *www.ocmag.com*

Maps:
USGS maps: Sand Lake, OR

Saddle Mountain

Hike Summary

This trail to the top of 3,283-foot Saddle Mountain, the highest point in the northern Coastal Mountains, begins in a thickly wooded expanse of alder forest. It then climbs through a beautiful Douglas fir forest with a thick understory of wood sorrel, trillium, Western columbine, coast penstemon, and many other unique wildflowers. Eventually, the trail becomes rocky and eroded and necessitates some careful navigation, but the effort is worth it, for those who make it to the top are rewarded with magnificent views.

Hike Specs

Start: From the Saddle Mountain State Park trailhead off U.S. 26

Length: 5.2-mile out-and-back

Approximate Hiking Time: 2–3 hours

Difficulty Rating: Difficult due to loose rocks and dirt on steep terrain. In winter the trail can be very icy and treacherous.

Trail Surface: The first half is an easy and well-maintained dirt path; the final 1.5 miles are very eroded but include cables, walkways, and stairs to aid travel.

Lay of the Land: Climbs through alder forests and open, alpine-like landscape to the summit where you can enjoy breathtaking views of the Coast Range on a clear day.

Elevation Gain: 2,221 feet

Land Status: State park

Nearest Town: Cannon Beach, OR

Other Trail Users: Hikers only

Canine Compatibility: Leashed dogs permitted

Getting There

From Portland: Drive 65 miles west on U.S. 26 to a sign for Saddle Mountain State Park. Turn right (north) on Saddle Mountain Road and drive seven miles to the trailhead.

From Cannon Beach: Drive 10 miles east on U.S. 101. Turn left (north) on Saddle Mountain Road and drive seven miles to the trailhead. *DeLorme: Oregon Atlas & Gazetteer:* Page 64 A3

One of the highest peaks in Oregon's northern Coastal Mountain range, Saddle Mountain rises 3,283 feet above sea level. The gray monolith juts its basalt head above its neighbors and stands testament to its volcanic beginnings. The peak is the eroded remnant of the Columbia basalt flows that poured through the area approximately 15 million years ago. The massive flows originated more than 250 miles away in Eastern Washington. When the lava came into contact with an ancient sea that covered the area, it cooled rapidly and formed fragmented layers. When North America pushed its way under the old Pacific seafloor, Saddle Mountain was born. Eventually, soft sedimentary rock eroded away to reveal the dark basalt mountaintop visible today.

Weathered basalt cliffs along the trail.

To see Saddle Mountain up close, try this strenuous 5.2-mile out-and-back trek to the summit. The trailhead is located at the base of the mountain, as are water and restroom facilities and 10 primitive campsites. The trail's first mile slips through a thick, secondary-growth forest of red alder that thrives in the moist environment. Red alders can be found in elevations of up to 3,000 feet and are easily identified by their grayish-white bark. They're often covered with a mottled coat of moss and lichen. The coastal Indian tribes steeped the tree's bark in hot water to cure rheumatic fever. (It contains salicin, which even today is used in prescription medication for treatment of this disease.) The wood of the tree was also used to make utensils and other tools.

The lower section of this route is a haven for wildflowers. The clover-like leaves and delicate white flowers of wood sorrel carpet the forest floor. You'll also find triangular trillium, pink Western columbine, and blue coast penstemon. Other botanical delights scattered throughout the woods include the hairy-stemmed checker-mallow, a high-stemmed plant with large, daisy-like purple flowers; the tooth-leafed monkey flower, a yellow, tubular flower with tooth-like petals; and goat's beard, recognizable for its white, feathery flowers.

Soon, the trail becomes steeper and the forest canopy thins to reveal many great views around almost every bend. The path also becomes more eroded and precipitous, and requires some careful footwork over rocky ledges. (Notice the firm grasp the thick red stems of Oregon stonecrop have

MilesDirections

0.0 START at the trailhead at the Saddle Mountain State Park parking lot. There are restrooms and water here. The trail begins with a climb through an alder forest.

1.5 The trail becomes steeper and, in parts, rocky and eroded.

1.7 Several bridges cross an alpine-like landscape of wildflowers. Look for blue iris, Indian paintbrush, white meadow chick-weed, chocolate lily, phlox, and larkspur.

2.2 Hike across a narrow saddle before climbing to the summit. The final stretch includes loose rocks and is very steep—use the stairs, walkways, and cables to ensure you don't slip.

2.6 Arrive at the summit and magnificent views of Nehalem Bay to the southwest, the Columbia River to the northwest, and other snow-capped Cascade peaks to the east. This is your turnaround point. Follow the trail back down the mountain to the starting point.

5.2 Reach the parking area and your vehicle.

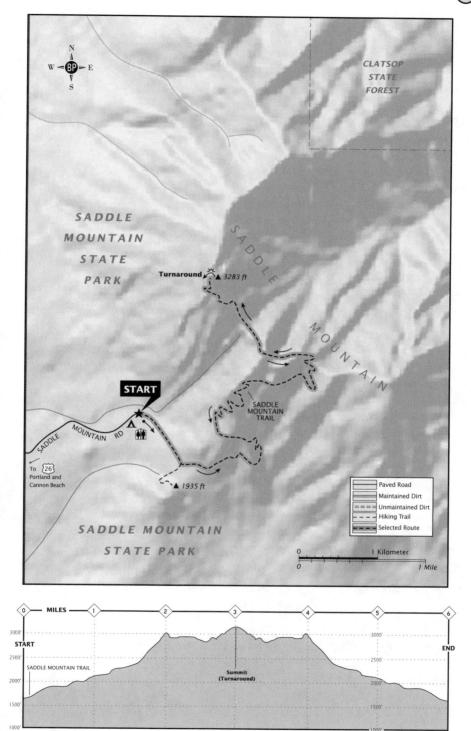

3,283 foot Saddle Mountain summit.

on the ledges. Don't you wish you had the same?) In an attempt to make navigating easier, stairs and walkways have been built over the more difficult sections of trail. The walkways also protect the wildflower meadows of blue iris, Indian paintbrush, meadow chickweed, phlox, and larkspur.

After about two miles, the trail crosses a narrow saddle then climbs to the dome-like summit. The push to the top is somewhat treacherous. The trail is steep and filled with loose rocks. Fortunately, stairs and cables are in place to make things easier. Still, these devices are not always reliable—some are loose and can be dangerous.

At the broad, flat summit there are grand views of Nehalem Bay to the southwest, the Columbia River to the northwest, and the snow-capped Cascade peaks of Mount Jefferson and Mount Hood to the east. Summertime crowds on this popular trek—especially at the summit—can be fierce. If you want solitude, come here on a weekday or off-season weekend in the spring or fall.

Hike Information

❶ Trail Contacts:
Oregon State Parks and Recreation Department, Salem, OR 1–800–551–6949 or www.prd.state.or.us

❷ Schedule:
Open year round

❸ Local Information:
Cannon Beach Chamber of Commerce and Information Center, Cannon Beach, OR (503) 436–2623 or www. cannonbeach.org

❹ Local Events/Attractions:
Sandcastle Day Festival, in June, Cannon Beach, OR (503) 436–2623

❺ Accommodations:
McBee Motel Cottages, Cannon Beach, OR (503) 436–2569

Saddle Mountain State Park Campground, Reservations Northwest, 1–800–452–5687 or www.ohwy.com/or/r/reservnw.htm · Stephanie Inn, Cannon Beach, OR 1–800–633–3466 or www.stephanie-inn.com

❻ Restaurants:
Bill's Tavern, Cannon Beach, OR (503) 436–2202 · Café de la Mer, Cannon Beach, OR (503) 436–1179 · Cannon Beach Bakery, Cannon Beach, OR (503) 436–0399

❼ Other Resources:
Oregon Coast Magazine, Florence, OR (541) 997–8401 or www.ocmag.com

❽ Maps:
USGS map: Saddle Mountain, OR

Yaquina Head Outstanding Natural Area

Hike Summary

The trails in the Yaquina Head Outstanding Natural Area take you through a rich coastal ecosystem, giving visitors an excellent opportunity to view seabirds, tidepool creatures, harbor seals, and migrating gray whales. The other main attraction at this special ocean oasis is the 93-foot Yaquina Head Lighthouse—the tallest lighthouse in Oregon. It's recommended that you bring a good pair of binoculars in order to get a close-up view of the abundance of wildlife this unique area has to offer.

Hike Specs

Start: From the trailhead off U.S. 101
Length: Trails vary from 0.2 miles to 1 mile in length, all are out-and-backs.
Cobble Beach Access–0.2-mile
Communications Hill Trail–1-mile
Lighthouse Trail–0.6-mile
Quarry Cove Trail–0.4-mile
Quarry Cove Tide Pools Trail–1-mile
Salal Hill Trail–0.8-mile out-and-back
Yaquina Head Lighthouse Trail–0.2-mile
Approximate Hiking Time: 15 min.–1 hour, depending on the trail selected
Difficulty Rating: Easy to Moderate

Trail Surface: Paved walkways, dirt path, wooden steps, and rocky beach
Lay of the Land: Hike to a majestic lighthouse that sits atop a scenic headland, home to tide pools, a cobblestone beach, and numerous species of sea birds and seals.
Land Status: Outstanding natural area
Nearest Town: Newport, OR
Other Trail Users: Hikers only
Canine Compatibility: Not dog friendly

Cobble Beach.

Getting There

From Newport: Drive two miles north on U.S. 101. Turn left onto Lighthouse Drive at the park sign. Drive one mile to the end of the road where you'll reach a parking area. Be prepared to pay a $5 entrance fee at the Entrance Station.
Delorme: Oregon Atlas & Gazetteer: Page 32 C1

E stablished in 1980, the Yaquina Head Outstanding Natural Area consists of 100 acres of rocky basalt cliffs, tide pools, rocky beaches, and grassy meadows that support a multitude of animal and aquatic life. Managed by the Bureau of Land Management, this seaside oasis has many trails that lead you through different coastal life zones. It's recommended that you begin your tour of the area by stopping first at the Interpretive Center located 0.7 miles from U.S. Route 101 on Lighthouse Drive. The Interpretive

Yaquina Head Lighthouse.

Center has exhibits, video presentations, and hands-on displays about the geology, and cultural and natural history of Yaquina Head. The Interpretive Center is open in the summer months from 10 A.M. to 6 P.M., and in the winter months from 10 A.M. to 4 P.M. Once you've filled up on facts at the Interpretive Center, turn right out of the Interpretive Center Parking Area and drive 0.3 miles to the end of Lighthouse Drive to the Yaquina Head Lighthouse Parking Area.

From the parking area, take a leisurely walk over to the 93-foot-tall Yaquina Head Lighthouse, the tallest lighthouse in Oregon. Construction on the classic seacoast tower lighthouse began in fall of 1871, taking two years to complete. Many of the building materials used for the lighthouse were shipped in from San Francisco and unloaded in Newport. They were then brought out to Yaquina Head by wagon over a crude, rough road along the coast. Amazingly, it took more than 370,000 bricks to build the tower. A two-story building was also constructed next door to house the lighthouse keepers and their families. (In 1872, a Fresnel lens arrived in sections from France; and on August 20, 1873, Fayette Crosby, a lighthouse keeper, lit the lamp for the first time.) In 1993, the lighthouse was refurbished by the Coast Guard and was officially named a part of the Yaquina Head Outstanding Natural Area. Tours of the lighthouse are available during the summer from 10 A.M. to 4 P.M., and in the winter from 12 noon to

MilesDirections

The Quarry Cove Parking Area is located on the left side of the road 0.5 miles from the intersection of Lighthouse Drive and U.S. 101. From this parking area, you can access the *Quarry Cove Trail*, *Communications Hill Trail*, and the wheelchair accessible *Quarry Cove Tide Pools Trail* (see map).

The Interpretive Center is located on the right side of the road 0.7 miles from the intersection of Lighthouse Drive and U.S. 101. From this parking area, you can access the *Lighthouse Trail* and the *Quarry Cove Trail* (see map).

The Yaquina Head Lighthouse parking area is located one mile from the intersection of Lighthouse Drive and U.S. 101. From this parking area, you can access the paved trail to Yaquina Head Lighthouse, a stairway that takes you to Cobble Beach, and the *Salal Hill Trail* (see map).

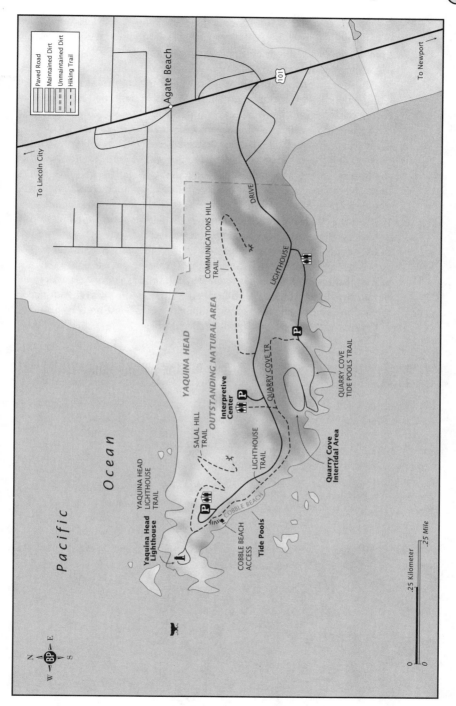

4 P.M. (weather permitting). From the viewpoint at the lighthouse, you may have the opportunity to see gray whales during their winter migration from December through mid February or during their spring migration, March through May.

After touring the lighthouse, take a walk down a long series of steps to Cobble Beach. This rocky beach and the offshore rocks and islands are all part of the Oregon Islands National Wildlife Refuge. While you're on the beach keep your eyes peeled, because you may spot black oyster catchers, easily recognized by their dark black plumage, gold eyes, bright red bills, and pink legs and feet. These birds feed on chitons, limpets, snails and other shellfish by picking the shellfish off the rocks with their long, sturdy beaks. In the rocky tide pools you may be lucky to see green anemones, prickly purple sea urchins, bright orange starfish, yellow sea lemons, oval shelled mussels, volcano shaped barnacles, turban snails, hermit crabs, and sculpin fish. Looking toward the offshore islands you may be lucky enough to spot some of the resident harbor seals. Your best chance at seeing harbor seal pups is between April and May. Taking a glance toward the offshore cliffs and islands will reveal multitudes of seabirds, comprised mainly of Brandt's cormorants, pelagic cormorants, tufted puffins, common murres, and pigeon guillemots. During the spring and summer over 24,000 birds nest on the cliffs and rocky islands surrounding Yaquina Head.

Cobble Beach.

32

Once you're back at your vehicle, drive 0.5 miles on Lighthouse Drive and turn right into the Quarry Cove parking area. The *Quarry Cove Tide Pools Trail* is wheelchair accessible and takes you on a tour of an area once quarried for the hard basalt rock used to build roads. Today, the area has evolved into a thriving intertidal ecosystem.

Hike Information

🌐 Trail Contacts:
Bureau of Land Management, Salem OR (541) 574–3100 or *www.or.blm.gov/salem/html/ yaquina/index.htm*

🕐 Schedule:
Open year round from dawn to dusk

$ Fees/Permits:
$5 entrance fee

❓ Local Information:
Greater Newport Chamber of Commerce, Newport, OR 1–800–262–7844 or *www.newportnet.com/newport/cc*

💡 Local Events/Attractions:
Newport Seafood and Wine Festival, in February, Newport, OR (541) 265–8801 · "Sea of Lights" Holiday Party, in December, Newport, OR (541) 867–3474

🛏 Accommodations:
Inn at Otter Crest, Newport, OR 1–800–452–2101 or *www. ottercrest.com* · Oar House Bed & Breakfast, Newport, OR 1–800–252–2358 or *www.oar-house-bed-breakfast.com/ home.htm*

📖 Other Resources:
Yaquina Lights, Inc., Newport, OR (541) 574–3100 or *www.yaquinalights.org*

🚌 Intercity Bus Service:
Valley Retriever Bus Service Albany Amtrak station to Newport (541) 265–2253 Schedule: *www.tripcheck.com/About/ valleyretriever.htm*

🚶 Hike Tours:
You can tour the Yaquina Head Lighthouse from 12 P.M. to 4 P.M. daily or call the BLM to schedule a private tour (541) 574–3100.

🏪 Local Outdoor Retailers:
Bittler Brothers Sport Center, Newport, OR (541) 265–7192

Ⓝ Maps:
USGS maps: Newport North, OR

33

Silver Falls State Park

Hike Summary

This 6.9-mile trail offers a tour of 10 waterfalls in Oregon's largest state park, Silver Falls. Begin the hike at South Falls, the park's most beautiful waterfall. From there, descend into Silver Creek Canyon for a walk along bubbling Silver Creek and its mesmerizing display of unique waterfalls. Take the time to learn about the tree fossils present in the caves behind the 136-foot-tall North Falls.

Hike Specs

Start: From the trailhead off OR 214
Length: 6.9-mile loop
Approximate Hiking Time: 4–5 hours
Difficulty Rating: Moderate due to a steep descent into Silver Creek Canyon and a steep ascent out of the canyon
Trail Surface: Paved path, well-maintained dirt trail, and stairs that can be slippery and wet
Lay of the Land: Forested canyons, steep ascents, and waterfalls
Elevation Gain: 515 feet
Land Status: State park
Nearest Town: Silver Falls, OR
Other Trail Users: Hikers only
Canine Compatibility: Dogs not permitted on the Silver Falls Canyon Trail

Getting There

From Interstate 5 in Salem: Turn east onto OR 22 at Exit 253 where a sign indicates "North Santiam Highway/ Stayton/Detroit Lake." Drive five miles east on OR 22 and turn off at Exit 7 onto OR 214 at the "Silver Falls State Park" sign. At the stop sign at the end of the off ramp, turn left onto OR 214 and proceed 4.5 miles to a stop sign. Turn left and continue driving 12.2 miles on OR 214 to the entrance of Silver Falls State Park. After you enter the park, turn left at the South Falls turnoff and drive 0.2 miles to the Entrance Station. You'll have to pay a $3 day-use fee to get in. Proceed to the parking area. *DeLorme: Oregon Atlas & Gazetteer:* Page 54 A3

Silver Falls State Park, which at 8,706 acres is Oregon's largest state park, is a canyon carved up by the North and South Forks of Silver Creek and loaded with waterfalls. It's thought that the creeks are named after James "Silver" Smith who traveled to the area with his pockets full of silver coins in the 1840s. The name lived on when Silver Falls was established in the 1880s— then consisting of nothing more than a sawmill, a hotel, and several hunting lodges. The land was overzealously logged for its timber until the late 1920s, when the state considered turning the area into a national park. This ground the area logging to a halt, but unfortunately, national-park status was never realized. Ironically, the land had been subjected to too much logging and farming and didn't pass muster for the National Park Service. The

federal government did purchase the land during the Depression and designated it as a Recreational Demonstration Area, which features recreational facilities, hiking trails, and the South Falls Lodge. All of what you'll find here was built by the Civilian Conservation Corps.

A classic 6.9-mile loop through a forested canyon of stately Douglas fir, Western hemlock, red cedar, maple, alder, and gregarious cottonwoods offers a tour of as many as 10 waterfalls. In the fall the maples are colored in brilliant reds, oranges, and yellows and contrast sharply with the dark green of the surrounding forest.

Middle North Falls (103 feet).

The Western Sword Fern

The Western sword fern is common in the coniferous forests of the Northwest. This striking fern, which can grow to be five feet tall, has sword-like fronds that project outward from the center of the plant. Native American tribes used the fronds from this plant to build sleeping platforms. They also roasted and ate the plant's rhizomes.

The trail begins at the South Falls parking area, where you'll find restrooms and the South Falls Lodge (inside is a gift shop and information on the park's plants, animals, and geology). Begin the hike by descending a steep trail into the canyon, where you'll be greeted by a stunning view of the roaring 177-foot South Falls. The trail leads behind the falls to a basalt cave. Be prepared to get wet. The large holes in the cave are formed as water trickles down through the cracks.

After the falls, the trail parallels the South Fork of Silver Creek and is lined with leafy vine maple, sweeping sword ferns, Oregon grape, salal, bigleaf maples, and Douglas firs. At 1.1 miles the path arrives at the picturesque 93-foot Lower South Falls, and at 1.4 miles it comes to an intersection. If you turn right at the junction you'll loop back to the starting point on the Ridge Trail.

Continue walking straight. In another mile you'll pass the 30-foot cascade of Lower North Falls. At the next intersection turn left and walk 0.1 miles to a view of the mesmerizing double cascade of 178-foot Double

On the Silver Falls Canyon Trail.

Falls. This waterfall is part of Hult Creek, which empties into the North Fork of Silver Creek. At mile 2.8 miles, you'll arrive at 27-foot Drake Falls—the namesake of June Drake, a photographer whose photos brought prominence to the area. At the three-mile mark stop and investigate the 106-foot Middle North Falls. Be sure to check out the side trail that leads behind the falls.

After 3.5 miles you'll come to 31-foot Twin Falls. From here, the trail continues to parallel the North Fork of Silver Creek for another mile until it arrives at North Falls, a thundering 136-foot cascade. The trail leads behind the falls to large oval depressions in a basalt cave—the last signs of ancient trees that once stood here. The casts were formed when lava cooled around the trees and, over time, the trees rotted away. If you look carefully you can see the bark ridges in the basalt.

At this point you have two options: Continue another 0.2 miles to 136-foot Upper North Falls, or return 2.2 miles along the Rim Trail back to the trailhead.

Hike Information

① Trail Contacts:
Oregon State Park Information Center 1–800–551–6949 or www.prd.state.or.us

① Schedule:
The park is open year round. However, the trail can be very icy and treacherous in the winter months.

⑤ Fees/Permits:
$3 day-use fee

② Local Information:
Salem Convention & Visitors Association, Salem, OR 1–800–874–7012 or www.scva.org

① Local Events/Attractions:
Oregon State Fair, August to September, Salem, OR (503) 378-3247 · Sliver Falls Musical Festival, in September, Sublimity, OR (503) 873-3495 • Mount Angel Oktoberfest, in September, Mount Angel, OR (503) 845-9440 or www.oktoberfest.org

② Accommodations:
You can camp at Silver Falls State Park. The main camping area is located upstream from the South Falls parking area. Call the Oregon State Park Information Center at 1–800–551–6949 or go to www.open.org/~slvrfall/index.htm for more information.

① Restaurants:
Jonathan's Oyster Bar, Salem, OR (503) 362–7219

① Local Outdoor Retailers:
Bike 'n Hike Centers, Salem, OR (503) 581–2707 or www.bikenhike.com

① Maps:
USGS maps: Drake Crossing, OR

MilesDirections

0.0 START from the parking area and walk on the paved path toward the South Falls trailhead and South Falls Lodge.

0.1 At the trailhead turn left onto the paved Canyon Trail and descend steeply down a series of wood and stone steps that take you into the canyon. *[FYI. If you go right, you'll go on the Ridge Trail.]*

0.2 The trail comes to a T-intersection. Turn left to walk behind the 177-foot South Falls. Walk behind the falls and be sure to stop and read the interpretive sign. Be prepared to get wet on this section of the trail.

0.3 You'll come to a trail junction. Stay to the left and continue on the trail (the trail turns to a dirt path here). *[FYI. If you go right you'll cross a wooden bridge over the North Fork of Silver Creek, which takes you back to your starting point on the canyon rim.]*

1.1 Arrive at 93-foot Lower South Falls.

1.4 Come to a trail junction with Ridge Trail. Continue straight. *[FYI. If you go right, the sign indicates "South Falls Trailhead via Ridge Trail 1.2 miles."]*

2.0 Cross a wooden bridge.

2.4 Arrive at 30-foot Lower North Falls. Continue walking a short ways and you'll come to a trail junction. Turn left and walk 0.1 miles to Double Falls.

2.5 Arrive at the 178-foot Double Falls viewpoint. When you're finished viewing the falls, turn around and walk back to the main trail.

2.6 Arrive at the main trail. Turn left and cross a wooden bridge over Hult Creek.

2.8 Arrive at 27-foot Drake Falls.

3.0 Arrive at 103-foot Middle North Falls.

3.2 Come to a trail junction. Continue straight. *[FYI. If you turn right, a sign indicates "Winter Falls 0.5 miles, North Falls 1.5 miles, South Falls 3.0 miles."]*

3.5 Arrive at 31-foot Twin Falls.

4.4 Arrive at 136-foot North Falls. Walk behind the falls and be sure to read the interpretive sign. Look for ancient tree casts on the ceiling of the basalt cave. Walk up a steep series of concrete steps to the canyon rim.

4.5 Take a sharp right and continue walking on the Rim Trail. *[FYI. If you go left, you'll continue another 0.2 miles to 136-foot Upper North Falls]*

5.3 Come to a trail junction where you'll continue straight at a sign indicating "South Falls Trailhead 1.6 miles." *[FYI. If you go right, you'll go to Winter Falls.]* Walk through a paved parking area and then continue following the trail 1.6 miles back to your starting point.

5.6 Come to a fork. Stay to the right.

6.1 Come to a fork. Stay to the left.

6.8 Cross a paved road.

6.9 Arrive back at the South Falls Parking Area and your starting point.

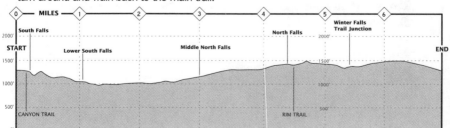

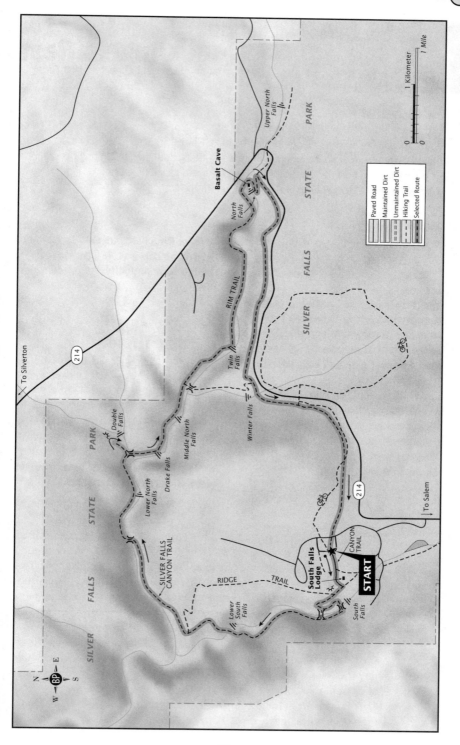

6

Angels Rest

Hike Summary

The rock cliffs of Angels Rest, accessible from a well-maintained trail, tower 1,500 feet above the Columbia River Gorge in the Columbia River Gorge National Scenic Area. The trail is certain to test your aerobic endurance but includes enough alluring distractions to keep your mind off the elevation gain. As a reward for all of your hard work, there is a first-rate view of the Columbia River Gorge from the top.

Hike Specs

Start: From the gravel parking area at the intersection of the I-84 Bridal Veil Falls exit and the Columbia River Highway

Length: 4.4-mile out-and-back

Approximate Hiking Time: 2–3 hours

Difficulty Rating: Moderate due to a steep ascent to the top of Angel's Rest

Trail Surface: Dirt trail with occasional rocky and muddy sections

Lay of the Land: Climb through a big-leaf maple and fern-filled forest to a great view of Coopey Falls. It's steep climbing up a series of switchbacks and a large boulder field before reaching the summit.

Elevation Gain: 1,674 feet

Land Status: National scenic area

Nearest City: Portland, OR

Other Trail Users: Hikers only

Canine Compatibility: Leashed dogs permitted

Getting There

From Portland: Drive 28 miles east on I-84. Take the Bridal Veil Falls exit (Exit 28) and drive a quarter mile to a gravel parking lot on the right side of the road. The trailhead is directly across the Columbia River Highway from the parking area. Look for a concrete trail marker and trailhead sign. *DeLorme: Oregon Atlas & Gazetteer:* Page 67 D7

R ising almost 1,500 feet from the Old Columbia River Highway, the rocky summit of Angels Rest offers stunning views of the Columbia Gorge. The basalt cliffs and ridges visible on this hike are the result of a 30-million-year struggle between fire and water. The cliffs are the eroded remnants of the Columbia lava flows that poured through the region over millions of years and originated from volcanic eruptions in eastern Oregon and Washington. Approximately 15,000 years ago, huge floods poured through the Columbia Gorge, widening the river channel and polishing the lofty walls visible today. This trail is one of many in the gorge leading from the Columbia River to magnificent cliff-top viewpoints.

The Angels Rest Trail begins with a steep traverse across a short hill to a forest of broadleaf maple trees. The jumble of mossy logs and rocks and the

fern-covered forest floor are a masterful mosaic of Mother Nature's handi-work. In early spring you'll see a colorful carpet of white Western trillium, delicate pink Barrett's penstemon, and the bluish-pink petals of the smooth-leaf Douglasia.

Just over half a mile up the trail, there's an excellent view of Coopey Falls. The falls, which plunge over the basalt cliff in a mesmerizing cascade, are the namesake of Charles Coopey, an English tailor who owned land in the area.

The trail continues past the falls through a mostly deciduous forest to tumbling Coopey Creek. If you're hiking with a dog, stop here for a cool-down. This is the path's only watering hole.

After the creek, the trail becomes steeper—gear up for a thigh-burning, heart-pumping ascent. A series of serpentine switchbacks slither through the skeletal remains of trees torched in a 1991 forest fire. The charred trees aren't exactly pretty, but the views certainly are.

Soon the trail arrives at a boulder field, home to the cute and cuddly pika. These small, gray-brown rodents, which look like rabbits, have short,

Views of the Columbia River from the Angel's Rest Trail are outstanding.

rounded ears. You'll hear their distinct "eep" warning call as you near. During the spring and summer you'll see them busily gathering grasses and seeds as they prepare for the coming winter.

Many hikers take a break to soak up the sun on the table-like boulders on this hillside. If you choose to rest here, be sure to look for turkey vultures soaring on the air currents above. Turkey vultures are easily recognized by their dark brown bodies, red featherless heads, and up to six-foot wing spans. Named for their likeness to the domestic turkey, these graceful soaring birds are actually scavengers and feed on carrion of amphibians, fish, and mammals.

Hike Information

● Trail Contacts:
Columbia River Gorge National Scenic Area, Hood River, OR (541) 386-2333 or *www.fs.fed.us/r6/columbia*

● Schedule:
Open year round

● Local Information:
Mount Hood National Forest, Gresham, OR (503) 668-1700 or *www.fs.fed.us/r6/mthood*

● Local Events/Attractions:
Columbia Gorge Sternwheeler, June to September, Cascade Locks, OR (503) 223-3928 or *www.sternwheeler.com* · **Mount Hood Railroad**, Hood River, OR (541) 386-3556 or *www.mthoodrr.com*

● Accommodations:
The Columbia Gorge Hotel, Hood River, OR 1-800-345-1921 or *www.columbiagorgehotel.com*

● Restaurant:
Multnomah Falls Lodge, Bridal Veil, OR (503) 695-2376

● Organizations:
Mazamas, Portland, OR (503) 227-2345 or *www.mazamas. org* · **Sierra Club Columbia Group**, Portland, OR (503) 231-0507 or *www.spiritone.com/~orsierra/columbia.html*

● Other Resources:
Eagle Newspapers, Salem, OR (503) 393-1774 or *www. gorgenews.com—for news and information about the Columbia Gorge.*

● Hike Tours:
Friends of the Columbia Gorge, Portland, OR (503) 241-3762 or *www.gorgefriends.org*

● Local Outdoor Retailers:
Great Outdoor Clothing Company, Troutdale, OR (503) 666-1543 or *www.greatoutdoorclothing.com*

● Maps:
USGS maps: Bridal Veil, OR
USFS maps: Trails of the Columbia Gorge

At the end of the boulder field, the trail forks. Follow the left branch for a short scramble to a basalt plateau—with top-notch views of the Columbia River Gorge—and the hike's turnaround point.

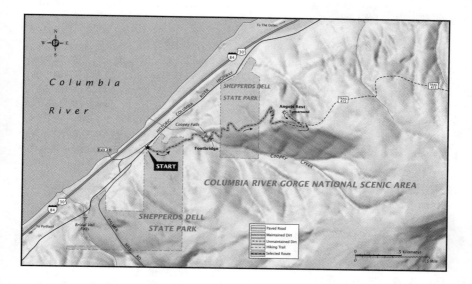

MilesDirections

0.0 START at the trailhead, located directly across the Columbia River Highway from the gravel parking area.

0.2 If you're lucky enough to be here in the spring, check out the delicate, white, triangular flowers of Western trillium along this section of trail.

0.6 Enjoy an excellent view of Coopey Falls on the left side of the trail.

0.7 Cross a wooden footbridge over tumbling Coopey Creek.

0.8 Ascend a series of switchbacks with magnificent views of the Columbia River Gorge.

2.1 Walk across a boulder field, keeping your eyes peeled for rock pikas. The trail comes to a fork—turn left and hike the remaining distance to the summit.

2.2 Reach the summit and a spectacular view of the Columbia River Gorge. This is your turnaround point.

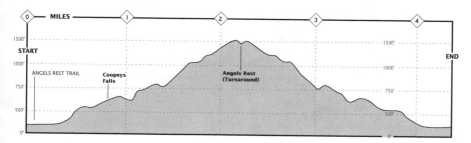

Larch Mountain

Hike Summary

Deep, mossy, green forests, pristine creeks, and cascading waterfalls—the natural beauty of the Columbia River Gorge National Scenic Area is spectacular. The Larch Mountain Trail 441 begins as a paved path that winds steeply up a ridge to a high point above Multnomah Falls Lodge. It's here that you're treated to grand views of 642-foot Multnomah Falls, one of Oregon's leading tourist attractions. Continuing past the Falls, the trail parallels Multnomah Creek, traversing up the side of Larch Mountain to yet another unforgettable view, this time of several of the Cascade's major volcanic peaks.

Hike Specs

Start: From the trailhead at Multnomah Falls Lodge
Length: 13.6-mile out-and-back
Approximate Hiking Time: 6–8 hours
Difficulty Rating: Difficult due to steep treks to the top of Multnomah Falls and Larch Mountain
Trail Surface: Pavement and dirt with occasional rocky sections
Lay of the Land: The trail begins as a paved path and winds steeply up a ridge to a high point above Multnomah Falls Lodge and Multnomah Falls. It then parallels Multnomah Creek through a mossy green forest, traversing steeply up the side of Larch Mountain.
Elevation Gain: 4112 feet
Land Status: National scenic area

Nearest Town: Portland, OR
Other Trail Users: Hikers only
Canine Compatibility: Dog friendly

Getting There

From Portland: Drive 30 miles east on I-84 to the Multnomah Falls Exit (Exit 31). Park you car in the large parking area in front of the lodge and gift shop. A paved path leads you to Multnomah Falls Lodge and the Multnomah Falls Lodge Gift Shop. The trail starts adjacent to the lodge. *DeLorme: Oregon Atlas & Gazetteer:* Page 67 D7

The mile-wide Columbia River carves through the Columbia River Gorge as it races west to meet the Pacific Ocean at Astoria in the northwest corner of Oregon. The mighty river, made famous by Lewis and Clark, separates Oregon from Washington and has served as a major transportation route for hundreds of years.

Basalt cliffs and 2,000- to 5,000-foot-tall peaks frame this magnificent gorge. Covering these mountains and the surrounding ridges is a thick canopy of Douglas fir, red alder, big-leaf maple, and red cedar. Through it all, tumbling down the cliffs of the River Gorge, are Oregon's magnificent waterfalls. One of the area's most spectacular is 642-foot Multnomah Falls,

the fourth highest year-round falls in the United States and one of the top tourist attractions in Oregon. Fed by Multnomah Creek, which drains snowmelt from Larch Mountain, Multnomah Falls plunges 560 feet from the top of the cliff onto a rock ledge and then drops another 82 feet to a deep pool.

The Larch Mountain Trail 441 starts at the base of the falls at the historic Multnomah Falls Lodge. The lodge, built in 1925, is now listed in the National Register of Historic Places. It was built from several different kinds of rock and was originally intended to serve as a place for travelers to spend the night. Today it houses a restaurant, gift shop, and Forest Service visitor center.

Just 0.1 miles from the lodge, the trail crosses Benson Bridge, built in 1914 by Italian stonemasons. This concrete bridge offers a splendid view of the long, billowing cascade of Multnomah Falls—as well as a good mist to get you a bit wet. Continue hiking up the steep paved path another

Columbia River Gorge.

MilesDirections

0.0 START walking on the paved trail adjacent to Multnomah Falls Lodge. Walk up a series of steps to a viewpoint.

0.1 Cross a wood footbridge over Multnomah Creek and then cross a large concrete bridge over Multnomah Creek. You'll have a breathtaking view of Multnomah Falls from the bridge.

0.2 The trail comes to a T-intersection. Turn right onto Larch Mountain Trail 441. *[FYI: Gorge Trail 400 continues to the left.]*

0.3 Pass a good viewpoint of Multnomah Falls.

0.7 The trail begins descending down a series of switchbacks that take you to Multnomah Creek.

0.8 The trail comes to a T-intersection. Turn left. The trail changes to gravel at this point. *[FYI. If you turn right the trail takes you to an overlook of Multnomah Falls.]* Proceed on the gravel path and cross a stone bridge over Multnomah Creek.

1.1 The trail comes to a T-intersection. Turn left. *[FYI. If you turn right you'll head to Wahkeena Trail 420 and Angels Rest.]* Cross a wooden bridge over Multnomah Creek.

3.0 The trail intersects with a double-track road. Continue straight. Proceed a few steps to another trail junction. Turn right at the sign that reads "Larch Mountain Trail 441 – 4 miles."

3.3 The trail comes to a fork. Continue straight (right). *[FYI. If you turn left, you'll see a sign that reads "Franklin Ridge Trail 427/Oneonta Trail 2.2."]*

3.4 Cross a log bridge.

4.2 Cross a log bridge.

4.5 Walk through a large boulder field.

5.0 The trail comes to a fork. Turn right and continue walking on Larch Mountain Trail 441.

5.5 The trail intersects with a double-track dirt road. Cross the road and continue another 1.3 miles to the top of Larch Mountain and your turnaround point.

6.5 Reach a trail junction. Stay left.

6.6 Arrive at a paved parking area. Turn left onto the paved trail that leads to the summit.

6.8 Arrive at the 4,055-foot summit of Larch Mountain where you'll have a commanding view (on a clear day) of Mount Hood, Mount Jefferson, Mount St. Helens, Mount Adams, Mount Rainier, the Columbia River Gorge, and the Bull Run Watershed.

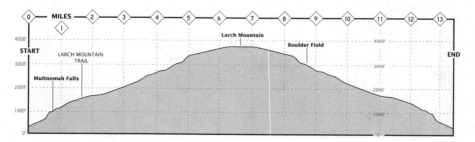

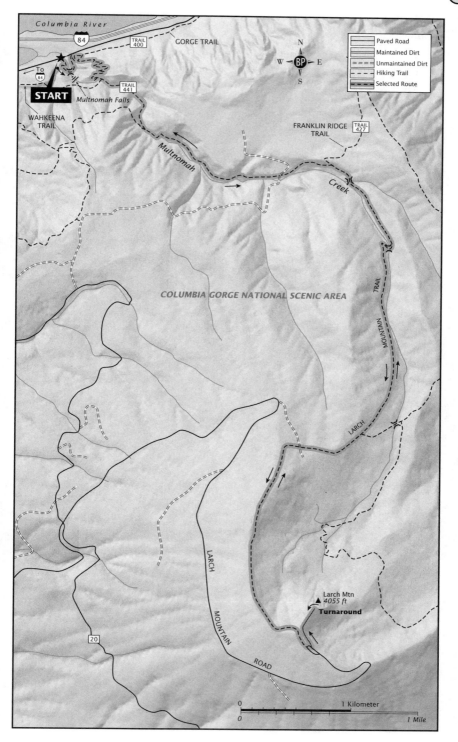

Columbia River

84

TRAIL 400

GORGE TRAIL

	Paved Road
	Maintained Dirt
	Unmaintained Dirt
	Hiking Trail
	Selected Route

To 84

START   *Multnomah Falls*

TRAIL 441

WAHKEENA TRAIL

Multnomah

FRANKLIN RIDGE TRAIL

TRAIL 427

Creek

COLUMBIA GORGE NATIONAL SCENIC AREA

MOUNTAIN   TRAIL

LARCH

LARCH

MOUNTAIN

ROAD

20

Larch Mtn
4055 ft
Turnaround

0   1 Kilometer

0   1 Mile

0.7 miles to the top of a ridge above the falls. There, at a trail junction, turn right for a quick detour to a dizzying cliffside view down the falls as it plunges over the high basalt cliff.

On September 4, 1995, a tour bus-size rockslide rumbled down the upper section of the falls. The slide, weighing almost 400 tons, plunged 225 feet and sent water, rocks, and debris more than 70 feet into the air from the valley floor. Twenty people suffered minor injuries from flying rocks. Imagine the mayhem.

642-foot Multnomah Falls.

After viewing the falls, head back to the trail junction. From there, continue walking on the Larch Mountain Trail. Over the next three miles the trail parallels Multnomah Creek and its charming waterfalls and mossy boulders and winds through a botanical wonderland filled with ferns, wildflowers, and other forest greenery.

The last 2.8-mile section of trail is a steep climb up the side of 4,055-foot Larch Mountain. At the top you'll find a picnic area and spectacular views of Mount Hood, Mount Jefferson, Mount St. Helens, Mount Adams, Mount Rainier, the Columbia River Gorge, and the Bull Run Watershed. Soak in the scenery then return to your vehicle the way you came.

Hike Information

● Trail Contacts:
USDA Forest Service, Columbia River Gorge National Scenic Area, Hood River, OR (541) 386-2333 or www.fs.fed.us/r6/columbia

● Schedule:
Open year round

● Local Information:
Mount Hood National Forest, Gresham, OR (503) 668-1700 or www.fs.fed.us/r6/mthood

● Local Events/Attractions:
Columbia Gorge Sternwheeler, June to September, Cascade Locks, OR (503) 223-3928 or www.sternwheeler.com · Mount Hood Railroad, Hood River, OR (541) 386-3556 or www.mthoodrr.com

● Accommodations:
The Columbia Gorge Hotel, Hood River, OR 1-800-345-1921 or www.columbiagorgehotel.com

● Restaurant:
Multnomah Falls Lodge, Bridal Veil, OR (503) 695-2376

● Organizations:
Mazamas, Portland, OR (503) 227-2345 or www.mazamas.org · Sierra Club Columbia Group, Portland, OR (503) 231-0507 or www.spiritone.com/~orsierra/columbia.html

● Other Resources:
Eagle Newspapers, Salem, OR (503) 393-1774 or www.gorge-news.com—for news and information about the Columbia Gorge.

● Hike Tours:
Friends of the Columbia Gorge, Portland, OR (503) 241-3762 or www.gorgefriends.org

● Local Outdoor Retailers:
Great Outdoor Clothing Company, Troutdale, OR (503) 666-1543 or www.greatoutdoorclothing.com

● Maps:
USGS maps: Multnomah Falls, OR · USFS maps: Trails of the Columbia Gorge

Horsetail, Oneonta and Triple Falls

Hike Summary

If you love waterfalls this hike is for you. This route through the Columbia River Gorge National Scenic Area visits four unique waterfalls, offers a great view of the narrow chasm of Oneonta Gorge, and snakes through a lush, mossy forest filled with wildflowers in the spring and summer months. It also climbs up a ridge to the long, sweeping cascade of Horsetail Falls, passes behind the broad cascade of Ponytail Falls, parallels swift Oneonta Creek, and travels along the tall, mossy walls of Oneonta Gorge.

Hike Specs

Start: From the trailhead off Columbia River Highway
Length: 5.4-mile out-and-back
Approximate Hiking Time: 2–3 hours
Difficulty Rating: Moderate due to some steep climbing
Trail Surface: Maintained dirt path with some rocky sections
Lay of the Land: Steep ridge trails with waterfalls and stunning views.
Elevation Gain: 1,173 feet
Land Status: National scenic area
Nearest City: Portland, OR
Other Trail Users: HIkers only
Canine Compatibility: Leashed dogs permitted

Getting There

From Portland: Drive 35 miles east on I-84 and take the Ainsworth State Park turnoff (Exit 35). Proceed 1.5 miles west on the Columbia River Highway to the Horsetail Falls parking lot located on the left (south) side of the road. **DeLorme: Oregon Atlas & Gazetteer:** Page 67 C8

The steep and scenic Columbia River Gorge, carved by the Columbia River, is filled with miles of hiking trails, lush forest, and unique and beautiful waterfalls. The main highway that travels through the orge, Interstate 84, allows easy access to many trails leading to dramatic vistas, through mossy forests, and along bubbling creeks.

In the early 1900s, travel through the gorge was difficult if not impossible. Without a road the trip was dangerous, tedious, and was usually avoided. So when two Portland businessmen, Simon Lancaster and Sam Hill, convinced the government to build a highway that would match the gorge's natural beauty while allowing easy access to and through the area, many people were thankful. The resulting Columbia River Highway, which stretched for 196

Triple Falls.

miles from Portland to The Dalles, was built at a cost of $11 million and was completed in 1922. Today drivers still travel on sections of the original highway. Old bridges, walls, and public buildings from the project are still standing, built from locally quarried basalt to last forever.

There are dozens of waterfalls in the area, and this hike takes you to four of the best: Horsetail, Ponytail, Oneonta, and Triple falls. The trail starts beside 176-foot Horsetail Falls. As its name implies, the plunging water mimics the swishing motion of a horse's tail. Moving on, the trail climbs a ridge along a series of steep switchbacks, past ferns clinging tightly to a hill-

MilesDirections

0.0 START at the Horsetail Falls Trailhead, which is accessed by crossing the Columbia River Highway from the parking area. Be sure to read the interpretive signs at the beginning of the hike that describe plant and animal species that you may see along this hike. And while here, it'll be hard to miss the charming cascade of 176-foot Horsetail Falls. Begin hiking on Trail 438 up a series of steep switchbacks through a fern-filled hillside dotted with bunches of candy flowers and geraniums.

0.1 Come to a T-intersection. Turn right and continue walking on Gorge Trail 400.

0.4 Arrive at cascading Ponytail Falls. The trail continues behind the falls.

0.8 Come to a fork and turn left. *[**FYI.** If you turn right you can view a memorial plaque for a hiker who fell from a cliff east of Horsetail Falls in April 1988.]*

1.3 Pass a good viewpoint of Oneonta Gorge. The trail begins to descend steeply here.

1.4 Cross over a metal bridge from which you can view 60-foot Oneonta Falls to your left. Once you cross the bridge, the trail begins to climb steeply.

1.5 The trail comes to a T-intersection. Turn left and continue hiking on Oneonta Trail 424.

2.0 Cross a wooden footbridge.

2.5 Pass a side trail that leads to a good viewpoint of Triple Falls.

2.7 Reach a wooden footbridge above Triple Falls. This is your turnaround point. Head back the way you came.

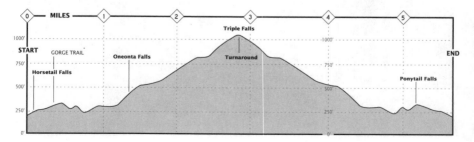

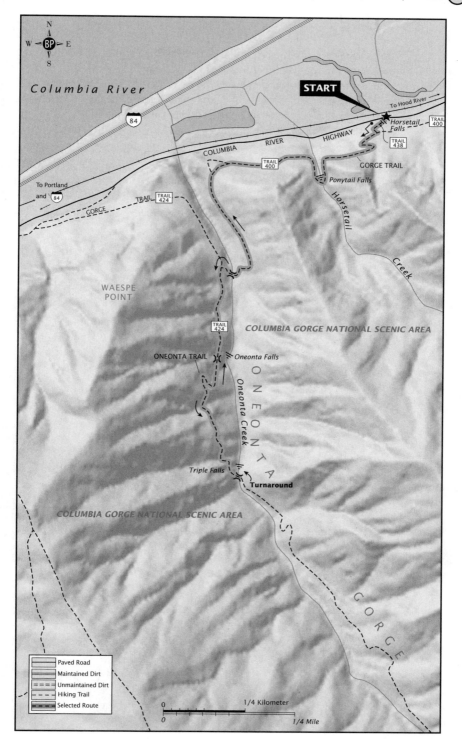

side dotted with candy flowers and geraniums. After 0.4 miles the trail passes Ponytail Falls (also known as Upper Horsetail Falls). This quick cascade drops from a rocky cirque into a deep, rounded pool. An open, circular cave has formed in the basalt behind the falls, allowing hikers to see the action from a new angle. If you step inside the cave, be sure to check out the cave roof—fractures seen in the ceiling (and the blocks on the floor) are a result of water penetrating from above then freezing and expanding.

Admiring Ponytail Falls.

At 1.3 miles you'll have a stunning view of narrow Oneonta Gorge and Oneonta Creek. Big-leaf maples, beautiful ferns, moss, and rare, cliff-dwelling plants that cling to the gorge's 100-foot rock walls are protected as part of the Oneonta Gorge Botanical Area. At 1.4 miles you'll cross a bridge offering excellent views of 60-foot Oneonta Falls.

At 2.5 miles you'll have a great view of the three-tiered cascade of Triple Falls. Like three long fingers, the triple cascade dangles over a basalt ledge and dips into the creek far below. From here, hike another 0.2 miles to a wooden footbridge, a good place to enjoy a well-deserved break and admire bubbling Oneonta Creek before turning around for the trek back to the trailhead.

Hike Information

🍂 Trail Contacts:
Columbia River Gorge National Scenic Area, Hood River, OR (541) 386–2333 or *www.fs.fed.us/r6/columbia*

🕐 Schedule:
Open year round

❓ Local Information:
Mount Hood National Forest, Gresham, OR (503) 668–1700 or *www.fs.fed.us/r6/mthood*

🍂 Local Events/Attractions:
Columbia Gorge Sternwheeler, June to September, Cascade Locks, OR (503) 223–3928 or *www.sternwheeler.com* · **Mount Hood Railroad,** Hood River, OR (541) 386–3556 or *www.mthoodrr.com*

🛏 Accommodations:
The Columbia Gorge Hotel, Hood River, OR 1–800–345–1921 or *www.columbiagorgehotel.com*

🍴 Restaurant:
Multnomah Falls Lodge, Bridal Veil, OR (503) 695–2376

👥 Organizations:
Mazamas, Portland, OR (503) 227–2345 or *www.mazamas.org* · **Sierra Club Columbia Group,** Portland, OR (503) 231–0507 or *www.spiritone.com/~orsierra/columbia.html*

📖 Other Resources:
Eagle Newspapers, Salem, OR (503) 393–1774 or *www.gorgenews.com*—for news and information about the Columbia Gorge.

🚶 Hike Tours:
Friends of the Columbia Gorge, Portland, OR (503) 241–3762 or *www.gorgefriends.org*

🏕 Local Outdoor Retailer:
Great Outdoor Clothing Company, Troutdale, OR (503) 666–1543 or *www.greatoutdoorclothing.com*

ⓝ Maps:
USGS maps: Multnomah Falls, OR

Munra Point

Hike Summary

This hike, one of the most challenging in the Columbia River Gorge National Scenic Area, throws just about everything at you at once: dense forest; steep ascents and descents on slippery, often muddy slopes; rock scrambling; steep drop-offs; and stunning views of the gorge. The hike starts by heading west on Gorge Trail 400, a dirt path that turns into a doubletrack dirt road. After half a mile it hooks up with the relentlessly steep Munra Point Trail, which winds its way up a ridge to the top of Munra Point.

Hike Specs

Start: From the Gorge Trail trailhead off I-84

Length: 2.0-mile out-and-back

Approximate Hiking Time: 4–5 hours

Difficulty Rating: Difficult due to a steep ascent to the top of Munra Point on an eroded, rocky trail

Trail Surface: Dirt path, doubletrack dirt road, and large rocks

Lay of the Land: Dirt paths and steep, unrelenting trails that wind up to the top of Munra Point

Elevation Gain: 2,110 feet

Land Status: National scenic area

Nearest Town: Portland, OR

Other Trail Users: Hikers only

Canine Compatibility: Not dog friendly

Warning!

This trail has several sections of rock scrambling and is recommended for advanced hikers only.

Getting There

From Portland: Drive east on I-84 for approximately 40 miles, exiting at Bonneville Dam (Exit 40). At the stop sign, turn right (south) and pull into the gravel parking lot at the Wahclella Falls trailhead. *DeLorme: Oregon Atlas & Gazetteer:* Page 68 C1

The Columbia River Gorge stretches east from Portland and is a popular destination for those living and visiting northwest Oregon. On its banks are over 40 million years' worth of Mother Nature's forces at work. High cliff walls and ridges covered with forest greenery and magnificent waterfalls are found between Troutdale and Hood River off Interstate 84. East from Hood River toward the community of The Dalles, sagebrush- and oak-covered slopes prevail thanks to decreased rainfall and the resulting hotter, drier climate.

For early settlers traveling along the Oregon Trail, The Dalles was a main stopping point—a place to rest and refuel before attempting the most difficult part of their journey, a dangerous rafting trip down the rapids of the

Columbia River (overland travel was, at the time, impossible). These huge rafts were built from logs up to 40 feet in length and were manned by skilled river-runners. The trip downriver was slow and tiring and the water was icy cold. Often the rafts traveled just a few miles per day, and on dangerous sections of the river, rafts, wagons, and other gear had to be portaged.

Elizabeth Smith made it to The Dalles in the fall of 1847. Her journey west to Portland took her and her family 26 days. This brave woman wrote about this difficult journey in her journal, as recorded in Bill Gulick's *Roadside History of Oregon*:

> **Nov. 2, 1847:** *We took off our wagon wheels, laid them on the raft, placed the wagon beds on them, and started. There are three families of us, Adam Polk, Russell Welch, and ourselves, on twelve logs eighteen inches through and forty feet long. The water runs three inches over our raft.*
>
> **Nov. 7, 1847:** *Put out in rough water. Moved a few miles. The water became so rough that we were forced to land. No one to man the raft but my husband and my oldest boy, sixteen years old.*
>
> **Nov. 18, 1847:** *My husband is sick. It rains and snows. We started around the falls this morning with our wagons. We have five miles to go. I carry my babe and lead, or rather carry, another through snow, mud, and water almost to my knees.*
>
> **Nov. 20, 1847:** *I froze or chilled my feet so that I can not wear a shoe, so I have to go around in the cold water in my bare feet.*
>
> **Nov. 27, 1847:** *Passed Fort Vancouver in the night. Landed a mile below. My husband has never left his bed since he was taken sick.*

Munra Point.

Elizabeth and her family finally reached Portland but their hardships did not end. She wrote:

Feb. 1, 1848: *Rain all day. This day my dear husband, my last remaining friend, died.*

Feb. 2, 1848: *Today we buried my earthly companion. Now I know what none but widows know: that is, how comfortless is a widow's life; especially when left in a strange land without money or friends, and the care of seven children.*

(Source: *Roadside History of Oregon*, Bill Gulick, Mountain Press Publishing Company)

As Smith's journal entries show, traveling down the Columbia River was not exactly a picnic. So it's no surprise that Portland settlers sought to find an overland route. One eventual alternative, discovered by Samuel Barlow and Joel Palmer in 1845, was what came to be known as Barlow Road.

Built the following year, in 1846, the road proved to be almost as diffi-

MilesDirections

0.0 START at the Wahclella Falls Trailhead parking lot. Walk back up the paved entrance road and turn left at the Gorge Trail 400 sign and walk over the concrete bridge over Tanner Creek.

0.1 Turn left at the Gorge Trail 400 sign and begin weaving your way up the hill on the dirt footpath lined with sword fern, big leaf maple and cedar trees.

0.2 Pass through an area dominated by blackberry bushes. These hardy and prickly plants bear tasty berries starting in mid-to-late August.

0.3 The trail forks; stay left.

0.5 Turn left onto an unmaintained dirt trail that begins climbing fairly steeply.

There is poison oak scattered everywhere along this section of the trail. Be sure to wear long pants and wear Ivy Block™ to protect exposed skin from this obnoxious plant!

0.7 You'll scramble up two consecutive rocky sections. Watch your footing if the rocks are wet! As you scramble up these rocks you'll see bunches of Oregon stonecrop clinging to the rocky ledges.

0.9 Scramble up a series of rocks through a narrow and steep gully.

1.0 Reach the small, flat summit and soak in the views of the magnificent Columbia River Gorge.

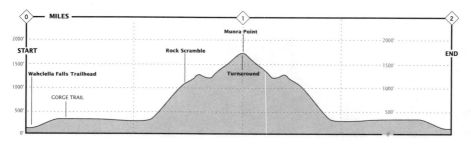

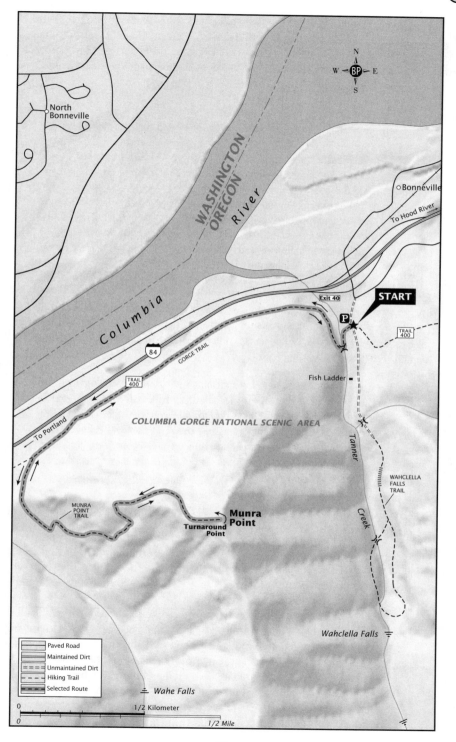

N
W —⊕BP⊕— E
S

North
Bonneville

WASHINGTON
OREGON
River

○ Bonneville

To Hood River

Exit 40

START

Ⓟ

TRAIL
400

Columbia

I-84

GORGE TRAIL

TRAIL
400

Fish Ladder ▪

To Portland

COLUMBIA GORGE NATIONAL SCENIC AREA

Tanner

WAHCLELLA
FALLS
TRAIL

MUNRA
POINT
TRAIL

**Munra
Point**

Turnaround
Point

Creek

Wahclella Falls ≡

	Paved Road
	Maintained Dirt
	Unmaintained Dirt
	Hiking Trail
	Selected Route

≡ Wahe Falls

0
1/2 Kilometer
0
1/2 Mile

cult as the trip down the river, as settlers were faced with the challenge of sending wagons and gear up and down 60 percent grades. A toll was charged to users, including a $5 fee for each wagon and $1 for each head of stock. Many settlers could not afford to pay, so Barlow made them sign a note that promised payment in the future.

Here are a traveler's comments:

"Some men's hearts died within them and some of our women sat down by the roadside and cried, saying they had abandoned all hope of ever reaching the promised land. I saw women with babies but a week old, toiling up the mountains in the burning sun, on foot, because our jaded teams were not able to haul them.

We went down mountains so steep that we had to let our wagons down with ropes. My wife and I carried our children up muddy mountains in the Cascades, half a mile high, and then carried the loadings of our wagons by piecemeal, as our cattle were so reduced that they were hardly able to haul up our empty wagon."

(Source: *Roadside History of Oregon*, Bill Gulick, Mountain Press Publishing Company)

One particularly hazardous section of the road was at Laurel Hill, located above Government Camp off present-day U.S. Route 26. This stretch was so steep that it filled the travelers' hearts with fear. Here are one settler's remarks from 1853:

"The road on this hill is something terrible. It is worn down into the soil from five to seven feet, leaving steep banks on both sides, and so narrow that it is almost impossible to walk alongside of the cattle for any distance without leaning against the oxen. The emigrants cut down a small tree about ten inches in diameter and about forty feet long, and the more limbs it has on the better. This tree they fastened to the rear axle with chains or ropes, top end foremost, making an excellent brake."

(Source: *Roadside History of Oregon*, Bill Gulick, Mountain Press Publishing Company)

Today nothing remains of this route but old wagon ruts. Visitors can now make the journey over Mount Hood in about an hour via U.S. Route 26. While pale in comparison, the hike to the top of the scenic Munra Point is physically demanding, even to experienced hikers, with its relentlessly steep grade and large, loose rocks.

The trail starts out innocently enough. Hike south from the Wahclella Falls trailhead on Gorge Trail 400 and climb up the side of a ridge. Eventually the trail flattens out and becomes a doubletrack road. You'll find juicy blackberries here during the months of August and September.

After half a mile, a side trail ascends Munra Point Ridge, but Gorge Trail 400 continues straight. The trail is lined with big-leaf maple, Oregon grape, and other forest greenery. And the higher the trail goes, the steeper and more eroded it becomes. Soon the vegetation is primarily scrub oak and poison oak, but splashes of Indian paintbrush, purple lupine, and wild roses keep things cheery. At 0.7 miles some rock scrambling is required, and at 0.9 miles there's a steep, narrow, and rocky gully. Finally, after a mile, the trail arrives at the small, flat summit. The reward for all your hard work: Spectacular views of the Columbia River Gorge and a steep descent back to your car.

Hike Information

◐ Trail Contacts:
Columbia River Gorge National Scenic Area, Hood River, OR (541) 386–2333 or *www.fs.fed.us/r6/columbia*

◐ Schedule:
Open year round

⑤ Fees/Permits:
Requires a Northwest Forest $5 day pass or $30 annual pass. You can purchase a pass online at: *www.fs.fed.us/r6/feedemo* or by call calling 1–800–270–7504.

❓ Local Information:
Mount Hood National Forest, Gresham, OR (503) 668–1700 or *www.fs.fed.us/r6/mthood*

◐ Local Events/Attractions:
Columbia Gorge Sternwheeler, June to September, Cascade Locks, OR (503) 223–3928 or *www.sternwheeler.com* · **Mount Hood Railroad,** Hood River, OR (541) 386–3556 or *www.mthoodrr.com*

◐ Accommodations:
The Columbia Gorge Hotel, Hood River, OR 1–800–345–1921 or *www.columbiagorgehotel.com*

◐ Restaurant:
Multnomah Falls Lodge, Bridal Veil, OR (503) 695–2376

◐ Organizations:
Mazamas, Portland, OR (503) 227–2345 or *www.mazamas.org* · **Sierra Club Columbia Group,** Portland, OR (503) 231–0507 or *www.spiritone.com/~orsierra/columbia.html*

◐ Other Resources:
Eagle Newspapers, Salem, OR (503) 393–1774 or *www.gorgenews.com—for news and information about the Columbia Gorge.*

◐ Hike Tours:
Friends of the Columbia Gorge, Portland, OR (503) 241–3762 or *www.gorgefriends.org*

◐ Local Outdoor Retailers:
Great Outdoor Clothing Company, Troutdale, OR (503) 666–1543 or *www.greatoutdoorclothing.com*

Ⓝ Maps:
USGS maps: Bonneville Dam, OR

Wahclella Falls

Hike Summary

This short-but-sweet hike takes you along the edge of Tanner Creek to a roaring two-tiered waterfall, which plunges into a deep rocky pool. Shady maples, wild raspberries and splashes of wildflowers decorate this fun, family hike. An optional loop takes you down to the creek's edge where you can wade in the cool, clear water on those hot summer days.

Hike Specs

Start: From the Wahclella Falls trailhead off I-84 (Exit 40)

Length: 2.2-mile out-and-back (with an optional loop)

Approximate Hiking Time: 1 hour

Difficulty Rating: Easy

Trail Surface: Combination well-graded gravel and dirt path

Lay of the Land: This fairly flat trail parallels the scenic Tanner Creek to the base of Wahclella Falls.

Elevation Gain: 384 feet

Land Status: National scenic area

Nearest Town: Portland, OR

Other Trail Users: Hikers only

Canine Compatibility: Leashed dog permitted

Getting There

From Portland: Drive east on I-84 for approximately 40 miles and exit at Bonneville Dam (Exit 40). At the stop sign, turn right (south) and pull into the gravel parking lot at the Wahclella Falls Trailhead. *DeLorme: Oregon Atlas & Gazetteer:* Page 68 C1

> *If you want to tour more magnificent waterfalls in a different part of Oregon, be sure to check out Silver Falls State Park [see Hike 5].*

Head east from Portland on Interstate 84 and you'll reach The Columbia River Gorge in about 30 minutes. The Gorge is chockfull of scenic hiking trails that wind through mossy, green forests and lead you to spectacular ridge-tops and cascading waterfalls. The Gorge has one of the highest concentrations of waterfalls in the United States. Over 77 falls make a roaring dive over basalt cliffs in a 420-square-mile area. The most well known waterfall in the Columbia Gorge is Multnomah Falls, located off Exit 31 on Interstate 84. The long, thin, two-tiered cascade of this magnificent waterfall plunges 620 feet into a deep, rocky pool.

Another magnificent river falls that could be seen in the Gorge during the first part of the century is the now extinct Celilo Falls, located 12 miles east of The Dalles on the Columbia River. This 20-foot falling torrent of

Wahclella Falls.

water was a favorite fishing spot for the local Native Americans, who'd seasonally congregate here to spear exhausted salmon making their way up the falls to spawn. This attractive fishing area was also a trading post of sorts. Native Americans from California, Canada, and the Rockies would assemble here to trade goods and gamble. Lewis and Clark passed through the area in 1805 and noted seeing over 10,000 pounds of dried salmon here. This spectacular falls all but disappeared in the 1950s when The Dalles Dam was built. Today, Celilo Park is all that remains of the falls. You can view pictures of Celilo Falls and learn more about its history by visiting the Columbia Gorge Discovery Center located three miles west of The Dalles off Interstate 84.

Other well-known waterfalls in the Columbia River Gorge include Horsetail and Ponytail falls [see Hike 8]. The concentration of these magnificent waterfalls is due to the 2,000- to 3,000-foot basalt cliff walls that line the Gorge. Huge basalt lava flows poured through the area between 10 and 17 million years ago, creeping toward the sea. For millions of years now the Columbia River has carved the beautiful gorge you see today. A few massive floods (we're talking of geologic proportions) following periods of glaciation made abrupt changes in the landscape. One such flood occurred as recently as 13,000 years ago. A natural dam broke on the Clark Fork River in Montana, unleashing a massive wall of water through the narrow gorge. The enormous wave acted like a natural bulldozer, gouging out hundreds of thousands of tons of earth and rock as the water rushed to the sea.

MilesDirections

0.0 START the hike at the wooden trailhead sign at the south end of the parking lot. Begin walking on a wide, well-graded gravel path next to picturesque Tanner Creek.

0.3 Come to a cement fish ladder.

0.4 Cross a wooden bridge and notice the splashing falls on your left.

0.6 Walk up a flight of wooden steps.

0.8 Come to a fork and go left. *[**Option.** The right fork takes you on the optional loop section of the trail.]*

0.9 Cross a wooden bridge.

1.1 Reach the roaring Wahclella Falls and turn around.

2.2 Arrive back at the parking lot.

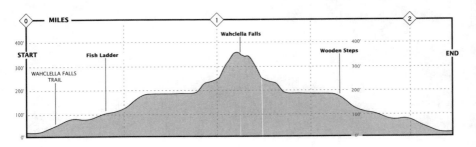

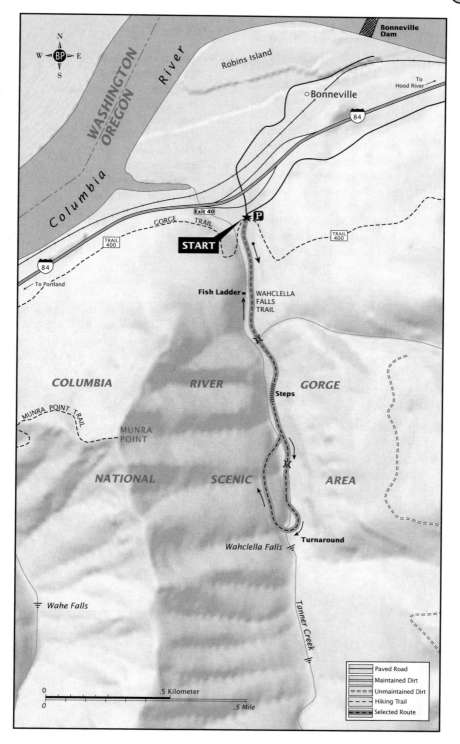

If you're still in the mood for waterfalls, take the time to do this easy, 2.2-mile out-and-back hike to the base of Wahclella Falls. The trail parallels tree-lined Tanner Creek. During July and August keep your eye out for wild raspberries along the trail. The half-sphere shaped berries range in color from light pink to a darker red and make a sweet treat as you stroll down the trail. If it's a hot summer day, be sure to bring along some sandals so you can wade in the creek and cool off on the way back to

Quick Oregon Facts

- **State Animal:** beaver
- **State Beverage:** milk
- **State Bird:** Western meadowlark
- **State Capital:** Salem
- **State Dance:** square dance
- **State Fish:** Chinook salmon
- **State Flower:** Oregon grape
- **State Gem:** sunstone
- **State Insect:** swallowtail butterfly
- **State Mushroom:** Pacific golden chanterelle
- **State Tree:** Douglas fir

Fish ladder for migrating salmon.

your car. If you still haven't had your fill of some of Oregon's most scenic waterfalls, head west on Interstate 84 and take the Warrendale exit (Exit 37). Turn left, proceed under the highway, and take another left. Drive approximately a half mile to a parking area located on the right side of the road. You'll hike a little under a mile to the base of the striking Elowah Falls, which pushes its way over a high cliff wall in a long, thin cascade.

Hike Information

📞 Trail Contacts:
Columbia River Gorge National Scenic Area, Hood River, OR (503) 668–1700 or *www.fs.fed.us/r6/columbia*

🕐 Schedule:
Open year round

💲 Fees/Permits:
Requires a Northwest Forest $5 day pass or $30 annual pass. You can purchase a pass online at: *www.fs.fed.us/r6/feedemo* or by call calling 1–800–270–7504.

❓ Local Information:
Mount Hood National Forest, Gresham, OR (503) 668–1700 or *www.fs.fed.us/r6/mthood*

💡 Local Events/Attractions:
Columbia Gorge Sternwheeler, June to September, Cascade Locks, OR (503) 223–3928 or *www.sternwheeler.com* · **Mount Hood Railroad,** Hood River, OR (541) 386–3556 or *www.mthoodrr.com*

🛏 Accommodations:
The Columbia Gorge Hotel, Hood River, OR 1–800–345–1921 or *www.columbiagorgehotel.com*

🍴 Restaurant:
Multnomah Falls Lodge, Bridal Veil, OR (503) 695–2376

👥 Organizations:
Mazamas, Portland, OR (503) 227–2345 or *www.mazamas.org* · **Sierra Club Columbia Group,** Portland, OR (503) 231–0507 or *www.spiritone.com/~orsierra/columbia.html*

📖 Other Resources:
Eagle Newspapers, Salem, OR (503) 393–1774 or *www.gorgenews.com*—for news and information about the Columbia Gorge.

🚶 Hike Tours:
Friends of the Columbia Gorge, Portland, OR (503) 241–3762 or *www.gorgefriends.org*

🛍 Local Outdoor Retailers:
Great Outdoor Clothing Company, Troutdale, OR (503) 666–1543 or *www.greatoutdoorclothing.com*

🗺 Maps:
USGS maps: Bonneville Dam, OR **USFS maps:** Trails of the Columbia Gorge

Eagle Creek to High Bridge

Hike Summary

This trail through the Columbia River Gorge National Scenic Area leads through a deep, scenic canyon carved by the bubbling Eagle Creek and shaded by a canopy of oak, big-leaf maple, and cedar. Along the route, hikers are rewarded with views of half a dozen cascading waterfalls and a creek perfectly suited for a swim during the hot summer months. Backpackers can hike in and camp at any one of the four established camp-sites along the first 7.5 miles of the trail—but keep in mind these sites fill up fast. For more solitude, forge ahead 13.3 miles from the Eagle Creek trailhead to Wahtum Lake and camp there.

Hike Specs

Start: From the trailhead off I-84
Length: 7.0-mile out-and-back
Approximate Hiking Time: 3–4 hours
Difficulty Rating: Moderate due to the long ascent up Eagle Creek Canyon to High Bridge
Trail Surface: Gravel and dirt path (with sections of cable handrail) along a deep canyon paralleling Eagle Creek
Lay of the Land: Deeply carved canyon walls and scenic waterfalls
Elevation Gain: 1,766 feet
Land Status: National scenic area
Nearest City: Portland, OR
Other Trail Users: Hikers only
Canine Compatibility: Leashed dog permitted

Getting There

From Portland: Drive east on I-84 for approximately 41 miles, exiting at the Eagle Creek Recreation Area sign (Exit 41). At the stop sign, turn right (south) and proceed toward the picnic area and trailhead. Drive approximately half a mile and park in the paved parking area. *DeLorme: Oregon Atlas & Gazetteer:* Page 68 C1

E agle Creek is a classic gorge hike that should not be overlooked by hikers of any level. As you hike this trail, it's hard not to appreciate the time and effort spent creating this engineering marvel that sweeps along the high cliff walls, offering spectac-ular views of many of the area's different waterfalls. Be fore-warned, though, if you're planning on hiking Eagle Creek with children: There are many steep drop-offs along the route and unsupervised children could easily fall from one of the trailside cliffs. If you're determined

to take your child with you, be sure to keep a close eye on him or her at all times. (Of course, this same philosophy also applies to dogs. If you must take your dog with you, keep it leashed at all times.) Because of the trail's spectacular scenery and fairly easy grade, this very popular hike is often crowd-

Eagle Creek Trail.

ed—especially on sunny summer weekends—so consider making the trip on a weekday to avoid the crowds. Otherwise, be prepared to share this trail with a slew of outdoor enthusiasts.

At the start of the trail, don't pass up the opportunity to visit the Cascade Fish Hatchery (near a picnic area and a campground). Many visitors choose to explore the hatchery before setting out on the trail because of the unique role it plays in the fish supply of the Columbia River. Built in 1957 in connection with the Columbia River Fishery Development Program, the

MilesDirections

0.0 START hiking on Eagle Creek Trail 440, beginning at the wooden trailhead sign at the far end of the paved parking area. There is drinking water and an interpretive sign at the trailhead.

0.6 Eagle Creek Trail becomes very narrow with a steep drop-off to the right. Steel cables are provided to help negotiate this part of the trail.

0.7 The trail narrows again and has more steep drop-offs. Cables and handrails are again provided to help with trail negotiation.

1.5 Walk down the side trail to view Metlako Falls.

1.6 Reach the viewpoint for Metlako Falls. When you're finished viewing the falls, continue following the side trail as it loops back to Eagle Creek Trail.

1.9 Walk over a series of concrete steps that cross a scenic cascading stream. Eagle Creek Trail intersects with the Lower Punch Bowl Falls Trail. Turn right

on this trail and descend steeply to the creek bed for a view Lower Punch Bowl Falls.

2.3 Reach Lower Punchbowl Falls. This is a good place for a swim in the hot summer months. When you're ready to leave, turn around and hike back to the main trail.

2.7 Intersect with Eagle Creek Trail. Turn right to continue the hike toward High Bridge.

2.8 Turn right on the side trail to a small viewpoint of Upper Punchbowl Falls. When you're finished viewing the falls return to the main trail.

2.9 Cross a wooden bridge over Fern Creek.

3.5 Reach High Bridge where you can view the deep chasm carved by Eagle Creek. At this point turn around and head back along Eagle Creek to your starting point.

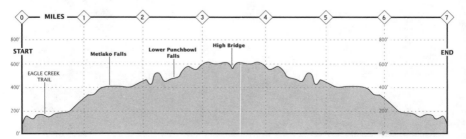

hatchery's primary purpose is to provide coho salmon for the ailing salmon fishery in the Columbia River. Adult salmon, as many know, migrate up-river every year to spawn. Salmon that make it as far as the hatchery, however, are captured and killed so that their eggs and sperm may be collected. (While this may sound harsh, adult salmon die naturally in the wild after spawning anyway.) The eggs and sperm are mixed in a bucket allowing the eggs to become fertilized. The fertilized eggs are then placed in trays and moved to an incubation building for 12 weeks. At that point, baby fish fry

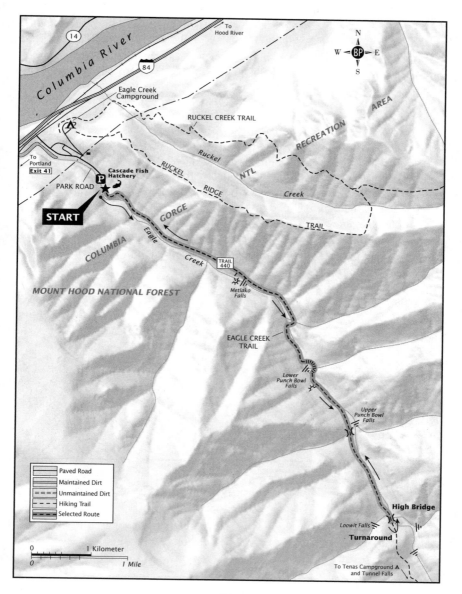

hatch and are moved to starter ponds where they are carefully monitored, fed, and raised. There are 30 raising ponds at the hatchery, and each pond is filled with 75,000 smolt (young salmon ready to migrate to the ocean). The fish are held in the raising ponds for a year, until they reach about six inches in length. Once the coho (also known as "silvers") are released, they migrate to the ocean. There they spend two to three years of their life before returning to the hatchery (nearly eight pounds at this point) to spawn and begin the cycle all over again.

The trail—remember, that's why you're here—is easy enough for just about anyone in the family to enjoy. It starts just above the creek and ascends very slowly over the next 3.5 miles to High Bridge (your turnaround point). Along the route you'll pass twisted oak trees and shady, big-leaf maples. In the spring and summer months, wildflowers along the trail compete amongst one another in a show of vibrant colors for all to enjoy.

At 0.6 miles there's a section of trail that often proves tricky to those unaccustomed to heights. Fortunately, cables are in place to help hikers navigate this precipitous stretch cliff-side trail. The trail is actually in good shape; it's just the steep drop-off to the right that makes your brain put on the brakes.

After 1.5 miles there's a very short, optional side trail to Metlako Falls, which takes its name from the Native American goddess of salmon (in fact, the falls seem to sweep off the basalt cliff like a salmon racing to the sea). At 1.9 miles you'll arrive at the Lower Punchbowl Falls Trail. Descend steeply here for 0.4 miles to the creek bed and falls, a broad cascade that tumbles into a rocky, circular bowl. If it's a hot summer day, this area will be packed with kids, dogs, and others splashing and wading in the water. Once you're back on the main trail you'll intersect with a side trail to 30-foot Upper Punchbowl Falls.

Eagle Creek.

As you continue on the trail the gorge becomes steeper and deeper until you reach the High Bridge, a long, skinny expansion bridge that stretches precariously across the canyon. From the middle of the bridge you'll have a giddy downward view into the deep chasm carved by Eagle Creek. The water rushing through the canyon over mossy boulders and ledges is absolutely mesmerizing.

Following the bridge, it's time to turn around and head back the way you came. If you still have some energy left, however, consider pressing on toward Tenas Campground and Skooknichuck Falls 0.4 miles up the trail. Two miles beyond that, you'll arrive at the roaring cascade of Tunnel Falls.

Hike Information

🕐 Trail Contacts:
Columbia River Gorge National Scenic Area, Hood River, OR (541) 386–2333 or *www.fs.fed.us/r6/columbia*

🕐 Schedule:
Open year round

💲 Fees/Permits:
Requires a Northwest Forest $5 day pass or $30 annual pass. You can purchase a pass online at: *www.fs.fed.us/r6/feedemo* or by call calling 1–800–270–7504.

❓ Local Information:
Mount Hood National Forest, Gresham, OR (503) 668–1700 or *www.fs.fed.us/r6/mthood*

💡 Local Events/Attractions:
[See Hike 10 for information.]

🛏 Accommodations:
The Columbia Gorge Hotel, Hood River, OR 1–800–345–1921 or *www.columbiagorgehotel.com*

🍴 Restaurant:
Multnomah Falls Lodge, Bridal Veil, OR (503) 695–2376

👥 Organizations:
Mazamas, Portland, OR (503) 227–2345 or *www.mazamas.org* · **Sierra Club Columbia Group,** Portland, OR (503) 231–0507 or *www.spiritone.com/~orsierra/columbia.html*

📖 Other Resources:
Eagle Newspapers, Salem, OR (503) 393–1774 or *www.gorgenews.com—for news and information about the Columbia Gorge.*

🏃 Hike Tours:
Friends of the Columbia Gorge, Portland, OR (503) 241–3762 or *www.gorgefriends.org*

🛍 Local Outdoor Retailers:
Great Outdoor Clothing Company, Troutdale, OR (503) 666–1543 or *www.greatoutdoorclothing.com*

🗺 Maps:
USGS maps: Bonneville Dam, OR; Tanner Butte, OR

Salmon River

Hike Summary

The Mount Hood National Forest's Salmon River Trail takes hikers on a journey through a mossy, old-growth forest next to the wild and scenic Salmon River. The trail begins by hugging the edge of the Salmon River. It then climbs a steep ridge, ending with a short loop that offers impressive views of the Salmon River Canyon and the surrounding forested ridges of the Salmon-Huckleberry Wilderness. Backpackers who follow the trail for 14.4 miles can look forward to spectacular scenery around every bend. Established campsites are available, but they fill up quickly on summer weekends.

Hike Specs

Start: From the Salmon River trailhead off U.S. 26
Length: 7.6-mile out-and-back
Approximate Hiking Time: 4–6 hours
Difficulty Rating: Easy the first 2.5 miles as the trail parallels the banks of the Salmon River; moderate the next 1.5 miles as it climbs a steep ridge at the base of 5,045-foot Devil's Peak
Trail Surface: Dirt path with some rocky sections and steep drop-offs
Lay of the Land: This trail parallels the Salmon River and then climbs a steep ridge to a scenic viewpoint of the Salmon River Canyon.
Elevation Gain: 2,060 feet

Land Status: National forest and wilderness area
Nearest Town: Zigzag, OR
Other Trail Users: Hikers only
Canine Compatibility: Dog friendly

Getting There

From Portland: Drive 41 miles east on U.S. 26 to the town of Zigzag. Turn right (south) on Salmon River Road (FS 2618) and drive 4.9 miles to the trailhead parking area on the left side of the road. *DeLorme: Oregon Atlas & Gazetteer:* Page 62 B1

Salmon River Trail 742 traipses through the 44,560-acre Salmon-Huckleberry Wilderness, which was established back in 1984. Located about an hour from the Portland metropolitan area, the Salmon River has carved a splendid canyon with prominent ridges, buttes, and pinnacles. Chinook and coho salmon spawn in its clear waters, and anglers enjoy casting for steelhead trout in its rushing currents.

Major landmarks in the Salmon-Huckleberry include Huckleberry Mountain to the north, 5,045-foot Devil's Peak to the east, and 4,877-foot Salmon Butte to the south. As its name implies, the wilderness is well known for its purplish, pea-size huckleberries, most abundant near Devil's

Hiking along the Salmon River.

Peak and Huckleberry Mountain. The enticing blue fruit, related to blueberries, is usually ripe by late August and makes for a delicious treat if you happen across some while out along the trail.

The Salmon River trailhead is approximately five miles south of Zigzag off Salmon River Road (Forest Service Road 2618). Large red alders, Douglas firs, and western hemlocks shade the trail, and towering old-growth trees give the forest a mystical quality. Beneath these giants are broad, fan-shaped leaves of vine maple and thick bunches of raspberry bushes. Wildlife includes black bear, mule deer, cougar, badger, and marten.

MilesDirections

0.0 START at the trailhead located on the far end of the parking area adjacent to the concrete bridge. Start hiking on Trail 742.

0.4 You'll pass by some rocky outcrops on your left as the trail skirts right the river. Notice the thick green stems and bright yellow flowers of Oregon stonecrop. Cross a wooden footbridge.

1.3 Cross a wooden footbridge.

1.5 Pass by Rolling Riffle Campground on your right. There's also a sign indicating a "Toilet Area" on your left.

1.7 Pass a picnic area on your right.

2.0 Cross a wooden footbridge and then come to a self-issue permit station. Wilderness permits are required from this point forward because you are about to enter the Salmon-Huckleberry Wilderness Area. Permits are free but there's a $100 fine if you do not have a

permit. After this point, the trail begins to fairly steeply ascend the ridge.

2.5 The trail crosses a creek.

2.8 The trail crosses a creek.

3.3 The trail crosses a creek.

3.4 The trail comes to a fork. Veer right to begin the loop portion of the trail.

3.5 Come out of the trees onto a steep grassy ridge with an excellent view of the Salmon River gorge.

3.6 Come to a T-junction. Turn left to complete the loop.

3.8 Complete the loop. Turn right and continue 3.8 miles back to your vehicle. If you're backpacking the trail you can continue another 10.5 miles along this trail toward Trillium Lake.

7.6 Arrive back at the trailhead and your vehicle.

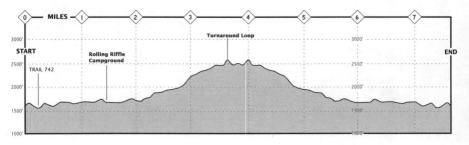

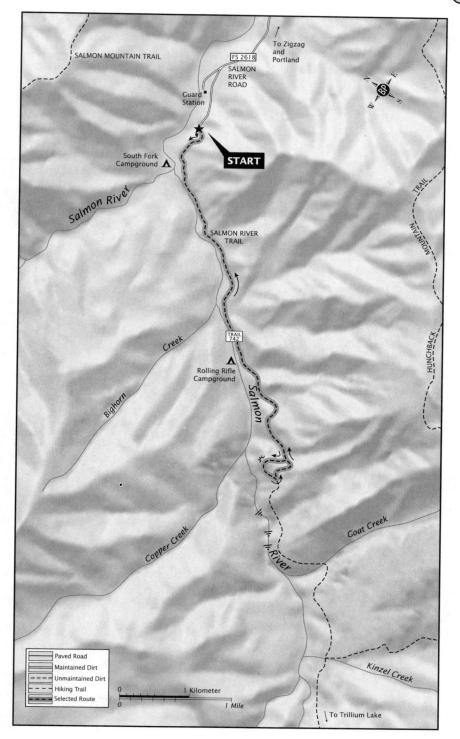

The trail begins by paralleling the shallow, boulder-strewn Salmon River, which carves its way westward and eventually empties into the Sandy River near Brightwood, four miles west of ZigZag off U.S. Route 26. The river, which flows for a total of 31 miles, receives its water as snowmelt from Mount Hood's Palmer Glacier. At 0.4 miles you'll pass a cliff where thick stems of Oregon stonecrop have a firm grasp on the rocky ledges. The bright-yellow flowers of this hardy plant thrive in the sunshine that basks the cliff walls.

A look into the Salmon River Canyon.

At 1.5 miles you'll come to Rolling Riffle Campground, a great place to pitch a tent (the 10 sites fill up fast, so come early), and after two miles you'll cross a footbridge and enter the Salmon-Huckleberry Wilderness. The trail climbs a steep ridge at the base of Devil's Peak for the next 1.5 miles. At the top of the ridge is an unsigned trail junction. Take a right and walk a short distance to a spectacular view of the canyon and the river far below.

From here the trail makes a loop along the edge of the ridge. When you've finished the loop, return to your vehicle the way you came. If you're backpacking, however, it's possible to follow the Salmon River for another 10.5 miles toward Trillium Lake. Plan a shuttle pick-up at the Salmon River trailhead near Trillium Lake.

To get to the Salmon River trailhead, drive three miles east of Government Camp on U.S. Route 26 to a road junction with Forest Service Road 2656 and turn right. Drive 1.7 miles and turn left at the Salmon River trailhead sign. Drive another 1.8 miles and take Forest Service Road 309 the remainder of the way to the trailhead.

Hike Information

Trail Contacts:
Mount Hood National Forest, Zigzag Ranger Station, Zigzag, OR (503) 622-3191 or (503) 668-1704 or www.fs.fed.us/r6/mthood/

Schedule:
June through October

Fees/Permits:
Requires a Northwest Forest $5 day pass or $30 annual pass. You can purchase a pass online at: www.fs.fed.us/r6/feedemo or by call calling 1-800-270-7504. A wilderness permit is also required to enter the Salmon-Huckleberry Wilderness Area.

Local Information:
Mount Hood Information Center, Welches, OR 1-888-622-4822 or

www.mthood.org · Portland Oregon Visitors Association, Portland, OR 1-877-678-5263 or www.pova.com/home/index.asp

Local Events/Attractions:
Portland Rose Festival in June, Portland, OR (503) 227-2681 or www.rosefestival.org

Accommodations:
Best Western Sandy Inn, Sandy, OR (503) 668-7100 · Old Welches Inn B&B, Welches, OR (503) 622-3754 or www.bbdirectory.com/inn/oldwelchesinn

Local Outdoor Retailers:
Cascade Ski & Sports, Sandy, OR (503) 668-9218

Maps:
USGS maps: Rhododendron, OR

Mount Hood National Forest Facts

- Mount Hood rises 11,235 feet above sea level; its base spreads over 92 miles.
- Mount Hood dates from the late Pleistocene Era.
- Mount Hood is the highest mountain in Oregon and the fourth highest in the string of Cascade Mountain Range volcanoes that stretch from Mount Garibaldi in British Columbia south to Mount Lassen in northern California.
- "Wy'East" is the Native American name for Mount Hood. (Mount Adams was "Klickitat" and Mount St. Helens was "Loowit," and the Great Spirit was called "Tyee Sahalie.")
- Mount Hood is a dormant or "sleeping" volcano, with steam constantly spewing from fumarole areas.
- Recent eruptions (all minor): 1804, 1853, 1854, 1859, 1865, and 1907. Scientists believe Mount Hood could have a significant eruption within the next 75 years.
- The first white men "discovered" the mountain on October 29, 1792, when British Navy Lt. William E. Broughton and his crew (representing King George III) saw it from the Columbia River near the mouth of the Willamette River. Broughton named the peak for famed British naval officer (and later, admiral) Alexander Arthur Hood (who never saw the mountain).
- In 1805 Lewis and Clark became the first Americans to see the mountain, first calling it "The Falls Mountain, or Timm Mountain", until learning of the prior naming by the British. Timm was the Indian name given to the falls area in the Columbia River Gorge just above The Dalles.
- In 1845 Oregon Trail pioneers Samuel K. Barlow, Joel Palmer, and their parties opened the first wagon trail over the Cascades on the south side of Mount Hood. While still a very difficult trail, the Barlow Trail became much preferred over the treacherous Columbia River rafting route to Oregon City.

- Oregon's first golf course was built in 1928 in Welches, at the base of Mount Hood.

- Mount Hood is the second-most climbed mountain in the world after Japan's Mount Fuji.

- The largest party to climb Mount Hood: 411 people on August 9, 1936.

- Ranger, the famed climbing dog born in 1925, climbed Mount Hood with his owner and friends 500 times during his life. Ranger made his last climb in 1938, died in 1939, and was buried on the peak's summit. Other animals seen on the summit of Mount Hood over the years include a badger, chipmunks, mice, a couple of bears, an elk, red foxes, a wolf, and three domestic sheep.

- The first wedding on Mount Hood's summit, held in July 1915, united Blanche Pechette and Frank Pearce.

- Mount Hood boasts five ski areas: Timberline Lodge Ski Area, Mount Hood Meadows, Mount Hood Ski Bowl, Cooper Spur Ski Area, and Summit Ski Area.

- Timberline Lodge was built at an elevation of 6,000 feet by the WPA (Work Projects Administration) and the CCC (Civilian Conservation Corps) and dedicated by President Roosevelt on September 28, 1937.

- Timberline Lodge Ski Area enjoys the only year-round ski season in North America. It's closed for just two weeks in late September. A record 318-inch base of snow was on the ground at Timberline during the winter of 1998–99.

- Timberline Lodge Ski Area hosts the longest continually run ski race in America, the Golden Rose Ski Classic, held every June.

- Timberline Lodge Ski Area's 1,000 skiable acres include the most vertical feet (3,590) of ski terrain in the Pacific Northwest.

- Timberline's Magic Mile chairlift, built in 1939, was the first chairlift in Oregon.

- Mount Hood Meadows Ski Area covers 2,159 acres and includes 240 acres for night skiing.

- Mount Hood Ski Bowl is the largest night-skiing area in North America.

- The Mount Hood National Forest encompasses 1.2 million acres, has four designated wilderness areas, and boasts more than 1,200 miles of hiking trails.

Source: Mount Hood National Forest Web site: www.fs.fed.us/r6/mthood/

Cooper Spur Trail

Hike Summary

This trek explores the high country on the east side of Mount Hood. The trail leads to the top of Cooper Spur for great views of the deep crevasses of Eliot Glacier and the snow-covered summits of Mount Hood, Mount Adams, and Mount Rainier. But don't worry about climbing any snow routes—the most dangerous part of this trail is the 45-degree snowfield far beyond where you'll be hiking, and high above this hike's turn-around point.

Hike Specs

Start: From the Trail 600 trailhead off Cloud Cap Road (FS 3512)

Length: 7.6-mile out-and-back

Approximate Hiking Time: 4–6 hours

Difficulty Rating: Difficult due to relentless switchbacks ascending a steep ridge

Trail Surface: Dirt path with some loose and rocky sections

Lay of the Land: Cooper Spur ascends through a thick cascade forest until climbing out above the treeline on volcanic Mount Hood. Snowfields and glaciers surround this spur trail.

Elevation Gain: 2,390 feet

Land Status: National forest and wilderness area

Nearest Town: Hood River, OR

Other Trail Users: Hikers only

Canine Compatibility: Dog friendly

Getting There

From Hood River: Drive 22.4 miles south on OR 35 to the junction with Cooper Spur Road and a sign that reads "Cooper Spur Ski Area." Turn right (west) where the sign reads "Cooper Spur Ski Area" and drive 2.4 miles to Cloud Cap Road (FS 3512). Continue straight (stay to the right) toward Cloud Cap and Tilly Jane Campground. Drive approximately eight miles, to a road junction. Turn right toward Cloud Cap and drive 0.6 miles to the trailhead parking on the right. *Delorme: Oregon Atlas & Gazetteer:* Page 62, A3

M ount Hood, a young Cascade volcano rising 11,235 feet above sea level, is the highest peak in Oregon and one of the most well-known landmarks in the Pacific Northwest. Covered with 12 glaciers and five unique ridges, Mount Hood—the second-most climbed mountain in the world after Japan's Mount Fuji—is a tantalizing quest for mountain climbers all over the world. Different historical records show that the first person to summit this lofty peak did so in either 1845 or 1857, and the first woman summitted in 1867.

Mount Hood.

MilesDirections

0.0 START hiking on Trail 600. Walk 100 yards and veer to the left.

0.8 The trail starts climbing out of the trees and you have a panoramic view of Mount Hood, Mount Rainier, and Mount Adams.

1.2 Come to a junction with the Timberline Trail (#600). Continue straight

on the Cooper Spur Trail as it switchbacks steeply up the ridge.

3.8 Arrive at the end of the trail and your turnaround point. There is a commemorative marker here dedicated to climbers who have lost their lives climbing to the summit of Mount Hood.

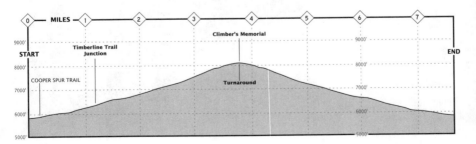

Today, many people each year reach Mount Hood's summit, but the climb is certainly not for novice mountaineers. And regardless of your experience, climbers will need special mountaineering equipment just to succeed. Many deaths and injuries occur each year when inexperienced or ill-equipped climbers got in over their heads, become lost when the weather turns bad, fall into crevasses, or develop frostbite when they wear improper clothing.

Mount Hood is located just 75 miles east of Portland in the Mount Hood Wilderness. Thick forests of Douglas fir, mountain hemlock, and noble fir characterize the wilderness area. And at its highest elevations, whitebark pine and high alpine meadows filled with bright splashes of white avalanche lilies, red Indian paintbrush, brilliant purple lupine, and Cascade aster, make up the summer scene.

Mount Hood—thought to be less than 780,000 years old—is young compared to other peaks in the area. Classified as a stratovolcano, the

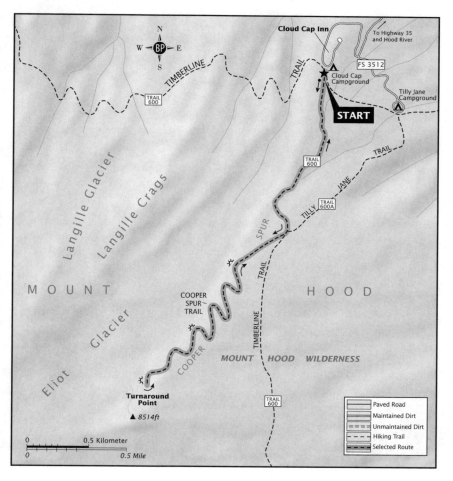

mountain has had four eruptive periods over the last 15,000 years: Polallie (15,000 to 12,000 years ago), Timberline (1,800 to 1,400 years ago), Zigzag (600 to 400 years ago), and Old Maid (250 to 180 years ago). Evidence of recent volcanic activity is present at Crater Rock, a volcanic lava dome believed by geologists to be only 200 years old. The dome is located south of the summit, where you'll notice the emission of sulfur gas and steam.

Cooper Spur, located on the northeast side of the mountain, is a remnant of the massive proportions of this mountain before erosion whittled it down to its present size. The high ridge, sandwiched between Eliot Glacier and Newton Clark Glacier, is the namesake of David Rose Cooper, an early set-

View of Elliot Glacier and the summit of Mount Hood.

tler who often camped on the peak's east side in the mid 1800s. The trail offers close-up views of the two glaciers and their deep crevasses and jumbled ice. During the summer months local climbers learning crevasse rescue come to Eliot Glacier, the second largest glacier in Oregon and the largest glacier on Mount Hood, to practice rescue techniques.

The trail also includes outstanding views of Mount Hood's summit and of Mount Rainier and Mount Adams much further north in Washington State. A plaque at the turnaround point is dedicated to climbers who have died trying to climb up this side of Hood and is a somber reminder that weather conditions on the mountain are wild and unpredictable and can be fatal to hikers and climbers who come to this mountain unprepared.

Hike Information

Trail Contacts:
Hood River Ranger District, Mount Hood, Parkdale, OR (541) 352-6002 or *www.fs.fed.us/r6/mthood*

Schedule:
July through October

Fees/Permits:
Requires a Northwest Forest $5 day pass or $30 annual pass. You can purchase a pass online at: *www.fs.fed.us/r6/feedemo* or by call calling 1-800-270-7504.

Local Information:
Hood River Chamber of Commerce, Hood River, OR 1-800-366-3530

Local Events/Attractions:
Pear and Wine Festival, in May, Hood River, OR 1-800-366-3530
• Gorge Games, in July, Hood River, OR (541) 386-7774

Accommodations:
Gorge View B&B, Hood River, OR (541) 386-5770 or *www.gorge.net/gorgeview*

Restaurants:
Full Sail Brew Pub, Hood River, OR (541) 386-2247

Other Resources:
Friends of the Columbia Gorge, Portland, OR (503) 241-3762 or *www.gorgefriends.org*

Organizations:
Mazamas Mountaineering Club, Portland, OR (503) 227-2345

Local Outdoor Retailers:
Hood River Outfitters, Hood River, OR (541) 386-6202 or *www.hoodriveroutfitters.com*

Maps:
USGS maps: Parkdale, OR

Honorable Mentions

Northwest Oregon

Compiled here is an index of great hikes in Northwest Oregon that didn't make the A-list this time around but deserve recognition. Check them out and let us know what you think. You may decide that one or more of these hikes deserves higher status in future editions or, perhaps, you may have a hike of your own that merits some attention.

(1) Ecola State Park to Indian Beach

This is an easy, short-and-sweet 4.0-mile out-and-back trail. It begins at Ecola State Park's main parking area and passes through an old-growth fern-filled forest, and then takes you along a seaside cliff with some scenic viewpoints along picturesque Indian Beach. At this secluded, cobblestone beach, you can watch surfers and boogie boarders catching the waves offshore. When you're finished exploring the beach, head back on the same trail.

To get there from U.S. 101 in Cannon Beach, take the Ecola State Park Exit and drive 2.3 miles to the park entrance. You'll have to pay a $3 entrance fee to park here. For more information, contact the Oregon State Parks and Recreation, Salem, OR; 1–800–551–6949; *www.prd.state.or.us.* *DeLorme: Oregon Atlas & Gazetteer:* Page 64 A1

(2) Haystack Rock

Haystack Rock is a well-known landmark in the small, artsy coastal community of Cannon Beach. This 235-foot rock is situated 1.1 miles south of downtown Cannon Beach on a scenic stretch of flat, sandy beach. This

striking rock is part of the Oregon Islands Wildlife Refuge and is home to nesting pigeon guillemots, pelagic cormorants, tufted puffins, and Western gulls. The rocky tide pools at the base of the rock are filled with colorful creatures such as sea green anemones, bright orange starfish, and prickly, purple sea urchins. To explore this scenic landmark, take the easy 2.2-mile out-and-back beach walk from downtown Cannon Beach.

To get to Cannon Beach and Haystack Rock, drive 90 minutes west of Portland on U.S. 26 to U.S. 101 South. Take the Ecola State Park/Cannon Beach exit off U.S. 101. Head into downtown Cannon Beach, to the intersection with 2nd Street. You can park in a public parking area. From the parking area, head west on 2nd Street to the beach. Walk south along the beach about a mile to Haystack Rock. Before you head out be sure to grab lunch to go at Osburne's Grocery Store & Delicatessen, on Hemlock Street just north of 2nd Street. For more information, contact the Cannon Beach Chamber of Commerce, Cannon Beach, OR; (503) 436–2623. *DeLorme: Oregon Atlas & Gazetteer:* Page 64 A1

③ Neahkahnie Mountain

This difficult, 3.0-mile out-and-back trail climbs through forests of Sitka spruce and open meadows to the 1,631-foot summit of Neahkahnie Mountain, where you'll have far reaching views of the scenic Oregon coastline. Follow the trail as it switchbacks up the steep mountainside for about a mile to a trail junction. Go straight and walk another 0.5 miles up the spiny ridge of the mountain to a magnificent viewpoint.

To get there, drive approximately 10 miles south of Cannon Beach on U.S. 101 and look for the hiker symbol just after milepost 41. Turn left (east) on a gravel road and drive just under a half mile to a trailhead parking area. For more information, contact Oregon State Parks and Recreation, Salem, OR; 1–800–551–6949; *www.prd.state.or.us. DeLorme: Oregon Atlas & Gazetteer:* Page 64 B1 C1

④ King Mountain

The 4.8-mile King Mountain Trail is a difficult, strenuous trek through a red alder and spruce forest to a viewpoint atop King Mountain, with spectacular 360-degree views of the Coast Range and Cascade Mountains. This hike will turn your thighs to noodles but the view from the top is worth the effort.

To get there from Portland, drive 30 miles west on U.S. 26 to its junction with OR 6. Exit and drive 27 miles west to a dirt pullout and the trailhead on the right (north) side of the road. For more information, contact Tillamook State Forest, Forest Grove District Office, Forest Grove, OR; (503) 359–7401; *www.odf.state.or.us/tsf/tsfhome.htm. DeLorme: Oregon Atlas & Gazetteer:* Page 64 C4

5 Munson Falls

The 0.4-mile out-and-back trail to Munson Falls is an easy family hike to a spectacular waterfall. From the parking area, follow the trail 0.2 miles to a grand viewpoint of this scenic cascade. The waterfall plunges over the cliff an astounding 266 feet, making it the highest waterfall in Coast Mountain Range.

To get there, drive south of Tillamook on U.S. 101 for 7.2 miles to a turnoff for Munson Falls. Turn left and drive 1.6 miles to a parking area. For more information, contact the Tillamook Chamber of Commerce, Tillamook, OR; (503) 842-7525; *www.tillamookchamber.org*. **DeLorme:** *Oregon Atlas & Gazetteer:* Page 58 A2

6 Beverly Beach Sate Park to Devil's Punchbowl

Take a 3.4-mile walk along a scenic, shoreline to Devil's Punchbowl—a rock bowl created from collapsed sea caves. You begin this hike from the campground, walk 0.2 miles west, and proceed through a tunnel under U.S. 101. You cross Spencer Creek and then walk 1.5-miles north on the beach. Here you'll have outstanding views of Otter Rock. You also may see surfers catching a good break. After 1.5 miles you reach a series of stairs that take you to the top of the headland of Otter Rock to rocky tide pools and to Devil's Punchbowl. Turn around and retrace your route back to the campground.

To get there, drive seven miles north of Newport on U.S. 101 to the state park entrance. While in the area, you might also want to take a short 0.7-mile hike on a self-guided nature trail that takes you along Spencer Creek through an alder and spruce forest. Brochures for this hike are available at the entrance booth to the campground. For more information, contact Oregon State Parks and Recreation, Salem, OR; 1-800-551-6949; *www.prd.state.or.us*. **DeLorme:** *Oregon Atlas & Gazetteer:* Page 32, Inset 1, C1

7 Warrior Rock Lighthouse

This easy 7.0-mile out-and-back hike takes you along the shores of Sauvie Island and the mighty Columbia River to the Warrior Rock Lighthouse. You walk through the Sauvie Island Wildlife Area, where opportunities to spot ducks, and geese, and blue herons abound. You'll also be able to watch massive freighters pass by on their way to Portland and Astoria. After 3.5 miles you arrive at Warrior Rock Lighthouse, located at the north tip of the island. To start, walk across an open field to the beach. Walk along the beach for the fist half mile and then pick up the trail (which is an old road) as it parallels the shore until you reach the lighthouse at the halfway point.

To get to Warrior Rock Lighthouse from Portland, drive approximately 11 miles north on U.S. 30 and cross the bridge to Sauvie's Island. After you cross the bridge, turn north on Sauvie Island Road and be sure to stop at the small grocery store to get a day-use permit for $3. Proceed 1.8 miles on Sauvie Island Road to the intersection with Reeder Road. Turn right and drive 12.6 miles to the end of the road and a parking area. For more information, contact the Oregon Fish & Wildlife Department, Portland, OR; (503) 872–5268; *www.dfw.state.or.us*. **DeLorme: Oregon Atlas & Gazetteer:** Page 66 B2

⑧ Wildwood Trail to Pittock Mansion

This moderate 4.0-mile out-and-back trail takes you on a section of the 27-mile-long Wildwood Trail, which begins at the Vietnam Memorial in Washington Park and winds uphill through scenic forest to the historic Pittock Mansion. The trail begins opposite the parking area, with a sign indicating the beginning of the Wildwood Trail. The trail traipses through Hoyt Arboretum and has several intersections. Keep following the signs for Wildwood Trail. After 1.1 miles, you have to cross Burnside Street. After crossing the busy road, the trail winds steeply on several switchbacks to the Pittock Mansion, where you can enjoy a one-of-a-kind view of downtown Portland and Mount Hood.

To get there from Portland, take OR 26 west toward Beaverton. Take the Oregon Zoo exit and follow the road as it winds past the main zoo parking area to the Vietnam Memorial parking area on the right side of the road. For more information, contact Portland Parks and Recreation Department, Portland, OR; (503) 823–PLAY; *www.parks. ci.portland.or.us*. **DeLorme: Oregon Atlas & Gazetteer:** Page 66 D3

⑨ Bagby Hot Springs

Take an easy three-mile out-and-back hike through a majestic old-growth forest to a free hot springs bathhouse. Bagby Hot Springs is found along the shores of a fork of the Collawash River. Take a hot, relaxing soak in the public tubs or a private log-bath. Keep in mind this area is very popular, and probably not the best place for small children as there's frequent nudity. Due to the number of people, taking your dog along is also not wise. To shorten your wait-time for a private bathing room, try visiting the springs on a weekday. Incidentally, don't leave valuables in your car—there's been a rash of car burglery. In order to park at this trailhead, you'll need a $5 Northwest Forest Pass—available at *www.fs.fed.us/r6/feedemo* or by calling 1–800–270–7504.

To get there from Estacada, drive south on OR 224 for 26 miles to the bridge at Ripplebrook. Proceed straight on FS 46 for 3.6 miles. Turn right on to FS 63 and drive 3.5 miles. Turn right on to FS 70 and drive six miles to the parking area on the left side of the road. For more information, contact the Estacada Ranger Station, Estacada, OR; (503) 630–8700. *DeLorme: Oregon Atlas & Gazetteer:* Page 55 A8

⑩ Hamilton Mountain

The 7.6-mile Hamilton Mountain loop trail takes you on a tour through a Douglas fir forest, past Hardy Falls and mesmerizing Rodney Falls. From Rodney Falls the trail begins ascending steeply on switchbacks to a trail junction. Stay to the right to begin the loop portion of the hike and climb steeply past some precipitous sections with great views of the Columbia Gorge. You reach the brushy summit ridge after about 1.8 miles. You can continue to the left and stay left at each trail junction until you reach the main trail, completing the loop. You then walk 1.4 miles back to your car.

To get there from downtown Portland, drive approximately seven miles east on I-84 to the intersection with I-205. Turn north onto I-205 and cross the Columbia River. Take the WA 14 exit in Washington and follow the road east as it parallels the Columbia River for about 29 miles to the parking area for Beacon Rock Park. Turn left onto a paved road opposite the Beacon Rock Park parking area and drive approximately 0.3 miles to a paved parking area adjacent to a campground. For more information, contact the USDA Forest Service, Columbia River Gorge National Scenic Area, Hood River, OR; (541) 386–2333; *www.fs.fed.us/r6/columbia.* *DeLorme: Oregon Atlas & Gazetteer:* Page 67 C8

⑪ Beacon Rock Trail

The 1.8-mile out-and-back Beacon Rock Trail winds up side of the 848-foot basalt block of Beacon Rock. This trail contains almost 50 switchbacks and numerous handrail sections as it winds up to the top, where you'll have a scenic viewpoint of the Columbia River Gorge. This rock impressed Lewis and Clark so much when they floated by this area in 1805 that they named it "Beacon Rock." This trail is located in Beacon Rock Park, which has roadside restrooms.

To get there from downtown Portland, drive approximately seven miles east on I-84. Turn north on to I-205 and cross the Columbia River. Take the WA 14 east and follow it as it parallels the Columbia River for about 29 miles to the parking area for Beacon Rock Park, located on the right side of the road. For more information, contact the USDA Forest Service, Columbia River Gorge National Scenic Area, Hood River, OR; (541) 386–2333; *www.fs.fed.us/r6/columbia. **DeLorme: Oregon Atlas & Gazetteer:** Page 67 C8

⑫ Bridal Veil Falls

Bridal Veil Falls is an easy 1.0-mile out-and-back that takes you up a set of stairs to a viewpoint where you can enjoy the big, billowy cascade of Bridal Veil Falls. This trail is located in Bridal Veil State Park and is short enough and easy enough for children to come along. If your children are of the canine variety, be sure to keep him or her on a leash. Another trail you'll want to check out in this state park is the upper trail, which has interpretive signs that describe native plants such as camas, lupine, trillium, and bleeding heart. From the top of this trail you'll have a grand view of the gorge and the striking 120-foot rock tower called Pillars of Hercules.

To get there from downtown Portland, drive east on I-84 for 28 miles to Exit 28 (Bridal Veil Falls). Turn west on the Columbia River Highway and drive approximately 0.75 miles to Bridal Veil State Park. For more information, contact Oregon State Parks and Recreation, Salem, OR; 1–800–551–6949; *www.prd.state.or.us. **DeLorme: Oregon Atlas & Gazetteer:** Page 67 D2

⑬ Latourell Falls

The 2.3-mile Latourell Falls loop trail takes you on an easy walk to view the upper and lower cascades of Latourell Falls. The trail heads left from the parking area and takes you 0.3 miles to a viewpoint of the 249-foot cascade of Lower Latourell Falls. After the viewpoint, you come to a trail junction. Stay to the left and continue another half mile to view the 100-foot cascade of the upper falls. From the upper falls descend a half mile to a trail junction. Stay to the left and descend to a scenic viewpoint of the Columbia River Gorge. Keep following the trail as it descends down to the highway. Cross the highway and walk through a picnic area where you may want to stop for lunch. Follow the path as it turns right, takes you under an artistic arched tunnel, and ends back at Lower Latourell Falls. Then it's back to your starting point.

To get there from downtown Portland, drive east on I-84 for 28 miles to Exit 28 (Bridal Veil Falls). Turn right and drive 2.8 miles to the Latourell parking area, located on the left side of the road. For more information, contact the USDA Forest Service, Columbia River Gorge National Scenic Area, Hood River, OR; (541) 386–2333; *www.fs.fed.us/r6/columbia. **DeLorme: Oregon Atlas & Gazetteer:** Page 67 D7

Ruckel Ridge/Ruckel Creek Trail

This 9.6-mile difficult loop takes you to some scenic viewpoints of the Columbia River Gorge. From the parking area, walk toward the campground and look for the sign for the Buck Point Trail. Follow the trail 0.6 miles to Buck Point. You'll head to the right and walk past a rockslide and a sign that indicates that the trail is not maintained. Begin hiking up the rockslide and continue up the Ruckel Ridge Trail for another 4.2 miles to the intersection with the Ruckel Creek Trail atop the Benson Plateau. Turn left on to the Ruckel Creek Trail and descend back to your starting point. In order to park at this trailhead, you'll need a $5 Northwest Forest Pass— available at *www.fs.fed.us/r6/feedemo* or by calling 1–800–270–7504.

To get there from Portland, drive east on I-84 for approximately 41 miles, exiting at the Eagle Creek Recreation area sign (Exit 40). At the stop sign, turn right (south) and proceed to a parking area. For more information, contact the USDA Forest Service, Columbia River Gorge National Scenic Area, Hood River, OR; (541) 386–2333; *www.fs.fed.us/r6/columbia.*
DeLorme: Oregon Atlas & Gazetteer: Page 68 C1

⑮ Clackamas River

The 15.6-mile out-and-back Clackamas River Trail clings to the edge of the beautiful Clackamas River Canyon. There are several opportunities to take a refreshing swim during the summer months. After hiking 3.6 miles, you cross Pup Creek with a spur trail leading to Pup Creek Falls. A little over halfway through the hike you come to a deep river gorge where white water passes through a 20-foot wide slot. The trail continues to parallel the river through the greenery of a cedar forest until you reach Indian Ford Campground at mile 7.8, your turnaround point.

To get there from Estacada, drive 15 miles southeast on OR 224 and turn right (south) on to Fish Creek Road 54. Cross the Clackamas River on a wide bridge and park in the parking area on the right side of the road. The trailhead begins across the road from the parking area. For more information, contact the Estacada Ranger Station, Estacada, OR; (503) 630–8700.
DeLorme: Oregon Atlas & Gazetteer: Page 61 D7

⑯ Lost Lake

The 3.5-mile Lost Lake Trail circles Lost Lake through groves of old-growth cedars and offers picture-perfect views of Mount Hood. This lake is a good family hike due to the easy, flat terrain.

To get there from Portland, drive east on U.S. 26 for about 41 miles to the town of Zigzag. Turn left on East Lolo Pass Road (FS 18) and drive 10.5 miles. Turn right on to McGee Creek Road (FS 1810) and proceed for 7.7 miles. At this point the road hooks up again with FS 18. Drive seven miles to the junction with FS 13. Turn left on FS 13, and drive six miles to the entrance booth at Lost Lake. The trailhead begins on the other side of the lake at a picnic area at the end of the road. For more information, contact the Mount Hood National Forest Information Center, Welches, OR; (503) 622–7674; *www.fs.fed.us/r6/mthood*. **DeLorme: Oregon Atlas & Gazetteer:** Page 62 A2

(17) McNeil Point

The McNeil Point is a difficult 9.0-mile hike that takes you to an historic stone shelter at the base of spectacular Mount Hood. You start the hike on the dirt path located straight across from the parking area. After 0.5 miles, come to a T-junction and turn right. (Going left leads to Lolo Pass.) Walk 60 yards and come to a three-way trail junction. Proceed on the center trail where the sign reads "Pacific Crest Trail 2000/Timberline Trail 600." Walk 30 yards and be sure to fill out a wilderness permit at the self-registration station, located on the left side of the trail. After 0.8 miles, emerge from the forest and walk along the wildflower filled slopes of Bald Mountain, with outstanding views of Mount Hood in front of you. At mile 1.1, look for an unmarked dirt path and turn left onto it. Climb over a small ridge to where the trail intersects with the unmarked Timberline Trail 600. Turn right onto Timberline Trail 600 and hike

0.2 miles to a fork. Stay to the right—sign reads "Cairn Basin." (Going left leads to McGee Creek Trail 625 and Ramona Road 1810-620.). After 3.0 miles, take the left fork in the trail. Over the next 0.5 miles you'll cross several creeks. At 3.6 miles, stay to the left. At mile 3.7, pass by two scenic ponds. At mile 3.8, stay to the right at the trail intersection. (Mazama Trail 625 goes left). At mile 4.2, stay to the right and at mile 4.5, reach the McNeil Shelter, which on a clear day will offer up spectacular views of Mount Hood, Mount Adams, Mount Rainier and Mount St. Helens. After you've admired the view you have the option of returning the way you came. Or, you can proceed down a steep, 0.5-mile rock scramble back to the Timberline Trail, where you can retrace your track to your car.

To get there from downtown Portland, drive east on U.S. 26 for 42 miles to Zigzag. Turn left (north) on to East Lolo Pass Road (FS 18) and drive 4.2 miles to FS 1825. Turn right on FS 1825 and drive 0.7 miles to a junction with FS 1828. Proceed straight (stay to the left) on FS 1828 and drive 5.6 miles to a road junction. Stay to the right (the road turns to gravel here) and continue driving on FS 1828 where the sign indicates "Top Spur Trail 788." Drive 1.6 miles to the trailhead parking area on the left side of the road. For more information, contact the Mount Hood National Forest Information Center, Welches, OR; (503) 622–7674; *www.fs.fed.us/r6/mthood*. *DeLorme: Oregon Atlas & Gazetteer:* Page 62 A2

(18) East Zigzag Mountain Loop

The 7.7-mile East Zigzag Mountain Loop is a difficult hike. It begins with a two-mile hike along Burnt Lake Trail to Devil's Meadow, an area bursting with wild flowers in June and July. You continue straight past the Devils Tie Trail junction. After a series of switchbacks, the trail skirts the crest of a high ridge, affording a grand view of Mount Hood and Burnt Lake. You turn left at the next junction onto the Zigzag Mountain Trail, which climbs unrelentingly to a magnificent viewpoint on the summit of 4,941-foot East Zigzag Mountain. From this viewpoint, hike downhill 0.7 miles to the Cast Creek Trail junction. Turn left and hike a short ways to the Cast Lake Trail junction (you have the option here of turning right and heading 0.7 miles to view Cast Lake). Continue straight to a junction with the Devil's Tie Trail. Turn left and hike 0.4 miles on the Devil's Tie Trail to the intersection with the Burnt Lake Trail. Turn right at the Burnt Lake Trail and hike the 2.6 miles back to your car.

To get there from Rhododendron, drive east on U.S. 26 for 1.5 miles and turn left (north) onto FS 27. Proceed 0.6 miles and turn left on FS 207. Drive 4.5 miles to a parking area at the end of the road. Note that the last half-mile section of this route is rough. In order to park at this trailhead, you'll need a $5 Northwest Forest Pass—available at *www.fs.fed.us/r6/feedemo* or by calling 1–800–270–7504. For more information, contact the Mount Hood National Forest, Hood River Ranger District, Parkdale, OR; (541) 352–6002; *www.fs.fed.us/r6/mthood*. *DeLorme: Oregon Atlas & Gazetteer:* Page 62 A2

(19) Elk Meadows Loop

The 6.8-mile Elk Meadows loop is a moderate trail that takes you on a scenic journey on the southeast side of majestic Mount Hood. The trailhead is located at the Clark Creek sno-park area. The trail begins by paralleling the clear, rocky Clark Creek. You hike along the creek for almost a mile and then turn right at the trail junction, where you'll cross the creek over a bridge and proceed straight for 0.6 miles to the junction with the Newton Creek Trail. Continue straight and cross over rushing Newton Creek. Climb up long, wavy switchbacks through a forested area to a four-way junction. Continue straight and take a right on the 1.2-mile Elk Meadows

Perimeter Trail, which circles the delicate high alpine landscape of Elk Meadow. At the next two trail junctions, stay to the left. After about 0.6 miles of walking on this trail you arrive at a wooden shelter. Be sure to stop here and soak in the stunning view of Mount Hood. Follow the circuit trail for another 0.6 miles as it circles Elk Meadow. Come to a trail junction for Gnarl Ridge and stay to the left until you reach the next trail junction, where you'll turn right to return to your car.

To get there from Portland, drive east on U.S. 26 for about 90 minutes to the intersection with OR 35. Turn left (north) on OR 35 and drive toward Hood River for approximately eight miles to the Clark Creek sno-park sign. Enter the sno-park and drive about a quarter mile to the Elk Creek Meadows trail sign. In order to park at this trailhead, you'll need a $5 Northwest Forest Pass—available at *www.fs.fed.us/r6/feedemo* or by calling 1–800–270–7504. For more information, contact the Mount Hood National Forest, Hood River Ranger District, Parkdale, OR; (541) 352–6002; *www.fs.fed.us/r6/mthood*. **DeLorme: Oregon Atlas & Gazetteer:** Page 62 B3

20 Dog Mountain

This difficult, 6.0-mile out-and-back trail climbs 1,500 feet in three miles and deposits you at the summit of Dog Mountain. Along the way you pass through a thick Douglas fir forest and encounter open vistas and hillsides covered with bright springtime blooms of yellow balsamroot, purple lupine, and fiery Indian paintbrush. From the parking area, there are two trails. The quickest route to the top is along the trail that begins at the far right end of the parking area. If you take this route, after 2.6 miles you'll come to a trail junction. Continue to the right to reach the summit, where you'll enjoy a magnificent view of the Columbia River Gorge. If you want to take longer, easier trail to the top, head out on the Augspurger Mountain Trail. The start of this trail can be found in the middle of the parking area. In order to park at this trailhead, you'll need a $5 Northwest Forest Pass—available at www.fs.fed.us/r6/feedemo or by calling 1–800–270–7504.

To get there from Portland, drive east on I-84 to Cascade Locks (Exit 44). Proceed across the Bridge of the Gods to WA 14 (there's a 75-cent toll to cross the bridge). Turn (right) east on WA 14 and go 12 miles to the parking are on the left side of the highway. For more information, contact the USDA Forest Service, Columbia River Gorge National Scenic Area, Hood River, OR; (541) 386–2333; *www.fs.fed.us/r6/Columbia*. **DeLorme: Oregon Atlas & Gazetteer:** Page 68 C3

Mark O. Hatfield/Twin Tunnels Trail

This paved, multi-use 5.0-mile trail takes you along an old section of the historic Columbia River Highway in the Columbia River Gorge. There are two trailheads, one in Hood River and one in Mosier. Starting in Mosier, the trail heads west toward Hood River through a dry landscape of ponderosa pine and deciduous trees. There are numerous viewpoints along the trail that offer spectacular Columbia Gorge scenery. After about a mile, you pass through the historic Twin Tunnels. These tunnels take you directly through a basalt cliff. After you emerge, the trail continues to wind along the high edge of the Gorge for another four miles through a fir-filled forest. All along the way, you'll also pass by jumbled lava flows and spectacular cliffs. A $3 state park day-use permit is required to park at the Hood River or Mosier Trailheads. You can purchase a permit at the self-service pay station at either trailhead or at the visitor center at the Hood River trailhead. The trail ends at Hood River where there are restrooms, a visitor center, and water.

To get to the Mosier trailhead from Hood River, drive east on I-84 for about five miles to Exit 69. In downtown Mosier, turn west on Rock Creek Road and proceed about two miles to the trailhead parking area. To get to the Hood River trailhead, take Exit 64 and proceed through downtown Hood River. Turn left (east) on the Old Columbia River Highway and drive to the trailhead parking area on the left side of the road. For more information, contact the Oregon State Parks and Recreation Dept. Salem, OR; 1–800–551–6949; *www.prd.state.or.us*.

㉒ McCall Point

This moderate 3.4-mile out-and-back hike takes you on a journey through the Tom McCall Preserve in the Columbia River Gorge. On this trail you pass through an area of open grasslands and wildflower meadows to a scenic viewpoint atop McCall Point. The best time to hike this trail is in the spring when the wildflowers are blooming. Beware of poison oak along the trail.

To get there from Portland, take the Mosier exit (Exit 69) off I-84 east. Drive 6.6 miles to the Rowena Crest Viewpoint parking area. The trail starts on the opposite side of the road from the parking area entrance. For more information, contact the USDA Forest Service, Columbia River Gorge National Scenic Area, Hood River, OR; (541) 386–2333; *www.fs.fed.us/r6/columbia*. **DeLorme: Oregon Atlas & Gazetteer: Page 69 C5**

㉓ Lookout Mountain to Palisade Point

The moderate 6.4-mile out-and-back Lookout Mountain Trail starts on a road and then ascends 1.2 miles to the top of 6,525-foot Lookout

Mountain. From the summit you have a spectacular view of the Hood River Valley and Mount Hood. From the summit, travel another 1.75 miles on the Divide Trail to the junction with the Fret Creek Trail, which takes you 0.25 miles to shimmering Oval Lake. After viewing the lake, return to the Divide Trail and trek another 0.25 miles east to Palisade Point.

To get there from Portland, go east on I-84 to Exit 64 (OR 35/White Salmon and Government Camp). Drive 26.6 miles south on OR 35 to FS 44 (Dufur Mill Road). Turn left (east) and drive four miles to High Prairie Road (FS 4410). Turn right and drive almost five miles south to a T-junction. Turn left. The trailhead is located on the right. For more information, contact the Hood River Ranger District, Parkdale, OR; (541) 352–6002; *www.fs.fed.us/r6/mthood*. **DeLorme: Oregon Atlas & Gazetteer:** Page 62 A4

(24) Deschutes River State Park

At Deschutes River State Park, set along the banks of the Deschutes River, miles of hiking trails await the hiker. You can walk on a multi-use double-track road that parallels the Deschutes River for over 20 miles though sagebrush covered hills and gray lava cliffs. Along this multi-use trail there are old railroad cars that serve as wildlife viewing platforms at miles 6.0 and 8.2. Here you can try to spot deer, rabbits, and migrating birds. Several side trails lead off the main trail up canyons and down to the river's edge. Another popular walk is the Atiyeh Deschutes River Trail that parallels the Deschutes River and has many good swimming holes on hot summer days. There is also an  overnight campground in this state park if you want to stay for a few days.

To get there from The Dalles, drive east on I-84 for 12 miles to Exit 97 (OR 206, Celilo Park/Deschutes River State Park). Turn right at the end of the exit, and take and immediate left onto OR 206. Drive three miles eastbound and then turn right into the Deschutes River State Park entrance. Park in the gravel lot on the left side of the road just after you enter the park entrance. The double-track multi-use trail starts here. For more information, contact Oregon State Parks and Recreation, Salem, OR; 1–800–551–6949; *www.prd.state.or.us*. **DeLorme: Oregon Atlas & Gazetteer:** Page 84 B1

Southwest

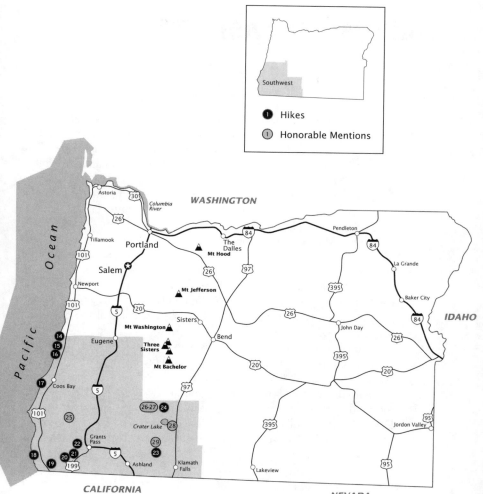

Southwest

● Hikes

① Honorable Mentions

WASHINGTON

Astoria
Columbia River
30
26
Tillamook
Portland
101
Salem
Newport
101
5
20
Sisters
Mt Washington ▲
Eugene
Three Sisters ▲
Mt Bachelor ▲
Coos Bay
5
101
25
Grants Pass
22
18
20 21
19 199
5
Ashland

The Dalles
Mt Hood ▲
84
Pendleton
84
26
97
La Grande
26
Mt Jefferson ▲
395
Baker City
Bend
John Day
26
84
IDAHO
20
395
20
97
26-27 24
Crater Lake 28
29
23
Klamath Falls
395
Jordon Valley
95
95
Lakeview
95

Pacific Ocean

14
15
16
17

CALIFORNIA

NEVADA

Oregon

101

Southwest Oregon

Southwest Oregon is a collage of scenic coastline, rugged mountains, wild and remote rivers, unusual endemic plants, and, of course, the astonishing Crater Lake National Park. The renowned Rogue River plunges through its namesake valley, home to the cultured towns of Ashland and Medford. When you're tired of walking, stop by the uncommon Ashland and join thousands of tourists and performers for a taste of the Oregon Shakespeare Festival.

The best-known attraction in Southwest Oregon is Crater Lake National Park, host to the impossibly blue waters of the deepest lake in the United States. Surrounding the park are the mighty volcanic peaks of Mount McLoughlin and Mount Thielsen, each rising abruptly from the nearby forests. You can hike to the summit of both of these lofty peaks and get a bird's-eye view of the nearby lakes and mountains of the Sky Lakes Wilderness and the Mount Thielsen Wilderness.

Highlights along the southwest coast include Cape Perpetua, the Sutton Creek Recreation Area, Sunset State Park, Shore Acres State Park, Cape Arago State Park, and Alfred A. Loeb State Park. Visit the Cape Perpetua Natural Area and walk through a botanical wonderland of coastal forest, rocky tide pools, spouting geysers, and watch the waves as they crash into Devil's Churn, a collapsed sea cave. If you want to hike a section of the Oregon Coast Trail, be sure to visit Sunset Bay State Park. Here are opportunities to view the Cape Arago Lighthouse, admire golden sandstone cliffs, tour a botanical garden at Shore Acres State Park, and observe sea lions at Cape Arago State Park. Go to Alfred A. Loeb State Park to see two rare tree species. Located about eight miles east of Brookings, this state park has two nature trails that take you on a journey through groves of rare Oregon myrtle and coastal redwoods. The park also has a campground that serves as a good base camp for exploring the immediate area, as well as other hiking trails in the Kalmiopsis Wilderness.

Moving farther east, the wild and rugged Kalmiopsis Wilderness and the Siskiyou National Forest dominate, each offering a unique array of plants and animals that call the Illinois River home. Take a tour along the Illinois River Trail to get a closer look at the deep canyon it has carved over the millennia. For a different perspective of this wilderness area, hike into Babyfoot Lake to glimpse a hard-to-find grove of old-growth Brewers spruce. For greater variety, hike to the glacier-carved basin that is home to Vulcan Lake.

The weather on the southern coast is typically warmer than on the northern coast. Expect temperatures in the 60s and 70s during the summer months, dropping slightly to the 50s and 60s in the winter months. Most rain falls from November through May—the clearest days are in September and October.

14

Cape Perpetua Scenic Area

Hike Summary

Take your pick of 10 trails that wind through the 2,700-acre Cape Perpetua Scenic Area. Depending on the trail(s) you select, you can experience a botanical wonderland of coastal forest, rocky tide pools, and other ocean spectacles such as the geyser-like Spouting Horn and the narrow rock channel of Devil's Churn. While you're here, plan on spending a few hours at the Cape Perpetua Interpretive Center. The center provides a good introduction to the plants and animals that live here as well as a look into the area's rich history.

Hike Specs

Start: From the trailhead off U.S. 101 at the Cape Perpetua Interpretive Center
Length: Trails vary in length from 0.2 miles to 10 miles

- A. *Whispering Spruce Trail*–0.25-mile loop
- B. *Saint Perpetua Trail*–2.6 miles out-and-back
- C. *Trail of Restless Waters*–0.4-mile loop
- D. *Cape Cove Trail*–0.3 miles
- E. *Giant Spruce Trail*–2.0-mile out-and-back
- F. *Captain Cook Trail*–0.6-mile loop
- G. *Oregon Coast Trail*–2.6-mile out-and-back
- H. *Discovery Loop Trail*–1.0-mile loop
- I–J. *Cooks Ridge/Gwynn Creek Loop Trail*–6.4-mile loop
- K. *Cummins Creek Loop Trail*–10.0-mile loop

Approximate Hiking Time: 1–6 hours depending on the trail selected
Difficulty Rating: Easy to Difficult depending on the trail selected

- A. *Whispering Spruce Trail*–Easy
- B. *Saint Perpetua Trail*–Moderate to difficult
- C. *Trail of Restless Waters*–Easy
- D. *Cape Cove Trail*–Easy
- E. *Giant Spruce Trail*–Easy
- F. *Captain Cook Trail*–Easy
- G. *Oregon Coast Trail*–Moderate
- H. *Discovery Loop Trail*–Moderate
- I–J. *Cooks Ridge/Gwynn Creek Loop Trail*–Moderate
- K. *Cummins Creek Loop Trail*–Moderate to difficult

Trail Surface: Combination of forest paths and paved paths. On the Restless Waters Trail, the stairs that lead down to Devil's Churn can be wet and slippery. Sneaker-waves can also catch you off guard at Devil's Churn, and dogs and children should be supervised at all times!
Lay of the Land: Hike through a variety of landscapes including old-growth coastal forest, rocky tide pools, and sandy beach.
Land Status: National forest
Nearest Town: Yachats, OR
Other Trail Users: Hikers only
Canine Compatibility: Leashed dog permitted

Getting There

From Yachats: Drive three miles south on U.S. 101 to the Cape Perpetua Interpretive Center located on the left side of the highway.
From Florence: Drive 22.5 miles north on U.S. 101 to the Cape Perpetua Interpretive Center located on the right side of the highway. ***DeLorme: Oregon Atlas & Gazetteer:*** Page 32, Inset 2 B2

If you're looking to explore the diversity of the Oregon Coast, you'll want to stop by the Cape Perpetua Scenic Area, located three miles south of Yachats and approximately 23 miles north of Florence off U.S. Route 101. This 2,700-acre area preserves large stands of coastal forest and rocky tide pools. First, stop in and explore the Interpretive Center, where you'll receive a comprehensive overview of coastal ecology, tides and weather, whale migration, and the history of the Alsea Indian tribe. You'll find interpretive exhibits, films, naturalist lectures, and a good selection of books about coastal ecology.

Each of the 10 trails in the Cape Perpetua Scenic Area has something different to offer. For craggy tide pools, sea-life, and a bit of Native American culture, hit the 0.6-mile *Captain Cook Trail*. The trail takes you past the historic Cape Creek Camp building, used by the Civilian Conservation Corp (CCC) from 1933 to 1942 to house the workers who built many of the park's trails and structures. The trail then dips under U.S. Route 101 past an Indian-shell middens site—where Native Americans discarded shells from the mussels they collected for food. The trail ultimately

Devil's Churn.

leads to rocky tide pools where you'll be able to view all kinds of colorful sea creatures like sea stars, mussels, hermit crabs, sea anemones, and purple sea urchins. Once you've finished exploring the tide pools, continue on to a viewpoint where you can watch for the geyser-like spray of Spouting Horn, an old sea cave with a small opening in its roof. Waves surge into this cave and shoot out of the small opening, creating a spectacular sea spray.

If you want to see a 500-year-old spruce tree, take the easy, 2.0-mile (round trip) walk on the *Giant Spruce Trail*. The trail parallels Cape Creek and leads you through an old-growth forest filled with ferns, salal, thimbleberry, and skunk cabbage. At the turn-around point is the trail's prize feature, an ancient Sitka spruce tree that's about 15 feet in diameter. Another shorter trail that also gives you a feel for the diversity of the coastal forest is the 1.0-mile *Discovery Loop Trail*. If you love sweeping views, you'll want to hike on the 2.6 mile round trip *Saint Perpetua Trail* that ascends the south side of Cape Perpetua on a series of fairly steep switchbacks and rewards you with excellent views (on a clear day) of Cape Foulweather to the north and Cape Blanco to the south. For great views without the long hike, walk the easy, 0.25-mile *Whispering Spruce Trail*. This trail promises spectacular ocean views (on a clear day) and an opportunity to explore the West Shelter, a stone building built by the CCC. If you're in for a longer hike, try the combination *Cooks Ridge/Gwynn Creek Loop Trail*. This 6.4-mile loop departs from the Interpretive Center and winds through old-growth forests, offering up several sneak peaks at the ocean. If you're interested in similar scenery but a lengthier hike, pack a lunch and strike out on the 10-mile *Cummins Creek Loop Trail*. From the Interpretive Center, the hike heads up the *Cooks Ridge Trail* and eventually hooks up with the Cummins Creek Trail for a return back to the *Oregon Coast Trail*. Then it's straight back to the Interpretive Center.

If you love to watch the churning ocean, head down the 0.4-mile *Trail of Restless Waters* loop to the rocky tide pool known as Devil's Churn. The rough, porous texture of the shoreline rock here is evidence of its volcanic past. Roughly 40 million years ago, offshore volcanoes deposited lava along the shoreline. As the molten rock cooled, hot gases within forced their way to the surface, giving it the porous texture. The pounding surf carved into the rock to form a sea cave. At some point, the roof of the cave collapsed, leaving behind the long, wide rock channel that forms Devil's Churn. The force of the waves crashing in the channel sends spectacular sprays of water dozens of feet into the air. If you're hiking with children or dogs, keep a close eye on them. The slippery surface of the rocks and sneaker-waves can catch you off balance if you get to close to the edge of the channel.

MilesDirections

The *Whispering Spruce Trail* is accessed 2.25 miles from the Interpretive Center via FS 55 and then FS 5553. The *Saint Perpetua Trail*, *Cape Cove Trail*, *Giant Spruce Trail*, *Captain Cook Trail*, *Oregon Coast Trail*, *Discovery Loop Trail*, *Cooks Ridge/Gwynn Creek Loop Trail*, and the

Cummins Creek Loop Trail can be accessed from the Interpretive Center. The *Trail of Restless Waters* starts from the Devil's Churn parking area, 0.7 miles north of the Interpretive Center off U.S. 101.

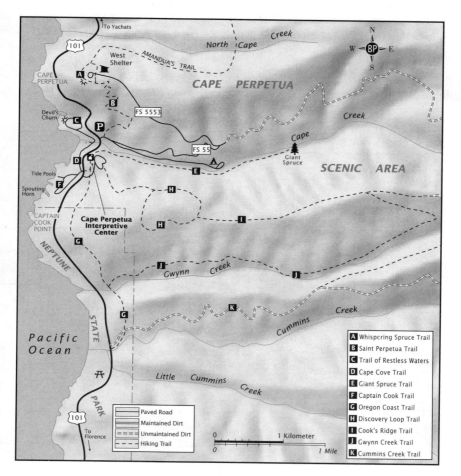

107

Coastal Sea Creatures

Cape Perpetua is home to a number of fascinating sea creatures. The easily recognizable, five-legged sea star (also known as the Ochre sea star) varies in color from orange to purple and can grow up to 40 centimeters in width. Feasting primarily on mussels and other shellfish, the sea star employs a rather curious method of consumption. It pries apart its victim's shell with its tube feet and inserts its stomach into the shell, secreting enzymes that help digest the soft tissue.

Mussels are another common tide pool resident. You'll find the mussels clinging tightly to the rocks by threadlike appendages called "byssus threads." These black, oval shaped mollusks obtain their food by filtering microscopic organisms from the water at high tide.

You'll likely see the industrious hermit crab scurrying about the shoreline in search of shelter. These comical creatures lack a hard shell for protection, so they're constantly looking for cover, often in abandoned snail shells. It's not uncommon to see two hermit crabs fighting fiercely over the rights to a prize shell.

Another tide pool inhabitant is the bright green sea anemone, which resembles a shimmering sea flower. This interesting creature has long tube-like feet that wave with the rise and fall of the tide. The feet contain stinging cells that can stun small fish and sea creatures, allowing the sea anemone to wrap itself around the victim and digest it.

Sea urchins frequent the rocky tide pools and can be identified by their purple, round bodies, which are covered with short, sharp spines. These industrious creatures eat just about anything, including seaweed, dead animal matter, and microorganisms.

Hike Information

Trail Contacts:
Cape Perpetua Interpretive Center, Yachats, OR (541) 547–3289 or *www.newportnet.com/capeperpetua*

Schedule:
Trails are open year round. The Interpretive Center is open from 9 A.M. to 5 P.M. daily, from Memorial Day through Labor Day. During the rest of the year, it's open weekends from 10 A.M. to 4 P.M.

Fees/Permits:
$3 day-use fee. Permits can be obtained in the upper parking lot or in the Interpretive Center.

Local Information:
Florence Chamber of Commerce, Florence, OR (541) 997–3128 or *www.florencechamber.com* · **Yachats Chamber of Commerce,** Yachats, OR (541) 547–3530 or *www.pioneer.net/~yachat*

Local Events/Attractions:
Rhododendron Festival, third weekend in May, Florence, OR (541) 997–3128 · **Sea Lion Caves,** Yachats, OR (541) 547–3111 or *www.sealioncaves.com* · **Siuslaw Pioneer Museum,** Florence, OR (541) 997–7884

Accommodations:
Heceta Head Lighthouse B&B, Yachats, OR (541) 547–3696 or *www.hecetalighthouse.com* · **Best Western Pier Point Inn,** Florence, OR (541) 997–7191

· **The Edwin K B&B,** Florence, OR 1–800–8 EDWIN K or *www.edwink.com* · **The Fireside Motel,** Yachats, OR 1–800–336–3573—*they allow dogs.* • **Cape Perpetua Campground,** Yachats, OR (541) 822–3799 · **Rock Creek Campground,** Yachats, OR (541) 822–3799–located 7.3 miles south of Cape Perpetua · **Tillicum Campground,** Yachats, OR (541) 822–3799—*located seven miles north of Cape Perpetua* · **Washburne State Park Campground,** 1–800–551–6949 —*located 14 miles north of Florence off U.S. 101* · **Sutton Creek Campground,** (541) 268–4473—*located five miles north of Florence off U.S. 101*

Restaurants:
Bridgewater Seafood Restaurant, Florence, OR (541) 997–9405

Other Resources:
To see more information about Heceta Head Lighthouse visit *www.hecetalighthouse.com/links.html* · To find out more about Oregon's Historic bridges visit *www.odot.state.or.us/eshtm/br.htm* · **Oregon Coast Magazine,** Florence, OR (541) 997–8401 or *www.ocmag.com*

Maps:
USGS maps: Yachats, OR

Heceta Head Lighthouse

Hike Summary

Take a picturesque walk to one of Oregon's most photographed lighthouses. Nestled on the edge of the coastal protrusion Heceta Head, the 205-foot-tall Heceta Head Lighthouse is a welcoming beacon to ships and hikers alike.

Hike Specs

Start: From the Heceta Head Lighthouse State Scenic Viewpoint parking area off U.S. 101

Length: 1.0-mile out-and-back

Approximate Hiking Time: 1 hour

Difficulty Rating: Easy due to the well-maintained gravel path

Trail Surface: Gravel path

Lay of the Land: Hike up a hillside and through coastal forest

Elevation Gain: 188 feet

Land Status: State park

Nearest Town: Florence, OR

Other Trail Users: Hikers only

Canine Compatibility: Leashed dogs permitted

Getting There

From Florence: Drive 12 miles north on U.S. 101 to the Heceta Head Lighthouse State Scenic Viewpoint (also known as Devil's Elbow State Park) sign. Turn left (west) and proceed 0.3 miles to the parking area. The hike begins on the north end of the parking lot.

From Yachats: Drive 14 miles south on U.S. 101 to the Heceta Head Lighthouse State Scenic Viewpoint (also known as Devil's Elbow State Park) sign. Turn right (west) and proceed 0.3 miles to the parking area. The hike begins on the north end of the parking lot. *DeLorme: Oregon Atlas & Gazetteer:* Page 32, Inset 2 C2

The Heceta Head Lighthouse (that's "huh-SEE-tuh") stands as a quiet sentinel on the central Oregon coast shining its beacon 21 miles out to sea. This magnificent structure was built in 1894 over a period of two years and at a cost of $80,000. The stone was shipped to the site from Oregon City, and the bricks and cement were brought in from San Francisco. Local sawmills supplied the wood, and the two-ton Fresnel lens was handcrafted and brought in by boat. The lighthouse and the scenic headland on which it sits owe their name to Captain Bruno Heceta, a Spanish captain who sailed his ship *Corvette* from Mexico to this part of the Oregon coast. George Davidson, of the Coastal Survey, officially named the point in 1862.

The whitewashed lighthouse is accessed by a one-mile out-and-back trail that starts at the north end of the Heceta Head Lighthouse State Scenic

Heceta Head Lighthouse.

Viewpoint parking lot. The wide gravel path begins by climbing through a thick coastal cedar and fir forest dotted with sword fern, wild iris, and salal. Picnic tables have been set up so visitors can enjoy the sweeping view of the rocky shore and rugged cape, as well as the 220-foot crowning arch of the Cape Creek Bridge. This bridge is just one of 162 bridges designed and built by Conde McCullough, head of the bridge division for the Oregon Department of Transportation from 1920 to 1935. In fact, McCullough designed virtually all of the bridges on the Oregon Coast Highway, using innovative techniques to overcome the many challenges of building coastal bridges. One of the biggest challenges he faced was how to design bridges that used materials other than steel, which doesn't hold up well in the stormy, salty air of the Oregon coast. He also needed a material that was strong enough to span the region's wide estuaries. His solution was to use the Freyssinet method, developed in France, to build bridges that used arches made of pre-stressed concrete. Construction on this scenic highway began in 1927, and by 1936 the final bridges were finished.

At mile 0.2, you pass the immaculately maintained light keeper's house. Built in 1893, this lovely Queen Anne-style house is now being used by the U.S. Forest Service as an interpretive center and bed & breakfast. In the spring, you may spot the teardrop-shaped petals of white lilies scattered along this section of trail. A white picket fence surrounds the Victorian house and its three upper-story rooms. Picture windows offer a grand view of the rocky coast and lighthouse, and everything is topped off with a bright-red roof.

Continue another 0.3 miles to reach the lighthouse and your turnaround point. After you've soaked in the views of the lighthouse glance to the offshore promontory called Parrot Rock, which is an important nesting area for the Brandt's cormorants. Tours of the lighthouse are offered daily and include climbs to the top, where the intricate Fresnel lens is on display.

MilesDirections

0.0 START at the north end of the parking area. *[**Note**. Before you begin, check out the interpretive signs that give you an in-depth view of the history of the lighthouse and light keeper's house.]*

0.2 Pass the light keeper's house on your right.

0.5 Reach 205-foot Heceta Head Lighthouse, your turnaround point.

1.0 Arrive back at the parking area.

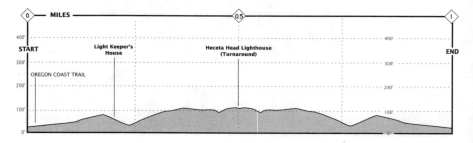

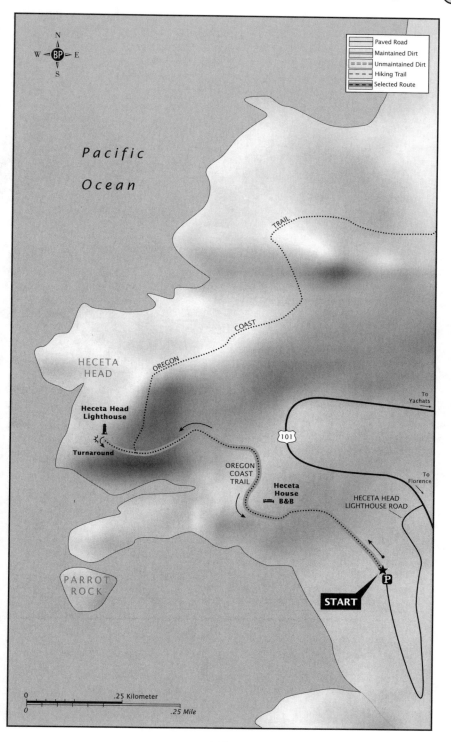

Pacific

Ocean

HECETA
HEAD

Heceta Head
Lighthouse

Turnaround

OREGON
COAST
TRAIL

Heceta
House
B&B

PARROT
ROCK

OREGON

COAST

TRAIL

To
Yachats

101

To
Florence

HECETA HEAD
LIGHTHOUSE ROAD

P

START

Paved Road
Maintained Dirt
Unmaintained Dirt
Hiking Trail
Selected Route

N
W E
S
BP

0   .25 Kilometer
0   .25 Mile

Hike Information

❶ Trail Contacts:
Siuslaw National Forest, Waldport Ranger District, Waldport, OR (541) 563–3211 or *www.fs.fed. us/r6/siuslaw*

❷ Schedule:
Open year round

❸ Fees/Permits:
$3 day-use fee

❹ Local Information:
Florence Chamber of Commerce, Florence, OR (541) 997–3128 or *www.florencechamber.com* · **Yachats Chamber of Commerce,** Yachats, OR (541) 547–3530 or *www.pioneer.net/~yachat*

❺ Local Events/Attractions:
Rhododendron Festival, third weekend in May, Florence, OR (541) 997–3128 · **Sea Lion Caves,** Yachats, OR (541) 547–3111 or *www.sealioncaves. com* · **Siuslaw Pioneer Museum,** Florence, OR (541) 997–7884

❻ Accommodations:
Best Western Pier Point Inn, Florence, OR (541) 997–7191 · **The Edwin K B&B,** Florence, OR 1–800–8EDWINK or *www.edwink. com* · **Heceta Head Lighthouse B&B,** Yachats, OR (541) 547–3696 or *www.hecetalighthouse.com* · **The Fireside Motel,** Yachats, OR 1–800–336–3573—*they allow dogs.*

· **Cape Perpetua Campground,** Yachats, OR (541) 822–3799 · **Rock Creek Campground,** Yachats, OR (541) 822–3799—*located 7.3 miles south of Cape Perpetua* · **Tillicum Campground,** Yachats, OR (541) 822–3799— *located seven miles north of Cape Pertpetua* · **Washburne State Park Campground,** 1–800–551–6949 or *www.prd.state.or.us—located 14 miles north of Florence off U.S. 101* · **Sutton Creek Campground,** (541) 268–4473—*located five miles north of Florence off U.S. 101*

❼ Restaurants:
Bridgewater Seafood Restaurant, Florence, OR (541) 997–9405

❽ Other Resources:
To see more information about Heceta Head Lighthouse visit *www.hecetalighthouse.com/links. html* · To find out more about Oregon's Historic bridges visit *www.odot.state.or.us/eshtm/br. htm* · **Oregon Coast Magazine,** Florence, OR (541) 997–8401 or *www.ocmag.com*

❾ Maps:
USGS maps: Heceta Head, OR

16

Sutton Creek Recreational Area

Hike Summary

The Sutton Creek Recreation Area has over six miles of trails to explore, giving you a close up view of a diverse coastal ecosystem made up of sand dunes, coastal forest, freshwater lakes, a coastal stream, and sandy beach. The Sutton Creek Campground has a short walk through a wet bog where you can view the interesting insect-eating plant, the cobra lily.

Hike Specs

Start: From the trailhead off U.S. 101
Length: Varies depending on the trails selected
Approximate Hiking Time: 1–4 hours depending on the trails selected
Difficulty Rating: Easy to moderate. The trail through the sand dunes is moderately hard. The hike to Sutton Beach requires that you ford Sutton Creek.
Trail Surface: Sand, dirt path, wooden walkway, and beach walking
Lay of the Land: You can hike through a coastal forest along Sutton Creek, walk through loose sand through the Sutton Creek Sand Dunes, or look at rare and interesting plants on a wooden walkway on the Bog Trail.
Land Status: National forest
Nearest Town: Florence, OR
Other Trail Users: HIkers only
Canine Compatibility: Leashed dog permitted

Getting There

To the Sutton Creek Campground Trailhead: Drive 4.2 miles north of Florence on U.S. 101 to Sutton Beach Road and turn right (west) at the "Sutton Recreation" sign. Proceed 0.7 miles and turn right into the Sutton Creek Campground. At the T-intersection, turn left (toward the "A loop" of camp sites) and drive approximately 0.2 miles to the Sutton Group Camp parking area, located between campsites A18 and A19. The trailhead is located on the right side of the Sutton Group Camp parking area.
To the Holman Vista Day-use Parking Area: Drive 4.2 miles north of Florence on U.S. 101 to Sutton Beach Road and turn right (west) at the "Sutton Recreation" sign. Drive two miles west to the day-use parking area. There's a $3 day-use fee. You can obtain a day-use permit at the self-service pay station in the parking area. *DeLorme: Oregon Atlas & Gazetteer:* Page 32, Inset 2 D2

The roughly 2,700-acre Sutton Creek Recreation Area preserves a unique coastal environment within Oregon's Siuslaw National Forest. Protected within the recreation area are fragile coastal forests and freshwater lakes, not to mention the region's trademark dunes. If you're of the mind that a sand dune is a sand dune is a sand dune, you're

missing out on some interesting distinctions. The Sutton Creek area contains a variety of sand dunes, including foredunes, traverse dunes, oblique dunes, and parabola dunes.

You begin with the foredune, and as you move inland, you find hummocks, a deflation plain, transverse dunes, tree islands, oblique dunes, parabola dunes, and transition forest. Foredunes parallel the ocean and can form 20 to 30 feet high. Nowadays you'll find these dunes covered with European beach grass, a non-native plant species introduced by settlers in the early 1900s to stabilize the soil. Since being sown, the European beach grass has spread rapidly, interrupting the natural movement of sand—the mark of an active dune—and altering the landscape.

Following the foredunes are hummocks, which form when sand collects around vegetation. In winter you may notice these as small sand islands, the result of the water table rising to fill the depressions around the hummocks. Farther inland from the hummocks is the deflation plain. You can recognize

Cobra Lily.

117

a deflation plain by its fairly flat landscape. As the foredunes block new sand from moving inland, the wind carries off the remaining dry sand, leaving only wet sand behind—thus deflating the area. The wet sand is a great environment for plants such as bush lupine, Scotch broom, yarrow, and a variety of scented grasses like the large-headed sage, salt rush, and the European beach grass

Farther inland are traverse dunes, created when the northwesterly winds of summer sculpt wavy crests into five- to 20-foot sand hills. Traverse dunes are perpendicular to the wind direction, and during the winter months the southwesterly winds tend to flatten out the crests. The next transition zone is the tree island. These small stands of trees are remnants of a prior coastal forest that was buried by the moving sand. Tree islands have steep, unstable slopes, which are highly susceptible to erosion.

If you like to fish, be sure to check out 100-acre Sutton Lake, located on the east side of U.S. Route 101. The lake is stocked with feisty rainbow trout, largemouth bass, bluegill, panfish, and yellow perch. Three-acre Alder Lake (just north of the Sutton Creek Campground off U.S. Route 101) also has good rainbow fishing.

Even farther inland are oblique dunes. These sloped dunes can reach a height of 180 feet and can be up to a mile long. The west face of an oblique dune is long and gentle, and the east side is steep—this is due to the winds hitting the dunes from the northwest and southwest. The constant pushing of the sand from the west side creates a longer, gentler west face. Due to the winds that are constantly shaping this type of dune and its instability, plants do not grow on oblique dunes.

The transition forest zone is where the sand dune environment meets up with the land environment. This type of forest is filled with a variety of plants that thrive in the windy, sandy environment, like shore pines, rhododendrons, salal, and thimbleberry. The large, sandy, U-shaped ridge in the middle of the coastal forest is the parabola dune. Constant wind erodes away the soil so that plants can live here.

The Sutton Creek Recreation Area is filled with a variety of trail options to explore this diverse community. From Sutton Creek Campground you can hike the 2.25-mile trail to scenic Baker Beach, the breeding ground for the endangered Western snowy plover. [**Note:** *Dogs are not allowed off their leash from March 15th to September 30th because they may disturb the nesting of the these rare birds.*] Along the way you get a taste of ever-changing sand dunes and lush coastal forests of shore pine, rhododendrons, thimbleberry,

MilesDirections

You can access the trails in the Sutton Creek Area from the Sutton Creek Campground and the Holman Vista day-use parking area trailhead. Refer to the map for individual trails.

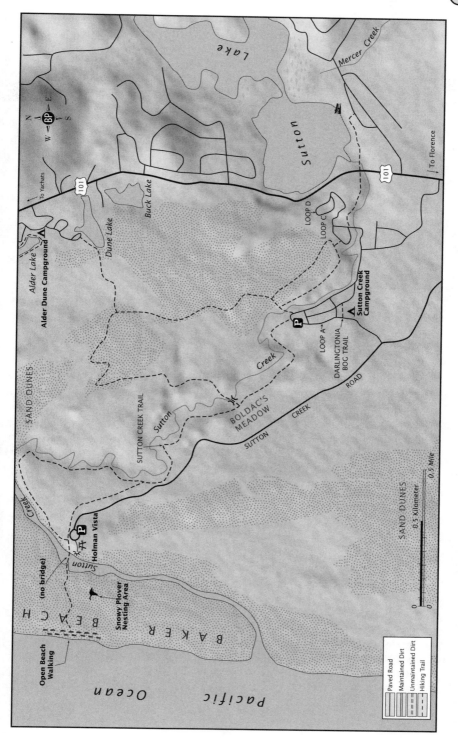

salal, and spruce trees. You might even see otter swimming in Sutton Creek or osprey fishing along its banks. Other trail options from Sutton Creek Campground include hiking 1.75 miles to Alder Dune Campground where you can hike to Dune Lake and Alder Lake.

If you want see the rare insect-eating cobra lily plant, hike the wheel-chair-accessible *Darlingtonia Bog Trail*, located just to the right of the Sutton Creek Campground entrance. These one-of-a-kind plants lure insects into their slow-but-sure traps and digest them slowly. The insects provide the much-needed nutrients that are lacking in the nutrient-poor coastal soil.

If you park at the Holman Vista day-use parking area, walk up the wheel chair-accessible walkway to Holman Vista where you have far reaching views of the rolling sand dunes, the scenic beach, and the rambling Sutton Creek. Notice the bent and twisted shore pine trees. These rugged trees are called *krumholzes* and their irregular shape is due to the constant wind and salt air that batter them on the windward side.

The Western Snowy Plovers

The Pacific Coast breeding colonies of Western snowy plovers can be found from southern Washington to Baja California. Snowy plovers are sparrow-sized birds with a dusty, sand-colored back and a white underside with a black chest band. They like to nest in open sandy areas next to the water. The plover's nesting season is from mid-March through mid-September. They usually lay two to three greenish-brown eggs in a sandy depression above the beach. According to Oregon Fish and Wildlife, the number of snowy plover nesting sites along the Oregon coast dropped from 29 to just six by 1990. Three of these sites (Bayocean Spit, North Spit at Coos Bay, and Floras Lake) supported 81 percent of the total Oregon nesting population.

The snowy plover's rapid decline is due to several different factors. The encroachment of European beach grass has caused a large amount of habitat loss. The grass stabilizes dunes and reduces the amount of un-vegetated area above the tide line, making the sandy beach narrower and steeper, and ultimately making the nesting area less suitable for the birds. Predators also play a role in the decline of the snowy plover. Ravens and crows eat eggs, chicks, and adult birds. The most preventable factor is human impact on nesting habitat. Off-road vehicle use, loose dogs, walking and running on the beach, beach raking, etc. have all taken their toll. Unfortunately, the nesting season for the snowy plover coincides with the highest traffic season of beachgoers.

Measures have been introduced to help protect the snowy plover. Nesting sites are now fenced off, thereby minimizing human impact, and nest enclosures have been introduced to protect the birds from predators. After you reach the beach, keep a lookout for these quick birds as they run up and down the beach feeding on flies and insects.

Hike Information

◐ Trail Contacts:
Siuslaw National Forest, Mapleton Ranger District, Florence, OR (541) 902–8526 or *www.fs.fed.us/r6/siuslaw*

◓ Schedule:
Open year round

Ⓢ Fees/Permits:
$3 day-use fee payable at the self-pay station at the Holman Vista Parking Area

❓ Local Information:
Florence Chamber of Commerce, Florence, OR (541) 997–3128 or *www.florencechamber.com* · **Yachats Chamber of Commerce,** Yachats, OR (541) 547–3530 or *www.pioneer.net/~yachat*

◉ Local Events/Attractions:
Rhododendron Festival, third weekend in May, Florence, OR (541) 997–3128 · **Sea Lion Caves,** Yachats, OR (541) 547–3111 or *www.sealioncaves.com* · **Siuslaw Pioneer Museum,** Florence, OR (541) 997–7884

⊜ Accommodations:
Best Western Pier Point Inn, Florence, OR (541) 997–7191 · **The Edwin K B&B,** Florence, OR 1–800–8EDWINK or *www.edwink.com* · **Heceta Head Lighthouse B&B,** Yachats, OR (541) 547–3696 or *www.hecetalighthouse.com* · **The Fireside Motel,** Yachats, OR 1–800–336–3573—*they allow dogs.*

• **Cape Perpetua Campground,** Yachats, OR (541) 822–3799 · **Rock Creek Campground,** Yachats, OR (541) 822–3799—*located 7.3 miles south of Cape Perpetua* · **Tillicum Campground,** Yachats, OR (541) 822–3799—*located seven miles north of Cape Pertpetua* · **Washburne State Park Campground,** 1–800–551–6949 or *www.prd.state.or.us*—*located 14 miles north of Florence off U.S. 101* · **Sutton Creek Campground,** (541) 268–4473—*located five miles north of Florence off U.S. 101*

⑪ Restaurants:
Bridgewater Seafood Restaurant, Florence, OR (541) 997–9405

◕ Other Resources:
To see more information about Heceta Head Lighthouse visit *www.hecetalighthouse.com/links.html* · To find out more about Oregon's Historic bridges visit *www.odot.state.or.us/eshtm/br.htm* · **Oregon Coast Magazine,** Florence, OR (541) 997–8401 or *www.ocmag.com*

Ⓝ Maps:
USGS maps: Mercer Lake, OR

Sunset Bay State Park to Cape Arago State Park

Hike Summary

Get your camera ready to snap great photos of the rocky coastline along this scenic stretch of the Oregon coast. This trail begins at Sunset Bay State Park and takes you on a journey along the cliff edges to Shore Acres State Park and to Cape Arago State Park. The rocky coastline is a haven to sea lions. As you near Cape Arago State Park, you can hear their noisy raucous from almost a mile away.

Hike Specs

Start: From the Oregon Coast Trail marker adjacent to the restrooms in the day-use picnic area in Sunset Bay State Park
Length: 8.8-mile out-and-back
Approximate Hiking Time: 4–5 hours
Difficulty Rating: Easy
Trail Surface: Dirt, gravel, and paved paths and roads
Lay of the Land: Hike through a coastal forest and along sandstone cliffs south to Cape Arago, your turnaround point.
Elevation Gain: 448 feet
Land Status: State parks
Nearest Town: Coos Bay, OR
Other Trail Users: None
Canine Compatibility: Not dog friendly. Dogs are not allowed in Shore Acres State Park.

Getting There

From Coos Bay: Follow the signs to "Charleston Harbor and Ocean Beaches." Drive southwest for 12 miles on the Cape Arago Highway to Sunset Bay State Park. When you reach the park, turn into the day-use picnicking area, located on the west side of the highway. Look for the Oregon Coast Trail marker located on the right side of the restrooms. *DeLorme: Oregon Atlas & Gazetteer:* Page 33 B5

Some of the most beautiful stretches of rocky coast and forest can be found along the Oregon Coast Trail between Sunset Bay State Park and Cape Arago State Park. Hemmed in and protected by golden sandstone cliffs, the beautiful Sunset Bay forms the focal point of Sunset Bay State Park. This secluded piece of the coast is thought to have served as a safe haven for ships waiting out the furious storms that often hit the Oregon coast. The park was once part of the enormous estate of lumberman, ship builder, and founder of North Bend, Louis B. Simpson. Simpson had his home two miles south in what is now Shore Acres State Park. In 1913, Simpson oversaw the building of the Sunset Bay Inn, situated on the edge of Sunset Bay.

The Oregon Coast Trail takes off from the day-use picnic area and parallels the cliff's edge through a thick Sitka spruce forest. As it winds its way south, you'll have sneak peaks at the golden, steep-walled sandstone cliffs.

Shore Acres State Park.

MilesDirections

0.0 START at the day-use picnicking area at Sunset Bay State Park. Look for the wooden Oregon Coast Trail located marker just to the right of the restrooms that indicates the start of the trail. As you begin walking on the trail you'll see a sign that reads "Shore Acres 2 miles."

0.1 Come to a fork and go right. (Left opens into a grassy picnic area.)

0.3 *[FYI. Good views of Sunset Bay and offshore rock formations.]*

0.6 Come to a trail junction and turn left. The trail winds up a fern-covered hillside to a paved road.

0.8 Reach the paved road and turn right. Walk along the road. Approach a set of wooden steps on your right and turn right. Take the steps over the metal road barrier.

1.3 Come to a fork and go right.

1.4 *[FYI. Good viewpoint of the bay and the Cape Arago Lighthouse to your right.]*

1.9 Cross two wooden bridges.

2.1 Reach Shore Acres State Park. The path turns from dirt to pavement when you enter the park. *[**Note.** Dogs are not allowed in the park.]*

2.2 Come to a fork and go right. (If you go left you'll enter a parking area). Come to another fork and stay right. The trail parallels a wood rail fence.

2.3 Come to an observation building on your left.

2.4 Come to a trail junction and veer right where the sign indicates "Simpson Beach." *[**Option.** You can turn left here and view the Botanical Garden.]*

2.7 Arrive at Simpson Beach. The paved path ends. Turn left and cross a stream. Continue walking on the trail and cross a second stream.

2.9 Come to a T-intersection and turn right.

3.5 Come to a fork and turn right. *[FYI. Listen closely for the calls from the sea lion colony in Cape Arago State Park.]*

3.6 Come to a T-intersection and turn right.

3.8 Come to a paved road and turn right. Walk into the paved parking area of Sea Lion Viewpoint. Continue walking parallel to U.S. 101 for 0.6 miles until you reach Cape Arago State Park.

4.4 Arrive at your turnaround point and retrace your tracks back to your vehicle.

8.8 Arrive back at the parking lot.

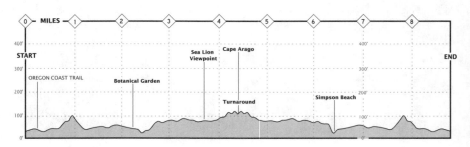

124

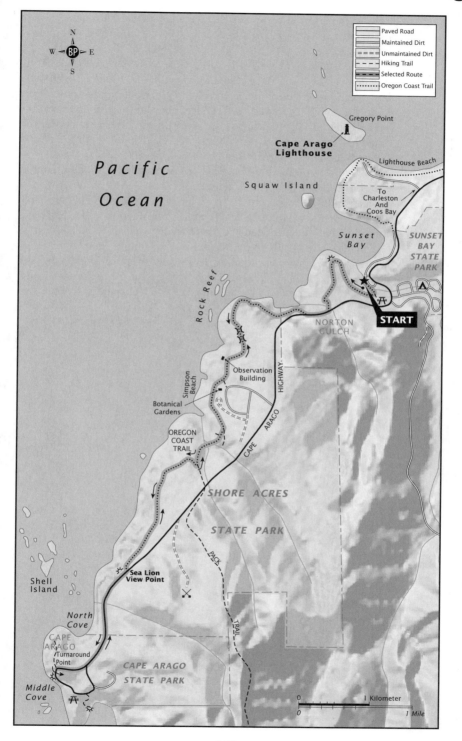

Many of the layers in these cliffs are curved, matching the ocean currents that formed them over 45 million years ago when this area was under a shallow sea.

After 1.4 miles, you'll have a scenic view of the bay and Cape Arago Lighthouse. The Cape Arago Lighthouse is one of only nine lighthouses that grace Oregon's coastline. Located on a rocky outcrop just off Gregory Point, the scenic lighthouse rises 100 feet above the ocean and stands 44 feet tall. Built in 1934, this lighthouse is the third lighthouse to occupy this same site. Its predecessors were built in 1866 and 1908—both fell prey to the harsh elements along this stretch of the Oregon Coast.

At mile 2.1 you reach 743-acre Shore Acres State Park, also formerly part of the Louis J. Simpson estate. Simpson discovered this scenic part of the coast in 1905 and bought 320 acres for $4,000. Simpson built an elaborate estate on the grounds: stables, a carriage house, tennis courts, and beautiful cultivated gardens. At mile 2.3, you come to a glass enclosed observation building that stands on the site of Simpson's former estate.

From this vantage point the wild, rocky coast stretches for miles in both directions and thundering waves create many great picture opportunities. From December through June you may also be lucky and spot some gray

whales on their semi-annual migration from Baja, Mexico to Alaska. At mile 2.4, you come to a view of the beautiful botanical gardens, which are meticulously maintained by Oregon State Parks and Recreation. These botanical gardens contain a Japanese garden, two rose gardens, and other formal flower gardens. From February through March, daffodils are in peak bloom; from April through mid-May, the azaleas and rhododendrons steal the show; and from June through September, roses are in full bloom.

You'll arrive at Cape Arago State Park after 4.4 miles. The 134-acre park sits atop a 200-foot rocky cliff. Offshore is Simpson Reef, home to large colonies of seals and sea lions. You'll be able to hear their raucous calling from several wildlife viewing points in the park. This scenic cape was named after Dominique F. J. Arago, a French physicist and geographer (1786–1853). This rocky headland was also once part of the large Simpson estate; It was handed over to the state of Oregon in 1932. There are three coves you can hike to in this park—North, Middle, and South. If you enjoy exploring tide pools, be sure to take a side trip to South Cove. North Cove is closed from March 1st to July 1st each year to protect sea lions and seal pups.

Hike Information

🕭 Trail Contacts:
Oregon Parks and Recreation Department, Salem, OR 1–800–551–6949 or www.prd.state.or.us

🕐 Schedule:
Open year round

❓ Local Information:
Bay Area Chamber of Commerce, Coos Bay, OR 1–800–824–8486

🅀 Local Events/Attractions:
4th of July Celebration in Mingus Park, Coos Bay, OR (541) 269–8912

🛏 Accommodations:
This Olde House B&B, Coos Bay, OR (541) 267–5224 or www.bnbweb.com/thisoldehouse.html
· Sunset Bay State Park Campground, Oregon State Parks and Recreation 1–800–551–6949 To make reservations call Reservations Northwest 1–800–452–5687 or www.prd.state.or.us

🍽 Restaurants:
Gourmet Coastal Coffees, Coos Bay, OR (541) 267–5004

🛒 Local Outdoor Retailers:
Fred Meyer, Coos Bay, OR (541) 269–4000

Ⓝ Maps:
USGS maps: Charleston, OR; Cape Arago, OR

Cape Ferrelo to Whalehead Beach

Hike Summary

This hike takes you on the Oregon Coast Trail through the heart of Samuel H. Boardman State Park. You'll walk through thick Sitka spruce forest, past bubbling coastal creeks, on wild and windy headlands with fantastic views of offshore sea stacks and rocky islands, and along an uncrowded sandy beach.

Hike Specs

Start: From the trailhead off the Cape Ferrelo Viewpoint parking area

Length: 9.4-mile out-and-back

Approximate Hiking Time: 4–6 hours

Difficulty Rating: Moderate due to the steep ascents and descents through forest and open headlands. The beach walking can be difficult due to high winds and soft sand.

Trail Surface: Well-maintained dirt path, short sections of pavement, stream crossings, and soft sandy beach hiking

Lay of the Land: Hike through a coastal forest and open, windy headlands and then descend several steep switchbacks to Whalehead Beach for a flat, sandy beach-walk to your turnaround point.

Elevation Gain: 1,271 feet

Land Status: State park

Nearest Town: Brookings, OR

Other Trail Users: Hikers only

Canine Compatibility: Dog friendly

Getting There

From Brookings: Drive 4.8 miles north on U.S. 101 and turn left (west) at the Cape Ferrelo Viewpoint. Drive 0.2 miles to the parking area. The hike begins in the northwest corner of the parking area.

DeLorme: Oregon Atlas & Gazetteer: Page 17 C13

The charming coastal town of Brookings lies six miles north of the California/Oregon border on the bay of the Chetco River and boasts uncrowded beaches, spectacular bluffs and offshore rock formations, a busy fishing harbor, prize fishing on the Chetco River, and some of the warmest weather on the Oregon coast. Established in 1908, Brookings is the namesake of the Brookings family who founded the Brookings Lumber & Box Company. In the past, logging was the chief industry here, but now tourism, Easter lily bulb production (Brookings is the nation's leader), and sport fishing are also major industries in this bustling seaport.

Large scale Easter lily bulb production in the Chetco Valley began during World War II when Japanese and Holland lily bulb imports were halted in the United States. Bulbs that sold for about a nickel apiece before the war

Whalehead Beach.

129

were going for $1 during the war. This high price soon made bulb production a profitable way to make a living in Curry County. During the war the amount of lily bulb growers exploded to about one thousand. Some growers were making $10,000 to $20,000 dollars per acre growing bulbs. Currently, 10 large production farms are active in the Brookings area, producing about 95 percent of the Easter lily bulbs worldwide.

Another highlight to the Brookings area is Samuel H. Boardman State Park. This 1,471-acre park stretches for over 12 miles along the rugged coastline north of Brookings and has several access points off U.S. Route

MilesDirections

0.0 START at the north end of the viewpoint parking area at the wooden Oregon Coast Trail marker.

0.3 Cross a concrete bridge over a creek.

0.5 Cross a bridge over a creek.

1.0 Cross a wooden bridge over a creek.

1.4 Reach the House Rock Viewpoint. Continue walking straight on the paved sidewalk. *[**Side-trip.** You can take a detour here by turning left and viewing the Samuel H. Boardman monument.]*

I.8 Cross a wood bridge over a creek.

2.0 Cross a wood bridge over a creek. Notice the small, cascading waterfall to your right.

2.3 *[**FYI.** There's a good viewpoint to your left.]*

2.5 Come to a fork and turn left. Cross a wooden bridge over a creek.

2.8 The trail takes you into an open area on a scenic headland above Whalehead Beach. Descend steeply down a series of switchbacks to Whalehead Beach.

3.1 Reach Whalehead Beach. Cross a small stream and continue walking north on the sandy beach.

4.2 Cross a stream.

4.3 Near the end of the beach. Veer to the right and look for the wooden Oregon Coast Trail marker.

4.4 Reach the marker indicating the continuation of the trail north.

4.6 Pass the wooden stairs to your left. *[**FYI.** If you take these stairs you'll walk through a 0.25-mile tunnel to an RV Park.]*

4.7 Comes to a paved parking and picnic area with restrooms. Turn around here.

9.4 Arrive back at the parking area.

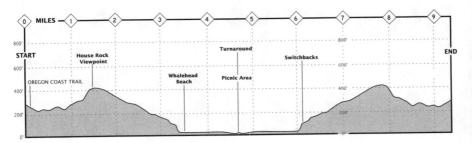

130

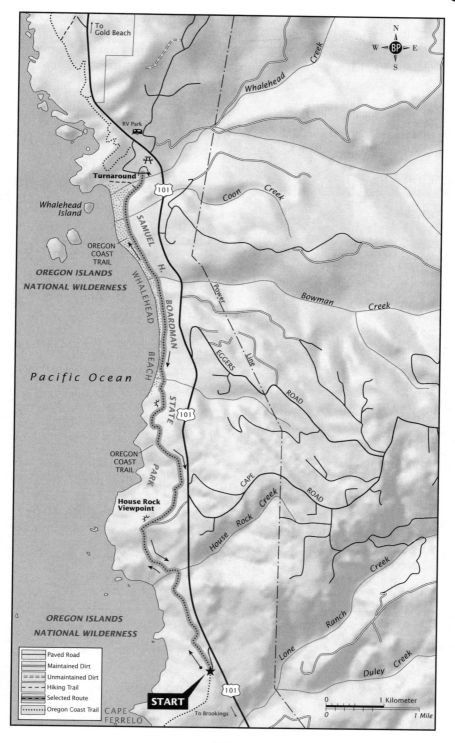

101. The Oregon Coast Trail runs right through the heart of this scenic area and promises you a pleasant, uncrowded coastal trek.

Begin the hike from the Cape Ferrelo parking area and wind through a Sitka spruce and red cedar forest interspersed with open meadows filled with vibrant purple lupine. There are also several viewpoints along this

section that give you a sneak peak at the rugged rocky sea stacks located just off of Whalehead Beach. After 1.4 miles you come to House Rock Viewpoint, an excellent vantage point for spotting migrating gray whales. As you continue north, the trail re-enters the forest and begins to descend steeply down a series of switchbacks. After 2.8 miles you emerge from the forest onto a scenic, open headland. The trail descends steeply to sandy Whalehead Beach. Continue walking north on the beach for another 1.6 miles, past large rocky outcrops, and offshore you'll see Whalehead Island—which clearly resembles the shape of a whale. At last you arrive at your turn-around point, where you'll find a scenic picnic spot and restrooms.

Hike Information

🕐 Trail Contacts:
Harris Beach State Park, Brookings, OR (541) 469–2021 or *www.prd.state.or.us*

🕑 Schedule:
Open year round

💲 Fees/Permits:
$3 day-use fee

❓ Local Information:
The Brookings-Harbor Chamber of Commerce, Brookings, OR 1–800–535–9469 or *www. brookingsor.com/BrookingsOR/ index.shtml*

📍 Local Events/Attractions:
Azalea Festival, Memorial Day Weekend, Brookings, OR (541) 469–9741 or 1–800–877–9741 · **Southern Oregon Kite Festival,** in July, Brookings, OR (541) 469–2218 · **Festival of the Arts,** in August, Brookings, OR (541) 469–6070 · **Chetco Valley Historical Society Museum,** Brookings, OR (541) 469–6651

⬤ Accommodations:
The South Coast Inn B&B, Brookings, OR 1–800–525–9273 · **Best Western Beachfront Inn,** Brookings, OR 1–800–468–4081 · **Alfred A. Loeb State Park Campground** (541) 469–2021 or *www.oregontrails.com/loeb.htm*

🍴 Restaurants:
Hog Wild Café, Brookings, OR (541) 469–8869 · **Rubio's Mexican Restaurant,** Brookings, OR (541) 469–4919 · **Wharfside Restaurant,** Brookings OR (541) 469–7316

🎣 Local Outdoor Retailers:
Loring's Lighthouse Sporting Goods, Brookings, OR (541) 469–2148

Ⓝ Maps:
USGS maps: Brookings, OR; Carpenterville, OR

19

Riverview & Redwood Trails

Hike Summary

This hike through Alfred A. Loeb State Park offers a rare glimpse of two hard-to-find tree species: the Oregon myrtlewood and the redwood. The Riverview Trail follows the banks of the salmon- and steelhead-rich Chetco River through an old grove of Oregon myrtle trees. The Redwood Nature Trail loops through a grove of immense coastal redwood trees. Both trails include numbered markers that correspond to a detailed brochure pointing out all the highlights. The state park also has a campground and all kinds of fun things to see and do. You can swim in the Chetco River, fish, or rent a charter boat in nearby Brookings Harbor. In addition, the park is the gateway to the 179,655-acre Kalmiopsis Wilderness and its hundreds of miles of trails, numerous lakes, and rugged river gorges *[see Hike 22]*.

Hike Specs

Start: From the parking area off North Bank Chetco River Road
Length: 4.2-mile out-and-back
Approximate Hiking Time: 2–3 hours
Difficulty Rating: *Riverview Trail*—easy due to the well-maintained dirt path, few trail obstacles, and flat terrain. *Redwood Nature Trail*—moderate due to how steep it is.
Trail Surface: Well-maintained dirt path
Lay of the Land: The *Riverview Trail* parallels the Chetco River through an old grove of myrtlewood trees. The *Redwood Nature Trail* loops through an ancient redwood grove.

Elevation Gain: 599 feet
Land Status: State park
Nearest Town: Brookings, OR
Other Trail Users: Hikers only
Canine Compatibility: Leashed dogs permitted

Getting There

From Brookings: Head east on North Bank Chetco River Road from U.S 101. Drive 7.5 miles and turn right into Alfred A. Loeb State Park. Come to a fork and go left. Proceed to the picnic area, and park in a parking area on your right. *DeLorme: Oregon Atlas & Gazetteer:* Page 17 D3

The Riverview and Redwood trails take you on a journey through groves of two hard-to-find tree species: the Oregon myrtle (also know as Coos Bay laurel) and the giant coastal redwood. Be sure to pick up the descriptive brochure at the trailhead, so you can identify these and other plant species found along the trails.

The trail begins as an easy ramble through a lush grove of Oregon myrtle, Douglas fir, Western hemlock, and red alder. As you walk the path, look for the distinctive gumdrop shape of the Oregon myrtle tree. This broad-leafed evergreen grows in small groves in the wet coastal regions of Oregon

and California and is a member of the laurel family—the same family as avocado, camphor, cinnamon, and sassafras. The oil from the myrtle's fragrant and spicy leaves is often used to scent candles and perfumes. The leaves are also an excellent seasoning for soups and sauces—Native Americans made a soothing tea from the leaves. The beautiful wood is used to make furniture and souvenirs.

The trees provide a shady canopy that creates a perfect growing environment for the feathery maidenhair fern, the spiked sword fern, deer fern, and the edible salmonberry. You'll also notice an abundance of English ivy, a nonnative plant that competes with the indigenous species for precious forest real estate. Poison oak can also be found lurking along this trail, so watch out.

As you walk you'll catch glimpses of the wide-running Chetco River. This calm, deep river meets the Pacific Ocean at Brookings Harbor—home to one of Oregon's largest fishing fleets. The river has some of the largest steelhead and salmon runs on the Oregon coast and is popular with sport fisherman. It's also home to several good swimming holes—keep your eyes peeled.

At mile 1.1, the Riverview Trail comes to a paved road. Across the road is the beginning of the Redwood Nature Trail. From here it's a series of steep switchbacks through a tall, silent grove of 300- to 800-year-old coastal redwood trees (*sequoia sempervirens*). Redwood trees (there are three varieties) are found in only three regions of the world: The coastal redwood is found along the Northern California coast and at the tip of the Southern Oregon

MilesDirections

0.0 START in the parking area for the Riverview Trailhead. Walk cross the paved road to the trailhead sign that indicates the start of the Riverview Trail. *[Note. Be sure to pick up a trail brochure. There are trail markers that correspond to descriptions in the brochure. Take the time to read about the plants and wildlife described in the brochure.]*

0.5 Walk through an area that has edible salmon berries.

0.8 Cross a wooden footbridge over a creek.

0.9 Cross a wooden footbridge over a creek.

1.0 Cross North Bank Chetco River Road and arrive at the Redwood Nature Trailhead. There are restrooms and a picnic table here.

1.1 The trail comes to a T-intersection. Begin the Redwood Nature Trail by going left on the trail. *[Note. This trail also has trail markers that are described in the brochure.]*

1.8 Cross a wooden footbridge over a creek.

2.3 Cross a wooden footbridge over a creek.

3.0 Cross a wooden footbridge over a creek.

3.1 The loop trail ends. Turn left and walk 1.1 miles on the Riverview Trail back to your car.

4.2 Arrive back at your car.

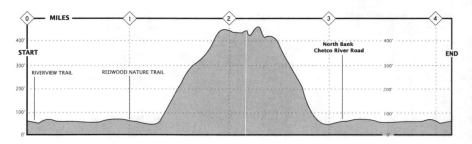

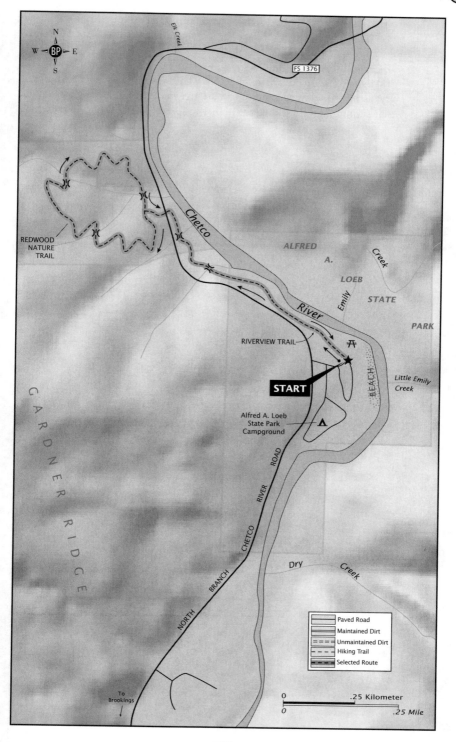

coast; the Sierra redwood (*sequoiadendron gigantia*) is found in a small section of the Sierra Nevada Mountains; and the dawn redwood (*meta sequoia*) is found in a remote area in China.

Coastal redwoods can live for more than 2,000 years, growing as high as 300 feet and with a diameter of 20 feet. These hardy trees have several survival strategies that account for their longevity. Their thick bark is fire and rot resistant, and they have the ability to grow a lateral root system, which

allows them to re-establish themselves after floods. If a redwood tree falls over, new trees spring up from the limbs of the parent tree to create a grove of small trees in fairly straight rows.

As you continue walking up the path, you'll see native rhododendrons and tanoak trees, which commonly grow in the company of redwoods. The bright-red and pink flowers of the rhododendron can be seen blooming in early spring. The tanoak tree can be identified by its fuzzy acorns. Finally, you'll see the delicate pink flowers and clover-like leaves of redwood sorrel. The Redwood Loop ends after 1.9 miles. Continue back to your starting point on the Riverview Trail.

Hike Information

🕐 Trail Contacts:
Siskiyou National Forest, Chetco Ranger District, Brookings, OR (541) 469–2196 or *www.fs.fed. us/r6/siskiyou*

🕐 Schedule:
Open year round

Ⓢ Fees/Permits:
$3 day-use fee. Requires a Northwest Forest $5 day pass or $30 annual pass. You can purchase a pass online at: *www.fs.fed.us/r6/feedemo* or by call calling 1–800–270–7504.

❓ Local Information:
The Brookings-Harbor Chamber of Commerce, Brookings, OR 1–800–535–9469 or *www. brookingsor.com/BrookingsOR/index.shtml*

◉ Local Events/Attractions:
Azalea Festival, Memorial Day Weekend, Brookings, OR (541) 469–9741 or 1–800–877–9741 · **Southern Oregon Kite Festival,** in July, Brookings, OR (541) 469–2218 · **Festival of the Arts,** in August, Brookings, OR (541) 469–6070 · **Chetco Valley Historical Society Museum,** Brookings, OR (541) 469–6651

🛏 Accommodations:
The South Coast Inn B&B, Brookings, OR 1–800–525–9273 · **Best Western Beachfront Inn,** Brookings, OR 1–800–468–4081 · **Alfred A. Loeb State Park campground** (541) 469–2021 or *www.oregontrails.com/loeb.htm*

🍴 Restaurants:
Hog Wild Café, Brookings, OR (541) 469–8869 · **Rubio's Mexican Restaurant,** Brookings, OR (541) 469–4919 · **Wharfside Restaurant,** Brookings OR (541) 469–7316

🌲 Local Outdoor Retailers:
Loring's Lighthouse Sporting Goods, Brookings, OR (541) 469–2148

Ⓝ Maps:
USGS maps: Mount Emily, OR

Vulcan Lake

Hike Summary

Experience the raw beauty of the rugged and remote Kalmiopsis Wilderness. This scenic hike takes you over an open, windswept ridge to a viewpoint of a spectacular glacier-carved basin that cradles Vulcan Lake. Once you reach this scenic lake, after descending down the ridge, you'll want spend hours sitting atop the boulder-strewn lakeshore staring at the crystal-clear water of the high alpine lake.

Hike Specs

Start: From the trailhead off FS 260
Length: 2.2-mile out-and-back
Approximate Hiking Time: 2–3 hours
Difficulty Rating: Moderate due to a fairly steep ascent up a ridge
Trail Surface: Graded dirt path with some rocky sections
Lay of the Land: Hike up an open, prominent ridge and then descend into a scenic rock basin to the shore of Vulcan Lake.
Elevation Gain: 1,052 feet
Land Status: Wilderness area
Nearest Town: Brookings, OR
Other Trail Users: Hikers only
Canine Compatibility: Dog friendly

Getting There

From Brookings: Turn onto North Bank Chetco River Road from U.S. 101 and drive 15.8 miles to FS 1909. Turn right. At mile 18.4, come to a fork and go right. Follow the signs indicating "Vulcan Peak and the Kalmiopsis Wilderness." At mile 23.6, the road comes to a T-intersection. Turn right where a sign indicates "Vulcan Lake." The road becomes very rough and rocky. At mile 25.6, come to a fork and turn left. At mile 28.4, pass Red Mountain Prairie Campground on your left. At mile 29.1, come to a fork and turn left on to FS 260, where the sign indicates "Vulcan Lake." The road becomes rougher and rockier and narrow, making it difficult to turn around. At mile 30.8, reach the trailhead at the road's end. *DeLorme: Oregon Atlas & Gazetteer:* Page 18 C1

Established in 1907, the 1,163,484-acre Siskiyou National Forest contains within its boundaries the Klamath, Coast, and Siskiyou mountain ranges. The wild and rugged million-acre Siskiyou National Forest boasts five wilderness areas: Grassy Knob, Red Buttes, Siskiyou, Wild Rogue, and the Kalmiopsis. Of these five, the 179,655-acre Kalmiopsis Wilderness is the largest.

The Kalmiopsis Wilderness is the namesake of a pre-ice-age shrub named *kalmiopsis leachiana*—one of the oldest members of the heath family. Over 153 miles of trails wander through this rugged area of steep ridges and

Vulcan Lake.

rugged river gorges. This diverse wilderness area is also known for its rare and unique plants, many of which have adapted to the harsh soils derived from peridotite and serpentinite rocks. Weather, climate, and geological forces have also played a role in the type of plants that live in this remote corner of southern Oregon. Some of the hardwood tree species you'll find here include golden chinkapen, Pacific madrone, Oregon myrtle, California black oak, tanoak, canyon live oak, and Oregon white oak. Woody shrubs found here that are considered rare and sensitive include Howell's man-

Spring snow on the Vulcan Lake Trail.

MilesDirections

0.0 START from the trailhead sign located at the end of FS 260. Be sure to fill out a self-issue wilderness permit.

0.1 Come to a fork and go right.

0.9 Come to a fork and go right, where a sign indicates "Trail 1110A." *[FYI: Trail*

1110B goes left and takes you to Little Vulcan Lake.]

1.1 Reach Vulcan Lake and your turn-around point.

2.2 Arrive back at the parking area.

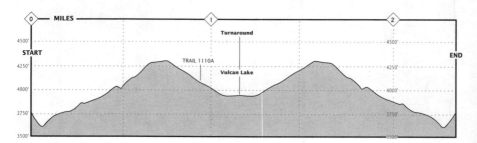

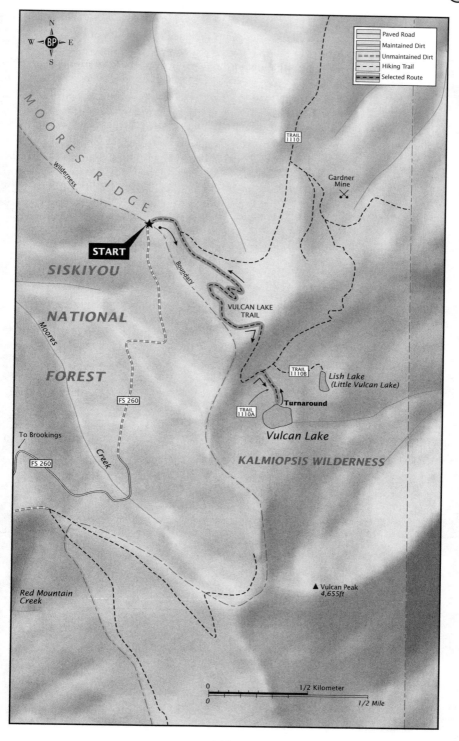

zanita, kalmiopsis plant, Sierra-laurel, Del Norte willow, and Tracy's willow. Rare and sensitive herbaceous plants include Bolander's onion, Waldo rock-cress, Siskiyou sedge, purple toothwort, short-lobed paintbrush, clustered lady's-slipper, rigid willow-herb, deer fleabane, Siskiyou fritillaria, and Siskiyou monardella, plus many more.

Millions of years by erosional forces have been shaping the Kalmiopsis Wilderness. Now extinct glaciers carved many of the lake basins, such as Babyfoot Lake, Vulcan Lakes, Rough and Ready Lakes, and Chetco Lake. The hike to Vulcan Lake gives you an inside look at the geological forces that have shaped this area. The trail begins by switchbacking steeply up an open ridge to a spectacular overlook. The trail then crosses a saddle on the ridge and descends across an open slope filled with different species of manzanita plants. There are numerous viewpoints of the lake along the way. After a mile you reach Vulcan Lake. This seven-acre lake rests at an

elevation of approximately 4,000 feet in a spectacular red rock basin at the foot of 4,655-foot Vulcan Peak. The blue-green lake is stocked with rainbow trout and is the home to the California newt. The lake's shoreline is strewn with large, oddly shaped boulders that make wonderful places to hang out, eat your lunch, and gaze at the lake before heading back to your car.

Hike Information

⊙ Trail Contacts:
Siskiyou National Forest, Chetco Ranger District, Brookings, OR (541) 469-2196 or *www.fs.fed.us/r6/siskiyou*

⊙ Schedule:
July through October

⑤ Fees/Permits:
Requires a Northwest Forest $5 day pass or $30 annual pass. You can purchase a pass online at: *www.fs.fed.us/r6/feedemo* or by call calling 1-800-270-7504.

❓ Local Information:
The Brookings-Harbor Chamber of Commerce, Brookings, OR 1-800-535-9469 or *www. brookingsor.com/BrookingsOR/ index.shtml*

⚲ Local Events/Attractions:
Azalea Festival, Memorial Day Weekend, Brookings, OR (541) 469-9741 or 1-800-877-9741 · **Southern Oregon Kite Festival,** in July, Brookings, OR (541) 469-2218 · **Festival of the Arts,** in August, Brookings, OR (541) 469-6070 · **Chetco Valley Historical Society Museum,** Brookings, OR (541) 469-6651

⊖ Accommodations:
The South Coast Inn Bed & Breakfast, Brookings, OR 1-800-525-9273 · **Best Western Beachfront Inn,** Brookings, OR 1-800-468-4081 · **Alfred A. Loeb State Park campground** (541) 469-2021 or *www.prd.state.or.us*

⑪ Restaurants:
Hog Wild Café, Brookings, OR (541) 469-8869 · **Rubio's Mexican Restaurant,** Brookings, OR (541) 469-4919 · **Wharfside Restaurant,** Brookings OR (541) 469-7316

⊛ Local Outdoor Retailers:
Loring's Lighthouse Sporting Goods, Brookings, OR (541) 469-2148

Ⓝ Maps:
USGS maps: Chetco Peak, OR

21

Babyfoot Lake

Hike Summary

This easy, 2.0-mile out-and-back trail takes you through part of the Babyfoot Lake Botanical Area, home to many rare plant species that are only found in the unspoiled Kalmiopsis Wilderness. After one mile of hiking you reach Babyfoot Lake, which sits in a dramatic glacial cirque surrounded by timbered hillsides that contain a large population of the rare Port Orford cedar and Brewers spruce trees.

Hike Specs

Start: From the trailhead off FS 140
Length: 2.0-mile out-and-back
Approximate Hiking Time: 1–2 hours
Difficulty Rating: Easy
Trail Surface: Maintained forest path
Lay of the Land: Hike through an old-growth forest to Babyfoot Lake
Elevation Gain: 510 feet
Land Status: Wilderness area
Nearest Town: Cave Junction, OR
Other Trail Users: Hikers only
Canine Compatibility: Dog friendly

Getting There

From Cave Junction: Drive north for four miles on U.S. 199 (The Redwood Highway) and turn left (west) on to Eight Dollar Road (this turns into FS 4201 after you enter the Siskiyou National Forest). Drive on FS 4201 for 11.3 miles to the intersection with FS 140. Turn left on to FS 140 and drive 0.3 miles to the trailhead on the right side of the road. *DeLorme: Oregon Atlas & Gazetteer:* Page 18 C2

Babyfoot Lake is located in a glacial cirque surrounded by forested hills and rocky bluffs. This high mountain lake is situated in the wild and rugged 179,655-acre Kalmiopsis Wilderness—one of five wilderness areas located in the Siskiyou National Forest. A short, easy one-mile trail leads you to this quiet lake through an old-growth forest—part of the 352-acre Babyfoot Lake Botanical Area, which was established in 1963 to protect the Brewers spruce and other rare plant species.

Due to its gentle terrain and easy access off Forest Service Road 140, the Babyfoot Lake Trail can be crowded during the summer months. The trail begins by winding through an old-growth forest of Brewers spruce, Douglas fir, Shasta red fir, sugar pine, Port Orford cedar, and incense cedar. Interspersed on the forest floor are vine maple, western sword fern, parsley fern, and fragile fern. In open areas you may see the bright colors of wildflowers such as bleeding hearts, rattlesnake orchid, Siskiyou iris, Newberry's penstemon, pussy paws, spreading phlox, and twinflower.

When you reach the lake you'll want to plan on staying for a while. You may want to take a refreshing swim, search for rare endemic plants (be sure

to bring your plant field guide), or have a picnic. If you love to fish, try your luck at catching some Eastern brook trout, which are present in small quantities in the lake.

While you are in the Caves Junction Area, be sure to check out Oregon Caves National Monument, located 20 miles east of Cave Junction on Oregon 46. This national monument was established in 1909 to showcase

Levi and Sage at Babyfoot Lake.

MilesDirections

0.0 START from the wooden trailhead sign. A sign indicates "Babyfoot Lake ¾/Canyon Peak Trail 4." (Note that the trail is actually a mile in length.) Be sure to fill out a self-issue wilderness permit at the trailhead.

0.3 Come to a fork and turn right. (If you go left here a sign indicates "Ridge Trail 1124.3.")

1.0 Reach Babyfoot Lake and your turn-around point.

2.0 Arrive back at the trailhead.

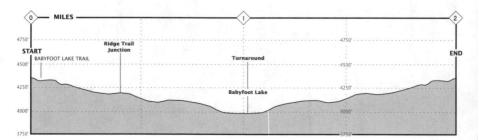

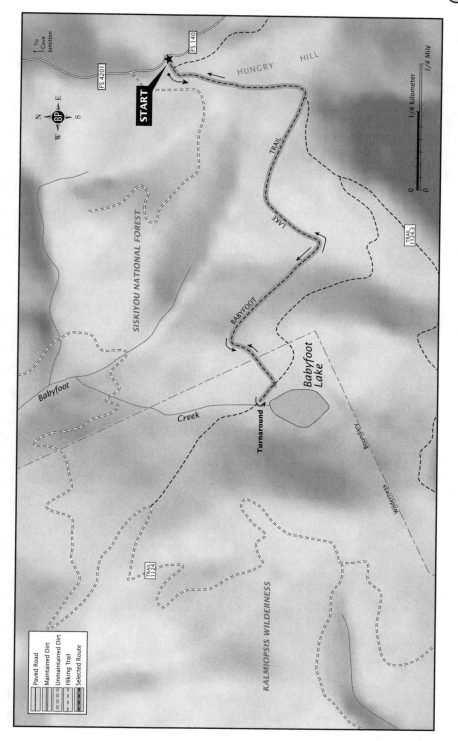

START

FS 140

FS 4201

To
Cave
Junction

HUNGRY HILL

BABYFOOT LAKE TRAIL

SISKIYOU NATIONAL FOREST

TRAIL
1124.3

Babyfoot

Creek

Babyfoot
Lake

Turnaround

Wilderness Boundary

TRAIL
1124

KALMIOPSIS WILDERNESS

N
W — E
S

1/4 Kilometer
0

1/4 Mile
0

Paved Road
Maintained Dirt
Unmaintained Dirt
Hiking Trail
Selected Route

The author enjoying the view at Babyfoot Lake.

its main attraction, a large cave carved by the Styx River. You can see this magnificent cave by taking the 90-minute guided tour. You'll see almost a half mile of fascinating rock chambers filled with stalactites and intricately carved rock columns. This national monument also contains nature trails that will help you learn about the 80 species of birds, 35 species of mammals, and more than 110 species of plants present in the park. The 3.3-mile Big Tree Trail loop trail takes you on a tour of an old-growth Douglas fir forest. The one-mile Cliff Nature Trail has interpretive signs that help you learn about the geology, plants, and animals present in the Siskiyou Mountains.

Hike Information

● Trail Contacts:
Illinois Valley Ranger District, Cave Junction, OR (541) 592–4000 or *www.fs.fed.us/r6/siskiyou*

● Schedule:
June through October

● Fees/Permits:
Requires a Northwest Forest $5 day pass or $30 annual pass. You can purchase a pass online at: *www.fs.fed.us/r6/feedemo* or by call calling 1–800–270–7504.

● Local Information:
Grants Pass/Josephine County Chamber of Commerce, Grants Pass, OR 1–800–547–5927 or *www.grantspasschamber.org*

● Local Events/Attractions:
Illinois River Celebration & Parade, in June, Cave Junction, OR (541) 592–4344 · **Bear Creek Winery,** Cave Junction, OR (541) 592–3977 · **Oregon Caves National Monument,** Cave Junction, OR (541) 592–2100 or *www.oregoncaves.com*

● Accommodations:
The Junction Inn, Cave Junction, OR (541) 592–3106 · **Grayback Campground,** Illinois Valley Ranger District, Cave Junction, OR (541) 592–4000 or *www.fs.fed.us/r6/siskiyou—To get there from Cave Junction and U.S. 199, drive 11 miles east on OR 46 to the campground entrance located on the right side of the highway.*

● Restaurants:
Pietros Italian Restaurant, Cave Junction, OR (541) 592–3228

● Local Outdoor Retailers:
Big Five Sporting Goods, Grants Pass, OR (541) 955–9519

● Maps:
USGS maps: Josephine Mountain, OR

Illinois River

Hike Summary

Take a tour in a rugged gorge carved by the wild and scenic Illinois River. This remote, well-maintained trail follows the Illinois River for 27 miles and gives you a unique glimpse into the wonders of the Kalmiopsis Wilderness. This 179,655-acre wilderness is filled with deep gorges and rocky ridges and is home to many rare plant species. Be prepared for a long, twisty drive to the trailhead. Due to this trail's remoteness, we recommend that you plan on backpacking this trail. If you don't want to backpack, the 8-mile out-and-back section of the trail described here gives you a good introduction to this beautiful, uncrowded wilderness area. If you care to stay the night, there's a campground at the trailhead.

Hike Specs

Start: From the trailhead off U.S. 199 (The Redwood Highway)

Length: 8.0-mile out-and-back

Approximate Hiking Time: 4–6 hours

Difficulty Rating: Moderate

Trail Surface: Well-maintained dirt and gravel path

Lay of the Land: The hike parallels the designated Wild and Scenic Illinois River—the trail itself is high on a ridge above the river.

Elevation Gain: 1,787 feet

Land Status: Wilderness area

Nearest Town: Selma, OR

Other Trail Users: Hikers only

Canine Compatibility: Leashed dog permitted

Getting There

From Grants Pass: Take I-5 Exit 55, indicated by the "Oregon Caves and Crescent City" sign. Turn south on U.S. 199 (The Redwood Highway) and drive 21.6 miles to Selma. From U.S. 199 in Selma, turn right (west) on FS 4103 (Illinois River Road) at the flashing yellow light. The pavement ends and turns to a rough, rocky dirt road after 11 miles. At mile 17.8, the road forks; go left. At mile 18, the road forks again; go right. There is a sign here that warns you that this road is "Not recommended for low clearance vehicles." If you are driving a passenger car, it is recommended that you park here and walk the remaining mile to the trailhead. *DeLorme: Oregon Atlas & Gazetteer:* Page 18 A2

The Illinois River Trail is located in the 179,655-acre Kalmiopsis Wilderness—one of Oregon's biggest and least crowded wilderness areas. Two words describe this wilderness best: rugged and remote. Characterized by deep river and creek gorges and high ridges, this part of Oregon is home to many rare plant species. The namesake of the Kalmiopsis Wilderness, the pink flowering *kalmiopsis leachiana*, can be found clinging to rocky ridges and hillsides. This plant begins blooming in late April through

Illinois River.

the end of June. Plants that live in this region of Oregon are tolerant of the high rainfall in the winter months—the average winter rainfall can range from 100 to 150 inches—and the dry, scorching summers when temperatures can reach the mid to upper 90s.

The Kalmiopsis Wilderness is part of the ancient Klamath Mountains. The mountains were formed when the North American plate pushed up against the Pacific Ocean bottom approximately 200 million years ago. This push-and-shove affair produced high mountain ridges where ocean fossils have been found. The rocks found in this wilderness area are of varied origins, from oceanic crust to ocean floor lavas. This mountainous region is also rich in metals such as copper, cobalt, platinum, chromite, nickle, iron, manganese, and gold. Old mining operations are dotted throughout the region; the largest producing mine, Gold Peck (located north of Baby Creek), was shut down in 1952.

The Illinois River Trail takes you right through the heart of this wilderness. The trail follows the river along a high ridge, taking you over Bald Mountain on a well-graded path for 27 miles to its terminus at Oak Flat, near Agness. Before you begin hiking on the trail, be sure to fill out a wilderness permit. You begin by walking on a path that crosses over Briggs Creek and then slowly ascends through a forest of Douglas fir, canyon live oak, and orange madrone trees (identifiable by their rusty orange-colored, papery bark). Along the way you'll see the low-growing, bushy manzanita and chinkapin. Another plant to look out for, though you may not appreciate it as much, is poison oak. When you catch your first glimpse of the Illinois

MilesDirections

0.0 START at the wooden trailhead marker at the end of FS 4103. Start walking on the Illinois River Trail (Trail 1161) and cross a wood bridge spanning Briggs Creek.

0.7 Cross a wooden bridge over Panther Creek.

2.2 Cross a wooden bridge over Hayden Creek.

4.0 Cross a bridge over Clear Creek. This is your turnaround point. After you cross the bridge there are some campsites to your left. There is also an unmaintained trail that leads down to the creek if you want to cool off.

8.0 Arrive back at the trailhead.

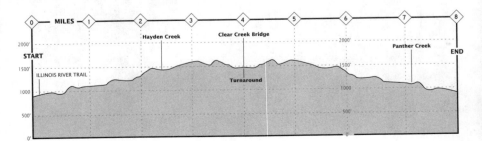

154

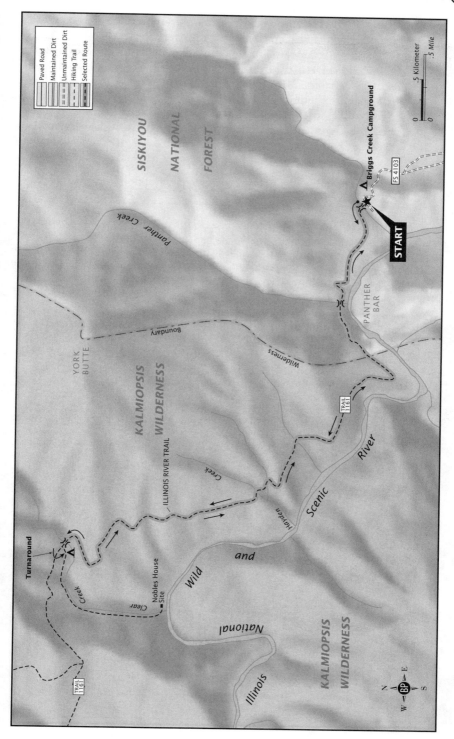

155

River, you'll notice its dark green color. The water's color is due to the serpentinite rock that's present along the river's course.

As the trail climbs you'll pass rough, rocky outcrops of lava rock that offer scenic viewpoints of the river and the river gorge. The river flows over large boulders and through narrow shoots filling the current with huge, challenging rapids. Not surprisingly, this river is the most difficult whitewater rafting river in Oregon and attracts a few brave rafters and kayakers to run its rapids. The greatest obstacle on the river is the Green Wall—a rip-roaring, class-five, boulder-strewn rapid that tests even the most experienced rafters

The Cobra Lily

The odd-looking cobra lily (pitcher plant) grows in boggy areas along the Illinois River and other places in the Kalmiopsis Wilderness. This ingenious plant lures unwary insects into its bulb-like opening and then traps them. The insect is then digested with enzymes, making a tasty meal that provides many needed nutrients.

and kayakers. (This rapid is located several miles away from the section of trail on which you're hiking, but you'll see many rapids along this section of the trail).

If you plan on backpacking this trail, you'll reach a good camping spot at Clear Creek (the hike's turnaround point). You cross a bridge over the creek and there are some level campsites to your left. There is also an unmaintained trail that leads down to bubbling Clear Creek where you can wade or filter water if you're running low. Keep in mind that black bears live in this wilderness area, so you should hang your food if you are camping. Other critters you may see on your journey include blue-tailed skinks, chattering Douglas squirrels, western fence lizards, and (last but certainly not least) rattlesnakes.

Hike Information

Trail Contacts:
Siskiyou National Forest, Galice Ranger District, Grants Pass, OR (541) 471–6500 or *www.fs.fed.us/ r6/siskiyou*

Schedule:
May through October

Fees/Permits:
Requires a Northwest Forest $5 day pass or $30 annual pass. You can purchase a pass online at: *www.fs.fed.us/r6/feedemo* or by call calling 1–800–270–7504.

Local Information:
Grants Pass/Josephine County Chamber of Commerce, Grants Pass, OR 1–800–547–5927 or *www.grantspasschamber.org*

Local Events/Attractions:
Wild Rogue Balloon Festival, first weekend in June, Grants Pass, OR 1–800–547–5927 · **Josephine County Fair,** in mid August, Grants Pass, OR (541) 476–3215

Accommodations:
Briggs Creek Campground, located at the trailhead, (541) 471–6500 · **Pine Meadow Inn B&B,** Grants Pass, OR 1–800–554–0806 or *www.pinemeadowinn.com*

Restaurant:
Wild River Brewing Co., Grants Pass, OR (541) 471–7487

Local Outdoor Retailers:
Big Five Sporting Goods, Grants Pass, OR (541) 955–9519

Maps:
USGS maps: York Butte, OR

Mount McLoughlin

Hike Summary

Located in the heart of volcano country, 9,495-foot Mount McLoughlin rises above the pristine Sky Lakes Wilderness. It's a difficult trek to the top of this Cascade volcano. Along the way you pass through a scenic forest of Douglas fir and Western red cedar and have many opportunities to view the lakes of the surrounding wilderness area. While you're in the area, be sure to visit Crater Lake National Park, located about 75 miles to the north via Oregon 62.

Hike Specs

Start: From the Trail 3716 trailhead off OR 140
Length: 11.0-mile out-and-back
Approximate Hiking Time: 6–8 hours
Difficulty Rating: Difficult due to the length and elevation gain
Trail Surface: Dirt path, and rocky, boulder-filled trail
Lay of the Land: Hike up a steep ascent to the top of 9,495-foot Mount McLoughlin.
Elevation Gain: 3,855 feet
Land Status: National forest and wilderness area
Nearest Town: Klamath Falls, OR
Other Trail Users: Hikers only
Canine Compatibility: Dog friendly

Getting There

From Klamath Falls: Drive approximately 38 miles west on OR 140 and turn right (north) on FS 3661 at the "Four Mile Lake" sign. Drive 2.9 miles on this gravel road to the junction with FS 3650. Turn left on FS 3650 and drive 0.2 miles to the Trail 3716 trailhead. **DeLorme: Oregon Atlas & Gazetteer:** Page 21 A6

The famous Pacific Crest Trail, which skirts the east flank of Mount McLoughlin, stretches over 2,650 miles from Canada to Mexico.

At 9,495 feet, Mount McLoughlin stands prominently above the pristine Sky Lakes Wilderness. The 113,590-acre wilderness area, established in 1984, stretches 27 miles by six miles and is bordered to the east by the 1.1 million-acre Winema National Forest and to the west by the 630,000-acre Rogue River National Forest. To the north is Crater Lake National Park, home to the deep blue waters of Crater Lake—the deepest lake in the United States at 1,932 feet.

Mount McLoughlin has gone by a variety of names. Native Americans called the volcano M'laiksini Yaina because of its steep slopes. Early on, settlers dubbed it Mount Pit (also spelled "Pitt"), borrowing on the nearby Pit River moniker, a name derived from the game-trapping pits that Native Americans dug out along its banks. Snowy Butte and Big Butte were also

Summit viewpoint.

tossed around from time to time, but in 1905 Congress officially named the mountain after Dr. John McLoughlin, a valued administrator in the Hudson's Bay Company from 1824 to 1849. McLoughlin established the company's Fort Vancouver outpost in 1824. He retired to Oregon City (southeast of Portland), where he ran a milling business until his death in 1857.

Geologically speaking, Mount McLoughlin is quite young—only about 700,000 years old. When viewed from the south or southeast, the mountain has a very symmetrical shape, characteristic of a young volcano. Glaciers

MilesDirections

0.0 START hiking on Trail 3716 and cross a bridge over Cascade Canal. [**Note**. *Be sure to sign in at the climber's register.*]

0.2 Enter the Sky Lakes Wilderness.

1.0 Come to a trail junction with the Pacific Crest Trail. Turn right onto the Pacific Crest Trail where a sign indicates "Mount McLoughlin Trail."

1.5 Come to a fork and turn left at the "Mt. McLoughlin Trail" sign. (The Pacific Crest Trail goes right here.) After this point the trail becomes rocky. Look for carvings in the trees for trail directions; in some places the trail is lined with rocks.

2.3 The trail becomes very steep and is scattered with boulders and other large rocks.

3.5 There are great views of Fourmile Lake and Pelican to the northeast and Lake of the Woods Lake to the south.

4.2 Look for rocks with spray-painted red arrows to guide you on the trail.

4.5 Reach the top of a ridge. If you look at the north slope of the mountain you can see the summit. Make a note of your position here because at this point many hikers become lost during their descent.

4.7 The trail is very hard to distinguish in this section. Head to the right (uphill) and follow the ridge. Eventually a faint trail leaves the ridge paralleling it to the south and then after 200 yards comes back to the ridge.

5.5 Reach the summit and a foundation of the old lookout. Here are grand views of the surrounding Sky Lakes Wilderness.

11.0 Arrive back at the trailhead.

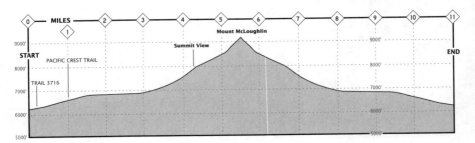

have carved large cirques on the mountain's northeast side, exposing rock within the volcano's cone that geologists have dated to as recently as 200,000 years ago.

To see this mountain for yourself, take the strenuous 11.0-mile out-and-back trek to the mountain's summit. The hike begins by winding through a forest of mixed

Quick Oregon Facts

- The Columbia River Gorge is the country's only national scenic area.
- Oregon has over 6,000 lakes, plus 112,000 miles of rivers and streams. It also has more than 7,000 bridges (51 of these bridges are covered).
- Oregon's statehood was recognized on Valentine's Day, February 14, 1859.
- Oregon has over 200 golf courses.
- Oregon has 16 hot springs.
- Oregon's leading industries are tourism, high technology, forest products, agriculture, biotechnology, metals, fisheries, and aerospace and environmental sciences.
- Nearly half of Oregon's 97,073 square miles is covered with forests.
- There are more than 5,800 registered campsites in Oregon.
- Mount Hood is the highest point in Oregon at 11,235 feet.
- Portland has more microbreweries per capita than any other major city.
- Oregon has no sales tax.
- Oregon has the fourth highest gas prices in the nation. And, get this: You can't pump your own gas!

Source: *The Official 2000 Travel Guide Oregon*, published by the Oregon Tourism Commission.

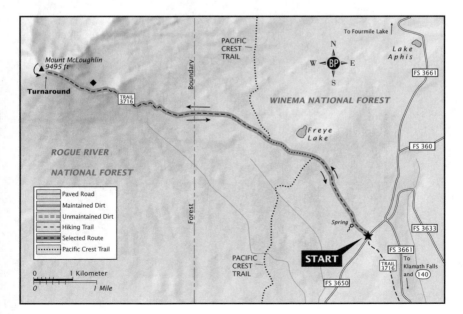

Crater Lake

Southern Oregon is marked by a violent geologic past, and there's no better example of that violence than Crater Lake—which at 1,932 feet is the deepest lake in the U.S. The deep blue lake is all that remains of Mount Mazama, an ancient volcano that once rose to 12,000 feet. After thousands of years of dormancy, the volcano suddenly blew in 4860 BC. The explosion was catastrophic, hurling super-heated lava down its slopes and spewing ash and debris for hundreds of miles in all directions—debris fell as far away as British Columbia. After erupting, the drained magma chambers within the volcano collapsed, creating a deep caldera. Over the years, the chasm slowly filled with water to form what is today the seventh deepest lake in the world.

Douglas fir and Western hemlock, ascending at a moderate-level pace. As you approach the southeast side of the mountain, the trail encounters a number of ups and downs and becomes scattered with rocks and boulders. After approximately 3.5 miles you're afforded great views of Fourmile Lake and Pelican Butte to the northeast and Lake of the Woods to the south. At mile 5.5, you reach the summit to grand views of the surrounding Sky Lakes Wilderness. Pay close attention to the route on the way up because many people lose the trail on the way down due to the numerous spur trails.

Hike Information

ⓒ Trail Contacts:
Rogue River National Forest, Medford, OR (503) 858–2200 or *www.fs.fed.us/r6/rogue* · **Winema National Forest,** Klamath Falls, OR (503) 883–6714 or *www.fs.fed.us/r6/winema/ recreation/index.shtml*

ⓞ Schedule:
June through October

ⓢ Fees/Permits:
Requires a Northwest Forest $5 day pass or $30 annual pass. You can purchase a pass online at: *www.fs.fed.us/r6/feedemo* or by call calling 1–800–270–7504.

❓ Local Information:
Klamath County Dept. of Tourism, Klamath Falls, OR 1–800–445–6728 or *www.klamath.org*

ⓠ Local Events/Attractions:
Great Northwest Pro Rodeo, second weekend in June, Klamath Falls, OR (541) 882–8833 · **Crater Lake National Park,** Crater Lake, OR (541) 594–2211 or *www.nps.gov/crla*

ⓔ Accommodations:
Lake of the Woods Resort, Klamath Falls, OR (541) 949–8300 or *www.lakowoods.com* · **The Running Y Ranch Resort,** Klamath Falls, OR 1–888–850–0275 or *www.runningy.com* · **Fourmile Campground,** Winema National Forest, Klamath Falls, OR (503) 883–6714–*to get to the campground from the trailhead, drive 0.2 miles north on FS 3650 to FS 3661. Turn left and drive 2.7 miles north on FS 366. You'll see the campground.*

ⓘ Restaurant:
Silvia's Restaurant, Klamath Falls, OR (541) 850–2445

ⓡ Local Outdoor Retailers:
Big R, Klamath Falls, OR (541) 882–5548

ⓝ Maps:
USGS maps: Lake of the Woods, OR

24

Mount Thielsen

Hike Summary

This hike takes you through the pristine Mount Thielsen Wilderness and challenges you with a thrilling rock scramble and technical Class-4 rock climb to the pinnacled summit of 9,182-foot Mount Thielsen. From this high vantage point you'll have outstanding views of the surrounding Cascade peaks and Diamond Lake to the west.

Hike Specs

Start: From the trailhead off OR 138
Length: 8.4-mile out-and-back
Approximate Hiking Time: 6–8 hours
Difficulty Rating: Moderate up to the junction with the Pacific Crest Trail, then the trail becomes difficult due to a rock scramble and a technical Class 4 rock climb to the summit
Trail Surface: Maintained dirt; rough, rocky trail; rock scrambling; technical Class-4 rock climbing to the summit—a belayed ascent (rope and harness with protection) is recommended, as is a helmet
Lay of the Land: Hike through an open Douglas fir forest. The trail transitions to rocky pumice and becomes indistinct as you proceed to the summit. The final 30 feet is a technical Class 4 rock climb.

Elevation Gain: 3,653 feet
Land Status: Wilderness area and national forest
Nearest Town: Chemult, OR
Other Trail Users: Equestrians
Canine Compatibility: Not dog friendly

Getting There

From Chemult: Drive 10 miles south on U.S. 97. Turn west on to OR 138 and drive about 20 miles to the Mount Thielsen trailhead located on the right (east) side of the road. *DeLorme: Oregon Atlas & Gazetteer:* Page 37 C8

M ount Thielsen is located in the Mount Thielsen Wilderness, north of Crater Lake National Park and just east of Diamond Lake. The 55,100-acre Mount Thielsen Wilderness, established in 1984, contains over 78 miles of hiking trails, including a 26-mile section of the famed Pacific Crest Trail. The wilderness area falls under the management of the Deschutes, Umpqua, and Winema national forests.

Portlander John A. Hurlburt named the peak in 1872 after prominent railroad engineer and builder Hans Thielsen, but prior to its official

Summit viewpoint.

naming, locals referred to the peak as Big Cowhorn. Native Americans called it His-chok-wol-as. Mount Thielsen is often referred to as the "lightning rod of the Cascades" because of its pointed summit, which tends to attract numerous lightning strikes each year.

Technically speaking, Mount Thielsen is a shield volcano (a broad, domed-shaped cone made up of solidified layers of lava) thought to be 290,000 years old—relatively young on a geologic time scale. The volcano is composed of a central pyroclastic (rock formed by a volcanic explosion) cone that consists of tuff (rock formed from fine-grained ash and dust particles) and breccia (fragmented pieces of volcanic rock). Some of the breccia present on this ancient mountain forms layers up to 100 meters thick. The north and east sides of this peak have spectacular cirque walls that were carved by now-extinct glaciers.

MilesDirections

0.0 START hiking from the Mount Thielsen trailhead (Trail 1456/1458) and hike through an open Douglas fir forest.

1.8 Come to a junction with the Spruce Ridge Trail (Trail 1458). Continue straight (right) on the Mount Thielsen Trail (Trail 1456).

2.0 Enter the Mount Thielsen Wilderness.

3.0 Enjoy views of Mount Thielsen. Pass through a popcorn pumice-like area.

3.8 Come to a junction with the Pacific Crest Trail. Continue straight. *[**Option.** Those not wanting to make the summit attempt should turn around at this point.]*

4.0 The trail becomes indistinct. There are several "goat" trails to the summit. You can either switchback to the right on looser scree or scramble directly up the ridge along a steep route. Stay on the right side of the ridge and ascend to a notch at the southwest edge of the summit plug. *[**WARNING:** The final 30 feet to the summit is a Class 4 technical rock climb and a belayed ascent (rope and harness with protection) is recommended. Also, due to the eroding rock conditions near the summit, a helmet is recommended.]*

4.2 Reach the 9,182-foot summit. There are stunning views of Diamond Lake to the west and of the surrounding Mount Thielsen Wilderness.

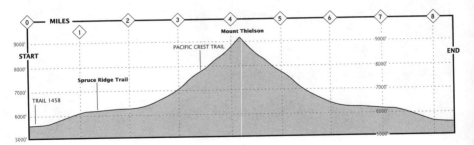

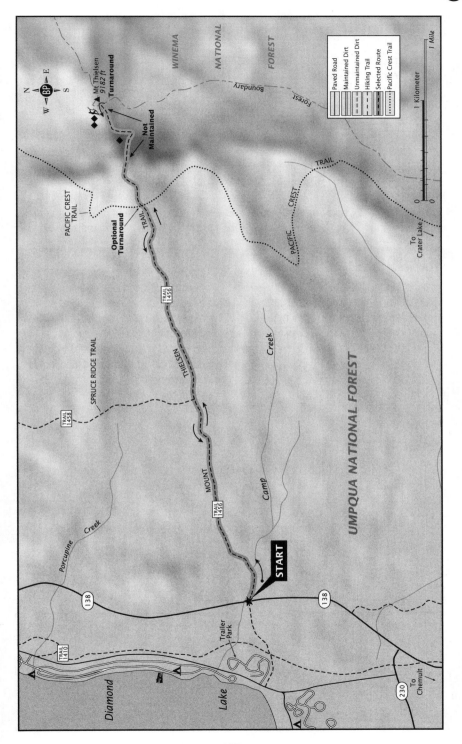

The Future of Trout Fishing in Diamond Lake

Located west of Mount Thielsen is Diamond Lake, a major natural landmark in this area that attracts thousands of outdoor enthusiasts each year. This 3,200-acre lake was formed by the gouging action of now-extinct glaciers. The lake is best known for its outstanding rainbow trout fishing. Stocked with rainbow trout since 1910, Lake Diamond has attracted thousands of anglers over the years. In recent years, however, the introduction of the tui chub has threatened the trout population.

According to the Oregon Department of Fish & Wildlife, tui chub were probably introduced to the lake by anglers using the fish as live bait in the late 1980s or early 1990s. Since that time, Diamond Lake's tui chub population has exploded. Fingerling rainbow trout have to compete with the tui chub for food and are losing the battle. The Department of Fish & Wildlife estimates that there are approximately three million chub age two and older (one million of which are mature spawners) living in the lake, while rainbow trout number about 300,000. Several million more chub under two years old are also in the lake.

Scientists have determined that there are three options for dealing with the tui chub problem: 1) Do nothing; 2) Treat the lake with the fish toxicant Rotenone, and start over; 3) Control the tui chub by disrupting the fish's spawning cycle, introducing predators, and/or selectively harvesting the fish out. The reigning wildlife authorities are currently preparing an environmental impact statement (EIS) to be completed in the fall of 2000 to determine the impact of the different alternatives. Based on the findings of this study and input from the public, the Oregon Fish & Wildlife Commission will make their final decision on how to proceed.

View of Diamond Lake.

The hike described here takes you through the Mount Thielsen Wilderness to the summit of 9,182-foot Mount Thielsen. You begin by hiking through an Douglas fir forest and after about three miles you enjoy your first views of the sharp, pointed summit of the volcano's central basalt plug. At mile 3.8, you cross the Pacific Crest Trail. If you're not planning to attempt the rock climb to the summit, this is a good place to turn around. After four miles, the trail becomes hard to distinguish, so you'll have to navigate your way to the summit on one of several unmaintained trails. A helmet is advised beyond this point, and you'll need to use your hands to scramble over large rocks. If you don't have rock climbing experience, do NOT attempt to climb to the summit of this peak—exposure, falling rock, and the chance of falling yourself make it too dangerous.

Hike Information

● Trail Contacts:
Umpqua National Forest, Diamond Lake Visitor Center, Diamond Lake, OR (541) 793–3310 or www.fs.fed.us/r6/umpqua

● Schedule:
July through October

● Fees/Permits:
Requires a Northwest Forest $5 day pass or $30 annual pass. You can purchase a pass online at: www.fs.fed.us/r6/feedemo or by call calling 1–800–270–7504.

● Local Information:
Bend Chamber of Commerce, Bend, OR 1–800–905–2363 or www.visitbend.org

● Local Events/Attractions:
Bend Summer Festival, in July, Bend, OR (541) 385–6570

● Accommodations:
Diamond Lake Resort, Diamond Lake, OR 1–800–733–7593 or www.diamondlake.net

● Hike Tours:
Wanderlust Tours, Bend, OR (541) 389–8359

● Organizations:
Pacific Crest Trail Association (PCTA), Sacramento, CA (916) 349–2109 or www.pcta.org

● Local Outdoor Retailers:
G.I. Joe's, Inc., Bend, OR (541) 388–3773

● Maps:
USGS maps: Mount Thielsen, OR

Southwest Oregon

Compiled here is an index of great hikes in Southwest Oregon that didn't make the A-list this time around but deserve recognition. Check them out and let us know what you think. You may decide that one or more of these hikes deserves higher status in future editions or, perhaps, you may have a hike of your own that merits some attention.

25 Hanging Rock

This difficult 21.6-mile trail takes you on a journey up the designated Wild & Scenic Rogue River. Beginning at Buck Point, this trail travels high above the river and heads south on Panther Ridge to the amazing Hanging Rock. You continue south, past Devil's Backbone, and end not far from Tate Creek.

To get there from Grants Pass, head north on I-5 to Exit 76. Take this exit and then hang a left on Glendale Valley Road. Drive west on Glendale Valley Road to Glendale and turn right. Cross over the river and then turn left on Cow Creek Road. Drive west on Cow Creek Road until you reach the intersection with Dutch Henry Road (FS 3348). Turn left and take Dutch Henry Road to the Buck Creek Campground and FS 5520. Turn left on FS 5520 and proceed to the junction with FS 230. Turn left on FS 230 and drive to the trailhead on the right. For more information, contact the Siskiyou National Forest, Powers Ranger District, Powers OR; (541) 439–3011; *www.fs.fed.us/r6/siskiyou. DeLorme: Oregon Atlas & Gazetteer:* Page 26 C3

26 Umpqua Hot Springs

This short path takes you along the North Umpqua Trail to a hot spring pool 150 feet above the North Umpqua River.

To get there from Roseburg, drive east on OR 138 for 60 miles to the junction with Toketee Rigdon Road (FS 34). Turn left on Toketee Rigdon Road. At the next fork in the road, bear left. After 2.3 miles turn right on to Thorn Prairie Road (FS 3401) and drive two miles to the trailhead parking area. In order to park at this trailhead, you'll need a $5 Northwest Forest Pass—available at *www.fs.fed.us/r6/feedemo* or by calling 1–800–270–7504.

For more information, contact The Umpqua National Forest, Roseburg, OR; (541) 672–6601; *www.fs.fed.us/r6/umpqua*. *DeLorme: Oregon Atlas & Gazetteer*: Page 37 B6

27 Mount Bailey

This 10.6-mile out-and-back trail takes you through a lodgepole pine forest mixed with mountain hemlock and fir to the summit of 8,363-foot Mount Bailey. You reach the timberline after about four miles, with the last half mile being quite steep and rocky. From the summit, you can see Mount Thielsen, Diamond Lake, the Cascade Mountains, and Mount Shasta.

To get there from the junction of OR 138 and OR 230, turn left on OR 230 and drive 0.2 miles to a sign that reads "South Diamond Lake Recreation Areas." Turn right at this sign and drive about 0.8 miles to the junction with FS 4795. Turn left on FS 4795 and drive 1.8 miles to the junction with FS 300. Turn left on FS 300 and drive 0.5 miles to the trailhead on the right side of the road. For more information, contact the Umpqua National Forest, Diamond Lake Ranger District, Idleyld Park, OR; (541) 498–2531; *www.fs.fed.us/r6/umpqua*. *DeLorme: Oregon Atlas & Gazetteer*: Page 37 C7

28 Mount Scott

This trail takes you on a 5.0-mile out-and-back to the top of 8,929-foot Mount Scott. From the top you have a fantastic view of the deep blue waters of Crater Lake and Crater Lake National Park.

To get there from Fort Klamath, drive north on OR 62 for approximately 16 miles to Mazama Village. Turn right on Munson Valley Road and drive about six miles to the junction with Rim Drive. Turn right on Rim Drive and continue east for 14 miles to the trailhead on the right. For more information, contact Crater Lake National Park, Crater Lake, OR; (541) 594–2211; *www.craterlake.com*. *DeLorme: Oregon Atlas & Gazetteer*: Page 29 A8

Sky Lakes Wilderness Loop

This 25.0-mile loop trail takes you through the (not surprisingly) lake-filled Sky Lakes Wilderness. The loop begins on Cold Springs Trail 3710. After 0.2 miles, take a left and continue on Trail 3710. You travel another two miles and reach the Sky Lakes Trail junction. Take a left on Sky Lakes Trail 3762. Along this section you pass by scenic Dee Lake. After 3.8 miles, come to a trail junction with the Pacific Crest Trail; turn right and follow the trail as it traipses through forest and open areas, providing views of the massive Klamath Lake. At mile 11.9, the trail eventually leads to a saddle sandwiched between Devil's Peak and Lee Peak. Here you have the option of climbing to the top of 7,582-foot Devil's Peak, which offers a panoramic view of the Sky Lakes Wilderness. From this saddle, turn around and head south on the Pacific Crest Trail. When you reach Snow Lakes Trail 3739, turn left. In the next three miles you reach Martin Lake and eventually pass the scenic Snow Lakes, Margurette Lake, and Trappers Lake. When you reach Trappers Lake, continue hiking south on Sky Lakes Trail 3762. At the 21.0-mile mark, take a right on the Isherwood Trail 3729; this will take you past Isherwood, Natasha, and Elizabeth Lakes. At mile 22.5, turn left on Sky Lakes Trail 3762 to the South Rock Trail junction. Turn right on South Rock Creek Trail 3709 and continue until you reach the Cold Springs Trail 3710. Take a left onto 3710 and head back to your car.

To get there from Lake of the Woods, drive east on OR 140 for approximately five miles to the junction with FS 3651. Turn left (north) on FS 3651 and proceed 10 miles to the trailhead at Cold Springs Camp. For more information, contact Supervisor's Office, Winema National Forest, Klamath Falls, OR; (541) 883–6714; *www.fs.fed.us/r6/winema*. **DeLorme: Oregon Atlas & Gazetteer:** Page 29 C7

Central

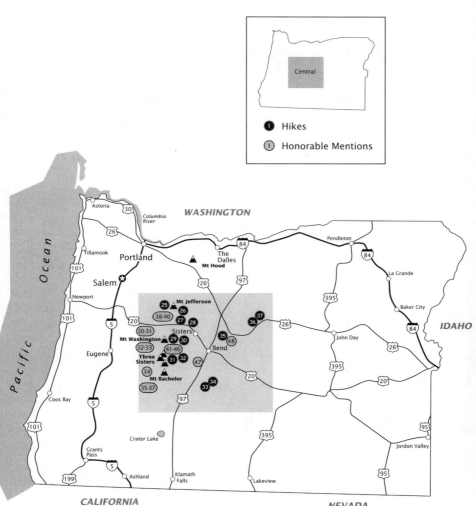

Central

- ● Hikes
- ① Honorable Mentions

WASHINGTON

Astoria
30
Columbia River
26
Tillamook
Portland
The Dalles
Mt Hood
Pendleton
84
84
La Grande
Salem
97
26
Baker City
Newport
101
84
IDAHO
5
20
Mt Jefferson
25
38-40
26
27 28
30-31
Sisters
36
37
35
John Day
26
Mt Washington
29 30
48
Bend
32-33
41-46
Eugene
Three Sisters
31 32
47
20
395
34
Mt Bachelor
33 34
26
20
35-37
97
Coos Bay
5
395
Pacific Ocean
101
Crater Lake
95
Grants Pass
395
Jordon Valley
5
199
Ashland
Klamath Falls
Lakeview
95
CALIFORNIA
NEVADA

Oregon

Central Oregon

A high desert ecosystem of sagebrush, juniper, and ponderosa pine characterize the dry, central part of this state where volcanic activity and erosion have formed amazing gorges and unique rock formations. Coursing through all of this is the mighty Deschutes River, beginning high in the Cascade Mountains and traveling north to south through the heart of Bend, Central Oregon's largest city.

Many consider Bend the gateway to the High Cascade Lakes Region and Deschutes National Forest. It serves as the geographic and popular center to this area of the state. Just northwest of here is the small western town of Sisters, a major access point to both the Mount Washington and Mount Jefferson wilderness areas—serious volcano country.

Here, two trails not to be missed are the Black Crater Trail and the Little Belknap Crater Trail. The eight-mile out-and-back Black Crater Trail winds its way through a mountain hemlock forest to the craggy, red-cinder summit of Black Crater, providing a panoramic view of the Three Sisters, Belknap Crater, Mount Washington, Mount Jefferson, and Mount Hood. The seven-mile out-and-back Little Belknap Crater Trail takes you across the moon-like landscape of an ancient lava flow to the summit of Little Belknap Crater. From the summit of the crater you can enjoy sweeping views of the snow-topped Three Sisters Mountains, Mount Washington, and the surrounding lava flows and craters that make up the Mount Washington Wilderness. For a pristine river hike, be sure to take a tour on the West Metolius River Trail and admire the lush, spring-fed river ecosystem.

Afterwards, consider the Three Sisters Wilderness and the Newberry National Volcanic Monument; both of these areas can be easily accessed from the city of Bend. To experience one of the best views in the Central Cascade Range, try hiking to the top of 10,358-foot South Sister (located in the Three Sisters Wilderness). This strenuous 11-mile out-and-back trail can be found approximately 27 miles west of Bend off the Cascade Lakes Highway. From the summit you'll have a panoramic view to the north of Middle Sister, North Sister, and Chambers Lakes; to the southeast you'll be able to see Broken Top, Mount Bachelor, and Green Lakes.

The Newberry National Volcanic Monument (southeast of Bend off U.S. Route 97) is home to Newberry Caldera—a 500-square-mile crater that houses Paulina and East lakes. This national monument has a rich geologic history, evident in its hot springs, lava flows, and cinder cones. The one-mile Big Obsidian Flow Trail takes you on a fascinating tour of

Oregon's youngest lava flow. To see the national monument from a different perspective, tackle the strenuous, six-mile Paulina Peak Trail. This trail climbs to the summit of 7,984-foot Paulina Peak, where from the top you'll have quite a view of the magnificent caldera, as well as vistas of Paulina and East lakes and the surrounding high-alpine country.

Smith Rock State Park is also located right in the center of this open, high-desert country and features spectacular pinnacles, columns, and cathedral-like cliffs that rise over 400 feet above a mammoth gorge carved by the Crooked River. Tour this unusual landscape on an eight-mile loop trail, located 10 miles northeast of Redmond off U.S. Route 97.

A less frequently visited but no less stunning area is Mill Creek Wilderness, located about 20 miles northeast of Prineville off U.S. Route 26. The Twin Pillars Trail takes you through this wilderness, which is characterized by open, park-like stands of ponderosa pine, grand fir, and Douglas fir forests.

Unlike the Willamette Valley to the west, the central part of the state is much sunnier and dryer. The average rainfall in this part of the state is about 12 inches, and blue skies are the norm. Summers are hot and winters are cold. Be prepared for a substantial amount of snow in the high mountain areas and periodic snow showers at lower elevations.

Triangulation Peak

Hike Summary

This trail begins in a lush forest filled, in summer, with colorful wildflowers and juicy raspberries. Near the summit of Triangulation Peak a side trail leads steeply downhill to Boca Cave, which is well worth exploring. From the cave's entrance there's a great view of the immense glaciated summit of Mount Jefferson. As you continue to the pointed summit of Triangulation Peak, you'll enjoy another sweeping view of Mount Jefferson and the surrounding Mount Jefferson Wilderness.

Hike Specs

Start: From the trailhead off FS 635
Length: 5.4-mile out-and-back (optional 0.6-mile side trail to Boca Cave)
Approximate Hiking Time: 3 hours
Difficulty Rating: Moderate due to a steep push to the summit. The trail to Boca Cave is challenging because it's steep, loose, and unmaintained.
Trail Surface: Forested dirt path and old doubletrack road. Large, rocky boulders at the summit. If you decide to hike to the cave, you'll navigate down an unmaintained, loose, rocky trail to the cave entrance.
Lay of the Land: Hike gently down a ridge and begin a steep ascent up the north slope of Triangulation Peak
Elevation Gain: 1,243 feet
Land Status: National forest and wilderness area

Nearest Town: Detroit, OR
Other Trail Users: Hikers only
Canine Compatibility: Dog friendly

Getting There

From Detroit: Drive six miles southeast on OR 22 and turn left on to FS 2233 (McCoy Creek Road). Drive 7.8 miles (the road turns to gravel after four miles) to a road junction. Stay to the right and drive another 1.3 miles to the junction with FS 635. Turn right on to FS 635 and park in the trailhead parking area on the right side of the road. *DeLorme: Oregon Atlas & Gazetteer:* Page 56 C1

Be sure to bring your camera on this hike!

The rocky summit of 5,434-foot Triangulation Peak rises prominently above the 1.6 million-acre Willamette National Forest, offering up a grand view of 10,497-foot Mount Jefferson. Jefferson is the second-highest peak in Oregon and one of 13 major cascade volcanoes in the Cascade Mountain Range. It forms the centerpiece of the 111,177-acre Mount Jefferson Wilderness. Sporting five glaciers (Jefferson Park, Milk Creek, Russell, Waldo, and Whitewater), Mount Jefferson is an

Climbing to the summit of Triangulation Peak.

active composite volcano, which has erupted periodically over the last 300,000 years. One of its largest eruptions occurred between 35,000 and 100,000 years ago, depositing ash as far away as southeast Idaho. Jefferson's last major eruption occurred almost 15,000 years ago. A more recent eruption, as early as 6,500 years ago, occurred about five miles south of Mount Jefferson at a Forked Butte cinder cone.

The base of this highly glaciated peak consists of picturesque alpine meadows and more than 150 small trout-stocked lakes. The high, park-like setting is popular with hikers and backpackers, as evidenced by the more heavily trafficked areas: Jefferson Park, Eight Lakes Basin, Marion Lake, Pamelia Lake, Jack Lake, Duffy Lake, and Santiam Lake. In an effort to control what could become a threat to the local ecosystem, the Forest Service now restricts camping to designated areas. Campfires are not permitted within 100 feet of lakes, and in many areas they're outright prohibited.

Begin this hike with a downhill walk along a gentle ridge surrounded by Douglas fir, subalpine fir, and mountain hemlock. Notice the showy pink blooms of wild rhododendrons, purple lupine, fiery Indian paintbrush, and other colorful wildflowers.

MilesDirections

0.0 START at the wooden trailhead sign off FS 635. *[**Note.** Be sure to fill out a wilderness permit at the trailhead.]*

0.2 Stay to the right. The trail turns into a doubletrack dirt road and changes back to a dirt path after approximately 50 yards.

1.8 Turn right onto Triangulation Trail. *[**FYI.** There are many wild raspberries present along this section of the trail that make a nice treat.]* You'll begin a steep ascent up the north slope of Triangulation Peak on a series of switchbacks.

1.9 Reach the base of Spire Rock.

2.6 Stay to the right. *[**Option.** If you go left, you can scramble 0.3 miles down a steep, rocky trail to Boca Cave.]*

2.7 Reach the pointed, rocky summit of Triangulation Peak. There are first class views of Mount Jefferson. Turn around here and retrace your route back to the trailhead.

5.4 Arrive back at the trailhead.

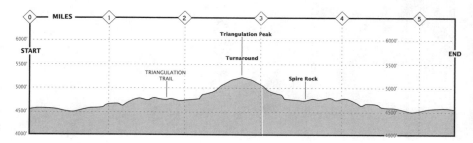

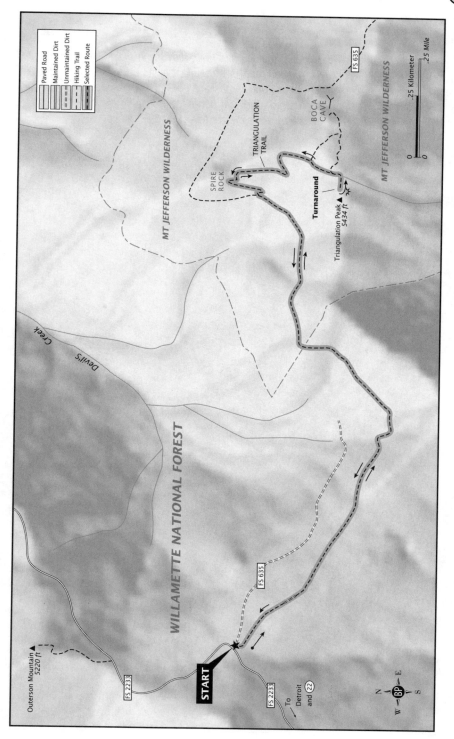

MT JEFFERSON WILDERNESS

FS 635

BOCA CAVE

TRIANGULATION TRAIL

SPIRE ROCK

MT JEFFERSON WILDERNESS

Turnaround

Triangulation Peak ▲ 5434 ft

.25 Mile

.25 Kilometer

Devil's Creek

WILLAMETTE NATIONAL FOREST

FS 635

Outerson Mountain ▲ 5220 ft

FS 2233

START

FS 2233

To Detroit and (22)

N
W — E
S

Paved Road
Maintained Dirt
Unmaintained Dirt
Hiking Trail
Selected Route

Raspberry Basics

Wild raspberries are common along this trail. They begin blooming in June and start to ripen in mid July. You can recognize the plant by its white petals and green clusters of three or five leaves. The berries are half-sphere shaped and range in color from light pink to dark red. The wild berries aren't quite as sweet as their domesticated cousins, but they are a delight to eat.

Curiously approaching Boca Cave.

The trail wanders at a pleasant pace for the first 1.8 miles. It then turns right at a junction with the Triangulation Trail and winds steeply up the north side of Triangulation Peak. At mile 1.9, you pass the rocky tower of Spire Rock. A little more than half a mile later, you arrive at a second trail junction where you have the option of turning left and scrambling down a steep, eroded trail to Boca Cave. Inside the cave, ferns cling precariously to jumbled rocks as water trickles from the sides and floor.

When you're through exploring the cave, climb back up to the main trail and turn left for a short hike and scramble over several large boulders to the summit of Triangulation Peak. Take in the sweeping views (especially of Mount Jefferson) before returning to the trailhead the way you came.

Hike Information

● Trail Contacts:
Detroit Ranger District, Mill City, OR (503) 854–3366

◔ Schedule:
June through October

⑤ Fees/Permits:
A free wilderness permit is required and is available at the trailhead. Requires a Northwest Forest $5 day pass or $30 annual pass. You can purchase a pass online at: *www.fs.fed.us/r6/ feedemo* or by call calling 1–800– 270-7504.

🛏 Accommodations:
Breitenbush Hot Springs Resort, Detroit, OR (503) 854–3314 or *www.breitenbush.com* · **Cove Creek,** Detroit, OR (503) 854–3366 — *To get there from Detroit: Drive three miles south-east on OR 22 and turn right on* to Blowout Road (FS 10). Drive 3.5 miles to the campground, which is located on the right side of the road. · **Detroit Lake State Recreation Area,** Detroit, OR (503) 854–9140 or *www. detroitlakeoregon.org* — *To get there from Detroit: Drive two miles southwest on OR 22 to the campground entrance, which is located on the left side of the road.*

❷ Other Resources:
USGS/Cascades Volcano Observatory, Vancouver, WA at *http://vulcan.wr.usgs.gov/ Volcanoes/Jefferson/description_jefferson.html* — *a good resource for information on Mount Jefferson.*

Ⓝ Maps:
USGS maps: Mount Bruno, OR

West Metolius River Trail

Hike Summary

This unique trail traces the banks of the clear, fast-moving Metolius River and meanders through a lush riparian ecosystem of bright wildflowers and riverside vegetation. The spring-fed river rushes over lava to create swirling rapids and big eddies that are home to various species of trout and Atlantic salmon. At the turnaround point is the Wizard Falls Fish Hatchery, home to millions of Atlantic and Kokanee salmon, Eastern brook trout, German brown trout, and rainbow trout.

Hike Specs

Start: From the trailhead parking lot off FS 400

Length: 4.2-mile out-and-back

Approximate Hiking Time: 2–3 hours

Difficulty Rating: Easy due to the well-graded path and flat terrain

Trail Surface: Dirt path over a few big tree roots, with an ascent up a few small hills. The majority of the trail is flat and makes for easy walking.

Lay of the Land: Dirt path parallels the crystal-clear Metolius River through an open ponderosa forest

Elevation Gain: 450 feet

Land Status: National forest

Nearest Town: Sisters, OR

Other Trail Users: Hikers only

Canine Compatibility: Leashed dogs permitted

Getting There

From Sisters: Drive 10 miles west on U.S. 20 to Camp Sherman Road (FS 14). Turn right (north) and drive 2.7 miles to a junction with FS 19. Turn left and drive 2.3 miles to another road junction and a stop sign. Continue straight (you're now on FS 1420) for another 3.4 miles to a junction with FS 400. Turn right, follow the signs for 0.7 miles to a fork, veer right again, and drive 0.2 miles through Canyon Creek Campground to the trailhead and parking area. *DeLorme: Oregon Atlas & Gazetteer:* Page 56 D3

The Metolius River, known for its world-class fly-fishing, originates as a natural spring at the base of Black Butte before winding its way north through the Metolius Basin and into Lake Billy Chinook. Numerous springs, fed via porous volcanic rock high in the Central Cascade Mountains, continue to feed the river along its length, keeping the flow rate fairly steady at 1,200 to 1,800 cubic feet per second.

The Northern Paiute and Tenino Indians were the first known people to inhabit the Metolius Basin. They fished for salmon, hunted deer and small game, and gathered nuts and berries on the slopes of Black Butte. In the mid

The spring-fed Metolius River.

19th Century several well-known explorers traveled through the area. Among them were Captain John Charles Fremont, who passed through in 1843, and Lieutenant Henry Larcom Abbott, who arrived in 1855 as a surveyor for the Pacific Railroad. In his journal, Abbott recorded a meeting with some of the local Native Americans:

> *Today we encamped, at the same place as before, in the Mpto-ly-as river canyon. Here we met a party of Indians, with their squaws and children, traveling north. They caught several salmon in the river; one of which, weighing about twenty-five pounds, we bought. They spear the fish with barbed iron points, fitted loosely by sockets to the end of poles about eight feet long.*

Homesteading in the Metolius Valley didn't occur until 1881. Settlers were attracted to the area by the thick timber and abundant grass that provided good grazing for livestock. The numerous springs and creeks in the valley also provided a plentiful supply of water. In 1893, with the passage of

MilesDirections

0.0 START at the wooden sign in the trailhead parking lot. The trail begins alongside the Metolius River.

1.7 Cross a small creek via a wooden footbridge.

2.0 Cross two more creeks.

2.1 Arrive at Wizard Falls Fish Hatchery and the turnaround point.

4.2 Arrive back at the trailhead.

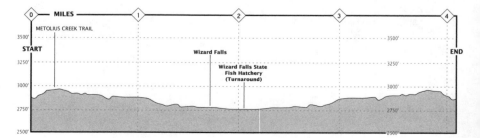

the Forest Reserve Act by President Grover Cleveland, the Metolius Valley became part of the Cascade Range Forest Reserve. Later, in 1908, the area was incorporated into Deschutes National Forest.

If you want to explore this beautiful river, the West Metolius River Trail is the easiest way to do it. The trail starts at Canyon Creek Campground, located approximately 20 miles northwest of Sisters, and proceeds on a scenic journey to Wizard Falls State Fish Hatchery. Along the way there is lush streamside greenery (including pinkish-lavender stream bank globe-mallow and bright orange, fragrant honeysuckle) as well as open forest dotted with purple lupine, crimson columbine, lavender-tufted thistle, and white-headed yarrow. Large ponderosa pines shade the path, and the river's deep rock pools and logs provide a haven for trout and salmon. After 2.1 miles the trail arrives at Wizard Falls Fish Hatchery, which raises almost 3.5 million salmon and trout every year. This is a great place to rest before the return trip to the trailhead.

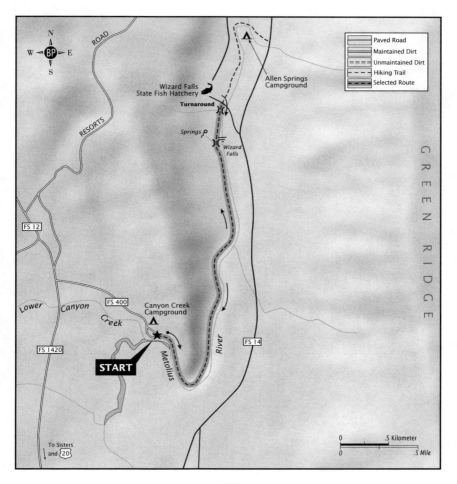

Metolious River.

Hike Information

Trail Contacts:
Deschutes National Forest, Sisters Ranger District, Sisters, OR (541) 549–2111 or *www.fs.fed.us/r6/deschutes/sisters/sisters.html*

Schedule:
May through October

Local Information:
Sisters Area Chamber of Commerce, Sisters, OR (541) 549–0251 or *www.sisters–chamber.com*

Local Events/Attractions:
Sisters Antique Festival, in August, Sisters, OR (541) 388–2082 · **Sisters Rodeo and Parade,** in June, Sisters, OR (541) 549–0121

Accommodations:
Best Western Ponderosa Lodge, Sisters, OR (541) 549–1234 or *www.bestwesternsisters.com* · **Sisters Motor Lodge,** Sisters, OR (541) 549–2551 · **Squaw Creek Bed & Breakfast,** Sisters, OR 1–800–930–0055 or *www.sisterslodging.com*

Restaurants:
Figaro's Italian Kitchen, Sisters, OR (541) 549–4661 · **Papandrea's Pizzeria,** Sisters, OR (541) 549–6081 · **Sisters Coffee Company,** Sisters, OR 1–800–524–JAVA or (541) 549–0527

Organizations:
Pacific Crest Trail Association, Sacramento, CA (916) 349–2109 or *www.pcta.org*

Other Resources:
Central Oregon Recreation Watch, Bend, OR (541) 318–2882 or *www.corw.com* · **The Nugget Newspaper,** Sisters, OR (541) 549–9941 or *www.nuggetnews.com* · **Paulina Springs Book Company,** Sisters, OR 1–800–397–0867 or *www.paulinasprings.com*

Local Outdoor Retailers:
Eurosports, Sisters, OR 1–800–382–3471 or (541) 549–2471

Maps:
USGS maps: Black Butte, OR; Candle Creek, OR; Prairie Farm Spring, OR · **USFS maps:** Deschutes National Forest

27 Three-Fingered Jack

Hike Summary

This hike follows the Pacific Crest Trail 2000 through a pristine forest of fragrant Douglas and alpine fir, blue spruce, and mountain hemlock to the base of 7,841-foot Three-Fingered Jack, an eroded remnant of an ancient volcanic plug. The plug itself is impressive, and if you have climbing experience and the appropriate gear you may be tempted to continue up its south ridge to the summit.

Hike Specs

Start: From the Pacific Crest Trailhead parking area off U.S. 20

Length: 11.6-mile out-and-back

Approximate Hiking Time: 4–6 hours

Difficulty Rating: Difficult due to a steep ascent to the base of Three-Fingered Jack

Trail Surface: Dusty dirt path with some steep and rocky sections

Lay of the Land: Hike a fairly flat course through a predominantly Douglas fir forest and then head up a ridge to the base of 7,841-foot Three-Fingered Jack.

Elevation Gain: 2,950 feet

Land Status: National forest and wilderness area

Nearest Town: Sisters, OR

Other Trail Users: Equestrians

Canine Compatibility: Dogs permitted

Getting There

From Sisters: Drive 20.4 miles west on U.S. 20 to a gravel parking area on the north side of the road and a trailhead for the Pacific Crest Trail. *DeLorme: Oregon Atlas & Gazetteer:* Page 50 A1

> *Bring mosquito repellant with you on this hike. There are plenty of hungry mosquitoes waiting for a good meal from unsuspecting hikers.*
>
> *This trail is a popular among horseback riders. If you encounter a horse, step off the trail and give it room to pass. If you can, sit down. The less imposing you appear, the less likely you are to spook a horse.*

The ragged spires of Three-Fingered Jack—named in honor of Joaquin Murietta, an aspiring gold rusher with a mutilated, three-fingered hand—rise abruptly out of Central Oregon's Mount Jefferson Wilderness to form a geologic slice of time. Hundreds of thousands of years ago, the mountain—formed by hot basaltic lava flows—resembled a broad, dome-shaped cone. Since that time, volcanic activity and glaciation have left the

southern side of the peak a skeleton of its previous majesty. Today the formation is what geologists call a shield volcano.

To view this decaying volcano for yourself, walk to its base on the Pacific Crest Trail 2000. The trail, which tends to be very dusty due to the area's soft volcanic soil, starts out fairly gently as it passes through a forest of Douglas and alpine fir, blue spruce, and mountain hemlock. Scattered along the path, resembling green, grassy wigs, are large clumps of bear grass. This

Summit view from Three-Fingered Jack.

interesting plant is a member of the lily family. When it blooms it produces tiny white flowers in dense clusters on top of a stout, leafy stem. Bears love to dig it up and munch on its succulent roots. Native Americans wove the plant's strong leaves into sturdy baskets. Interspersed among these green and groovy grass islands are showy clusters of bright-purple lupine and red Indian paintbrush.

After 5.8 miles the trail arrives at the base of 7,841-foot Three-Fingered Jack. From there, a climbers' trail ascends steeply up the south ridge of the mountain. If you want to climb to the summit, you should have rock-climbing experience and carry the appropriate gear. There are several places where the route is narrow and rocky and, if you're not accustomed to the breathtaking exposure, the hike is likely to be difficult.

While day hikers should turn around here, backpackers can continue along the trail as it dives deeper into the wilderness. For the next 15 miles the path parallels the Cascade Crest, switching back and forth between Deschutes and Willamette national forests before eventually traversing the west side of 10,497-foot Mount Jefferson. The mountain forms the center-piece of the magnificent Jefferson Wilderness, the second most visited wilderness area in Oregon—second to the Three Sisters Wilderness. In 1806, Lewis and Clark named Mount Jefferson in honor of President Jefferson who commissioned their famous expedition.

Hike Information

(C) Trail Contacts:

Deschutes National Forest, Sisters Ranger District, Sisters, OR (541) 549–2111 or *www.fs.fed.us/r6/deschutes/ sisters/sisters.html*

(O) Schedule:

June through October

(S) Fees/Permits:

A $3 Trail Park Pass can be purchased at the Sisters Ranger Station in Sisters. Also requires a Northwest Forest $5 day pass or $30 annual pass. You can purchase a pass online at: *www.fs.fed.us/r6/feedemo* or by call calling 1–800–270–7504.

(?) Local Information:

Sisters Area Chamber of Commerce, Sisters, OR (541) 549–0251 or *www.sisterschamber.com*

(Q) Local Events/Attractions:

Sisters Antique Festival, in August, Sisters, OR (541) 388–2082 · **Sisters Rodeo and Parade,** in June, Sisters, OR (541) 549–0121

(bed) Accommodations:

Best Western Ponderosa Lodge, Sisters, OR (541) 549–1234 or *www.bestwesternsisters.com* · **Sisters Motor Lodge,** Sisters, OR (541) 549–2551 · **Squaw Creek Bed & Breakfast,** Sisters, OR 1–800–930–0055 or *www.sisterslodging.com*

(fork) Restaurants:

Figaro's Italian Kitchen, Sisters, OR (541) 549–4661 · **Papandrea's Pizzeria,** Sisters, OR (541) 549–6081 · **Sisters Bakery,** Sisters, OR (541) 549–0361 · **Sisters Coffee Company,** Sisters, OR 1–800–524–JAVA or (541) 549–0527

(org) Organizations:

Pacific Crest Trail Association, Sacramento, CA (916) 349–2109 or *www.pcta.org*

(C) Other Resources:

Central Oregon Recreation Watch, Bend, OR (541) 318–2882 or *www.corw.com* · **The Nugget Newspaper,** Sisters, OR (541) 549–9941 or *www.nuggetnews.com* · **Paulina Springs Book Company,** Sisters, OR 1–800–397–0867 or *www.paulinasprings.com*

(retail) Local Outdoor Retailers:

Eurosports, Sisters, OR 1–800–382–3471 or (541) 549–2471

(N) Maps:

USGS maps: Three-Fingered Jack, OR · **USFS maps:** Deschutes National Forest

If you chose to continue past the turnaround point at mile 5.8, here's a list of all the trail junctions you'll find as you hike north for the next 15 miles. From the saddle on Cascade Crest, between Three-Fingered Jack and Porcupine Rock at mile 7.0, the trail passes around the west side of Three-Fingered Jack. At mile 10.2 you'll reach the junction with the Minto Pass Trail 3437 (on your left) and the Minto Pass Tie Trail 4015 (on your right). At mile 10.7, you'll arrive at a junction on your right with Summit Lake Trail 4014. At mile 13.9, you'll reach a junction on the right with Rockpile Lake Trail #4005. At mile 14.4, you'll come to Brush Creek Trail 4004, on your right. At mile 15.4, you'll reach Swallow Lake Trail 3488 on your left. At mile 17.5, you'll intersect with the Shirley Lake Trail 4003.1 on your right. And lastly, at mile 20.8 you'll arrive at a junction on your left that provides an alternate route to Pamelia Lake.

MilesDirections

0.0 START at the wooden trailhead sign adjacent to the gravel parking area. Fill out a free self-issue wilderness permit before you go. Walk a short distance and the trail comes to a T-intersection. Turn left and head north on the Pacific Crest Trail 2000. The trail surface is very soft and dusty.

0.1 Arrive at a second trail junction. Continue straight on the Pacific Crest Trail 2000.

1.0 Pass a small lake on the right side of the trail.

1.4 Arrive at a junction. Stay right and continue on the Pacific Crest Trail 2000.

3.6 The trail ascends from the thick forest for a grand view of the Central Cascade peaks.

3.7 That's Three-Fingered Jack straight ahead. There's also a good view of Summit Lake.

4.0 Enjoy a good view of Black Butte to the east. The trail begins to climb steeply here on a series of switchbacks. There are several rocky sections along this stretch.

5.8 Arrive at a good spot to view the eroding spires of Three-Fingered Jack and the Climbers' Trail that travels up the south side of the mountain. This is your turnaround point.

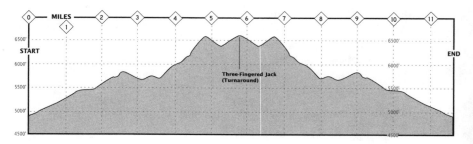

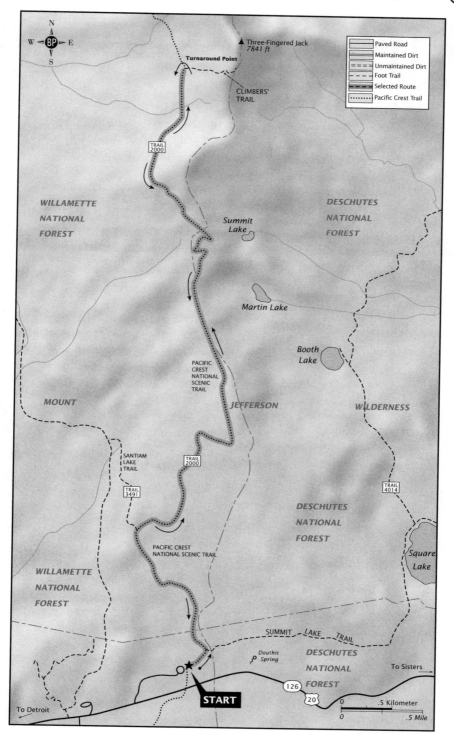

N
W — BP — E
S

▲ Three-Fingered Jack
7841 ft

Turnaround Point

CLIMBERS'
TRAIL

TRAIL
2000

WILLAMETTE
NATIONAL
FOREST

DESCHUTES
NATIONAL
FOREST

*Summit
Lake*

Martin Lake

*Booth
Lake*

PACIFIC
CREST
NATIONAL
SCENIC
TRAIL

MOUNT

JEFFERSON

WILDERNESS

SANTIAM
LAKE
TRAIL

TRAIL
3491

TRAIL
2000

TRAIL
4014

DESCHUTES
NATIONAL
FOREST

*Square
Lake*

PACIFIC CREST
NATIONAL SCENIC TRAIL

WILLAMETTE
NATIONAL
FOREST

SUMMIT   LAKE   TRAIL

DESCHUTES
NATIONAL
FOREST

*Douthit
Spring*

To Sisters

126
20

START

To Detroit

	Paved Road
	Maintained Dirt
	Unmaintained Dirt
	Foot Trail
	Selected Route
	Pacific Crest Trail

0   .5 Kilometer

0   .5 Mile

Black Butte

Hike Summary

This trail leads to the top of one of Central Oregon's best-known landmarks, 6,436-foot Black Butte. The summit includes three historic fire lookouts and fantastic views of several Cascade peaks to the west. Interpretive signs en route to the summit point out native plant and tree species.

Hike Specs

Start: From the Black Butte trailhead off FS 1110

Length: 3.8-mile out-and-back

Approximate Hiking Time: 2–3 hours

Difficulty Rating: Moderate due to the steep climb to Black Butte's summit

Trail Surface: Dusty dirt path

Lay of the Land: Hike up the side of a 1.5-million-year-old strato-volcano, through an open forest of ponderosa and white-bark pine and Douglas, sub-alpine, and grand fir.

Elevation Gain: 1,585 feet

Land Status: National forest

Nearest Town: Sisters, OR

Other Trail Users: Hikers only

Canine Compatibility: Leashed dogs permitted

Getting There

From Sisters: Drive six miles west on U.S. 20 to Green Ridge Road (FS 11). Turn right (north) onto Green Ridge Road (FS 11) and drive 3.8 miles to FS 1110. Turn left onto FS 1110 and proceed 4.2 miles to the junction with FS 700. Stay to the right and drive a rough and narrow 1.1 miles to the trailhead. *DeLorme: Oregon Atlas & Gazetteer:* Page 50 A3

Black Butte's summit can be windy and cold—be sure to pack extra layers of warm clothing.

Black Butte rises 6,436 feet above the Central Oregon landscape. This well-known geological landmark, a 1.5-million-year-old strato-volcano, was created by numerous basaltic lava flows over a period of hundreds of years. Because Black Butte stands in the rain shadow of the Cascade Mountains, it has not been exposed to the eroding forces of wind and water like its neighboring peaks and has therefore managed to maintain its conical shape.

Black Butte is located approximately 10 miles west of the small Western town of Sisters, established in 1888. The town's name was inspired by the Three Sisters Mountains, known to early settlers as Faith, Hope, and Charity, which rise impressively from the pine-filled valley surrounding Sisters. Before 1900 Sisters was the only settlement between Prineville and

the Cascade Mountains and was an important stopping point for people traveling through the state. It was also the local supply center for farmers and ranchers. In the early 1900s the town began to grow and soon it hosted a sawmill, hotel, saloon, blacksmith shop, real estate office, schoolhouse, and mercantile store.

Some of the first explorers to pass through the Sisters area mentioned Black Butte in their journals. In September of 1855 Lieutenant Henry Larcom Abbot, who was traveling through the area as a member of a survey party for the Pacific Railroad, wrote: "Today, we followed an old trail to the 'black butte'...."

That old trail has most likely faded away, but today there is a relatively new path to Black Butte's summit. The 1.9-mile trail begins at the end of Forest Service Road 1110 and winds through a dry, open forest of ponderosa and white-bark pine and Douglas, sub-alpine, and grand fir. Signposts along

Black Butte.

197

MilesDirections

0.0 START at the parking lot at the end of FS 1110.

0.2 Check out the greenleaf manzanita *(arctostaphylos patula)*. Proceed approximately 15 yards to a sign indicating snowbrush *(ceanothus velutinus)*.

0.4 Pass a sign indicating chinkapin *(castanopsis chrysophylla)*. There's a great view of Mount Washington to the left.

0.5 Arrive at a grand fir tree *(abies grandis)*.

0.8 Notice the white-bark pine *(pinus albicaulis)*.

0.9 Walk through a grove of aspen trees *(populus tremuloides)*. Notice the grand view of Mount Washington.

1.0 Squaw currant is a bushy plant with geranium-like leaves.

1.1 A sign on the right points out bitter cherry *(prunus emarginata)*, a bushy plant with white, feathery tufts.

1.2 That's bitterbrush *(purshia tridentata)* on the left.

1.5 A sign on the right points out pine-mat manzanita. This ground-hugging plant resembles a green-leafed mat. A few yards up the trail there's a sub-alpine fir *(abies lasiocarpa)*.

1.7 The trail forks. Turn right and continue toward the old lookout tower and viewpoint. (The trail to the left leads to Black Butte Lookout Tower.)

1.8 Pass the old Cupola and Lookout Tower on your right. This historic tower, built in 1934, took more than 1,000 packhorse loads of material to build.

1.9 Arrive at the 6,436-foot summit of Black Butte and the turnaround point. Before you leave, enjoy views of Broken Top (9,175 feet), South Sister (10,350 feet), North Sister (10,085 feet), Belknap Crater (6,872 feet), and Mount Washington (7,794 feet) to the southwest; and, to the northwest, views of Haystack Butte (5,523 feet), Three-Fingered Jack (7,841 feet), Mount Jefferson (10,497 feet), Mount Hood (11,235 feet), and Mount Adams (12,326 feet).

3.8 Arrive back at the parking lot.

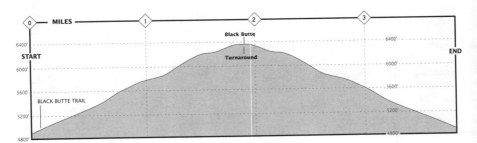

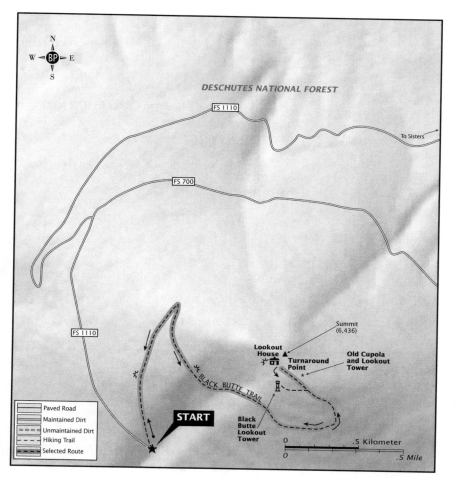

the trail point out these tree species as well as other indigenous plants including squaw currant, bitterbrush, and pinemat manzanita. Small groves of quaking aspens have also staked out territory along the trail. These silvery, shimmering trees have one of the largest footholds in the West and can be found from the Atlantic to the Pacific coast. French-Canadian trappers believed that Christ's crucifix was made of aspen, which accounted for why the trees are still trembling today.

After about a mile the trail becomes steeper, and soon there are gorgeous, sweeping views of Mount Washington and other Cascade peaks rising majestically to the west. At the butte's summit, there are signs indicating the names and elevations of the prominent peaks. There are also three fire towers of note: a 65-foot tower built in 1995 (mile 1.7); an 83-foot tower erected in 1934 by the Civilian Conservation Corps (mile 1.8); and, most important for history buffs, a 14'x14' cabin/fire tower erected in 1922. The old cabin/fire tower is one of only eight such buildings remaining in Oregon and is listed on the National Register of Historic Places. Soak up the sun and the views before you turn around and head back to your vehicle.

Fire tower on the summit.

Hike Information

ⓒ Trail Contacts:
Deschutes National Forest, Sisters Ranger District, Sisters, OR (541) 549–2111 or *www.fs. fed.us/r6/deschutes/sisters/ sisters.html*

🕐 Schedule:
May through October

Ⓢ Fees/Permits:
$3 permit available from the self-service pay station at the trailhead or from the ranger station in Sisters. Also requires a Northwest Forest $5 day pass or $30 annual pass. You can purchase a pass online at: *www.fs.fed.us/r6/feede-mo* or by call calling 1–800–270–7504.

❓ Local Information:
Sisters Area Chamber of Commerce, Sisters, OR (541) 549–0251 or *www.sisterschamber.com*

💡 Local Events/Attractions:
Sisters Antique Festival, in August, Sisters, OR (541) 388–2082 · Sisters Rodeo and Parade, in June, Sisters, OR (541) 549–0121

🛏 Accommodations:
Best Western Ponderosa Lodge, Sisters, OR (541) 549–1234 or *www.bestwesternsisters.com* · Sisters Motor Lodge, Sisters, OR (541) 549–2551 · Squaw Creek Bed and Breakfast, Sisters, OR 1–800–930–0055 or *www.sisterslodging.com*

🍴 Restaurants:
Figaro's Italian Kitchen, Sisters, OR (541) 549–4661 · Papandrea's Pizzeria, Sisters, OR (541) 549–6081 · Sisters Bakery, Sisters, OR (541) 549–0361 · Sisters Coffee Company, Sisters, OR 1–800–524–JAVA or (541) 549–0527

🏛 Organizations:
Pacific Crest Trail Association, Sacramento, CA (916) 349–2109 or *www.pcta.org*

ⓛ Other Resources:
Central Oregon Recreation Watch, Bend, OR (541) 318–2882 or *www.corw.com* · The Nugget Newspaper, Sisters, OR (541) 549–9941 or *www.nuggetnews.com* · Paulina Springs Book Company, Sisters, OR 1–800–397–0867 or *www.paulinasprings.com* · Oregon's Sisters Country by Ray Hatton

ⓕ Local Outdoor Retailers:
Eurosports, Sisters, OR 1–800–382–3471 or (541) 549–2471

Ⓝ Maps:
USGS maps: Black Butte, OR · USFS maps: Deschutes National Forest

Little Belknap Crater

Hike Summary

This rather difficult stretch of the Pacific Crest Trail traverses rock-strewn, moon-like terrain on its way to the summit of Little Belknap Crater. But the effort is worth it. Along the way you pass lava rock, lava tubes, and fascinating caves. And from the summit you can enjoy views of the Three Sisters, Mount Washington, Black Crater, and many other Cascade peaks.

Hike Specs

Start: From the Pacific Crest (Trail 2000) trailhead off the McKenzie Highway (OR 242)

Length: 7.2-mile out-and-back

Approximate Hiking Time: 3–4 hours

Difficulty Rating: Difficult due to an arduous ascent up a rough, sharp, and uneven lava flow

Trail Surface: Dirt path with sharp and loose lava rock. No shade and no water.

Lay of the Land: Hike along a dry and exposed route across a unique lava flow to the summit of Little Belknap Crater.

Elevation Gain: 1,032 feet

Land Status: National forest and wilderness area

Nearest Town: Sisters, OR

Other Trail Users: Hikers only

Canine Compatibility: Not dog friendly

Getting There

From Sisters: Drive 15.3 miles west on the McKenzie Highway (OR 242) to the Pacific Crest (Trail 2000) trailhead, located on the right (north) side of the road. (A very small hiker sign marks the trailhead.) If you need to purchase a Trail Park pass, there is a self-pay station located 1.4 miles west of Sisters on the McKenzie Highway on the left (south) side of the road. *[Note: The McKenzie Highway is closed in the winter and sometime does not reopen until late June to early July.]* **DeLorme: Oregon Atlas & Gazetteer:** Page 50 B2

T he rugged character of Central Oregon's lava country is nowhere better represented than on this hike to the summit of Little Belknap Crater. The rich history of the area begins with the highway to the trailhead. The McKenzie Highway (Oregon 242) is a gorgeous scenic byway with spectacular views of mountains, lava fields, and endless blue sky—a great introduction to the hike you're about to take. When gold was discovered in eastern Oregon and Idaho in the 1860s, settlers made a push to find a route that connected the Willamette Valley on the west side of the Cascades to the land on the east. In 1862 Felix Scott and his brother Marion led a party of 40 men, 60 oxen, and 900 head of cattle and horses across McKenzie Pass, blazing what would later become the Scott Trail.

An extremely rough trail, the Scott Trail required almost five days to travel from Eugene in the Willamette Valley to the small town of Sisters in central Oregon. For future travelers, a toll road was built in 1872 that traveled up Lost Creek Canyon, traversed over the rough lava beds, and ended at the Deschutes River.

Today the road is paved and toll-free. It also happens to pass the Dee Wright Observatory (11 miles west of Sisters), built by the Civilian Conservation Corps and named for an early-1900s Forest Service packer and mountain guide. The observatory's arched windows frame 11 Cascade peaks. A paved half-mile walkway offers an easy means to explore the eerie moonscape of the Belknap lava flow. The trail is complemented by interpretive signs detailing the area's unique geology.

When you've had enough of the observatory, continue on to the trailhead for Little Belknap Crater. The trail (95 percent of which is the Pacific Crest Trail), leads through the heart of the Mount Washington Wilderness and its rugged lava formations, craters, and extinct vol-

A WORD OF CAUTION:

Little Belknap Crater and the surrounding area are nothing short of brutal. There's no water. The sun is relentless. The rocky terrain is sharp as knives. It's critical that you pack plenty of water—at least two liters per person. Wear a hat. Slather on the sunscreen. And to avoid mauling your feet, wear sturdy boots or hiking shoes. Finally, if you have a dog, do it a favor and leave it at home. The razor-sharp rock will most certainly tear its paws to shreds.

MilesDirections

0.0 START at the wooden trailhead sign. *[Note. Be sure to fill out the free self-issue wilderness permit at the trailhead.]*

1.0 Begin walking on the lava flow.

3.2 Come to a trail junction and turn right to hike to the 6,057-foot summit of Little Belknap Crater.

3.5 Pass a lava tube on your left.

3.6 Reach the summit and enjoy sweeping views of Belknap Crater, Mount Washington, Black Crater, and The Three Sisters. Turn around here and retrace your route back to the trailhead. *[Option. If you came prepared, you can continue on the Pacific Crest Trail and explore more of the Mount Washington Wilderness.]*

7.2 Arrive back at the trailhead.

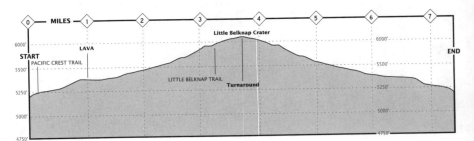

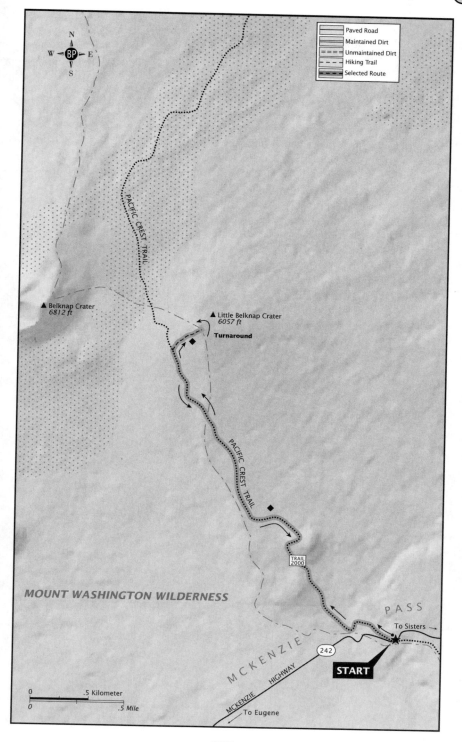

Paved Road
Maintained Dirt
Unmaintained Dirt
Hiking Trail
Selected Route

N
W — BP — E
S

PACIFIC CREST TRAIL

▲ Belknap Crater
6812 ft

▲ Little Belknap Crater
6057 ft
Turnaround

PACIFIC CREST TRAIL

TRAIL 2000

MOUNT WASHINGTON WILDERNESS

PASS
To Sisters →

242

START

MCKENZIE HIGHWAY

MCKENZIE
To Eugene

0   .5 Kilometer
0   .5 Mile

canoes. The route begins rather innocently as it winds through an open forest. But within a mile, things change drastically. Soon the forest is replaced by a grayish-black lava flow practically devoid of life, except for the rare hardy tree that has managed to sink its roots through the jumbled basalt rocks.

The flow was created more than 2,900 years ago when hot liquid basalt poured from Belknap Crater, the large cinder cone to the west. Approximately 20 years later a second eruption sprung from Little Belknap Crater, located directly north of the trailhead. A third phase of eruptions occurred a little more than a thousand years later from the northeast base of Belknap Crater, releasing lava nine miles west into the McKenzie River Valley.

After three miles of hiking through this mysterious maze of rock, you come to a trail junction and go right. In 0.3 miles you pass a deep lava tube on your left. If you approach the edge of the tube and look in (be careful—it's quite a drop-off), you can feel the cool air escaping from deep within the earth.

From the lava tube, hike a steep and dramatic 0.1 miles to the top of Little Belknap Crater. The trail surface is loose and crumbly, and piles of gray rock mingle with the bright red cinders that form much of the crater. When you reach the top you can enjoy magnificent views of Belknap Crater, Mount

Mount Washington.

Washington, Black Crater, and the Three Sisters Mountains. The summit of Little Belknap Crater is your turnaround point. If you're backpacking, continue on the Pacific Crest Trail as it winds its way north through the magnificent lava country of the Mount Washington Wilderness.

Hike Information

● Trail Contacts:
Deschutes National Forest, Sisters Ranger District, Sisters, OR (541) 549–7700 or www.fs.fed.us/r6/deschutes/sisters/sisters.html

● Schedule:
Late June through October

● Fees/Permits:
$3 Trail Park Pass fee. You can purchase a Trail Park Pass at the Sisters Ranger Station or at a self-pay station located 1.4 miles west of Sisters on OR 242 on the left (south) side of the road. Also requires a Northwest Forest $5 day pass or $30 annual pass. You can purchase a pass online at: www.fs.fed.us/r6/feedemo or by call calling 1–800–270–7504.

● Local Information:
Sisters Area Chamber of Commerce, Sisters, OR (541) 549–0251 or www.sisters-chamber.com

● Local Events/Attractions:
[See Hike 28: Black Butte]

● Accommodations:
[See Hike 28: Black Butte]

● Restaurants:
Figaro's Italian Kitchen, Sisters, OR (541) 549–4661 · Papandrea's Pizzeria, Sisters, OR (541) 549–6081 · Sisters Coffee Company, Sisters, OR 1–800–524–JAVA or (541) 549–0527

● Organizations:
Pacific Crest Trail Association, Sacramento, CA (916) 349–2109 or www.pcta.org

● Other Resources:
Central Oregon Recreation Watch, Bend, OR (541) 318–2882 or www.corw.com · The Nugget Newspaper, Sisters, OR (541) 549–9941 or www.nuggetnews.com · Paulina Springs Book Company, Sisters, OR 1–800–397–0867 or www.paulinasprings.com

● Local Outdoor Retailers:
Eurosports, Sisters, OR 1–800–382–3471 or (541) 549–2471

● Maps:
USGS maps: Mount Washington, OR · USFS maps: Deschutes National Forest

30 Black Crater

Hike Summary

This trail winds its way through a mountain-hemlock forest to the craggy red-cinder summit of Black Crater. At the prominent summit you can enjoy sweeping views of the snow-topped Three Sisters Mountains, Mount Washington, and the surrounding lava flows and craters that make up the Mount Washington Wilderness. The walk to the top is tough, but the view of the surrounding central Oregon volcanic landscape is well worth the effort.

Hike Specs

Start: From the Black Crater trailhead (Trail 58) off the McKenzie Highway (OR 242)

Length: 8.2-mile out-and-back

Approximate Hiking Time: 4–6 hours

Difficulty Rating: Difficult due to a very strenuous climb to the summit of Black Crater

Trail Surface: Dirt path

Lay of the Land: Hike a steep ascent through a mountain-hemlock forest up the north side of Black Crater.

Elevation Gain: 2,388 feet

Land Status: National forest and wilderness area

Nearest Town: Sisters, OR

Other Trail Users: Equestrians

Canine Compatibility: Leashed dogs permitted

Getting There

From Sisters: Drive 11.7 miles west on the McKenzie Highway (OR 242) to the Black Crater trailhead, on the left (south) side of the road. If you need to purchase a Trail Park pass, there's a self-pay station 1.4 miles west of Sisters on McKenzie Highway on the left (south) side of the road. *[**Note:** The McKenzie Highway is closed in the winter and sometime does not reopen until late June to early July.]* **DeLorme: Oregon Atlas & Gazetteer:** Page 50 B2

Central Oregon is truly the land of volcanoes, and the Sisters vicinity is, perhaps, its most shining example. One incredible hike is along the Black Crater Trail, which leads to the summit of 7,251-foot Black Crater. The difficult path, which climbs over 2,000 feet to the craggy, double-pinnacled summit, is a test of both strength and endurance.

The trail begins as a series of switchbacks through a mountain-hemlock forest. Mountain hemlock can be found growing at elevations of 3,500 to 6,000 feet and is often confused with Western hemlock. This hardy tree differs from the Western hemlock by having thick needles that fan out in bushy clusters. It also has two-inch-long cones and blue-green foliage.

View of the Three Sisters Mountains from the summit of Black Crater.

209

In contrast, the Western hemlock has flat needles that are shaped in an open spray, cones that are an inch or less in length, and yellow-green foliage. Mountain hemlocks are also characterized by their deep, furrowed bark and are usually the first trees to grow at timberline. It's not uncommon for a mature branch to touch the ground and take root as a new tree. The parent tree then shelters the new tree from the harsh high-altitude environment.

As you hike up this trail you may also notice the purple lupine and vibrant-red Indian paintbrush scattered about in grassy hillside meadows. After about three miles the trail emerges from the thick forest for great views to the north of Mount Jefferson and Mount Hood. As you climb higher notice the crooked whitebark pine trees (shaped by the prevailing southeasterly winds). Inhabiting elevations above 5,500 feet, these tough trees are sprinkled across hundreds of miles of high-country landscape from central British Columbia to California and as far east as Wyoming. At the edge of the treeline, these trees grow 40 to 80 feet tall and have thick, stout trunks with widespread branches. Above timberline, whitebark pines take on a totally different appearance. Growing to heights of only five to 12 feet the trees become more shrub-like. The branches and trunk are often twisted and bent and are known as krumholzes—German for "crooked wood." At higher elevations the trees become even smaller and are often referred to as alpine scrub.

As the trail nears the summit it crosses an alpine-like meadow sprinkled with purple, yellow, and white bouquets of wildflowers. At the summit are two prominent pinnacles that rise above the crater. From these spires you can enjoy a panoramic view of the Three Sisters to the south and Belknap Crater, Mount Washington, Mount Jefferson, and Mount Hood to the north. The spectacular scenery makes it obvious why so many other hikers are attracted to this spot. If you're looking for solitude, hike the trail on a weekday.

MilesDirections

0.0 START at the wooden the Black Crater trailhead (Trail 58). *[**Note.** Be sure to fill out a free wilderness permit at the trailhead sign.]*

3.3 Enjoy spectacular views of Mount Jefferson and Mount Hood to the north.

4.2 Reach the summit and your turn-around point.

8.4 Arrive back at the trailhead.

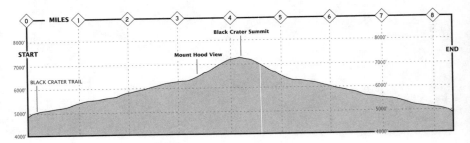

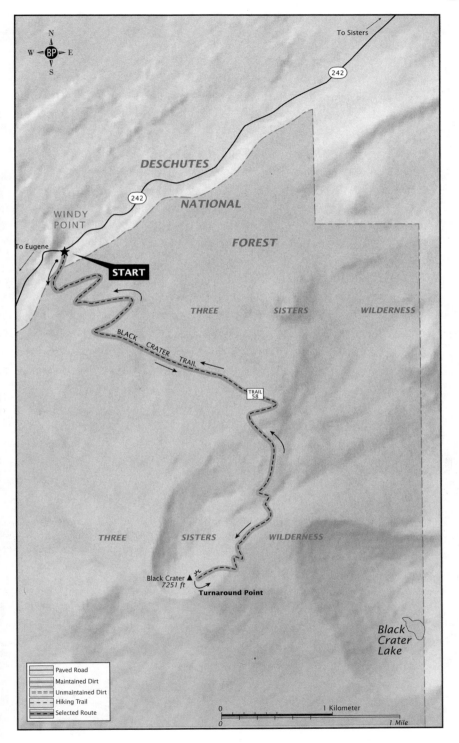

To Sisters

242

DESCHUTES

242

WINDY
POINT

NATIONAL

To Eugene

FOREST

START

THREE   SISTERS   WILDERNESS

BLACK   CRATER   TRAIL

TRAIL
58

THREE   SISTERS   WILDERNESS

Black Crater ▲
7251 ft
Turnaround Point

Black
Crater
Lake

Paved Road
Maintained Dirt
Unmaintained Dirt
Hiking Trail
Selected Route

0   1 Kilometer
0   1 Mile

Hike Information

🕐 Trail Contacts:
Deschutes National Forest, Sisters Ranger District, Sisters, OR (541) 549–7700 or *www.fs.fed.us/r6/deschutes/sisters/sisters.html*

🕐 Schedule:
Late June through October

💲 Fees/Permits:
$3 Trail Park Pass available at the Sisters Ranger Station or at the self-pay station 1.4 miles west of Sisters off the McKenzie Highway (OR 242) on the left (south) side of the road. Also requires a Northwest Forest $5 day pass or $30 annual pass. You can purchase a pass online at: *www.fs.fed.us/r6/feedemo* or by call calling 1–800–270–7504.

❓ Local Information:
Sisters Area Chamber of Commerce, Sisters, OR (541) 549–0251 or *www.sisters-chamber.com*

🎉 Local Events/Attractions:
Sisters Antique Festival, in August, Sisters, OR (541) 388–2082 · Sisters Rodeo and Parade, in June, Sisters, OR (541) 549–0121

🛏 Accommodations:
Best Western Ponderosa Lodge, Sisters, OR (541) 549–1234 or *www.bestwesternsisters.com* · Sisters Motor Lodge, Sisters, OR

(541) 549–2551 · Squaw Creek B&B, Sisters, OR 1–800–930–0055 or *www.sisterslodging.com*

🍴 Restaurants:
Figaro's Italian Kitchen, Sisters, OR (541) 549–4661 · Papandrea's Pizzeria, Sisters, OR (541) 549–6081 · Sisters Coffee Company, Sisters, OR 1–800–524–JAVA or (541) 549–0527

🏢 Organizations:
Pacific Crest Trail Association, Sacramento, CA (916) 349–2109 or *www.pcta.org*

📖 Other Resources:
Central Oregon Recreation Watch, Bend, OR (541) 318–2882 or *www.corw.com* · The Nugget Newspaper, Sisters, OR (541) 549–9941 or *www.nuggetnews.com* · Paulina Springs Book Company, Sisters, OR 1–800–397–0867 or *www.paulinasprings.com*

🍹 Local Outdoor Retailers:
Eurosports, Sisters, OR 1–800–382–3471 or (541) 549–2471

Ⓝ Maps:
USGS maps: Black Crater, OR; Mount Washington, OR · USFS maps: Three Sisters Wilderness *(available from the Sisters Ranger Station)*; Deschutes National Forest maps *(available from the Sisters Ranger Station)*

31

Tam McArthur Rim

Hike Summary

Tam McArthur Rim is a wide-open ridge that captures the true beauty of the high alpine country of the Three Sisters Wilderness. From a vantage point high on this prominent ridge you'll take in views of a lifetime of many well known Cascade peaks like the Three Sisters Mountains and Broken Top to the west, Mount Washington and Mount Jefferson to the northwest, and Mount Bachelor to the south.

Hike Specs

Start: From the Tam McArthur Rim trailhead (Trail 4078) off FS 16
Length: 5.6-mile out-and-back
Approximate Hiking Time: 3–4 hours
Difficulty Rating: Difficult due to a steep climb up multiple switchbacks
Trail Surface: Dirt path
Lay of the Land: Hike through a thick fir forest up Tam McArthur Rim
Elevation Gain: 1,507 feet
Land Status: National forest and wilderness area
Nearest Town: Sisters, OR
Other Trail Users: Equestrians
Canine Compatibility: Leashed dogs permitted

Getting There

From Sisters: Turn south on Elm Street (which turns into FS 16) and drive 15.6 miles (the road turns to gravel after 14 miles) to the trailhead located on the left (west) side of the road at Three Creeks Lake. *DeLorme: Oregon Atlas & Gazetteer:* Page 50 C3

ocated south of Sisters and east of Broken Top, Tam McArthur Rim is a windswept ridge offering outstanding views of Three Sisters country. This broad ridge is home to twisted whitebark pines that somehow manage to survive the brutal winds and harsh winters that frequent this moon-like landscape.

The Tam McArthur Rim Trail begins adjacent to Three Creeks Lake, approximately 16 miles south of Sisters off Forest Service Road 16. The lake resides in a basin carved by ice age glaciers and is a popular summer recreation spot for those living and visiting Central Oregon. It's stocked with rainbow and Eastern brook trout, which are raised at the Wizard Falls Fish Hatchery northwest of Sisters. Driftwood Campground, which has sites along the shores of Three Creeks Lake and in the adjacent Three Creeks Meadow, sells bait and tackle and rents rowboats. To the west

Three Creeks Lake.

of Three Creeks Lake is Little Three Creeks Lake, which can be reached via a 2.2-mile round-trip trail from Driftwood Campground. Mountain bikes are allowed on the trail to Little Three Creeks Lake, but not on the Tam McArthur Rim Trail.

Tam McArthur Rim takes its name from Lewis A. "Tam" McArthur, author of *Oregon Geographic Names*. Interest in Oregon ran deep in the McArthur family. Both of Tam's grandfathers were involved in

MilesDirections

0.0 START at the wooden Tam McArthur Rim trailhead sign. [**Note.** *Be sure to obtain a free self-issue wilderness permit at the trailhead.*]

1.8 Come to a trail junction. Continue straight.

2.5 Come to a trail junction and turn to your right.

2.6 Reach a scenic viewpoint with views of the surrounding Cascade Mountains. Turn around and retrace your route back to the trailhead.

5.2 Arrive back at the trailhead.

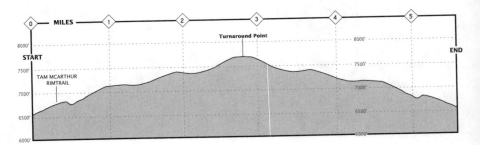

surveying Oregon and in Oregon politics. Born in The Dalles, Oregon, on April 27, 1883, McArthur worked for the Pacific Power & Light Company from 1923 to 1946. He also served as the secretary to the Oregon Geographic Board from 1914 to 1949. It was during this time that the idea of writing a book about Oregon's geographic names took shape. The first edition of *Oregon Geographic Names* was published in 1928. Today the book is in its sixth edition and is edited by McArthur's son, Lewis L. McArthur. After McArthur passed away in 1951, Robert W. Sawyer, a good friend of McArthur's, named the prominent ridge above Three Creeks Lake in his honor.

Begin this hike by heading south on steep switchbacks through a fir forest lined with grassy meadows and purple lupine. As the trail climbs, there are many opportunities to view the Three Creeks Lake basin to the east. When the path reaches the ridge crest, at mile 1.8, it forks. At this point the landscape is wide open with occasional groups of tough whitebark pines.

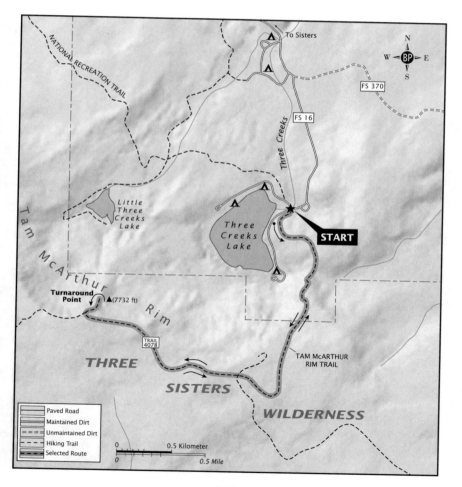

The views are endless. Go straight at the intersection and hike another 0.8 miles to a highpoint on the ridge. From there you can enjoy spectacular views of the Three Creeks Lake basin to the east, the Three Sisters Mountains and Broken Top to the west, Mount Washington and Mount Jefferson to the northwest, and Mount Bachelor to the south. From here it's all downhill. Turn around and head back to the trailhead the same way you came.

Hike Information

◕ Trail Contacts:
Deschutes National Forest, Sisters Ranger District, Sisters, OR (541) 549–7700 or *www.fs.fed.us/r6/deschutes/ sisters/sisters.html*

◷ Schedule:
July through October

⑤ Fees/Permits:
Free wilderness permits are required and are available at the trailhead. Also requires a Northwest Forest $5 day pass or $30 annual pass. You can purchase a pass online at: *www.fs.fed.us/r6/feedemo* or by call calling 1–800–270–7504.

❓ Local Information:
Sisters Area Chamber of Commerce, Sisters, OR (541) 549–0251 or *www.sisters-chamber.com*

💡 Local Events/Attractions:
Sisters Antique Festival, in August, Sisters, OR (541) 388–2082 · Sisters Rodeo and Parade, in June, Sisters, OR (541) 549–0121

🛏 Accommodations:
Squaw Creek B&B, Sisters, OR 1–800–930–0055 or *www. sisterslodging.com* · Best Western Ponderosa Lodge, Sisters, OR (541) 549–1234 or

www.bestwesternsisters.com · Sisters Motor Lodge, Sisters, OR (541) 549–2551

🍴 Restaurants:
Figaro's Italian Kitchen, Sisters, OR (541) 549–4661 · Papandrea's Pizzeria, Sisters, OR (541) 549–6081 · Sisters Coffee Company, Sisters, OR 1–800–524–JAVA or (541) 549–0527

👥 Organizations:
Pacific Crest Trail Association, Sacramento, CA (916) 349–2109 or *www.pcta.org*

🔄 Other Resources:
Central Oregon Recreation Watch, Bend, OR (541) 318–2882 or *www.corw.com* · The Nugget Newspaper, Sisters, OR (541) 549–9941 or *www.nuggetnews.com* · Paulina Springs Book Company, Sisters, OR 1–800–397–0867 or *www.paulinasprings.com*

🌴 Local Outdoor Retailers:
Eurosports, Sisters, OR 1–800–382–3471 or (541) 549–2471

Ⓝ Maps:
USGS maps: Tumalo Falls, OR; Broken Top, OR · USFS maps: Deschutes National Forest

South Sister

Hike Summary

This is a hike of a lifetime—long, tough, and with high-alpine scenery and spectacular summit views. The trek up 10,358-foot South Sister, the crown jewel of the Three Sisters Wilderness, is well worth the hard work. The trail starts out by heading through the high, open Wickiup Plains on the way to Lewis Glacier and, finally, the summit crater. At the peak you'll find gorgeous views of Middle and North Sister to the north and Green Lakes, Mount Bachelor, and Broken Top to the southeast. The weather on South Sister is notoriously erratic, so be prepared for anything. If the skies look threatening, don't attempt to summit. Keep in mind: You may find snow on the summit as late as mid July. If you climb the peak before the snow melts, you'll need waterproof mountaineering boots and an ice axe.

Hike Specs

Start: From the Devil's Lake trailhead off the Cascade Lakes Highway (OR 46)
Length: 11.0-mile out-and-back
Approximate Hiking Time: 8–10 hours
Difficulty Rating: Difficult due to a steep, unrelenting climb to the summit. The last two miles of trail on loose, rocky scree.
Trail Surface: Dirt path, steep switchbacks, loose and rocky in places
Lay of the Land: Hike toward Moraine Lake and ascend a high alpine landscape to the 10,358-foot summit of South Sister.

Elevation Gain: 5,400 feet
Land Status: National forest and wilderness area
Nearest Town: Bend, OR
Other Trail Users: Hikers only
Canine Compatibility: Not dog friendly

Getting There

From Bend: Drive 33.5 miles west on the Cascade Lakes Highway (OR 46) to the Devil's Lake trailhead. The trailhead is located in Devil's Lake Campground on the left (south) side of the highway.
DeLorme: Oregon Atlas & Gazetteer: Page 50 D2

The Deschutes National Forest encompasses 1.6 million acres in Central Oregon. The diverse woodland is home to lofty volcanic peaks, interesting lava formations, alpine lakes and forest, and sagebrush- and juniper-covered plateaus and canyons. Some of Oregon's highest peaks are found in this area, including the centerpieces of the 242,400-acre Three Sisters Wilderness: 10,085-foot North Sister, 10,047-foot Middle Sister, and 10,358-foot South Sister. More than 260 miles of trails, including 40 miles of the Pacific Crest Trail, wind through this scenic wilderness area.

Early settlers to the area called the North, Middle, and South Sister mountains Faith, Hope, and Charity, but these names never gained official

View of Middle and North Sister from the summit of South Sister.

recognition. Geologists believe each peak is a separate volcano. The oldest mountain, North Sister, has been dubbed by some mountaineers as "the Black Beast of the Cascades" due to the difficult route to its summit. The eroding mountain was once a broad shield volcano almost 20 miles wide and 8,000 feet tall. Eruptions added another 3,000 feet, but over the past 300,000 years it has suffered serious erosion. Middle Sister is the second oldest of the three. Though it's the smallest of the three peaks, it has the most symmetrical cone, and situated on the peak's western slope is the impressive Collier Glacier, a 1.5-mile long ice sheet that has been shrinking over the last century.

> If you're planning to camp overnight at Moraine Lake, bring mosquito repellant to ward off the swarms. Without it, you'll be miserable.

Its cone still filled with ice and snow, South Sister is the baby of the trio. It's thought to date back to the late Pleistocene era. During the warmer months of the summer, portions of the summit's ice and snow melts into a

MilesDirections

0.0 START from the Devil's Lake trailhead.

0.1 Cross OR 46. Continue on the trail.

2.0 Come to a trail junction. Continue straight. If you turn right, you'll reach Moraine Lake in 0.5 miles. If you plan on backpacking you can camp in one of 23 designated campsites surrounding Moraine Lake. If you turn left a sign indicates you'll be heading toward the Wickiup Plain.

4.4 Arrive at the southern tip of the Lewis Glacier. From this point, stay to the left of the glacier on an unofficial trail. The trail is very steep, and as you near the summit, it becomes loose scree.

5.4 Reach the south rim of the South Sister crater. Hike another 0.1 miles on the Rim Trail to the true summit.

5.5 Reach the true summit and your turnaround point. The view from this spectacular summit is one of the grandest in all of Oregon. You should be able to see 10,047-foot Middle Sister, 10,085-foot North Sister, and Chambers Lakes to the north and 9,152-foot Broken Top and Green Lakes to the southeast.

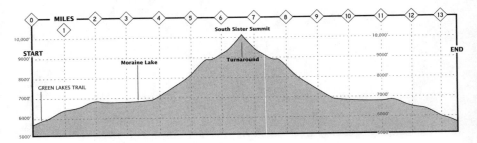

brilliant aqua-blue lake called Teardrop Pool. South Sister is also home to Oregon's largest glacier, Prouty, named after climber Harley Prouty, who served as president for the Mazamas, a Portland-based mountaineering group. He was the first person to ascend Prouty Pinnacles on North Sister in August of 1910, and is thought to be the first person to reach the summit of North Sister.

It's possible to reach South Sister's summit on a very strenuous out-and-back day-hike, but most people like to take it slow and camp along the way. Whatever you decide, begin at the Devil's Lake trailhead and start out climbing a steep series of switchbacks through a thick fir forest. After two miles you arrive at a junction. If you're climbing to the summit (on a day-hike), continue straight. If you're planning to camp for the night, turn right and continue half a mile to Moraine Lake and its 23 designated campsites. Watch your step here—the land is very delicate and vulnerable to misuse. Practice leave-no-trace camping, and make every effort to preserve the integrity of the area.

A spur trail leads around the lake and up a canyon and then rejoins the South Sister Trail. Back at the junction (two miles from the trailhead), continue across the wide-open Wickiup Plain—wickiup is the Native American term for a wigwam or teepee. This open alpine landscape is characterized by small islands of trees, long lava ridges, and smooth, glacier-carved basins.

At mile 4.4, you arrive at the southern tip of Lewis Glacier, named for explorer Meriwether Lewis, who traveled through Oregon in 1805 with his famous partner William Clark.

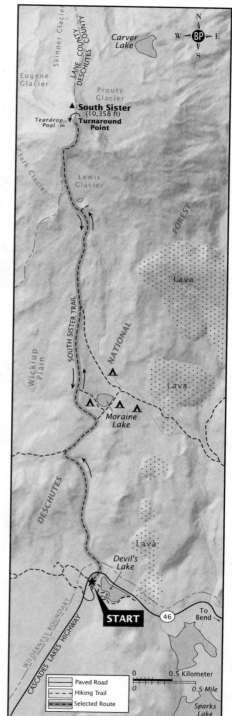

Stay to the left of the small lake at the base of the glacier and follow a steep and rocky trail about a mile to the south rim of South Sister crater. From there, continue another 0.1 miles on the Rim Trail to the true summit. Or, if there is still snow in the crater, access the summit by traversing the snowfield. On the way you'll pass Teardrop Pool, the state's highest lake.

The views at the summit is fantastic. On a clear day, Mount Rainier is visible 180 miles to the north in Washington. There are also inspiring views of the Chambers Lakes and Middle and North Sisters to the north, and of

Green Lake, Mount Bachelor, and Broken Top to the southeast. It's often cold and windy at the summit, so bring extra clothing, plenty of food and water, and aspirin if you are prone to altitude sickness.

Hike Information

🕽 Trail Contacts:
Deschutes National Forest, Bend-Fort Rock Ranger District, Bend, OR (541) 388–5664 or *www.fs.fed.us/r6/deschutes*

🕐 Schedule:
July through October

💲 Fees/Permits:
You'll need a free wilderness permit to hike on the trail, which is available at the trailhead for day hikers. Overnight backpackers will have to obtain their permits from the Deschutes National Ranger station in Bend. Also requires a Northwest Forest $5 day pass or $30 annual pass. You can purchase a pass online at: *www.fs.fed.us/r6/feedemo* or by call calling 1–800–270–7504.

❓ Local Information:
Bend Chamber of Commerce, Bend, OR 1–800–905–2363 or *www.bendchamber.org*

🟡 Local Events/Attractions:
High Desert Museum, Bend, OR (541) 382–4754 *www.highdesert.org* · **Cascade Festival of Music in Drake Park**, Bend, OR (541) 382–8381 or *www.cascademusic.org*

🛏 Accommodations:
Lara House B&B, Bend, OR 1–800–766–4064 · **East Lake Resort**, La Pine, OR (541) 536–2230 or *www.eastlakeresort.com* · **Paulina Lake Resort**, La Pine, OR (541) 536–2240 or *http://usa10.com/paulina/cabins.html* · **Soda Creek Campground**, Bend-Fort Rock Ranger District, Bend, OR (541) 388–5664 or *www.fs.fed.us/r6/deschutes*

🍴 Restaurants:
Deschutes Brewery & Public House, Bend, OR (541) 382–9242 · **East Lake Resort**, La Pine, OR (541) 536–2230 · **Paulina Lake Resort**, La Pine, OR (541) 536–2240

🏃 Hike Tours:
Wanderlust Tours, Bend, OR (541) 389–8359 or *www.wanderlusttours.com*

🛍 Local Outdoor Retailers:
G.I. Joe's, Inc., Bend, OR (541) 388–3773

🅝 Maps:
USGS maps: South Sister, OR · **USFS maps:** Deschutes National Forest

Paulina Peak

Hike Summary

This hike to the top of Paulina Peak begins with an easy jaunt through a beautiful pine and fir forest. But don't be deceived. After half a mile the terrain gets steep and you'll have to shift gears for the thigh-burning ascent to the summit. There, 7,984 feet above sea level, you'll be rewarded with gorgeous views of Paulina and East Lakes, Newberry Caldera, and the Big Obsidian lava flow.

Hike Specs

Start: From the Crater Rim Trail 57 trailhead off Paulina Lake Road (FS 21)
Length: 6.0-mile out-and-back
Approximate Hiking Time: 3–4 hours
Difficulty Rating: Difficult due to the very steep and strenuous nature of the trail
Trail Surface: Dirt path over fairly flat terrain. Becomes a steep climb up a ridge to the summit of Paulina Peak.
Lay of the Land: Hike along a fairly flat forested path through a Douglas fir and lodgepole pine for the first half mile, before climbing steeply up a ridge through a few loose, rocky sections to the top of 7,984-foot Paulina Peak.
Elevation Gain: 1,641 feet
Land Status: National monument
Nearest Town: Bend, OR
Other Trail Users: Equestrians
Canine Compatibility: Leashed dogs permitted

Getting There

From Bend: Drive south on U.S. 97 from the intersection of Greenwood Avenue and U.S. 97 for 23.1 miles to a sign for Newberry Caldera National Monument and Paulina and East lakes. Turn left on Paulina Lake Road (FS 21) and drive 14 miles to the visitor center. The trailhead is 50 feet before the visitor center on the right side of the road. *DeLorme: Oregon Atlas & Gazetteer:* Page 45 C7

The climate at Paulina Lake can be cool and brisk even in the middle of summer. Bring extra layers of clothing to be safe.

Established in 1990, the 55,000-acre Newberry National Volcanic Monument showcases Newberry Caldera, a 500-square-mile volcanic crater. This area is absolutely teeming with geologic history. You'll find hot springs, lava flows, and cinder cones, all of which can be explored on well-established trails.

One particularly noteworthy trail is the three-mile path to the summit of 7,984-foot Paulina Peak, the highest point in the monument. The trail

Hiking up the Paulina Peak Trail.

begins just to the right of the visitor center in a lodgepole-pine forest; the straight and slender lodgepole pines grow in thick stands and are distinguished by their prickly cones and pairs of two-inch-long needles. After half a mile over fairly flat terrain, the path begins a steep climb. The higher it gets, the better the views become, and soon you'll see Paulina and East lakes below. At the summit you'll find restrooms and, sadly for some, a large parking lot. Yes, you can choose to drive to the top via Forest Service Road 500.

Ignore the crowds. Instead, focus on your surroundings. Rising prominently from Paulina Lake, Paulina Peak offers spectacular views of the mountains and high-desert country of Central Oregon. The peak is what remains of ancient Mount Newberry, which, at 10,000 feet above sea level, was once the highest volcano in the Paulina Mountains. About 200,000 years ago, Newberry erupted and collapsed. The huge caldera left in its place eventually filled with water to create an enormous lake. Thousands of years later, more eruptions split the water into two separate lakes (Paulina and East) and left a central cone and several obsidian flows. The most recent eruption, which occurred about 1,300 years ago, resulted in the Big Obsidian Flow [see Hike 34], visible to the east.

Despite the area's remarkable geologic history, it's the wildlife that often proves to be the biggest draw here. Each year the Oregon Fish & Wildlife

MilesDirections

0.0 START at the Paulina Peak trailhead sign located approximately 50 feet to the right of the visitor center. The sign reads: "Crater Rim Trail 57. Paulina Peak 3 miles."

0.7 Cross FS 500. Continue straight on the trail.

1.5 Enjoy good views of Paulina and East Lakes.

2.7 Arrive at a trail junction. Continue straight toward Paulina Peak.

3.0 Arrive at the top of Paulina Peak. This is your turnaround point. There are a viewpoint and restrooms here. *[FYI. You can also drive to this viewpoint on FS 500.]*

6.0 Arrive back at the trailhead and your vehicle.

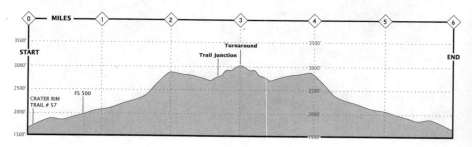

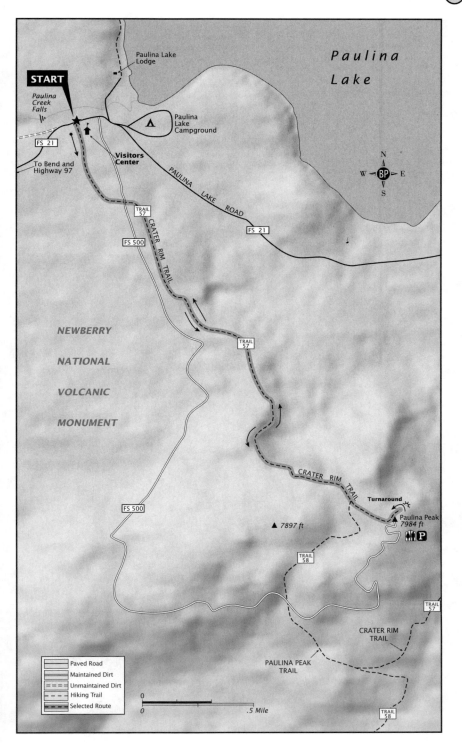

START

*Paulina
Creek
Falls*

Paulina Lake
Lodge

*Paulina
Lake*

Paulina
Lake
Campground

FS 21

To Bend and
Highway 97

**Visitors
Center**

PAULINA LAKE ROAD

FS 21

N
W — BP — E
S

TRAIL
57

FS 500

CRATER RIM TRAIL

NEWBERRY

NATIONAL

VOLCANIC

MONUMENT

TRAIL
57

CRATER RIM TRAIL

Turnaround

Paulina Peak
7984 ft

FS 500

▲ *7897 ft*

TRAIL
58

TRAIL
57

CRATER RIM
TRAIL

PAULINA PEAK
TRAIL

TRAIL
58

Paved Road
Maintained Dirt
Unmaintained Dirt
Hiking Trail
Selected Route

0
0   .5 Mile

Summit view.

Service stocks more than 200,000 trout and salmon in Paulina and East Lakes to satisfy the annual onslaught of 60,000 anglers. Campers must fend off black bears in search of edible delicacies in coolers and trailers. Other wild critters include badgers, deer, elk, and pine marten, as well as a variety of chipmunks and squirrels.

Before you trek to the top of Paulina Peak, stop in at the visitor center near the trailhead. There you'll find informative brochures (including advice on what to do about the bears), the lowdown on camping, and ideas on other things to see and do while at the monument.

Hike Information

◐ Trail Contacts:
Newberry National Volcanic Monument, Bend-Fort Rock Ranger District, Bend, OR (541) 388–5664 or *www.fs.fed.us/ r6/deschutes/monument/ monument.html*

◑ Schedule:
June through October

⑤ Fees/Permits:
Requires a Northwest Forest $5 day pass or $30 annual pass. You can purchase a pass online at: *www.fs.fed.us/r6/feedemo* or by call calling 1–800–270–7504.

❷ Local Information:
Bend Chamber of Commerce, Bend, OR 1–800–905–2363 or *www.bendchamber.org*

◉ Local Events/Attractions:
High Desert Museum, Bend, OR (541) 382–4754 *www. highdesert.org* · Cascade Festival of Music in Drake Park, Bend, OR (541) 382–8381 or *www.cascademusic.org*

⊖ Accommodations:
[See Hike 32: South Sister]

⑪ Restaurants:
Deschutes Brewery & Public House, Bend, OR (541) 382–9242 · East Lake Resort, La Pine, OR (541) 536–2230 · Paulina Lake Resort, La Pine, OR (541) 536–2240

⑥ Hike Tours:
Wanderlust Tours, Bend, OR (541) 389–8359 or *www.wanderlusttours. com*

⑳ Local Outdoor Retailers:
G.I. Joe's, Inc., Bend, OR (541) 388–3773

⑭ Maps:
USGS maps: Paulina Peak, OR · USFS maps: Deschutes National Forest

Big Obsidian Flow Trail

Hike Summary

The 0.7-mile Big Obsidian Flow Trail is an easy and convenient way to check out Oregon's youngest lava flow. Located in the Newberry National Volcanic Monument, this fascinating path crosses the lava flow and highlights the volcanic history of the area. Interpretive signs along the way explain how Native Americans visited the area to collect obsidian for making jewelry and tools.

Hike Specs

Start: From the Big Obsidian trailhead parking area off Paulina Lake Road FS 21)

Length: 0.7-mile loop

Approximate Hiking Time: 1 hour

Difficulty Rating: Easy due to the relatively flat terrain

Trail Surface: Pavement, gravel, and sand path over a large lava flow of pumice and obsidian

Lay of the Land: Hike on a large lava flow that is comprised of pumice and shiny obsidian.

Elevation Gain: 386 feet

Land Status: National monument

Nearest Town: Bend, OR

Other Trail Users: HIkers only

Canine Compatibility: Not dog friendly. Sharp rocks can slice dogs' feet.

Getting There

From Bend: Drive south on U.S. 97 from the intersection of Greenwood Avenue and U.S. 97 for 23.1 miles to a sign for Newberry Caldera National Monument and Paulina and East lakes. Turn left on Paulina Lake Road (FS 21) and drive 9.8 miles to the Big Obsidian Trailhead parking area on the right side of the road.

DeLorme: Oregon Atlas & Gazetteer: Page 45 C7

One of the main attractions at the 55,000-acre Newberry National Volcanic Monument is the Big Obsidian Flow Trail, which provides a fascinating tour of Oregon's youngest lava flow. The trail, which begins as a flat, paved path, offers panoramic views of the flow and includes interpretive signs along the way. The lava rock is very sharp, so be sure to wear sturdy shoes—*not sandals.*

After a short distance the path ascends a steep set of metal stairs and, at the top, arrives at the flow itself, a vast spread of gray pumice interspersed with shiny glass-like boulders of obsidian. Just past the stairs, the trail comes to a T-intersection. From here you can go right or left to begin

a 0.3-mile loop. The loop offers outstanding views of 7,984-foot Paulina Peak and the Paulina and East Lakes, located at the center of 500-square-mile Newberry Crater.

The 1,300-year-old flow, which covers 1.1 square miles and has an average thickness of 150 feet, began as extremely hot magma (up to 1,600 degrees Fahrenheit) trapped by the earth's crust two to four miles underground. The magma eventually found weak points in the earth's surface and a violent eruption ensued. Later, as the eruption slowed, the sticky magma began oozing out of the earth and crawling over the landscape.

MilesDirections

0.0 START on the paved path by the parking area.

0.1 Ascend a set of metal stairs to the lava flow.

0.2 Arrive at a junction. Turn right to begin the loop portion of the trail.

0.5 Turn right (this is the end of the loop).

0.7 Arrive back at the parking area.

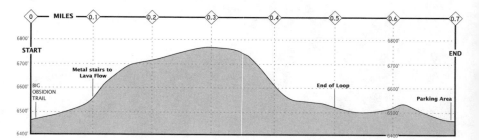

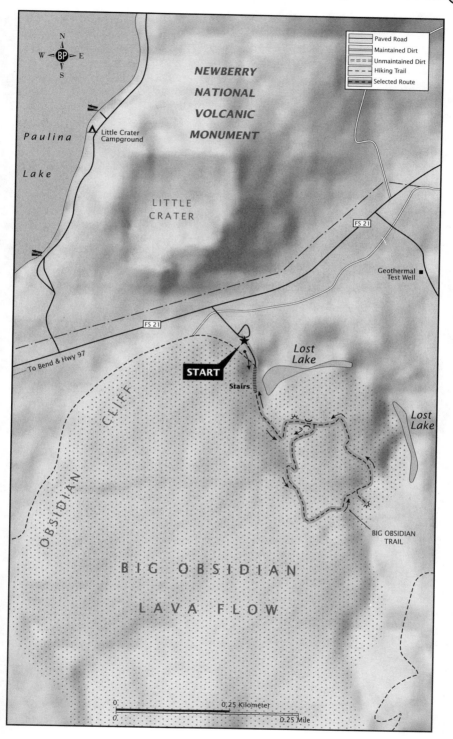

Paved Road
Maintained Dirt
Unmaintained Dirt
Hiking Trail
Selected Route

NEWBERRY
NATIONAL
VOLCANIC
MONUMENT

N
W · BP · E
S

Paulina
Lake

△ Little Crater
Campground

LITTLE
CRATER

FS 21

Geothermal
Test Well

FS 21

To Bend & Hwy 97

★
START

Stairs

Lost
Lake

Lost
Lake

O
B
S
I
D
I
A
N
·
·
C
L
I
F
F

BIG OBSIDIAN
TRAIL

BIG   OBSIDIAN

LAVA   FLOW

0   0.25 Kilometer
0   0.25 Mile

One of the more interesting features of the present-day rough and jumbled flow is the glass-like obsidian found on its surface. Due to the way obsidian is formed (through rapid cooling of the lava), it is very hard and extremely sharp. These properties were highly valued by Native Americans, who called the rock *isukws* (pronounced "eshookwsh"). They made arrowheads, knives, jewelry, ornaments, sculptures, ceremonial objects, and tools out of the obsidian to trade with other tribes for fish, shells, and roots. Artifacts dating back 10,000 years have been found in the monument and surrounding areas. You can read about these relics of the past as you walk the trail.

Hike Information

● Trail Contacts:
Newberry National Volcanic Monument, Bend-Fort Rock Ranger District, Bend, OR (541) 388–5664 or *www.fs.fed.us/r6/ deschutes/monument/ monument.html*

● Schedule:
Open June through October

● Fees/Permits:
Requires a Northwest Forest $5 day pass or $30 annual pass. You can purchase a pass online at: *www.fs.fed.us/r6/feedemo* or by call calling 1–800–270–7504.

● Local Information:
Bend Chamber of Commerce, Bend, OR 1–800–905–2363 or *www.bendchamber.org*

● Local Events/Attractions:
High Desert Museum, Bend, OR (541) 382–4754 *www. highdesert.org* · Cascade Festival of Music, Bend, OR (541) 382–8381 or *www.cascademusic.org*

● Accommodations:
[See Hike 32: South Sister]

● Restaurants:
Deschutes Brewery & Public House, Bend, OR (541) 382–9242 · East Lake Resort, La Pine, OR (541) 536–2230 · Paulina Lake Resort, La Pine, OR (541) 536–2240

● Hike Tours:
Wanderlust Tours, Bend, OR (541) 389–8359 or *www.wanderlusttours. com*

● Local Outdoor Retailers:
G.I. Joe's, Inc., Bend, OR (541) 388–3773

● Maps:
USGS maps: East Lake, OR · USFS maps: Deschutes National Forest

Smith Rock

Hike Summary

The main hiking trail through 623-acre Smith Rock State Park descends into a canyon carved by the Crooked River before climbing steeply to the top of Staender Ridge on a dirt road. From the top of the ridge a dirt trail swings around to the backside of the park's magnificent, multicolored cliffs, home to peregrine falcons and other raptors. It then drops back down to the canyon floor to complete a scenic loop.

Hike Specs

Start: From the trailhead adjacent to the self-pay station at the north end of Smith Rock's main parking area

Length: 8.4-mile loop

Approximate Hiking Time: 4–5 hours

Difficulty Rating: Difficult due to a very steep ascent up Staender Ridge, rock scrambling, and an unstable trail surface

Trail Surface: Dirt path with some loose and crumbly rocks; some rock scrambling

Lay of the Land: Millions of years of volcanic activity and the erosive power of the Crooked River have worked to form the park's jagged canyon walls and dihedrals.

Elevation Gain: 1,541 feet

Land Status: State park

Nearest Town: Terrebonne, OR

Other Trail Users: Equestrians and cyclists

Canine Compatibility: Leashed dogs permitted

Getting There

From Redmond: Take U.S. 97 north seven miles to the small town of Terrebonne. At the flashing yellow light in Terrebonne, turn right (east) on B Avenue, which becomes Smith Rock Way after the first stop sign. Follow the signs for 2.5 miles to Smith Rock State Park and continue to the trailhead at the self-pay station at the north end of the main parking area. *DeLorme: Oregon Atlas & Gazetteer: Page 51 A7*

Watch out for rattlesnakes. Smith Rock State Park is full of them. Also, if you bring along your dog, check it for ticks when you're through hiking.

S mith Rock State Park, nestled in the heart of the Central Oregon farming and ranching community of Terrebonne, is one of those places you just have to see if given the chance.

The sightseeing begins in the main parking area. You'll see climbers sorting through their gear and chatting about the routes they've planned for the day. You'll also see families, photographers, mountain bikers, hikers, and dogs (keep yours on a leash or you'll be slapped with a $65 fine). Before you even leave your

car, you'll enjoy spectacular views of the park's colorful 400-foot-tall cliffs. These volcanic masterpieces started to take shape in the Miocene period, nearly 17 to 19 million years ago, when hot steam and ash spewed from the

ground. Traces of basalt can be found from the Newberry Volcano eruption 1.2 million years ago that formed Paulina and East Lakes [see Hikes 33 and 34]. Since this volcanic activity, the Crooked River has eroded the rock to form the columnar shapes that you see in the upper gorge today.

The main trail through the park, an eight-mile highlight reel of the area's major attractions, begins with a steep, rocky descent to the canyon floor. Want to snap a photo? Stop at the maintained overlook, and while you're at it, read about the park's geologic history on the interpretive sign.

Upon reaching the canyon floor, the path crosses a bridge, turns right, and parallels the Crooked River. Along this stretch of the trail watch for Canadian geese, whose striking white throat patch and black head and neck make them easy to spot. The geese feed on the riverside vegetation and are apt to honk in alarm as you approach. Also keep an eye out for porcupines, but don't go too close if you see one. These animals have hundreds of loosely attached quills on their back and tail and when provoked aren't afraid to use them.

Peregrine Falcons

Peregrines are the high-speed flyers of the raptor world. With their sharp, pointed wings they can dive up to 275 miles per hour. In addition to their stunning speed and agility, peregrines have remarkably keen eyes. Their eyesight is eight times sharper than ours, and two times that of a golden eagle's. They can spot a bird up to five miles away. The peregrines feed primarily off of small- to medium-size birds which they carefully pick from the air. The flocks of pigeons that nest in the park are a favorite meal of the resident clan of peregrines.

After following the Crooked River for 1.4 miles on relatively flat terrain, the trail turns to climb Staender Ridge. Atop of the ridge are spectacular views of Black Butte, the Three Sisters, Mount Jefferson, and the sage- and juniper-covered landscape of Central Oregon. Here, too, wildlife is abundant. Perhaps most intriguing are the peregrine falcons [see Sidebar]. They nest high up on the cliff faces and are protected by climbing restrictions during the nesting season.

Eventually the trail arrives at an excellent view of Monkey Face, a 350-foot-tall volcanic monolith with multiple climbing routes and an enormous cave. Look for climbers clinging to the wall's features as they attempt to reach the summit. From here it's a steep 0.9-mile descent back to the Crooked River and the canyon floor. The trail then continues another 3.1 miles back to the parking area.

Hike Information

☏ Trail Contacts:
Smith Rock State Park, Redmond, OR (541) 548–7501 or *http://ohwy.com/or/s/smithrck.htm* · **Oregon State Parks and Recreation Department,** Salem, OR 1–800–551–6949 or *www.prd.state.or.us*

◷ Schedule:
Open year round

⑤ Fees/Permits:
$3 day-use fee and $4 camping fee

❓ Local Information:
Redmond Chamber of Commerce, Redmond, OR (541) 923–5191 or *www.redmondcofc.com*

💡 Local Events/Attractions:
Deschutes County Fair, in July, Redmond, OR (541) 548–2711 · **Walk the Art Beat,** in July, Redmond, OR (541) 923–5191

🛌 Accommodations:
Redmond Super 8 Motel, Redmond, OR 1–800–800–8000 · **Smith Rock Bivouac Area** (walk-in camping only), Smith Rock State Park 1–800–551–6949 or *www.prd.state.or.u* · **Skull Hollow Campground,** Crooked River National Grassland (541) 475–9272

🍴 Restaurants:
La Siesta Mexican Restaurant, Terrebonne, OR (541) 548–4848 · **Seventh Street Brew House,** Redmond, OR (541) 923–1795 – *Sample Redmond's own micro-brewed beers.*

✏ Other Resources:
Climber's Guide to Smith Rock by Alan Watts – *available at Redpoint Climbers Supply*

⛏ Local Outdoor Retailers:
The Big R, Redmond, OR (541) 548–4095 · **Redpoint Climbers Supply,** Terrebonne, OR (541) 923–6207 or 1–800–923–6207 or *www.crag.com/store/redpoint.html*

Ⓝ Maps:
USGS maps: Gray Butte, OR; O'Neil, OR; Redmond, OR · **USFS maps:** Ochoco National Forest; Crooked River National Grassland

MilesDirections

0.0 START at the trailhead adjacent to the self-pay station at the north end of the main parking area. Follow the paved path to a T-intersection and turn right.

0.1 The paved path ends. Pass an interpretive sign and viewpoint on your right. Soon, the trail forks. Stay right and take the steep trail to the canyon floor.

0.4 Arrive at a collection of picnic tables and a drinking fountain—your last chance for water. Follow a bridge across the Crooked River and arrive at a three-way junction. Turn right and follow the dirt path along the river.

0.8 Walk beneath a huge ponderosa pine. There's a bench here if you need a rest.

1.2 Cross a talus slope.

1.4 Turn left and follow the trail as it winds up a small canyon. *[FYI. There are many side trails that lead off the main trail to different climbing areas.]*

1.5 Arrive at an intersection with Burma Road. Turn left and follow the road up the North Bank Canal to the top of Staender Ridge.

2.0 Go around a green gate.

2.7 Arrive at the top of Staender Ridge and a three-way junction. This is a good place to take a breather and enjoy a panoramic view of the Three Sisters Mountains, Black Butte, Mount Jefferson, and the other Central Cascade

peaks to the west. When you've had your fill, turn left and continue along the ridge. *[FYI. If you go right you'll intersect with the Gray Butte Trail, and if you go straight you'll follow a doubletrack road that leads you into Sherwood Canyon.]*

2.9 Arrive at three-way junction. Turn right.

4.0 Arrive at a trail junction. Stay to the right. *[FYI. If you go left, you'll hook up with the Misery Ridge Trail.]*

4.1 The trail forks. Go left.

4.2 The trail forks again. Go left.

4.3 The trail becomes very rough and requires a bit of scrambling over rocks. Look for yellow ribbons that mark the way—and watch for rattlesnakes. The trail cuts across a ridge and then begins a steep descent.

4.4 The trail comes to a T-intersection. To the left is the 350-foot rock tower called Monkey Face. Turn right and descend a series of switchbacks on a well-maintained trail to the canyon floor.

5.3 Arrive at a junction. Turn left.

7.4 Descend a series of steps.

7.6 Pass a restroom on your left. Check out the climbers ascending the cliff walls.

8.0 Turn right and cross the Crooked River via a wooden footbridge. Begin the steep ascent back up the ridge to the main parking area.

8.4 Arrive at the main parking area.

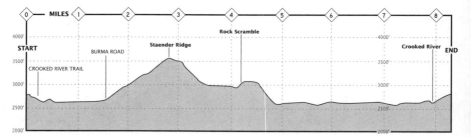

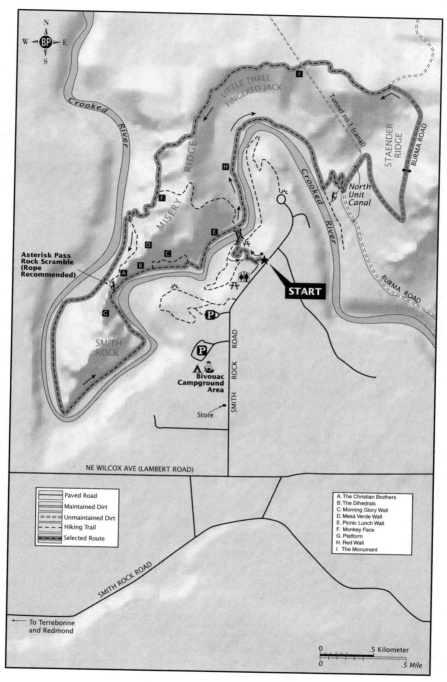

Asterisk Pass Rock Scramble (Rope Recommended)

START

SMITH ROCK

MISERY RIDGE

LITTLE THREE FINGERED JACK

STAENDER RIDGE

BURMA ROAD

Crooked River

Tunnel no.1 (canal)

North Unit Canal

BURMA ROAD

Bivouac Campground Area

SMITH ROCK ROAD

Store

NE WILCOX AVE (LAMBERT ROAD)

SMITH ROCK ROAD

To Terrebonne and Redmond

Paved Road
Maintained Dirt
Unmaintained Dirt
Hiking Trail
Selected Route

A. The Christian Brothers
B. The Dihedrals
C. Morning Glory Wall
D. Mesa Verde Wall
E. Picnic Lunch Wall
F. Monkey Face
G. Platform
H. Red Wall
I. The Monument

0   .5 Kilometer
0   .5 Mile

243

Steins Pillar

Hike Summary

If peace and solitude are what you need, this uncrowded trail through the heart of Central Oregon's Ochoco National Forest is your answer. The trail starts out fairly flat as it winds its way through a Douglas fir and ponderosa pine forest. It then descends an open high-desert ridge covered with juniper and sagebrush, eventually arriving at the base of 350-foot-tall Steins Pillar. The hike can be completed in a couple hours and is a great introduction to the diverse landscapes present in this part of the state.

Hike Specs

Start: From the Steins Pillar trailhead off FS 500

Length: 5.2-mile out-and-back

Approximate Hiking Time: 2 hours

Difficulty Rating: Moderate due to some short hill climbs and moderate descents

Trail Surface: Dirt path

Lay of the Land: Hike through a Douglas fir and ponderosa pine forest, along a ridge of juniper and sagebrush, and down a steep series of log stairs to the base of Steins Pillar.

Elevation Gain: 1,268 feet

Land Status: National forest

Nearest Town: Prineville, OR

Other Trail Users: Equestrians and cyclists

Canine Compatibility: Dog friendly

Getting There

From Prineville: Drive 9.1 miles east on U.S. 26 and turn left (north) on to Mill Creek Road (FS 33)—this road turns to gravel after 5.2 miles. Drive 6.7 miles on Mill Creek Road and turn right on FS 500. Drive 2.1 miles to the trailhead on the left side of the road. Primitive camping is available at the trailhead, but there are no restroom facilities or running water. *DeLorme: Oregon Atlas & Gazetteer:* Page 80 C2

Steins Pillar is a fascinating rock formation located in the heart of the Ochoco National Forest in the Ochoco Mountains. The 350-foot pillar is an important geologic remnant of the area's rich volcanic history.

Nearly 50 million years ago this was volcano land. Eruptions layered the area in volcanic tuff, andesite, and ash. The Clarno and John Day formations, world famous for their many fossils remains, were created as a result of these eruptions. James Condon, a young Congregational minister and naturalist, first discovered fossils in the area in the 1860s. His first find was an ancient tortoise shell in Picture Gorge in the John Day Valley. Over the next several years, Condon

Steins Pillar.

245

and others uncovered many more plant and animal fossils. This became the precursor to research and cataloging of hundreds of specimens in the area over the next century. Examples of fossils that have been discovered include amynodonts and brontotheres of the Clarno Formation period (37 to 54 million years ago) and dogs, cats, camels, oreodonts, swine, rhinoceroses, and rodents of the John Day Formation period (20 to 39 million years ago).

A great way to get a feel for the geologic history of the area is by hiking the moderate 2.6-mile trail to the base of Steins Pillar. The trail starts out fairly flat through a dry, open forest of Douglas fir trees and then transitions into an open rocky landscape filled with sagebrush and Western juniper trees. The small, fragrant, bluish berries of the juniper are a favorite food of small birds and other small mammals. In the spring and summer wildflowers are scattered along the trail—bright-red Indian paintbrush, bluish-purple lupine, and bright-yellow mule's ears are just a few of the varieties you'll see.

After 1.2 miles, the trail begins to descend the ridge and the landscape shifts back to Douglas fir and ponderosa pine. Tree debris scattered on the forest floor along this section of trail appears to be the result of an old burn and frequent winter storms. Another mile up the trail you'll catch your first glimpse of Steins Pillar, as it rises prominently above the Mill Creek Valley and Steins Ranch. To reach the base of the pillar, descend a long series of steps for the remaining 0.3 miles. While at the pillar's base, look up to see why rock

MilesDirections

0.0 START the trail at the wooden trailhead sign that indicates "Steins Pillar," adjacent to the parking area. You have the option of filling out a visitor registration card at the trailhead.

0.3 The trail starts ascending a ridge.

1.2 The trail begins descending the other side of the ridge.

1.6 Walk through what appears to be an old burn area. Branches and debris cover the forest floor.

2.3 Reach a rocky outcrop and viewpoint of Steins Pillar on your left.

2.4 Descend a series of log steps.

2.6 Walk down more log steps and reach the base of Steins Pillar, your turnaround point. From this vantage point you have views of the Steins Ranch below you and the Mill Creek Valley. Turn around and retrace your route back.

5.2 Arrive back at the trailhead.

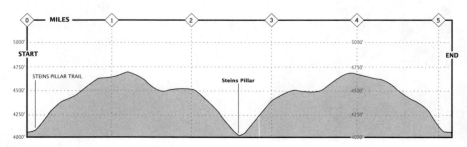

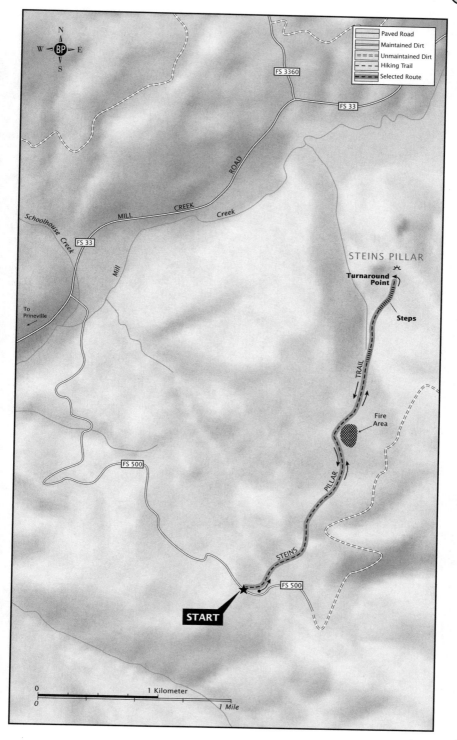

Paved Road
Maintained Dirt
Unmaintained Dirt
Hiking Trail
Selected Route

N
W BP E
S

FS 3360

FS 33

ROAD

MILL CREEK Creek

Schoolhouse Creek

FS 33

Mill

STEINS PILLAR

Turnaround
Point

To
Prineville

Steps

TRAIL

Fire
Area

FS 500

PILLAR

STEINS

FS 500

START

0   1 Kilometer
0   1 Mile

Steins Pillar Trail.

climbers find it such a tempting challenge. The pillar was first climbed in 1950. A 5.11A route heads up the northeast face and a 5.10D climb shoots up the southeast face. These climbs are very difficult and some of the pitches are overhanging and cross over sections of crumbly, rotten rock.

Hike Information

⏱ Trail Contacts:
Ochoco National Forest, Prineville, OR (541) 416–6500 or www.fs.fed.us/r6/ochoco

🕐 Schedule:
May through October

❓ Local Information:
Prineville Chamber of Commerce, Prineville, OR (541) 447–6304 · **Eastern Oregon Visitor's Association,** Baker City, OR 1–800–523–1235 or www.eova.com

💡 Local Events/Attractions:
Crooked River Rodeo, in June, Prineville, OR (541) 447–4479 · **High Desert Celtic Celebration,** in August, Prineville, OR (541) 447–3561 or users.bendnet.com/celtic · **Old-fashioned Fourth of July Celebration,** Prineville, OR (541) 447–6307 · **Rockhounds Association Powwow,** in June, Prineville, OR (541) 548–7477 · **AR Bowman Museum,** Prineville, OR (541) 447–3715

🛏 Accommodations:
Best Western, Prineville, OR (541) 447–8080 · **Carolina Motel,** Prineville, OR (541) 447–4152 · **Ochoco Inn,** Prineville, OR (541) 447–6231 or www.ochocoinn.com

· **Wildcat Campground,** northeast of Prineville – *To get there from Prineville, drive 9.1 miles east on U.S. 26 to Mill Creek Road (FS 33). Turn left (north) and drive 10.6 miles (the road turns to gravel after 5.2 miles) to a fork. Veer right following the sign to Wildcat Campground. Drive another 0.3 miles to the campground entrance. Campsites are $8 per night. There are primitive campsites at the trailhead, but there are no water or restroom facilities.*

🍴 Restaurants:
Cinnabar Restaurant, Prineville, OR (541) 447–3880

🏪 Local Outdoor Retailers:
Prineville Sporting Goods, Prineville, OR (541) 447–6883

🗺 Maps:
USGS maps: Salt Butte, OR; Steins Pillar, OR · **USFS maps:** Ochoco National Forest; Crooked River National Grassland

Twin Pillars

Hike Summary

The first three miles of this hike, a beautiful and peaceful walk through the Mill Creek Wilderness, includes wildlife, wildflowers, and a meandering stream. The remaining portion of the trail traverses a ponderosa pine forest interspersed with grassy meadows before arriving at the base of Twin Pillars, the eroded remnant of a volcano that erupted 40 to 50 million years ago.

Hike Specs

Start: From the trailhead parking area off Mill Creek Road (FS 33)

Length: 10.6-mile out-and-back

Approximate Hiking Time: 5–7 hours

Difficulty Rating: Easy for first three miles along Mill Creek; difficult for final 2.3 miles due to a very steep ascent up a series of switchbacks to the base of Twin Pillars

Trail Surface: Dirt path with loose and crumbly rock near the base of Twin Pillars and numerous stream crossings

Lay of the Land: Forested valley filled with ponderosa pines, wildflowers, and the meandering Mill Creek

Elevation Gain: 1,944 feet

Land Status: National forest and wilderness area

Nearest Town: Prineville, OR

Other Trail Users: Equestrians

Canine Compatibility: Dog friendly

Getting There

From Prineville: Drive 9.1 miles east on U.S. 26 to Mill Creek Road (FS 33). Turn left (north) and drive 10.6 miles to a fork in the road. Turn right at the sign for Wildcat Campground. Drive 0.1 miles and turn right into a gravel parking area at the trailhead. Wildcat Campground is another 0.3 miles past the parking area. *DeLorme: Oregon Atlas & Gazetteer:* Page 80 B2

L ocated in the 17,000-acre Mill Creek Wilderness of Ochoco National Forest, the Twin Pillars Trail is a 10.6-mile out-and-back path along bubbling Mill Creek. The route passes through a forest of ponderosa pine, grand fir, and Douglas fir; and up a steep ridge to the base of Twin Pillars—the double-spiked rock formation that constitutes the trail's namesake.

The trail begins with a series of creek crossings, so be sure to bring an old pair of tennis shoes or sandals to wear in the water. As you walk along the creek you'll hear the cries of kingfishers protesting your presence on their home turf. Other birds in the area include pileated woodpeckers, wild turkeys, and Northern goshawks. Pileated woodpeckers are the largest species of woodpecker and can be identified by their prominent red crests,

Twin Pillars.

black feathers, and white undersides. Northern goshawks, which weigh between six and eight pounds and live up to 10 years, have slate-gray feathers and bright orange-red eyes outlined in white. You'll most likely see them weaving in and out of the woodlands with great speed and finesse as they hunt for small birds and mammals. If you don't first see a Northern goshawk, you may hear its distinctive "ca-ca-ca" hunting cry. Other wildlife in this pristine wilderness area include Rocky Mountain elk, mule deer, bobcats, cougars, and black bears.

MilesDirections

0.0 START at the trailhead for Twin Pillars Trail 380.

0.1 Cross Mill Creek Road (FS 33) and continue straight.

0.2 Proceed through a green metal gate and enter the Mill Creek Wilderness.

0.3 Wade across Mill Creek. After the creek the trail forks. Turn left.

0.8 Cross the creek.

0.9 Cross the creek.

1.1 Navigate another stream crossing.

1.2 Cross the creek. Proceed approximately 100 yards and cross again.

1.5 Cross the creek.

2.1 The trail forks. Turn left and continue along the main trail.

2.2 Arrive at another stream crossing. Logs are in place to help you cross. Walk another 50 yards and cross the stream again.

2.4 Cross the creek and arrive at a trail junction. Belknap Trail (Trail 832A) veers right. Ignore it and stay to the left.

2.5 Pass a sign on the left that reads, "Twin Pillars 2 miles."

2.7 Cross the creek on a log bridge.

2.9 The trail climbs steeply then veers away from the creek.

3.1 Cross Brogran Creek.

3.4 Enjoy a view of the Twin Pillars rock formation.

3.6 Cross a side creek.

4.0 Cross a very small side creek. As you hike this section, you'll pass by open slopes of tall bunch grass filled with purple aster, Indian paintbrush, and wild iris.

5.1 Turn right at the trail junction and scramble up a steep rock-strewn slope to the base of the pillars.

5.3 Arrive at the base of Twin Pillars and your turnaround point. Enjoy a scenic view of the surrounding Ochoco Mountains.

10.6 Arrive back at the trailhead.

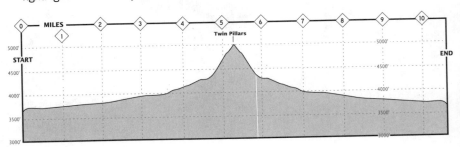

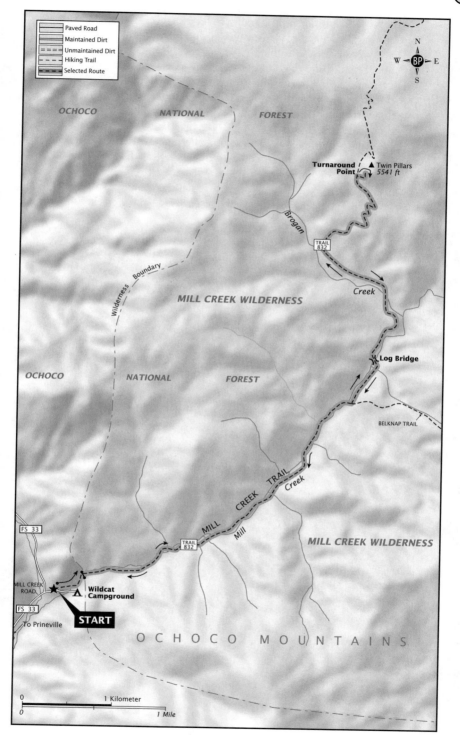

Legend:
- Paved Road
- Maintained Dirt
- Unmaintained Dirt
- Hiking Trail
- Selected Route

OCHOCO NATIONAL FOREST

Turnaround Point

▲ Twin Pillars
5541 ft

TRAIL 832

Brogan

Creek

MILL CREEK WILDERNESS

Wilderness Boundary

OCHOCO NATIONAL FOREST

Log Bridge

BELKNAP TRAIL

MILL CREEK TRAIL

Creek

Mill

MILL CREEK WILDERNESS

TRAIL 832

FS 33

MILL CREEK ROAD

▲ Wildcat Campground

FS 33

To Prineville

START

OCHOCO MOUNTAINS

0   1 Kilometer
0   1 Mile

As you continue on the trail, you'll pass green meadows of daises, delicate purple aster, crimson penstemon, and bright purple thistle. Tall stocks of woolly mullein with their bright bunches of yellow flowers are also common. Shimmering green aspen trees grow in clusters along the banks of the creek and cutthroat trout hang out in shady rock pools.

Three miles from the trailhead, the path turns away from Mill Creek and climbs steeply in a series of long and winding switchbacks for two miles up a ridge to the base of the 200-foot-tall Twin Pillars rock formation. Towering stands of Douglas fir and ponderosa pine grace the slopes of this ridge; below, wildflowers sprinkle open meadows with splashes of color.

Due to the length of this hike, you may want to complete the trail as an overnight backpack. There are many potential camping spots overlooking Mill Creek. Once you set up camp you can wade in the creek, fish for trout,

or just relax. The following day a light daypack is all you'll need for the remaining climb to the pillars' base. If you don't want to backpack, complete the trail in a day then pitch your tent at Wildcat Campground. The camping area is located just 0.3 miles northeast of the trailhead and sites cost $8 per night.

Hike Information

🌐 Trail Contact:
Ochoco National Forest, Prineville, OR (541) 416–6500 or *www.fs.fed.us/r6/ochoco*

🕐 Schedule:
May through October are the best months

❓ Local Information:
Prineville Chamber of Commerce, Prineville, OR (541) 447–6304 · **Eastern Oregon Visitor's Association,** Baker City, OR 1–800–523–1235 or *www.eova.com*

💡 Local Events/Attractions:
Crooked River Rodeo, in June, Prineville, OR (541) 447–4479 · **High Desert Celtic Celebration,** in August, Prineville, OR (541) 447–3561 or *users.bendnet.com/celtic* · **Old-fashioned Fourth of July Celebration,** Prineville, OR (541) 447–6307 · **Rockhounds Association Powwow,** in June, Prineville, OR (541) 548–7477 · **AR Bowman Museum,** Prineville, OR (541) 447–3715

🛏 Accommodations:
Best Western, Prineville, OR (541) 447–8080 · **Carolina Motel,** Prineville, OR (541) 447–4152 · **Ochoco Inn,** Prineville, OR (541) 447–6231 or *www.ochocoinn.com* · **Wildcat Campground,** northeast of Prineville – *To get there from Prineville, drive 9.1 miles east on U.S. 26 to Mill Creek Road (FS 33). Turn left (north) and drive 10.6 miles (the road turns to gravel after 5.2 miles) to a fork. Veer right following the sign to Wildcat Campground. Drive another 0.3 miles to the campground entrance. Campsites are $8 per night. There are primitive campsites at the trailhead, but there are no water or restroom facilities.*

🍴 Restaurants:
Cinnabar Restaurant, Prineville, OR (541) 447–3880

🏪 Local Outdoor Retailers:
Prineville Sporting Goods, Prineville, OR (541) 447–6883

🗺 Maps:
USGS maps: Steins Pillar, OR · **USFS maps:** Ochoco National Forest; Crooked River National Grasslands

Honorable Mentions

Central Oregon

Compiled here is an index of great hikes in Central Oregon that didn't make the A-list this time around but deserve recognition. Check them out and let us know what you think. You may decide that one or more of these hikes deserves higher status in future editions or, perhaps, you may have a hike of your own that merits some attention.

(30) Hackleman Creek Old-Growth Trail

Hackleman Creek Old-Growth Trail is an easy, self-guided 0.8-mile interpretive loop. On this hike you stroll through old-growth stands of Douglas fir, Western red cedar, and mountain hemlock. Pick up a brochure at the trailhead before beginning the hike to learn about the complexities of an old-growth forest. The trail is kid-friendly and wheelchair accessible. In order to park at the trailhead, you'll need a $5 Northwest Forest Pass—available at *www.fs.fed.us/r6/feedemo* or by calling 1–800–270–7504.

To get there from the junction of OR 228 and U.S. 20 in Sweet Home, drive east on U.S. 20 approximately 42 miles to the trailhead located on the right side of the road. For more information, contact the Sweet Home Ranger District, Sweet Home, OR; (541) 367–5168; *www.fs.fed.us/r6/willamette/contents.htm*. **DeLorme: Oregon Atlas & Gazetteer:** Page 49 A8

(31) Iron Mountain

The 3.4-mile out-and-back Iron Mountain Trail takes you to the upper slopes of Iron Mountain. Plant lovers will enjoy the over 300 species of flowering plants; keep in mind that peak blooming season is in July. Begin from the lower trailhead parking area and at mile 0.75 cross U.S. 20. Shortly thereafter is a trail intersection; stay to the left and you'll reach the Upper Trailhead parking area. Continue on the Iron Mountain Cutoff Trail as it switchbacks up the side of Iron Mountain. At the next junction, stay to the right (the left fork leads to Cone Peak) until you reach the exposed summit at mile 1.7, your turnaround point.

To get there from Sweet Home, drive 35 miles east on U.S. 20 to its junction with FS 15. Turn right on FS 15 and drive 0.2 miles to a parking area on the right. In order to park at this trailhead, you'll need a $5 Northwest Forest Pass—available at *www.fs.fed.us/r6/feedemo* or by calling 1–800–270–7504. For more information, contact the Sweet Home Ranger District, Sweet Home, OR; (541) 367–5168; *www.fs.fed.us/r6/willamette/contents.htm*. **DeLorme: Oregon Atlas & Gazetteer:** Page 49 A7

㉜ McKenzie River National Recreational Trail

The 26.4-mile McKenzie River National Recreational Trail twists and turns along the banks of the crystal-clear McKenzie River. Along this trail you walk through old-growth forest, past deep lava pools, and along cascading waterfalls.

To reach the lower trailhead, drive 50 miles east of Eugene on the McKenzie Highway (OR 126) to a marked trailhead on the left (north) side of the road, not far past McKenzie Bridge. In order to park at any McKenzie River trailhead, you'll need a $5 Northwest Forest Pass—available at www.fs.fed.us/r6/feedemo or by calling 1–800–270–7504. For more information, contact the Willamette National Forest, McKenzie Ranger District, McKenzie Bridge, OR; (541) 822–3381; *www.fs.fed.us/r6/willamette*. *DeLorme: Oregon Atlas & Gazetteer:* Page 49 C7

㉝ French Pete Creek

This 3.2-mile out-and-back trail meanders along bubbling French Pete Creek through an ancient grove of Douglas fir trees. Simply follow the trail for 1.6 miles to your turnaround point at a bridge.

To get there, drive five miles east of Blue River on OR 126. Turn right (south) on FS 19. Drive 0.4 miles, turn right, and continue driving another 11 miles on FS 19 to the trailhead on the left side of the road. In order to park at this trailhead, you'll need a $5 Northwest Forest Pass—available at www.fs.fed.us/r6/feedemo or by calling 1–800–270–7504. For more information, contact the Blue River Ranger District, Blue River, OR; (541) 822–3317; *www.fs.fed.us/r6/willamette*. *DeLorme: Oregon Atlas & Gazetteer:* Page 49 D7

㉞ Erma Bell Lakes

This moderate 8.0-mile loop travels past the high alpine Erma Bell Lakes, Williams Lake, and Otter Lake in the Three Sisters Wilderness. You begin walking through a predominantly Douglas fir forest. At 0.6 miles you come to the Otter Lake junction; stay to the right. At mile 1.7, you pass Lower Erma Bell Lake, and over the next mile, you pass Middle and Upper Erma Bell lakes. If you're backpacking into this area, camp at designated sites at the Erma Bell Lakes. At mile 3.3, you come to the Taylor Burn junction. Turn left. At the 4.0-mile mark you come to another trail junction; turn left and proceed 0.4 miles to Williams Lake. Continue on the trail to Otter Lake and a trail intersection. Stay to the left and then proceed to the Erma Bell Lakes Trail. Turn right and head back to your car. A wilderness permit is required for day hikes and overnight trips.

To get there from, McKenzie Bridge, drive south on FS 19 for 27 miles. Turn left on FS 1957 and drive 3.7 miles to the trailhead, located at the end of the road in Skookum Campground. For more information, contact the Willamette National Forest, Middle Fork Ranger District, Oakridge, OR; (541) 782–2283; *www.fs.fed.us/r6/willamette*. **DeLorme: Oregon Atlas & Gazetteer:** Page 43 A8

㉟ Wall Creek Warm Springs

This 0.6-mile out-and-back jaunt takes you to a rocky pool filled with bubbling hot springs on Wall Creek.

To get there from Eugene, drive 40 miles southeast to the town of Oakridge. In Oakridge, head for the city center and turn right on East 1st Street, which turns into Salmon Creek Road (FS 24). Drive nine miles on this road to the intersection with a gravel road where a sign reads "Blair Lake." Turn left on the gravel road and drive 0.4 miles to a parking area on the left side of the road (indicated by a hiker sign). Willamette National Forest, Middle Fork Ranger District, Oakridge, OR; (541) 782–2283; *www.fs.fed.us/r6/willamette*. **DeLorme: Oregon Atlas & Gazetteer:** Page 43 B6

㊱ The Twins

This moderate 6.6-mile hike is located in the Waldo Lake Wilderness and cuts through an open pine forest for 1.5 miles before intersecting with the Pacific Crest Trail. Continue straight and at mile 3.3 you reach the crater rim and the 7,360-foot summit of The Twins cinder cone, where you'll enjoy a spectacular view of Waldo Lake and Diamond Peak. You'll need a wilderness permit to hike in this area, and in order to park at the trailhead, you'll need a $5 Northwest Forest Pass—available at *www.fs.fed.us/r6/feedemo* or by calling 1–800–270–7504.

To get there from Willamette Pass, drive west on OR 58 for three miles to Waldo Lake Road (FS 5897). Turn right (north) on Waldo Lake Road and drive about six miles to the trailhead (following the signs to Waldo Lake Campground). For more information, contact the Willamette National Forest, Middle Fork Ranger District, Oakridge, OR; (541) 782–2283; *www.fs.fed.us/r6/willamette*. *DeLorme: Oregon Atlas & Gazetteer:* Page 43 C8

37 McCredie Hot Springs

A short-and-sweet 150-foot path leads you to the soaking pools of McCredie Hot Springs. These popular hot springs are located on Salt Creek, where the water temperatures hover between 95 and 105 degrees. Be forewarned that the atmosphere here is round-the-clock raucous; don't come here expecting a quiet soak—except possibly in the very early morning hours.

To get there from Eugene, drive southeast on OR 58 for 50.5 miles to a pullout on the right side of the road. This pullout is located about a half mile beyond the Blue Pool Campground. Follow the trail upstream to the hot springs. For more information, contact the Willamette National Forest, Middle Fork Ranger District, Oakridge, OR; (541) 782–2283; *www.fs.fed.us/r6/willamette*. *DeLorme: Oregon Atlas & Gazetteer:* Page 43 C6

38 Jefferson Park

This difficult 11.4-mile round trip takes you through the high alpine country of Jefferson Park in the Mount Jefferson Wilderness. It's highly recommended that you complete this hike as an overnight backpack so you can fully explore the area. Start the hike on the South Breitenbush Trail, located above the South Breitenbush River. The climb is steep and scenic and will give your quads a workout. After 1.7 miles, you come to The Bear Point Trail junction. Stay to the right and follow the trail as it ascends through a fir forest, past picturesque meadows. Your turnaround point is at 5.7 miles—the junction with the Pacific Crest Trail. A wilderness permit is required for day hikes and overnight trips, and in order to park at this trailhead, you'll need a $5 Northwest Forest Pass—available at *www.fs.fed.us/r6/feedemo* or by calling 1–800–270–7504.

To get there from Detroit, drive east on FS 46 for 11 miles to the junction with FS 4685. Turn right on FS 4685 and drive four miles to the trailhead parking area. For more information, contact Detroit Ranger District, Mill City, OR; (503) 854–3366; *www.fs.fed.us/r6/willamette*. *DeLorme: Oregon Atlas & Gazetteer:* Page 56 C1

39 Pamelia Lake/Grizzly Peak

This area of the Jefferson Wilderness is wild and beautiful, but it's also teeming with people. This 10.4-mile hike begins with a stroll through a mossy-green old-growth forest paralleling the boulder-strewn Pamelia

Creek; you reach Pamelia Lake in two miles. From the lake, follow signs toward Grizzly Peak. Over the next few miles there are gorgeous views of Pamelia Lake and Mount Jefferson. The only drawback to this area is the hordes of people that come during June, July, and August. So many people, in fact, that overnight access is restricted. Call ahead for permit information. If you're planning on backpacking, try to visit the area in mid to late September when the summer crowds are gone. In order to park at this trailhead, you'll need a $5 Northwest Forest Pass—available at *www.fs.fed.us/r6/feedemo* or by calling 1–800–270–7504. Other trail options here include a northern route to Jefferson Park or a southern route to Hunts Cove.

To get there from Sisters, drive west on U.S. 20 for 27 miles to its junction with U.S. 22. Turn right and drive for 20 miles to Pamelia Road (FS 2246). Turn right and drive four miles (the road turns to gravel after three miles) to the trailhead. This is a limited access trail; obtain a limited-entry permit and at the Detroit Ranger Station. For more information, contact the Detroit Ranger District, Mill City, OR; (503) 854–3366; *www.fs.fed.us/r6/willamette*. *DeLorme: Oregon Atlas & Gazetteer:* Page 56 C2

40 Canyon Creek Meadows Loop

This 5.8-mile loop trail takes you through spectacular wildflower meadows with stunning views of Three Fingered Jack's craggy spires. Start this

hike at the wooden trailhead sign adjacent to the parking area. Free wilderness permits are required and are self-issue at the trailhead. From the trailhead sign, take the trail that goes to the right toward "Canyon Creek Meadows." At 0.1 miles, you pass scenic Jack Lake on your left. At mile 0.3, you come to a trail junction; turn left toward Canyon Creek. After 1.7 miles, cross a small creek and come to a fork. Turn left and cross a log bridge over a creek. After 2.5 miles, reach a basin filled with a grassy meadow and colorful wildflowers. To the northeast you have a grand view of Three Fingered Jack; this is your turnaround point. A wilderness permit is required for day hikes and overnight trips, and in order to park at this trailhead, you'll need a $5 Northwest Forest Pass—available at *www.fs.fed.us/r6/feedemo* or by calling 1–800–270–7504.

To get there from Sisters, drive west on U.S. 20 for 12 miles to Jack Lake Road (FS 12). Turn right on Jack Lake Road (FS 12) and drive 4.3 miles to the junction with FS 1230. Turn left on FS 1230, drive 1.7 miles, and then turn left again (the road turns to gravel here) on FS 1234, following the signs toward Jack Lake. Drive 0.7 miles. Stay to the left when the road comes to a fork. Proceed another 5.2 miles on FS 1234 to Jack Lake and the trailhead. (The road becomes very rough and wash-boarded along this last section.) Deschutes National Forest, Sisters Ranger District, Sisters, OR; (541) 549–7700; *www.fs.fed.us/r6/deschutes/sisters/sisters.html. DeLorme: Oregon Atlas & Gazetteer*: Page 50 A2

41 Four-In-One Cone

This difficult 9.0-mile trek begins at the Scott Trailhead just off OR 242 in the Three Sisters Wilderness. You hike uphill for about four miles past jumbled lava flow rocks to a 0.25-mile spur trail that leads to the fascinating viewpoint of Four-In-One Cone—four cinder cones clustered together. This overlook also provides close-up views of North Sister and other prominent Central Cascade peaks. You have the option of continuing on the main trail for another mile to the intersection with the Pacific Crest Trail—this will lead you through more spectacular Three Sisters Wilderness backcountry. A wilderness permit is required for day hikes and overnight trips, and in order to park at this trailhead, you'll need a $5 Northwest Forest Pass—available at www.fs.fed.us/r6/feedemo or by calling 1–800–270–7504.

To get there from Eugene, drive east on OR 126 for approximately 55 miles to the junction with OR 242. Turn right (east) on OR 242 and drive about 10 miles to the intersection with the Scott Lake turnoff, on the left. The trail starts on the south side of the road. Please be aware that OR 242 is closed in the winter and sometimes doesn't open until late June. For more information, contact the Willamette National Forest, McKenzie Ranger District, McKenzie Bridge, OR; (541) 822–3381; *www.fs.fed.us/r6/willamette. DeLorme: Oregon Atlas & Gazetteer*: Page 50 C2

42 Camp Lake

The 14.0-mile out-and-back Camp Lake Trail is a strenuous yet spectacular trek through the Three Sisters Wilderness, providing first-rate views of the Three Sisters Mountains. This hike is best experienced as an overnight backpack trip, but energetic hikers can also complete this trail in a day. Begin at the Pole Creek Trailhead. At the first trail junction stay to the left (a trail leading to the right goes toward Matthieu Lakes). At the next trail junction, stay to the right (if you go left you'll be heading toward Green Lakes). At the third trail junction continue straight until you reach Camp Lake; that is your turnaround point. A wilderness permit is required for day hikes and overnight trips, and in order to park at this trailhead, you'll need a $5 Northwest Forest Pass—available at *www.fs.fed.us/r6/feedemo* or by calling 1–800–270–7504.

To get there from Sisters, drive west on OR 242 for 1.5 miles to the intersection with FS 15. Turn left on FS 15 and drive approximately 10.5 miles, following signs for Pole Creek Trailhead. For more information, contact the Deschutes National Forest, Sisters Ranger District, Sisters, OR; (541) 549–7700; *www.fs.fed.us/r6/deschutes/sisters/sisters.html*. **DeLorme: Oregon Atlas & Gazetteer:** Page 50 C3.

43 Broken Top Trail to Green Lakes

The difficult 11.4-mile Broken Top Trail rewards the tenacious hiker with a nice view of the jagged spires of 9,175-foot Broken Top. The trail meanders through open forest and meadows. After about the first mile you also get views of the south slopes of Broken Top. At mile 1.8, you come to

an intersection with the Soda Creek Trail; continue straight. At this point you pass by Cayuse Crater, and before long, you catch sight of South Sister. At mile 4.5, the trail intersects the Green Lakes Trail; this is your turnaround point. A wilderness permit is required for day hikes and overnight trips, and in order to park at this trailhead, you'll need a $5 Northwest Forest Pass—available at *www.fs.fed. us/r6/feedemo* or by calling 1–800–270–7504.

To get there from just outside of Bend, drive west on the Cascade Lakes Highway (a.k.a. OR 46 or Century Dive Highway) for 26 miles. Turn right at the sign for Todd Lake onto FS 370. Travel 4.2 miles on this very rough road to the intersection with FS 380. Turn left and continue 1.4 miles to the road's end and the trailhead. For more information, contact the Bend-Fort Rock Ranger District, Bend, OR; (541) 383–4000; *www.fs.fed.us/r6/deschutes*. **DeLorme: Oregon Atlas & Gazetteer:** Page 50 D3

44 Park Meadow

This moderate 9.8-mile hike takes you to open alpine meadows in the Three Sisters Wilderness with fantastic views of the knife-edge summit of 9,175-foot Broken Top. You reach Park Meadow after approximately 4.9 miles; this is the turnaround point. A wilderness permit is required for day hikes and overnight trips, and in order to park at this trailhead, you'll need a $5 Northwest Forest Pass—available at *www.fs.fed.us/r6/feedemo* or by calling 1–800–270–7504.

To get there from Sisters, drive south on Three Creek Road (FS 16) for approximately 14 miles to the trailhead. For more information, contact the Deschutes National Forest, Sisters Ranger District, Sisters, OR; (541) 549–7700; *www.fs.fed.us/r6/deschutes/sisters/sisters.html*. **DeLorme: Oregon Atlas & Gazetteer:** Page 50 D3

45 Three Sisters Loop

The Three Sisters Loop is a splendid backpack tour around the magnificent Three Sisters Mountains in the wilderness area of the same name. This loop travels about 43 miles and can easily be completed in four days. It begins at the Lava Lakes Trailhead off OR 242 (McKenzie Pass Highway). On this loop trail you follow the Pacific Crest Trail as it heads southwest past South Matthieu Lake, Yapoah Crater, Collier Cone, Glacier Creek, and the Obsidian area. Along the first half of this loop, there are many opportunities to gaze at the spectacular Three Sisters Mountains. After about 20 miles, turn left and hook up with the Moraine Lake Trail and follow it to Moraine Lake—which you'll reach that in about another 1.7 miles. From Moraine Lake, follow the trail east for another mile to Fall Creek—stay to the left. After another two miles heading northwest, you hook up with the Green Lakes Trail, at which point you pass through the Green Lakes Basin. Three miles later you find yourself at Park Meadow, an open grassy alpine meadow with superb views of Broken Top. From Park Meadow, turn left on the Pole Creek Trail (which heads north) and after about 31 miles you cross the south fork of Squaw Creek. Continue heading north and cross the north fork of Squaw Creek and Alder Creek. When you reach the Scott Trail junction—at about 38.7 miles—turn left (west). Follow this trail to the top of Scott Pass and the intersection with the Pacific Crest Trail. Turn right on the Pacific Crest Trail and continue straight until you hook back up with the Lava

Camp Trail; there you'll turn right and reach your car in another 0.2 miles.

There are many trail intersections on this loop trail, and it's highly recommended that you obtain a Three Sisters Wilderness map (available from the Sisters Ranger Station) before heading out. You'll also need a wilderness permit to hike in the Three Sisters Wilderness. Call ahead for information about obtaining an overnight permit. In order to park at this trailhead, you'll need a $5 Northwest Forest Pass—available at *www.fs.fed.us/r6/feedemo* or by calling 1–800–270–7504.

To get there from Sisters, drive 11 miles west on OR 242 (The McKenzie Highway) to the gravel road junction with signs to Lava Camp Lake. Turn left and drive about a half mile to the Pacific Crest Trail parking area, located on the right side of the road. Note that OR 242 is closed in the winter and is sometimes not open until late June. For more information, contact the Deschutes National Forest, Sisters Ranger District, Sisters, OR; (541) 549–7700; *www.fs.fed.us/r6/deschutes/sisters/sisters.html.* **DeLorme: Oregon Atlas & Gazetteer:** Page 49 A7

46 Obsidian/Sunshine Meadow Loop

This difficult 12.0-mile loop trail takes you through open and forested lava country in the Three Sisters Wilderness. The route passes through Sunshine Meadows, a high alpine meadow filled with bright-purple lupine. Here the trail hooks up with a loop that takes you past Obsidian Falls, back up Obsidian Trail, and back to your starting point. Along the way are gorgeous views of the Three Sisters Mountains. Many hikers climb to the top of Middle Sister from this trailhead. The area is very popular and it's recommended that you complete this loop as a long day hike and not as an overnight trip. A wilderness permit is required for day hikes and overnight trips. In order to park at this trailhead, you'll need a $5 Northwest Forest Pass—available at *www.fs.fed.us/r6/feedemo* or by calling 1–800–270–7504. We also recommend that you purchase a Three Sisters Wilderness map for a detailed profile of the trails in this area.

To get there from Eugene, drive east on OR 242 (The McKenzie Highway) for 55 miles to its junction with OR 242. Drive six miles east on OR 242 to the Obsidian Trailhead sign on the right side of the road. Note that OR 242 is closed during the winter months and is sometimes not open until mid June. For more information, contact the Willamette National Forest, McKenzie Ranger District, McKenzie Bridge, OR; (541) 822–3381; *www.fs.fed.us/r6/willamette.* **DeLorme: Oregon Atlas & Gazetteer:** Page 50 C1

47 Deschutes River to Benham Falls

This easy 17.0-mile out-and-back trail takes you along the shores of the moody Deschutes River. While at times it can be meandering and lazy, it can very quickly become roaring rapids over sharp lava ledges and falls. On this trail you follow the shores of the river 8.5 miles to Benham Falls, your turnaround point. Note that this trail is also popular with mountain bikers, so be on the lookout for bikes racing past. You may also want to complete this hike as a car shuttle. In order to park at this trailhead, you'll need a $5 Northwest Forest Pass—available at *www.fs.fed.us/r6/feedemo* or by calling 1–800–270–7504.

To get to the trailhead from Bend, drive west on the Cascade Lakes Highway (a.k.a. Century Drive Highway) for about six miles, toward Mount Bachelor. Turn left at a sign indicating "Meadow Picnic Area." Proceed to the trailhead at the end of the road. To leave a car at Benham Falls, follow U.S. 97 south of Bend and take the Lava Butte exit. Turn right into the Lava Lands Visitor Center and proceed on FS 9702 to the Benham Falls trailhead. For more information, contact the Bend-Fort Rock Ranger District, Bend, OR; (541) 383–4000; *www.fs.fed.us/r6/deschutes.* **DeLorme: Oregon Atlas & Gazetteer:** Page 45 A6

48 Gray Butte

The 5.6-mile Gray Butte Trail takes you on a tour of the high desert landscape of the Crooked River National Grasslands. This trail takes you around the base of 5,108-foot Gray Butte through a landscape of sagebrush and juniper. As you're walking on this trail, keep an eye out for a green gate at mile 0.9; you'll need to pass through it. At mile 2.8, you arrive at a T-intersection, your

turnaround point. You have the option of continuing on the trail and exploring Smith Rock State Park [see Hike 35].

To get there from Redmond, drive north on U.S. 97 for 4.5 miles to the small town of Terrebonne. At the flashing yellow light in Terrebonne, turn right (east) on B Avenue. After a short distance B Avenue turns into Smith Rock Way. Drive 4.9 miles on Smith Rock Way to Lone Pine Road and turn left. Drive 4.4 miles to FS 5710 and turn left—you'll pass Skull Hollow Campground on your left. Follow FS 5710 as it winds up Skull Hollow Canyon for 2.6 miles to a road intersection. Turn left on FS 57. Drive 0.6 miles to a gravel pullout on the left side of the road and the trailhead. For more information, contact the Ochoco National Forest, Prineville, OR; (541) 416–6500; *www.fs.fed.us/r6/ochoco/welcome.html.* **DeLorme: Oregon Atlas & Gazetteer:** Page 51 A7

Northeast

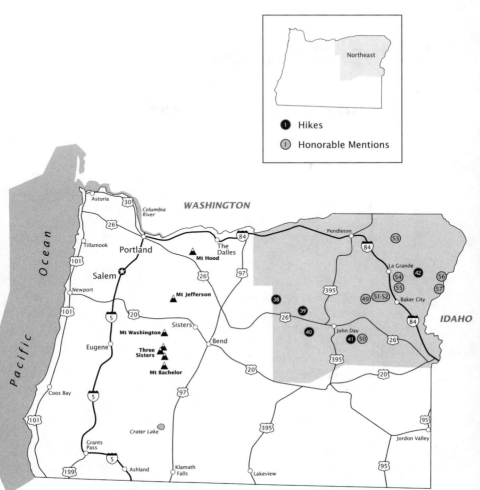

Oregon

Northeast Oregon

Northeastern Oregon has a rich pioneer history and is dotted with farms, ranches, imposing mountain ranges, deep river gorges, and picturesque canyons filled with fossilized treasures. The rugged country is bordered by the Wallowa Mountains and Hells Canyon, which, at over one mile deep, is the deepest canyon in North America.

First stop in this wide-open country should be the Sheep Rock Unit of the John Day Fossil Beds National Monument, located about 19 miles northwest of Dayville off Oregon 19. Here you can examine fossilized evidence of the prehistoric life that roamed the hills and valleys of the John Day area over 40 million years ago. For a good introduction to this national treasure, stop by the Sheep Rock Unit Visitor Center, two miles northwest of the intersection of U.S. Route 26 and Oregon 19. After touring the visitor center, try hiking the short Islands in Time Trail, which winds through an intricately carved canyon embedded with fossils.

Don't miss the Painted Hills Unit of the John Day Fossil Beds. This spot is filled with color-splashed hills that vary from red and pink to bronze and tan—occasionally even black. Several trails wander through the Painted Hills Unit, located 47 miles northeast of Prineville and 10 miles northwest of Mitchell off U.S. Route 26.

The Wallowa Mountains in the far northeast corner of Oregon contain some of Oregon's highest peaks. These jagged granite peaks resemble California's Sierra Nevada Mountains and contain hundreds of miles of trails to high alpine lakes and glacier-carved meadows. These peaks are part of the Eagle Cap Wilderness, just south of the small towns of Lostine, Enterprise, and Joseph off Oregon 82. Lakes Basin is one popular destination; to see this unique area you can backpack into the lakes and take a very long day hike on the Lakes Basin Trail. This difficult 20-mile trail leads you along the east fork of the Lostine River, through a spectacular glacial valley, and then loops through the scenic Lakes Basin at the base of 9,595-foot Eagle Cap.

The Blue Mountains and the Strawberry Mountains are part of the immense 1,460,000-acre Malheur National Forest, a rolling expanse of ponderosa pine, lodgepole pine, and a variety of firs. To see the Blue Mountains up close and personal, try hiking from Anthony Lake to Dutch Flat Lake. This 10-mile trail passes through ponderosa pine, lodgepole pine, spruce, and larch forests on its way to alpine meadows at the top.

You can take a jaunt to two high alpine lakes in the Strawberry Mountain Wilderness on the Strawberry Lakes hike. This seven-mile out-and-back takes you past Strawberry Lake and Strawberry Falls. Prairie City, located on U.S. Route 26, is one major access point into this area.

Of course, Hells Canyon is a must. The Snake River has been hard at work over the past two million years carving out the deepest river gorge in North America (over a mile deep). It flows swiftly through the canyon past high cliffs, grassy plateaus, ancient petroglyphs, lava flows, and serves as the dividing line between Oregon and Washington. If you want to get down into the canyon, try the 14-mile McGraw Creek Loop, which parallels the mighty Snake River and McGraw Creek. Keep in mind, however, that the temperatures in Hells Canyon vary by as much as 30 degrees from the canyon's rim to the canyon floor, rising as you descend. During the summer months, temperatures in the 70s on the rim may translate to temperatures in the 90s—sometimes topping 100 degrees—on the floor. Heat stroke is a big concern on trails in the canyon, so always carry at least a gallon of water per person per day (or carry a water filter). In addition, the trails in the canyon are isolated, rough, and poorly maintained. Other concerns include black bears and rattlesnakes. They don't call it Hells Canyon for nothing.

38

Painted Hills Unit
(John Day Fossil Beds N.M.)

Hike Summary

The short hikes in the Painted Hills Unit of the John Day Fossil Beds National Monument provide a close-up look at the area's beautiful color-splashed hills and fascinating fossil beds. The Painted Hills Overlook Trail is a one-mile out-and-back affair that takes you to the top of an overlook with views of the colorful surrounding hills. If you want more of an adventure, trek 1.5 miles to the top of Carroll Rim where you'll have a sweeping view of the painted hills and surrounding high-desert country. If you want to see one of these hills up close, stroll the quarter-mile Painted Cove Trail. To view fossils of plants that dominated this area 33 million years ago, walk the Leaf Hill Trail. It's possible to complete all four of the established trails in just a day.

Hike Specs

Start: From the Carol Rim parking area off Bear Creek Road

Length:
- A. *Carroll Rim Trail*—1.5-mile out-and-back
- B. *Painted Hills Overlook Trail*—1.0-mile out-and-back
- C. *Painted Cove Trail*—0.25-mile loop
- D. *Leaf Hill Trail*—0.25-mile loop

Approximate Hiking Time: 30–90 min.

Difficulty Rating: *Painted Hills Overlook*, *Painted Cove*, and *Leaf Hill* trails are easy due to the well-maintained trail surfaces and flat terrain. *Carroll Rim Trail* is moderate due to a steep climb up Carroll Rim.

Trail Surface: Graded dirt path, paved trail, and wooden ramp

Lay of the Land: The trails in the Painted Hills Unit are a part of the lower John Day Formation, which consists of a series of brightly colored hills and fossil beds.

Land Status: National monument

Nearest Town: Mitchell, OR

Other Trail Users: Hikers only

Canine Compatibility: Dog friendly

Getting There

From Prineville: Drive 40.5 miles east on U.S. 26 and turn left (north) on to Burnt Ranch Road at the "John Day Fossil Beds National Monument–Painted Hills Unit" sign. Proceed 5.5 miles and turn left on Bear Creek Road. Drive 0.3 miles to a road junction and stay right. (To the left is a day-use area with restrooms, picnic tables, and water.) Drive 0.8 miles to the Carroll Rim parking area, on the left. This trailhead gives you access to the *Painted Hills Overlook Trail* and the *Carroll Rim Trail*. The *Carroll Rim Trail* begins on the opposite side of the road from the parking area. Follow the road signs to reach the *Painted Cove Trail* and *Leaf Hill Trail*. **DeLorme: Oregon Atlas & Gazetteer:** Page 80 B3

The Painted Hills Unit of the John Day Fossil Beds National Monument has several hikes offering glimpses of the area's rich geologic history. The hikes are easy to moderately difficult and each provides a different perspective on the unique formations in this national monument.

The most striking feature you'll notice are the round, multicolored hills of colorful claystone. Thirty million years ago, layers of ash were deposited in this area from volcanoes erupting to the west. Over millions of years, the forces of nature have carved and shaped the hills that you see today. Different elements such as aluminum, silicon, iron, magnesium, manganese, sodium, calcium, titanium, and others have combined to produce minerals that have unique properties and colors.

271

MilesDirections

A. Carroll Rim Trail – 1.5-mile out-and-back trek to the top of Carroll Rim that offers sweeping views of the surrounding hills and valleys.

B. Painted Hills Overlook Trail – 1.0-mile out-and-back path with a panoramic view of the Painted Hills.

C. Painted Cove Trail – 0.25-mile loop that circles a painted hill and gives you a close up look at the unique properties that make up these interesting geologic formations.

D. Leaf Hill Trailhead – 0.25-mile loop that circles a hill where ancient plant fossils are abundant.

To get a bird's-eye view of these interesting hills, take a short jaunt on the 1.0-mile out-and-back *Painted Hills Overlook Trail*, which takes you up a gentle ridge and includes several viewpoints along the way. If you want a close-up view of one of these unique painted hills, take a walk on the 0.25-mile *Painted Cove Trail* loop. A brochure and corresponding trail markers offer an in-depth look at these geologic formations. For instance, the colors of the hills change with the weather. When it rains the clay absorbs water, causing more light reflection and changing the color of the hills from red to pink and from light brown to yellow-gold. As the hills dry out, the soil contracts, causing surface cracking that diffuses the light and makes the color of the hills deepen. The purple layer in the hill is the weathered remains of a rhyolite lava flow. Other colored bands in the hillside are due to differences in mineral content and weathering. Plants can't grow on the painted hills because the clay is so dense that moisture can't penetrate the surface. Also, the clay soil is nutritionally poor.

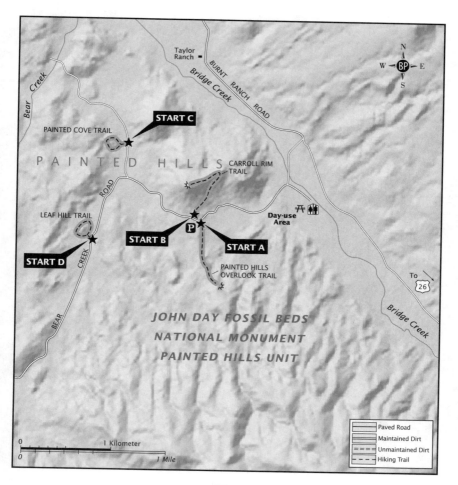

Another distinguishing landmark of the Painted Hills Unit is Carroll Rim, a high ridge consisting of John Day ignimbrite, better known as "welded tuff." More than 28 million years ago, a volcano to the west erupted and hurled hot ash, debris, and gases into the air, which then landed and cooled to form a glass-like layer. To reach the top of this landmark and excellent views of the surrounding hills and valleys, hike the 1.5-mile out-and-back up the *Carroll Rim Trail*. From the top you'll be able to see Sutton Mountain, which rises prominently to the east.

For fossils, check out the 0.25-mile-long *Leaf Hill Trail* and its collection of ancient plants. The trail circles a small hill of loose shale deposits. While at first the hill seems somewhat unremarkable, a closer look reveals secrets to the plants that once dominated here. The shales present in this hill were formed about 33 million years ago from lake-deposited volcanic ash. Thirty-five species of plants can be found at Laurel Hill with alder, beech, maple, and the extinct hornbeam most prevalent. Other specimens include elm,

rose, oak, grape, fern, redwood, and pine. Scientists have analyzed these plant fossils and concluded that this group of plants closely resembles two types of modern forests found in China—the mixed northern hardwood forest and the mixed mesophytic forest. Comparing the mix of plant species to these two modern forests indicates that this area had a much higher rainfall content (up to 40 inches), milder temperatures, and a warmer climate than the found here today. (Today the area receives about 12 to 15 inches of rain a year and experiences more extreme temperature variations.) In addition, the vegetation that grows here today is made up of high-desert-type plants—juniper, sagebrush, and grasses.

Hike Information

◐ Trail Contacts:
John Day Fossil Beds National Monument, Kimberly, OR (541) 987–2333 or *www.nps.gov/joda*

◑ Schedule:
Open year round

❓ Local Information:
Prineville Chamber of Commerce, Prineville, OR (541) 447–6304 · **Eastern Oregon Visitor's Association**, Baker City, OR 1–800–523–1235 or *www.eova. com*

◕ Local Events/Attractions:
Crooked River Rodeo, in June, Prineville, OR (541) 447–4479 · **High Desert Celtic Celebration**, in August, Prineville, OR (541) 447–3561 or http://users.bend-net. com/celtic · **Old-fashioned Fourth of July Celebration**, Prineville, OR (541) 447–6307 · **Rockhounds Association Powwow**, in June, Prineville, OR (541) 548–7477 · **AR Bowman Museum**, Prineville, OR (541) 447–3715

● Accommodations:
Best Western, Prineville, OR (541) 447–8080 · **Carolina Motel,** Prineville, OR (541) 447–4152 · **Ochoco Inn,** Prineville, OR (541) 447–6231 or *www.ochocoinn.com* · **Wildcat Campground,** northeast of Prineville – *To get there from Prineville, drive 9.1 miles east on U.S. 26 to Mill Creek Road (FS 33). Turn left (north) and drive 10.6 miles (the road turns to gravel after 5.2 miles) to a fork. Veer right following the sign to Wildcat Campground. Drive another 0.3 miles to the campground entrance. Campsites are $8 per night. There are primitive campsites at the trailhead, but there are no water or restroom facilities.*

ⓘ Restaurants:
Cinnabar Restaurant, Prineville, OR (541) 447–3880

ⓖ Local Outdoor Retailers:
Prineville Sporting Goods, Prineville, OR (541) 447–6883

ⓝ Maps:
USGS maps: Painted Hills, OR

Island in Time
(John Day Fossil Beds — Sheep Rock Unit)

Hike Summary

The Island in Time Trail leads you on a beautiful tour through a desert canyon filled with intricate rock terraces and high cliff walls that have been molded and shaped by wind and water. Interpretive signs posted along the trail describe different ancient fossils and offer interesting details about what the region's climate and landscape were like over 30 million years ago.

Hike Specs

Start: From the Blue Basin trailhead off OR 19
Length: 1.4-mile out-and-back
Approximate Hiking Time: 1 hour
Difficulty Rating: Easy due to the gentle grade
Trail Surface: Graded dirt path
Lay of the Land: Walk up a gentle grade through an intricately terraced canyon.
Elevation Gain: 450 feet
Land Status: National monument
Nearest Town: Dayville, OR
Other Trail Users: Hikers only
Canine Compatibility: Dogs permitted

Getting There

From Dayville: Drive 6.6 miles west on U.S. 26. At the junction with OR 19, turn right and drive 5.1 miles (you'll pass the Sheep Rock Unit Visitor Center after two miles) to the Blue Basin trailhead and parking area on the right side of the road. There are restrooms and interpretive signs at the trailhead. *DeLorme: Oregon Atlas & Gazetteer:* Page 81 B6

> Be sure to bring water on this trail. It can be very hot in the summer months.

Two paths can be accessed from the Blue Basin trailhead: the Blue Basin Overlook Trail and the Island in Time Trail. The 0.7-mile Island in Time Trail, recommended here, is located in the Sheep Rock Unit of the John Day Fossil Beds National Monument and highlights some of the species that roamed the area's hills and valleys more than 30 million years ago. The Sheep Rock Unit is one of three units in the national monument that cover a total of 14,000 acres—the other two units are Clarno, located 18 miles west of Fossil off Oregon 218; and Painted Hills, found nine miles northwest of Mitchell off U.S. Route 26. Established in 1975, this vast preserve offers a glimpse at the plants and animals that lived between the extinction of the dinosaurs and the Ice Age.

Before you embark on the Island in Time Trail, or any trail in the national monument, stop by the park's visitor center, located two miles northwest of the intersection of U.S. Route 26 and Oregon 19. It offers a good intro-

duction to the area and contains informative displays about the monument's fossils and the history of the John Day Valley. It also sells books and brochures and includes restrooms, water, and a shaded picnic area with superb views of Sheep Rock.

Hike Information

Trail Contacts:
John Day Fossil Beds National Monument, Kimberly, OR (541) 987–2333 or *www.nps.gov/joda*

Schedule:
Open year round

Fees/Permits:
No admission fees. Donations accepted at the visitor center.

Local Information:
Grant County Chamber of Commerce, John Day, OR 1–800–769–5664 or *www.grantcounty.cc*

Local Events/Attractions:
Dayville Fourth of July Celebration, Dayville, OR (541) 987–2375

Accommodations:
Fish House Inn B&B, Dayville, OR (541) 987–2124 or *www.grantcounty.cc/business/ dayville/fishhouse/index.htm*

Local Outdoor Retailers:
Dayville Mercantile, Dayville, OR (541) 987–2133 or *www.dayvillemerc.com*

Maps:
USGS maps: Picture Gorge East, OR; Picture Gorge West, OR

After soaking up the fun facts at the visitor center, proceed about three miles northwest on Oregon 19 to the Blue Basin trailhead and the start of the Island in Time Trail. According to an interpretive sign located just up the trail, the volcanic eruptions that occurred here millions of years ago covered the native plants and animals with wind-blown silt and washed them into ash-filled streams and ponds. Subsequent years of wind and rain have eroded the greenish clay rock in the basin to expose the fossils. The trail passes by several of these fossils, now enclosed in glass.

At mile 0.3, you can view a glass-encased fossil of an ancient tortoise, and at 0.4 miles you can gaze at the interesting fossil of an oreodont, a sheep-size leaf-eater that was abundant in this area. Lastly, you can see the fossil remains of a stabbing cat, which the park describes as a "saber-toothed cat" that preyed on "slow-moving and thick-skinned animals." What is especially interesting about these displays is that you are seeing the fossils as they were actually discovered in the greenish claystone rock.

If you're in the mood for a steeper, more challenging hike, try the Blue Basin Overlook Trail, a three-mile loop to a scenic vista overlooking the

MilesDirections

0.0 START at the large trailhead sign at the Blue Basin parking lot. Go right to begin the Island in Time Trail (the Blue Basin Overlook loop is to the left). Cross a bridge and pass an interpretive sign.

0.1 Pass a bench on your right.

0.2 Cross two wooden bridges and pass an interpretive sign on your right. An intersection with the Blue Basin Overlook Trail is on your right.

0.3 Cross two more bridges and arrive at an interpretive sign and bench on the right side of the trail. Next to the sign is a glass-enclosed fossil of an ancient tortoise. Continue past the fossil and cross three more bridges.

0.4 Cross two more bridges and ascend a set of stone steps. Arrive at an interpretive sign on your right and a glass-enclosed fossil of an oreodont.

0.5 Arrive at another interpretive sign and a stabbing cat fossil. Continue along the trail and cross a bridge.

0.7 Arrive at the end of the trail and the turnaround point.

1.4 Reach the Blue Basin parking lot and your car.

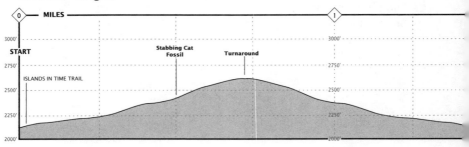

278

John Day River Valley. Still more trails, including the quarter-mile Flood of Fire Trail, which ascends a ridge for a view of the John Day Valley, and the Story in Stone Trail (wheelchair accessible), which features more fossils, can be found to the northwest in the national monument's Foree Area.

Fluidity of Place

"Our place is part of what we are. Yet even a 'place' has a kind of fluidity.... A place will have been grasslands, then conifers, then beech, and elm. It will have been half riverbed, it will have been scratched and plowed by ice. And then it will be cultivated, paved, sprayed, dammed, graded, built up. But each is only for a while, and that will be just another set of lines on the palimpsest. The whole earth is a great tablet holding the multiple overlaid new and ancient traces of the swirl of forces. Each place is its own place, forever (eventually) wild."

Gary Snyder, as recorded on a plaque on the Blue Basin Overlook Trail.

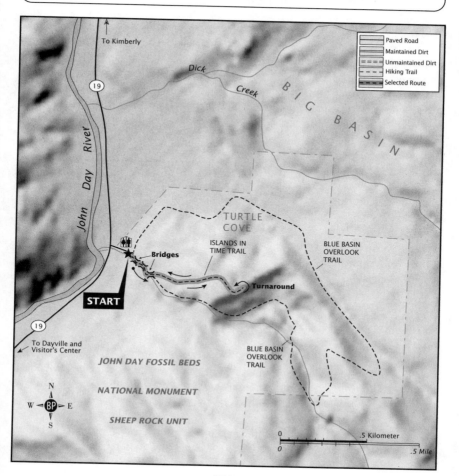

Black Canyon Trail

Hike Summary

The Black Canyon Trail takes you on a tour of the outback in the Black Canyon Wilderness. The trail follows Black Canyon Creek through a deep, rocky canyon filled with ponderosa pine and Douglas fir and numerous stream crossings. If you hike the trail during the mid summer months, don't miss the opportunity to feast on the wild red raspberries. If you are up for an adventure and want to get away from it all, backpack the entire 11.6-mile trail (and not just the 2.6 miles described below). Set up a shuttle by leaving a car at the Wolf Mountain trailhead.

Hike Specs

Start: From the Black Canyon Trailhead off South Fork John Day Road (FS 47)
Length: 5.2-mile out-and-back (11.6-mile shuttle option)
Approximate Hiking Time: 3–4 hours
Difficulty Rating: Difficult due to the many stream crossings and thick brush
Trail Surface: Rocky and uneven dirt path with multiple stream crossings and thick brush
Lay of the Land: Hike through heavy brush and ponderosa pine and fir forest along a deep, rocky canyon carved by Black Canyon Creek.
Elevation Gain: 670 feet
Land Status: Wilderness area
Nearest Town: Dayville, OR
Other Trail Users: Equestrians
Canine Compatibility: Dogs not permitted

Getting There

From Dayville: Drive south 0.5 miles on South Fork John Day Road (FS 47), from U.S. 26. Turn right and continue on South Fork John Day Road for another 13 miles until you reach a dirt pullout on the right side of the road. A sign reads "The Black Canyon Trailhead." *DeLorme: Oregon Atlas & Gazetteer:* Page 81 C6

> *This trail is infamous for its rattlesnakes, poison oak, and range cows. Wear long nylon pants and boots. Bring an extra pair of tennis shoes or sandals for the multiple stream crossings.*

The Black Canyon Trail cuts right through the heart of the 3,400-acre Black Canyon Wilderness. The area is a haven for more than 300 species of wildlife—black bear, elk, deer, cougar, rattlesnakes, and raptors to name a few. It's a true wilderness hike, guaranteed to make you feel like you're away from it all.

The trail is fraught with numerous stream crossings and lots of poison oak, so carry extra shoes and wear long pants to combat these obstacles.

Black Canyon Creek.

Also carry a sturdy walking stick in case you need to sweep a rattlesnake from your path. Check the trailhead for sticks used by previous hikers.

The first mile of trail leads through a thick layer of streamside plants, trees, and raspberry bushes. Begin by fording the South Fork of the John Day River. Cross the slippery rocks, using a walking stick for balance if you need it. In the spring months the river can be swift and high, so be careful. After the trail crosses the river it seems to disappear in a mass of streamside vegetation, but if you turn left and walk up the bank about 30 yards you'll find it again. In no time you become an expert at fording the creek. In just 2.6 miles, you'll get your feet wet 15 times. Tennis shoes (without socks) seem to work best for these crossings, but bring along a pair of sandals to wear during breaks.

Don't be surprised if you see range cows munching grass along the stream bank. Cows aren't supposed to be in the wilderness area, but the fence along the border is in disrepair. If you do see cows, by all means let the Forest Service know they're in the area so they can be safely returned back to their owners, the fences can be mended, and the wilderness can recuperate.

As the trail continues up the canyon it zigzags through thick brush and follows grassy ridges through a ponderosa pine, fir, and tamarack forest.

MilesDirections

0.0 START the hike at the Black Canyon Trailhead. *[**Note**. Be sure to grab a walking stick at the start. It'll help with stream crossings and brushing away an errant snake.]* Immediately cross the South Fork of the John Day River. This river can be very high in the spring months, but it's only usually calf deep beginning in July. After crossing the river, walk 30 feet to your left to hook up with the trail.

0.1 Cross Black Canyon Creek.

0.2 Cross the creek.

0.3 Navigate another stream crossing and then walk 25 yards and cross the creek again.

0.7 Cross the creek and walk 20 yards and cross the creek again.

0.9 Navigate another stream crossing.

1.0 Cross the creek three times.

1.2 Cross the creek.

1.3 Cross the creek again.

1.5 Cross the creek again.

1.9 Navigate another stream crossing.

2.4 Cross a side stream.

2.6 Cross a side stream and come to your turnaround point.

5.2 Arrive back at the trailhead.

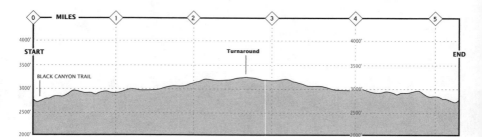

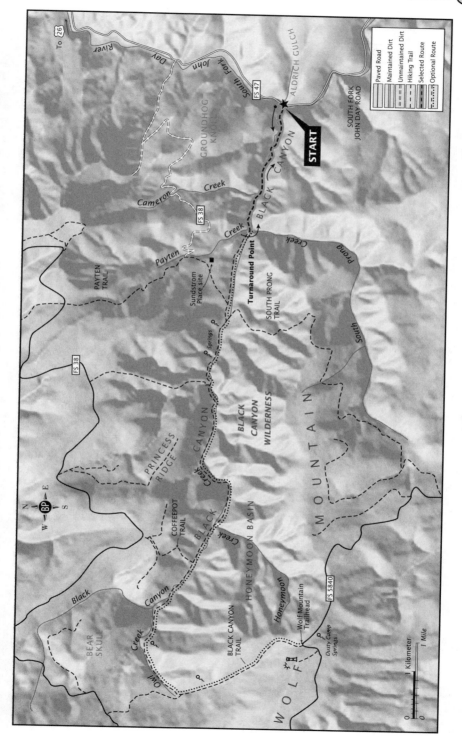

Black Canyon.

Interspersed amongst the tangles of bushes are sprinkles of crimson penstemon, bright-purple lupine, and vibrant Indian paintbrush. It's a beautiful place indeed.

If you want to complete the entire 11.6-mile trail through the canyon, you can set up a car shuttle. To get to the trailhead near Wolf Mountain, drive 14 miles west of Dayville (63 miles east of Prineville) on U.S. Route 26. Turn south on Forest Service Road 12 and drive 15.6 miles. Turn left on Forest Service Road 1250 and drive 3.9 miles to a road junction. Continue driving straight on Forest Service Road 090 for 3.6 miles. (The road becomes very rough here, but it's passable with a passenger car.) Turn left on Forest Service Road 5820 and drive 0.4 miles to a junction. Continue driving 2.5 miles on Forest Service Road 5840 to the trailhead.

Hike Information

🕐 Trail Contacts:
Ochoco National Forest, Paulina Ranger District, Paulina, OR (541) 477–3713

🕐 Schedule:
June through November

❓ Local Information:
Grant County Chamber of Commerce, John Day, OR 1–800–769–5664 or *www.grantcounty.cc*

📍 Local Events/Attractions:
Dayville Fourth of July Celebration, Dayville, OR (541) 987–2375

🛏 Accommodations:
Fish House Inn B&B, Dayville, OR (541) 987–2124 or *www.grantcounty.cc/business/dayville/fishhouse/index.htm*

🎒 Local Outdoor Retailers:
Dayville Mercantile, Dayville, OR (541) 987–2133 or *www.dayvillemerc.com*

🇳 Maps:
USGS maps: Wolf Mountain, OR; Aldrich Gulch, OR

Strawberry Lakes Trail

Hike Summary

This trail takes you on a tour of the scenic Strawberry Mountain Wilderness. Your tour begins at Strawberry Campground and takes you to a high glacial cirque that is the home to Strawberry Lake. The trail then leads you around the lake, taking you to the spectacular cascade of Strawberry Falls and ultimately to charming Little Strawberry Lake.

Hike Specs

Start: From the Strawberry Campground off CR 60

Length: 6.8-mile out-and-back

Approximate Hiking Time: 3–4 hours

Difficulty Rating: Moderate due to a challenging ascent to Strawberry and Little Strawberry lakes

Trail Surface: Well-maintained dirt trail with a switchback ascent

Lay of the Land: Hike through a thick fir forest to Strawberry Lake. Walk along the shore of the lake and then begins another ascent to scenic Strawberry Falls and Little Strawberry Lake.

Elevation Gain: 1,404 feet

Land Status: Wilderness area

Nearest Town: Prairie City, OR

Other Trail Users: Equestrians

Canine Compatibility: Leashed-dog friendly

Getting There

From Prairie City: Turn off U.S. 26 onto Bridge Street (CR 60) and head south. Drive approximately 11.5 miles to Strawberry Campground. (The road turns to gravel after 3.3. miles.) *DeLorme: Oregon Atlas & Gazetteer:* Page 82 C2

The vast Malheur National Forest, in the northeast corner of the state, encompasses nearly 1.5 million acres of the Blue Mountain Range, drawing together elevations from 4,000 to over 9,000 feet. Ponderosa and lodgepole pines and many different species of fir dominate the region's forests. The area supports five different eco-zones, and with that a diverse cast of animals—elk, mule deer, antelope, bighorn sheep, beaver, and pine marten. Among its notable raptors are the bald and golden eagles and sharp-shinned and red-tailed hawks.

Within Malheur National Forest is the 68,700-acre Strawberry Mountain Wilderness—characterized by its rugged, high-alpine country with lakes, jagged mountain peaks, and U-shaped glacial valleys. Old and young mountains make up the impressive peaks of the Strawberry Range. More than 200 million years ago, when the North America continent drifted westward, it pushed up a large section of the Pacific seafloor, creating the

western half of the Strawberry Range. The eastern half, created only 16 million years ago, took form when lava erupted from vents and spread east from John Day to Unity.

Strawberry Mountain, the forest's tallest point and star attraction, is the remnant of a much larger stratovolcano that once existed here. Nathan Wills Fisk, one of the area's first settlers, gave the 9,025-foot mountain its name because of the abundance of wild strawberries found in the area.

More than 100 miles of trail runs through the Strawberry Mountain Wilderness. Trail 375 offers a good introduction to the trail network and to

Strawberry Lake.

MilesDirections

0.0 START from the Strawberry Lakes campground at the Trail 375 trailhead. Voluntary registration cards are available at the trailhead.

1.0 Comes to a fork and go right. (Left goes to Slide Lake.)

1.3 Come to a T-intersection. Turn right toward Strawberry Lake. (Left goes to Slide Lake.)

1.4 Reach Strawberry Lake and come to a trail junction. Turn right and cross a log bridge over Strawberry Creek, and then start to follow the trail as it parallels Strawberry Lake.

2.0 Cross a log footbridge and then cross another log bridge.

2.1 Cross another log footbridge over a creek.

2.2 Cross two more bridges.

2.3 Come to a trail junction. Turn right toward Little Strawberry Lake. Walk a short ways and then come to another trail junction. Stay to the right.

2.4 Cross a log footbridge over a creek.

2.8 Reach Strawberry Falls.

3.0 Turn left toward Little Strawberry Lake.

3.4 Arrive at Little Strawberry Lake and your turnaround point. Return to the trailhead.

6.8 Arrive back at the trailhead.

Hike Information

Trail Contacts:
Prairie City Ranger District, Prairie City, OR (541) 820–3800 or *www.fs.fed.us/r6/malheur*

Schedule:
June through October

Local Information:
Eastern Oregon Visitor Association, Baker City, OR 1–800–332–1843 or *www.eova.org*

Local Events/Attractions:
Grant County 4th of July Celebration, Prairie City, OR (541) 820–3605

Accommodations:
Strawberry Mountain Inn, Prairie City, OR 1–800–545–6913 or *www.strawberrymountaininn.com*
• **Strawberry Campground,** Prairie City Ranger District, Prairie City, OR (541) 820–3800

Restaurants:
The Bakery, Prairie City, OR (541) 820–3674

Maps:
USGS maps:
Strawberry Mountain, OR

this unique wilderness. The route begins at Strawberry Lakes Campground in an aromatic fir forest and travels 1.4 miles to Strawberry Lake. It then loops around the lake, past shimmering groves of aspen trees, and follows a creek through thick forest for half a mile to Strawberry Falls, before coming to an end at Little Strawberry Lake, a great place to rest and enjoy lunch before turning back for the trek home.

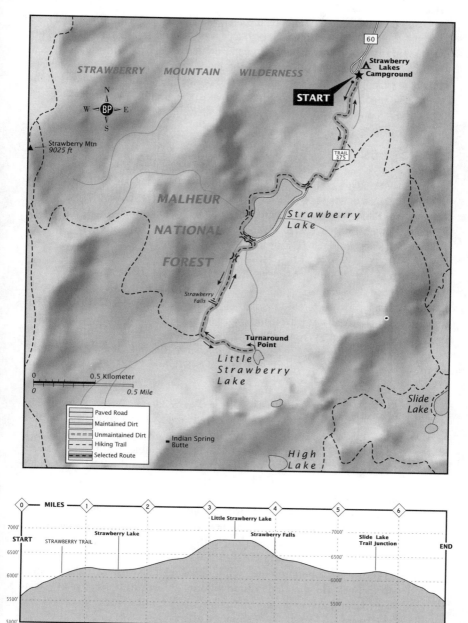

Lakes Basin

Hike Summary

The Lakes Basin hike is an adventure into Oregon's Little Switzerland. The jagged granite peaks of the Wallowa Mountains, high alpine lakes, and scenic glacial valleys are just a few of the spectacular natural landmarks on this classic trail. The route begins at the Two Pan trailhead and then parallels the East Fork of the Lostine River. Passing through an alpine valley, the hike then climbs to reveal the many beautiful lakes of the Lakes Basin area. Keep in mind that this is a very popular trail. If you're seeking solitude, come in early fall, after the summer crowds have gone.

Hike Specs

Start: From the Two Pan trailhead off Lostine River Road (FS 8210)
Length: 20.2-mile out-and-back
Approximate Hiking Time: 10–12 hours
Difficulty Rating: Difficult due to steep switchbacks along the East Fork of the Lostine River
Trail Surface: Dirt path with several rocky and eroded stretches
Lay of the Land: A dense forest trek up steep switchbacks to a high alpine meadow, ultimately arriving at high alpine lakes
Elevation Gain: 3,447 feet

Land Status: Wilderness area
Nearest Town: Lostine, OR
Other Trail Users: Equestrians
Canine Compatibility: Leashed-dog friendly

Getting There

From Lostine: Turn south off OR 82 onto Lostine River Road (FS 8210). Drive 17.8 miles—the road turns to gravel after seven miles—to the Two Pan trailhead. *DeLorme: Oregon Atlas & Gazetteer:* Page 87 D7

The 358,461-acre Eagle Cap Wilderness is one of Northeast Oregon's most treasured areas. The centerpiece of this magnificent area is the Wallowa Mountains, whose jagged, granite peaks and ridges resemble California's Sierra Nevada. Seventeen peaks, including the 9,826-foot, marble-topped Matterhorn and 9,595-foot Eagle Cap, top out at over 9,000 feet.

The limestone and marble rocks found here today are the remnants of an ancient seafloor. Yes, 200 million years ago this mountain range was entirely under water. When the North American continent shifted, this seafloor was pushed upward. About 100 million years ago, hot lava intruded into the surrounding underground sedimentary layers. It then cooled slowly over a long period of time to form granite. Millions of years of glacial erosion have since carved the Wallowa Mountains and its valleys and lake basins into spectacular granite masterpieces.

The Wallowa Mountains take their name from the Nez Perce word *wallowa*, meaning "fish trap." For hundreds of years the Wallowa band of the Nez Perce gathered plants, fished, and hunted game here in the summer months and then traveled to the warmer Hell's Canyon country in the winter months.

When gold was discovered in the region in the mid 1860s and settlers began to arrive, the federal government decided to take back land that was originally promised to the Nez Perce in treaties from a decade earlier. In 1863 a newly proposed treaty asked the Nez Perce to return more than six million acres of their native tribal land to the government. Native American chiefs felt the new treaty was unfair and refused to allow government officials to force their people to move. Eventually, the government agreed and announced that white settlers could not remain in the area. The land would continue to belong to the Nez Perce.

Unfortunately, settlers and politicians refused to accept it the decision. To avoid trouble, several bands of Nez Perce decided to relocate to a reservation in Idaho. But things didn't go so smoothly. On their way to the reservation, young braves from one of the bands killed four white settlers, kicking off the Nez Perce War of 1877.

Mirror Lake.

As the war began, the leader of the Wallowa band, In-mut-too-yah-lat-lat (translated as "Thunder Coming up Over the Land from the Water"), decided to lead his people to Canada. There, he thought, they would find freedom from persecution by the United States Army. He led 800 of his people on a 1,400-mile trek through Idaho and Montana, eluding and fighting U.S. soldiers until they were caught just 40 miles from the Canadian border in the Bear Paw Mountains of Montana. After their surrender, In-mut-too-yah-lat-lat and his people were moved to a reservation

MilesDirections

0.0 START hiking at the Two Pan trailhead. *[**Note.** Fill out a free self-issue wilderness permit at the trailhead.]*

0.1 Come to a fork and go right—the sign indicates "East Fork Lostine Trail 1662." Cross a stream and enter the Eagle Cap Wilderness.

0.3 Turn right and cross a log bridge over the East Fork of the Lostine River.

3.0 Begin walking through a high, scenic glacial meadow.

7.3 Come to a trail junction. Turn left where the sign indicates "Lakes Basin Trail 1810." Pass Mirror Lake on your right. *[**FYI.** If you are backpacking, this is a great place to set up base camp.]*

7.6 Come to a fork and go right—the sign indicates "Moccasin Trail 1810A." (The Lakes Basin Trail 1810 turns to the left here). Begin the loop portion of the trail here. Pass by Moccasin Lake on your right.

8.3 Come to a trail intersection. Turn left where the sign indicates "West Fork of the Wallowa River." (Going right here takes you to Glacier Pass.)

10.1 Walk by picturesque Douglas Lake and then come to a trail junction. Turn left where the sign reads "Hurricane Creek." (Turning right sends you toward the West Fork of the Wallowa River.)

11.5 Come to a fork and go left—the sign marks "Lakes Basin Trail 1810." (Going right leads you toward Hurricane Trail 1807.)

12.4 Pass Sunshine Lake on your left.

12.6 Complete the loop portion of the hike. Turn right on the East Fork Lostine Trail and proceed 7.6 miles back to the trailhead.

20.2 Arrive back at the Two Pan trailhead.

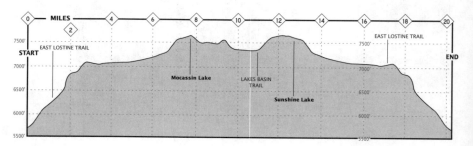

in Oklahoma. When In-mut-too-yah-lat-lat visited Washington, D.C. in 1879 to plead his case for his people, he spoke these words:

> *Whenever the white man treats the Indian as they treat each other then we shall have no more wars. We shall be all alike—brothers of one father and mother, with one sky above us and one country around us and one government for all. Then the Great Spirit Chief who rules above will smile upon this land and send rain to wash out the bloody*

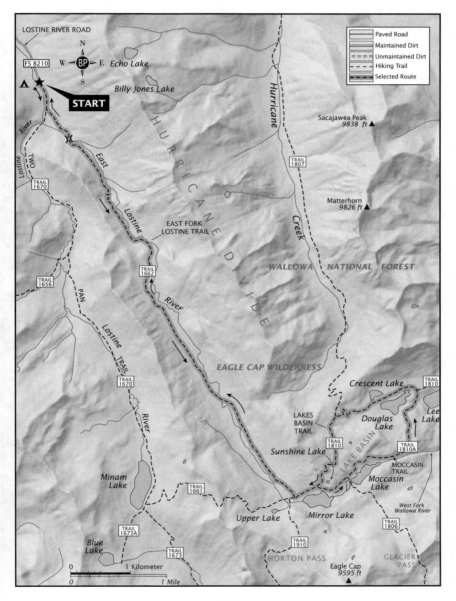

*spots made by brothers' hands upon the face of the earth. For this time
the Indian race is waiting and praying. I hope no more groans of
wounded men and women will ever go to the ear of the Great Spirit
Chief above, and that all people may be one people. . . .*

Chief Joseph: The Biography of a Great Indian by Chester Anders Fee,
Wilson-Erickson, 1936

Sadly, In-mut-too-yah-lat-lat's wishes were never realized, and in 1885
he and the rest of the Nez Perce were relocated to the Colville
Reservation in Washington State. It is said that the wise and peaceful
chief died of a broken heart because he was never allowed to return to his
homeland. Today, visitors to the Lakes Basin area of the Eagle Cap

Wilderness find it easy to see why the Nez Perce wished to remain in this stunning area.

The Two Pan Trail leads to the heart of the wilderness through a glaciated valley and an alpine lake basin. The trail begins by paralleling the East Fork of the Lostine River and ascends steeply through a thick forest of Engelmann spruce and Western larch. To the east is a good view of Hurricane Divide. After three miles, the trail arrives at a high, rock-strewn glacial valley. The trail skirts the western side of the valley for the next four miles and includes magnificent views of Eagle Cap rising prominently in the distance.

At the southern end of the valley, the trail begins to switchback steeply through a lodgepole pine and alpine fir forest to the upper Lakes Basin. At mile 7.3, you come to a junction and veer left. You pass Mirror Lake on your right and have a spectacular view of Eagle Cap to the south. At mile 7.6, you begin a five-mile loop, during which you pass Moccasin Lake, Douglas Lake, and Sunshine Lake. After the loop, it's another 7.6 miles back to the trailhead.

Hike Information

🕽 Trail Contacts:
Wallowa - Whitman National Forest, Eagle Cap Ranger District, Enterprise, OR (541) 426–4978 or *www.fs.fed.us/r6/w-w*

🕒 Schedule:
July through October

💲 Fees/Permits:
Requires a Northwest Forest $5 day pass or $30 annual pass. You can purchase a pass online at: *www.fs.fed.us/r6/feedemo* or by call calling 1–800–270–7504. The pass is also available at Wallowa-Whitman National Forest office in Enterprise or at certain local businesses in Wallowa, Enterprise, Joseph, and Wallowa Lake.

❓ Local Information:
Eastern Oregon Visitor Association, Baker City, OR 1–800–332–1843 or *www.eova.org*

💡 Local Events/Attractions:
Old Time Fiddlers Contest, June 9–10, Enterprise, OR (541) 426–4634 · **Wallowa Valley Arts Festival,** June 23–24, Joseph, OR (541) 432–1305 · **Wallowa County Fair,** June 6–12, Enterprise, OR (541) 426–3143

🛏 Accommodations:
Best Western Rama Inn & Suites, Enterprise, OR 1–888–RAMA–INN · **Two Pan Campground,** Eagle Cap Ranger District (541) 426–4978

🎿 Local Outdoor Retailers:
Wallowa Outdoors, Enterprise, OR (541) 426–3493

🆖 Maps:
USGS maps: Eagle Cap, OR

Honorable Mentions

Northeast Oregon

Compiled here is an index of great hikes in Northeast Oregon that didn't make the A-list this time around but deserve recognition. Check them out and let us know what you think. You may decide that one or more of these hikes deserves higher status in future editions or, perhaps, you may have a hike of your own that merits some attention.

(49) North Fork of the John Day River

This trail follows the meandering course of the North Fork of the John Day River for over 22 miles through the wilderness area of the same name. The path travels through scenic forest filled with deer, elk, and a variety of bird species. At one time, this area was a miner's mecca, and you'll find many miners' cabins dotted along the trail.

To get there from Ukiah, drive southeast on the Blue Mountain Scenic Byway (FS 52) for 40 miles until you reach the North Fork John Day Campground. The trailhead is located near the northwest corner of the campground. In order to park at this trailhead, you'll need a $5 Northwest Forest Pass—available at *www.fs.fed.us/r6/feedemo* or by calling 1–800–270–7504. For more information, contact the Umatilla National Forest, North Fork John Day Ranger District, Ukiah, OR; (541) 427–3231; www.fs.fed.us/r6/uma. *DeLorme: Oregon Atlas & Gazetteer:* Page 82 A3

(50) Skyline Trail

This 35.0-mile trail sweeps through the Strawberry Mountain Wilderness, promising vast views of the backcountry. The trail runs north along a ridge crest, passing Dead Horse Butte and Big Riner Basin, and then loops through the gorgeous Lakes Basin.

To get there from Prairie City, drive south on CR 62 for 18 miles to its junction with FS 101. Turn right on FS 101 and proceed two miles to the trailhead. For more information, contact the Prairie City Ranger District, Prairie City, OR; (541) 820–3800; *www.fs.fed.us/r6/malheur.* *DeLorme: Oregon Atlas & Gazetteer:* Page 82 C2

(51) Lakes Lookout

This 2.0-mile out-and-back trail takes you past bright bunches of wild-flowers and wind-blown trees to high granite country in the Umatilla National Forest. There's an old fire lookout at the end of the trail which serves up gorgeous views of the snow-capped Wallowa Mountains and the awesome granite peaks that surround the Anthony Lakes and Crawfish Basins.

To get there from Baker City, drive north on U.S. 30 for about 10 miles to the town of Haines. Turn left on the Elkhorn Drive Scenic Byway (CR 1146)—this road eventually turns into FS 73. Continue for 27.5 miles to the junction with FS 210—look for this junction 3.8 miles past the Anthony Lakes Campground. Turn left on FS 210 and drive two miles to the trailhead. For more information, contact the Wallowa-Whitman National Forest, Baker Ranger District, Baker City, OR; (541) 523–6391; *www.fs.fed.us/r6/w-w*. *DeLorme: Oregon Atlas & Gazetteer:* Page 82 A3

52 Anthony Lake to Dutch Flat Lake

This trek takes you on a section of the Elkhorn Crest National Recreation Trail through some scenic high country in the Blue Mountains. You begin this 10-mile out-and-back hike at the east end of Anthony Lake Campground. Hike along the trail through a mixed conifer forest for five miles to a side trail that takes you to Dutch Flat Lake; this is your turn-around. If you want to backpack for several days, follow the Elkhorn Crest National Recreational Trail through many more miles of this scenic high country. In order to park at this trailhead, you'll need a $5 Northwest Forest Pass—available at www.fs.fed.us/r6/feedemo or by calling 1–800–270–7504.

To get there from Baker City, drive north on U.S. 30 for about 10 miles to Haines. Turn left on the Elkhorn Drive Scenic Byway (CR 1146)—this road eventually turns into FS 73. Drive 24 miles to the Anthony Lakes Campground. For more information, contact the Wallowa-Whitman National Forest, Baker City, OR; (541) 523–6391; *www.fs.fed.us/r6/w-w*. *DeLorme: Oregon Atlas & Gazetteer: Page* 82 A4

53 Minam River

On the Minam River Trail you can enjoy a 44-mile hike along the scenic Minam River. The trail winds through undisturbed forest filled with deer, elk, black bears, and other wildlife. You can try your hand at catching feisty rainbow, brook, and cutthroat trout in this prize fishing stream. The trail ultimately ends at Minam Lake.

To get there from Wallowa, drive west on OR 82 for 19 miles to Minam Summit. A mile past the summit, turn left on Minam River Road. Follow the road until it ends at Mead's Flat. For more information, contact the Wallowa-Whitman National Forest, Wallowa Ranger District, Enterprise, OR; (541) 426–4978; *www.fs.fed.us/r6/w-w*. *DeLorme: Oregon Atlas & Gazetteer:* Page 87 B5 B6

(54) Echo/Traverse Lakes

This difficult 16.6-mile trail blazes through the high country of the Wallowa Mountains to offer stunning views of Echo and Traverse Lakes— lakes that rest in spectacular glacial-carved basins. This trail requires a free self-issue wilderness permit, which is available at the wood trailhead sign. Make sure you don't start the trail at the wooden trailhead sign. Start by walking up the dirt road at the north end of the parking lot. Follow this dirt road as it passes some walk-in campsites for about 0.2 miles. It then turns into the dirt path. At mile 0.3, cross a wooden bridge. The trail parallels an open grassy valley where you may see cows grazing. At mile 0.5, come to a fork and stay left. (Going right puts you on Fake Creek Trail 1914.) After another 1.2 miles you cross a stream. At mile 1.3, you'll have to ford a stream. You can either wade through the stream or walk across thin logs to get across. DO NOT continue following the trail as it parallels the stream. Pick the trail up on the other side. After 1.4 miles, you enter the Eagle Cap Wilderness. Another three miles and you cross Eagle Creek (using a log). The trail begins climbing steeply up an enormous granite canyon on a long

series of switchbacks. After 3.8 miles, the trail comes to a fork. Go right, where the sign indicates "Trail Creek." (If you turn left, you'll be headed toward Elk Creek.) After 6.1 miles, cross Eagle Creek again. At mile 6.3, there's a spectacular view of Echo Lake on your right. You can turnaround here, or, for an even more spectacular view, continue another two miles to Traverse Lake.

To get there from La Grande, take I-84 to OR 203 (Exit 265). Drive south on OR 203 for 11 miles to downtown Union. In Union, take a sharp left and continue following OR 203 south for 13.8 miles to the junction with FS 77 (a gravel road). Turn left on FS 77 and drive 15 miles to West Eagle Creek. The trailhead is located on the left side of the road. Note that the road becomes very rough after 9.6 miles. A sign warns that the road is not suitable for passenger cars; however, if you go slowly, the road is passable in a passenger car. For more information, contact the Wallowa-Whitman National Forest, La Grande Ranger District, La Grande, OR; (541) 963–7186; *www.fs.fed.us/r6/w-w.* *DeLorme: Oregon Atlas & Gazetteer:* Page 87 D7

55 Historic Oregon Trail

This easy 4.2-mile trail takes you back in time as it weaves through the old wagon ruts of the famous Oregon Trail, which during the 1800s brought thousands of settlers to Oregon. This route offers historic and natural wonders: You'll be able to check out historic pioneer home sites and defunct mines, as well as reward yourself with grand views of the Powder River Valley and the majestic Elkhorn Mountains. While you're here, be sure to take the time to visit the National Historic Oregon Trails Interpretive Center, which provides a wealth of displays about those who traveled the Oregon Trail, as well as the history and culture of the Native Americans impacted by this westward migration.

To get there from Baker City, drive east on OR 86 for six miles to the National Historic Oregon Trails Interpretive Center. The trailhead is in the back of the center. For more information, contact the National Historic Oregon Trail Interpretive Center at Flagstaff Hill, Baker City, OR; (541) 523–1843; *www.or.blm.gov/NHOTIC*. *DeLorme: Oregon Atlas & Gazetteer:* Page 83 A5

56 Hells Canyon Loop

Dive deep into Hells Canyon on this difficult 30.0-mile backpack trip. Start your journey on Saddle Creek Trail 1776 and follow it as it descends for 10 miles along the Saddle Creek Drainage, eventually joining up with the Snake River. Turn north on the Snake River Trail 1726 and follow it 14.5 miles until you reach the junction with Sluice Creek Trail 1748. There is very little shade along this section of the trail and summertime temperatures can reach over 100 degrees, so carry plenty of water—one gallon per person per day is recommended. Also be on the lookout for rattlesnakes, poison oak, and bears around creek drainages. Hike the steeply climbing Sluice Creek Trail up toward the rim of the canyon. At mile 18.3, intersect with the High Trail 1751—signs indicate this trail is 418, but don't be fooled. Continue on the High Trail 1751 to the junction with the Saddle Creek Trail 1776 at the 26-mile mark. Here you can hook up with the Saddle Creek Trail and head back to your car.

To get there from Joseph, drive east on Wallowa Road for 30 miles to Imnaha. In the town of Imnaha, turn right on Upper Imnaha Road (CR

727) and drive 12.7 miles to the intersection with FS 4230. Turn left and drive three miles to the trailhead. For more information, contact the Wallowa-Whitman National Forest, Hells Canyon National Recreation Area, Enterprise, OR; (541) 426–4978; *www.fs.fed.us/r6/w-w*. **DeLorme:** **Oregon Atlas & Gazetteer:** Page 88 C1

(57) McGraw Creek Loop

This difficult 14.0-mile loop takes you right through the heart of Hells Canyon Country. Begin this hike at the Freezeout Trailhead on Hells Canyon Trail 1890, which leads north to the Snake River Canyon. After two miles you reach a junction with the McGraw Creek Trail 1879. Stay to the right and continue hiking on Trail 1890. After another mile you come to another trail junction. Turn left onto Bench Trail 1884, and after a short ways, enter the Hells Canyon National Recreation Area. After about four miles, cross Spring Creek. This section of the trail is very overgrown and rough and you'll need to navigate carefully. At mile 5.6, reach the McGraw Creek Cabin Trail 1879 at a signed intersection. Continue on this trail through Hells Canyon Country until McGraw Cabin at mile 9.3. From the cabin, follow the trail that parallels the left side of the creek and cross McGraw Creek at about the 10-mile mark. After another two miles and many bridgeless stream crossings you reach the intersection with the Hells

---

Oregonian Tongue Twisters

Having trouble pronouncing your latest destination? This handy key should help.

Aloha—*Uh-Lo'-Uh*
Belknap—*Bell'-Nap*
Cape Arago—*Air'-Uh-Go*
Celilo Falls—*Seh-Lie'-Lo Falls*
Champoeg—*Sham-Poo'-Ee*
Chemult—*Sheh-Mult'*
Chiloquin—*Chill'-Oh-Quin*
Clatskanie—*Klats'-Kuh-Ni*
Coquille—*Ko-Keel'*
Deschutes—*Deh-Shoots'*
Gleneden—*Glen-Ee'-Den*
Grand Ronde—*Grand Rond*
Heceta—*Heh-See'-Tah*
La Grande—*La Grand'*

Madras—*Mad'-Russ*
Ochoco—*O'-Choh-Ko*
Owyhee—*O-Why'-He*
Paulina—*Paul-I'-Nah*
Siuslaw—*Sigh-Oo'-Slah*
The Dalles—*The Dals'*
Tillamook—*Till'-Uh-Muk*
Wallowa—*rhymes with Ka-Pow'-Uh*
Willamette—*Will-Lam'-It*
Winema—*Why-Nee'-Mah*
Yachats—*Yaw'-Hots*
Yaquina—*Ya-Quin'-Uh*

The Official 2000 Travel Guide Oregon

Canyon Trail 1890, which completes the loop portion of the trail. Turn right and follow the trail back to your car. Take note that the temperatures in Hells Canyon can exceed 100 degrees in the summertime, so be sure to carry plenty of water—one gallon per person per day is recommended. If you're completing this trail as an overnight backpack, hang your food and be sure to bring a water filter. Also, wear boots and long pants because rattlesnakes and poison oak are common. In order to park at this trailhead, you'll need a $5 Northwest Forest Pass—available at *www.fs.fed.us/r6/feedemo* or by calling 1–800–270–7504.

To get there from Baker City, drive east on OR 86 for 70 miles. Turn left on CR 1039 and proceed nine miles to the trailhead at the end of the road. For more information, contact the Wallowa-Whitman National Forest, Baker City, OR; (541) 523–6391; *www.fs.fed.us/r6/w-w. DeLorme: Oregon Atlas & Gazetteer:* Page 88 D1

Southeast

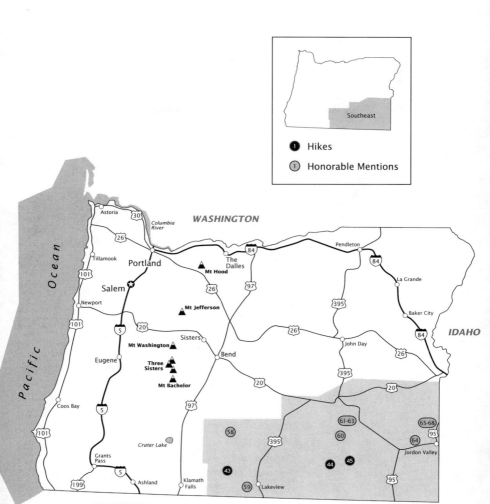

Southeast

● Hikes
① Honorable Mentions

Astoria
Columbia River
WASHINGTON
30
26
Tillamook
Portland
The Dalles
Mt Hood
84
Pendleton
84
101
Salem
26
97
La Grande
Newport
Mt Jefferson
395
Baker City
101
5
20
Sisters
26
84
IDAHO
Mt Washington
John Day
26
Eugene
Bend
Three Sisters
395
Mt Bachelor
20
20
Coos Bay
5
97
61-63
65-68
58
60
95
Crater Lake
395
64
Jordon Valley
Grants Pass
5
44
45
Ashland
Klamath Falls
43
95
199
59
Lakeview
Pacific Ocean
CALIFORNIA
NEVADA

Oregon

Southeast Oregon

Southeast Oregon is situated in a great basin of rugged fault-block mountains separated by large sagebrush valleys. A region of wonderful extremes, this least-populated part of the state promises a dry desert landscape, abundant wildlife, awe-inspiring scenery, and a sense of remoteness. In this wild and rugged country, there are more animals than people. If solitude is what you're after, this is the place to be. Almost two-thirds of the area is rangeland managed by the Bureau of Land Management (BLM). Not surprisingly, farms and ranches are common sites.

The town of Lakeview (Oregon's highest town at 4,800 feet) is located near the southern border and is a good place to stock up on supplies before setting out to explore the open sagebrush country. Aptly named, Lakeview is just a short drive from heavenly vistas of Summer Lake, Goose Lake, Drews Reservoir, and Warner Lake.

No place celebrates the beauty, remoteness, and ruggedness of the area like the nearby Hart Mountain National Antelope Refuge located approximately 60 miles northeast of Lakeview. This distinct refuge is comprised of sagebrush, hot springs, rugged canyons and ridges, and aspen-filled valleys. The refuge was established in 1936 by President Roosevelt to protect the pronghorn antelope. Today it supports a healthy antelope population as well as coyotes, jackrabbits, raptors, bighorn sheep, and mule deer. You'll also have to contend with rattlesnakes and mosquitoes—always wear leather boots and carry mosquito repellant. You can hike through this open sagebrush country along Poker Jim Ridge as it rises dramatically above the Warner Basin and the Warner Wetlands. These wetlands support dozens of species of migrating birds including Canadian geese, whistling swans, and white pelicans—keep an eye out.

Head northeast from Lakeview to the natural wonder of Steens Mountain, a fault-block mountain that showcases U-shaped, glacier-carved gorges and supports a variety of eco-zones. Take the summit hike to the top of 9,733-foot Steens Mountain for fantastic views of the surrounding lakes and mountains. Bring binoculars to spot the golden eagles riding the thermals and bighorn sheep grazing the slopes of the glacial gorges.

Backpackers and day hikers will enjoy trekking into the Gearhart Mountain Wilderness located 18 miles northeast of Bly off Oregon 140. This area is characterized by old-growth ponderosa, lodgepole, and white-bark pine. Take a walk to the top of Gearhart Mountain for magnificent views of Three Sisters, Steens Mountain, and California's Mount Lassen.

The weather in this part of Oregon can hover in the 80s and 90s at the lower elevations and drop 30 degrees at the higher elevations. Some trail-heads around this area are remote and often off roads that are in poor condition. Always carry extra water with you in your car as well as tools and a spare gallon of gas.

In some case the hiking is cross-country, such as the Leslie Gulch hike, the Three Fingers Gulch hike, and the Wall of Rome hike. It's recommended that you carry a well-stocked first aid kit, at least one gallon of water per person per day, sunscreen, a wide-brimmed hat, sunglasses, and a GPS unit.

43 Gearhart Mountain

Hike Summary

If you truly want to experience the beauty and solitude of pristine wilderness, this hike is for you. Old-growth ponderosa pine, lodgepole pine, and whitebark pine fill the Gearhart Mountain Wilderness with their stately beauty. This hike also takes you through the Palisades, a unique area of oddly shaped rock formations, and ends at a high pass with magnificent views of Steens Mountain to the east, the Three Sisters Mountains to the west, and California's Mount Lassen to the south. Backpackers have the option of continuing another 3.4 miles to Blue Lake, a high alpine lake stocked with rainbow trout.

Hike Specs

Start: From the Gearhart Mountain Trail 100 off Corral Creek Road
Length: 11.2-mile out-and-back
Approximate Hiking Time: 5–7 hours
Difficulty Rating: Difficult due to the steep ascent of Gearhart Mountain
Trail Surface: Dirt path, with occasional rocky sections and creek crossings. You may also have to climb over logs and other trail debris.
Lay of the Land: The trail ascends Gearhart Mountain along switchbacks through a ponderosa pine forest to a spectacular viewpoint.
Elevation Gain: 2,889 feet
Land Status: Wilderness area
Nearest Town: Bly, OR
Other Trail Users: None
Canine Compatibility: Dog friendly

Getting There

From Bly: Drive east 1.3 miles on OR 140 to Campbell Road. Turn left (north) on to Campbell Road and drive 0.5 miles. Turn right onto FS 34, where the sign indicates "Gearhart Wilderness 17 miles." Drive 14.3 miles on FS 34. At the fork, stay to the left. Drive an additional 0.2 miles and turn left onto Corral Creek Road (FS 012), a rough narrow dirt road. Drive 1.4 miles to Gearhart Mountain Trail 100 (You'll pass Corral Creek Forest Campground in 0.3 miles.) *DeLorme: Oregon Atlas & Gazetteer:* Page 72 C1

The bulk of Fremont National Forest lies in Lake County, one of Oregon's least populated areas. Though it's filled with scenic trails that offer both solitude and magnificent scenery, the 1,198,301-acre reserve is one of Oregon's most overlooked outdoor playgrounds. The forest borders California to the south, the Warner Range to the east, and the Deschutes and Winema national forests to the north and west. The dry, high-desert ecosystem can be both harsh and unpredictable, with temperatures varying from 30 to 100-plus degrees Fahrenheit and precipitation ranging from 16 to 40 inches. At the lower elevations, sagebrush and juniper trees dominate

The Dome.

the landscape, while at higher elevations you'll find thick stands of white fir, ponderosa pine, white pine, sugar pine, incense cedar, and lodgepole pine.

Over 300 species of fish, birds, and mammals flourish in this region. Among the large mammals, you might be lucky enough to spot while hiking are Rocky Mountain elk, mule deer, and pronghorn antelope. Mountain lions, black bears, and bobcats also roam the hills and valleys of this seemingly endless expanse of national forest. Mallard ducks, whistling swans, and Canadian geese are commonly found in the wetlands, and bald eagles and peregrine falcons nest here.

One of this national forest's hidden treasures is the 22,823-acre Gearhart Wilderness, the only wilderness area in the forest. The centerpiece of this wilderness area is Gearhart Mountain (8,364 feet), a shield-type volcano with glacier-carved valleys and well-known craggy cliffs (such as The Dome and Haystack Rock). Gearhart Mountain Trail 100 takes you right through

Fremont National Forest

Fremont National Forest takes its name from John C. Fremont (1813–1890), a topographical engineer for the U.S. Army who led many explorations throughout the West, among them an expedition through Oregon in 1843. One of Fremont's more notable assignments was to find a railroad route over the Rocky Mountains. In his later years, Fremont took to politics, becoming one of California's first senators in 1851. In 1856, Fremont showed up on the Republican Party ticket for president of the United States.

MilesDirections

0.0 START the hike at the wood trailhead sign. Voluntary registration cards are available to fill out at the trailhead. Begin walking on the Gearhart Mountain Trail 100. Shortly, you'll pass a sign on your left that reads: "Palisades, ¾ mile/The Notch, 6 miles/Blue Lake, 10 miles."

0.7 Come to the Palisades. Walk through these interesting rock formations for about 0.3 miles and then descend some switchbacks for about 0.2 miles.

3.4 Cross a creek.

3.6 Pass The Dome—an impressive wall of rock cliff that shoots skyward on your right.

4.9 The trail comes to a fork. Stay right.

5.5 Reach a spectacular view of the Gearhart Wilderness, California's Mount Lassen to the south, Steens Mountain to the east, and the Three Sisters Mountains to the west.

5.6 Reach a high pass and your turn-around point. *[**Option.** Backpackers may want to continue another 3.4 miles to Blue Lake.]*

11.2 Arrive back at the trailhead.

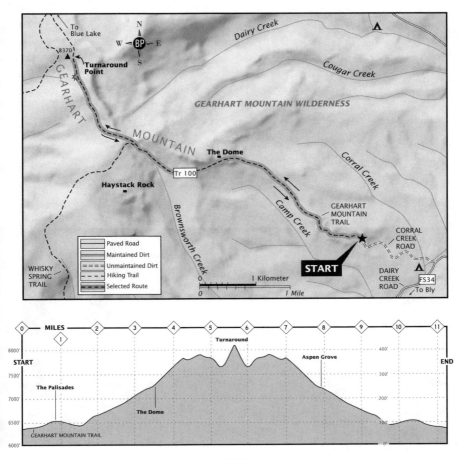

309

Old-growth ponderosa pine forest.

the heart of this pristine wilderness. The trail described here begins at the Gearhart Mountain Trail 100 trailhead and leads you through an open old-growth ponderosa pine forest scattered with wild flowers in the spring and summer months. In short order, you come to the Palisades, a mini rock city. Here you'll find balanced rocks, stacked rocks, and rocks in all sorts of unusual shapes. Next up is The Dome, a huge rock cliff that shoots skyward. Nearing the turn-around point, you'll reach an over-look with magnificent views of

The Lake County's largest town, Lakeview, is home to just 2,800 people, but don't let its size fool you. Lakeview is renowned for being the "Hang Gliding Capital of the West."

California's Mount Lassen to the south, Steens Mountain to the east, and the Three Sisters Mountains to the west. At the high pass and turnaround point, those backpacking may want to continue on the trail as it descends another 3.4 miles to the only lake in this wilderness area, Blue Lake. The lake is stocked with rainbow trout and makes a nice campsite after the nine-mile hike from the trailhead.

Hike Information

❶ Trail Contacts:
Bly Ranger District/Fremont National Forest, Bly, OR (541) 353–2427 or *www.fs.fed.us/ r6/fremont/welcome.htm*

☉ Schedule:
June to October

❷ Local Information:
Lake County Chamber of Commerce, Lakeview, OR 1–877–947–6040 or *www.lake-countychamber.org* · **Lakeview Ranger District**, Lakeview, OR (541) 947–3334

♀ Local Events/Attractions:
Festival of Flight, June 30–July 4, Lakeview, OR 1–877–947–6040

● Accommodations:
Corral Creek Forest Campground, Bly Ranger District, OR (541) 353–2427

⑩ Restaurants:
Tall Town Burgers and Bakery, Lakeview, OR (541) 947–3521

⑪ Clubs & Organizations:
The Desert Trail Association, Madras, OR at *www.madras.net/ dta/dtainfo.htm*

❽ Hike Tours:
The Desert Trail Association, Madras, OR at *www.madras.net/ dta/dtainfo.htm*

⑩ Maps:
USGS maps: Gearhart Mountain, OR

Poker Jim Ridge

Hike Summary

Escape to the wild expanse of the Southeast Oregon desert and the Hart Mountain National Antelope Refuge, home to over 330 species of animals, among them the elusive pronghorn antelope. This hike takes you on a cross-country adventure along the edge of Poker Jim Ridge. Loaded with magnificent views of dozens of seasonal lakes that dot the Warner Basin, the hike culminates in a relaxing soak in a hot springs.

Hike Specs

Start: From the trailhead off Hart Mountain Road
Length: 4.0-mile out-and-back
Approximate Hiking Time: 2 hours
Difficulty Rating: Moderate
Trail Surface: No established trail. Double-track road and cross-country travel over very rocky terrain through thick sagebrush.
Lay of the Land: Travel along the rim of Poker Jim Ridge through thick sagebrush and rocky terrain.
Elevation Gain: 240 feet
Land Status: National antelope refuge
Nearest Town: Plush, OR
Other Trail Users: Equestrians
Canine Compatibility: Not dog friendly. The rocky trail is rough on dog paws. Also, there are rattlesnakes and foxtails.

Getting There

From Lakeview: Drive 4.6 miles north on U.S. 395 to the OR 140 junction. Turn right (east) and drive 15.6 miles to the junction with Plush Cutoff Road (CR 313). Turn left (north) and drive 18.5 miles to the town of Plush. Continue driving through town for about a mile and turn right on Hart Mountain Road (CR 212). Drive 20 miles (the road turns to gravel at mile 13.1)) and park in the dirt pullout on the right side of the road where a sign reads "Restrict off-road travel to foot or horseback. Unload and case or dismantle all guns." *DeLorme: Oregon Atlas & Gazetteer:* Page 73 B6

idden away in the southeast corner of Oregon is the lake-filled Warner Basin. This remote and unpopulated part of Oregon is covered with miles of sagebrush, beveled fault-block mountains, and alkaline lakes. Near the end of the last ice age, a 500-square-mile lake covered the Warner Basin. This lake eventually receded leaving a succession of smaller lakes that rise and fall, appear and disappear, with the level of rainfall. Among them are Bluejoint, Stone Corral, Campbell, Flagstaff, Swamp, and Anderson—with Crump, Hart, and Pelican lakes sticking around on a more permanent basis. These lakes make up the Warner Wetlands, which support many species of migrating birds including Canadian geese, pied-billed grebes, white pelicans, snowy egrets, a variety of ducks, and whistling

Trekking along the edge of Poker Jim Ridge.

swans. This hike takes you along Poker Jim Ridge where you'll have far-reaching views of these numerous lakes and the vast landscape that make up the Warner Basin.

Poker Jim Ridge is located in the Hart Mountain National Antelope Refuge, a 430-square-mile preserve of sagebrush, hot springs, rugged canyons and ridges, and aspen-filled valleys. This vast, high-desert landscape supports over 330 species of animals, including coyotes, jackrabbits, raptors, pronghorn antelope, bighorn sheep, mule deer, and many others. The 275,000-acre refuge was established in 1936 by President Franklin D. Roosevelt to protect the pronghorn antelope—the fastest land mammal in North America. With a huge heart, powerful lungs, and padded hooves, and keen eyesight, the pronghorn is built for speed. It can storm across the desert at speeds up to 35 mph and can even manage short power surges of up to 70 mph. The pronghorn's natural enemies are coyotes and golden eagles. They can spot these predators up to three miles away, and at the slightest sign of trouble, they're off in a flash.

The number of pronghorn in the West once numbered over 40 million in the 1800s, but the animals were nearly wiped out by hunting. Now, several million pronghorns wander the high desert plains of southeast Idaho, eastern Washington, central and eastern Oregon, and Nevada and other western states, with one of the largest herds (about 1,700 animals) living in the Hart Mountain National Antelope Refuge. When hiking on Poker Jim Ridge, it's highly recommended that you carry a pair of binoculars and scan the horizon for these magnificent creatures. You can identify them by the two white chest bands on their light brown coat, the striking white rump, and the black, spiked horns. Pronghorn are very observant and terribly skit-

MilesDirections

0.0 START walking east on the double-track dirt road.

0.1 Turn left (north) and head cross-country along the edge of Poker Jim Ridge, where you'll have glorious views of Stone Corral, Campbell, Flagstaff, Swamp, Anderson, and many others lakes.

2.0 Turn around here and retrace your tracks. *[**Option**. You can continue farther, if you like, and turn around and any point.]*

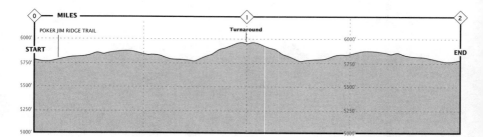

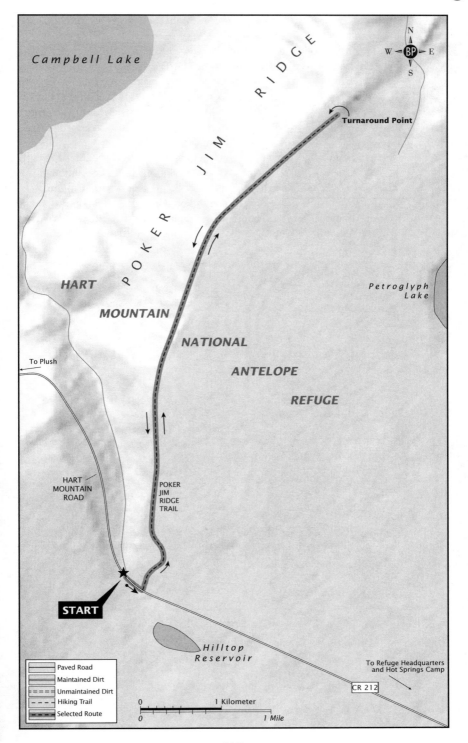

Campbell Lake

POKER JIM RIDGE

Turnaround Point

N
W — BP — E
S

HART
MOUNTAIN

Petroglyph
Lake

NATIONAL

ANTELOPE

REFUGE

To Plush

HART
MOUNTAIN
ROAD

POKER
JIM
RIDGE
TRAIL

START

Hilltop
Reservoir

To Refuge Headquarters
and Hot Springs Camp

CR 212

	Paved Road
	Maintained Dirt
	Unmaintained Dirt
	Hiking Trail
	Selected Route

0   1 Kilometer
0   1 Mile

tish, so if you see a cloud of dust form, more than likely it's from a pronghorn that spotted you.

This hike begins just off Hart Mountain Road, at the base of a broad plateau that forms the better part of the Hart Mountain National Antelope Refuge. From your car, you'll walk east along Hart Mountain Road for about 0.1 mile and then turn left and walk north over rough, sagebrush covered terrain along Poker Jim Ridge.

> Be sure to wear long pants on this hike. The sagebrush is very thick and can scratch your legs. It's also wise to wear boots because of the rocky terrain and potential rattlesnake encounters.

Be forewarned that you'll be hiking cross-country, which makes hiking here more challenging, if not more alluring. As you hike along the edge of the ridge, watch your footing on the numerous, loose lava rocks. To the west is a magnificent expanse of blue lakes that stretch out for miles.

Campbell Lake.

Wear long pants and tough footwear for this hike, and remember, rattlesnakes are found here. The boots will help protect your feet and ankles and long pants will shield your legs from the scratchy sagebrush. There are a dozen species of sagebrush that thrive in this high desert environment. In the spring and early summer months you'll also catch glimpses of larkspur and bright red Indian paintbrush dotting this expansive ridge.

Before or after your hike, be sure to stop by the refuge headquarters to learn about the region's plants and wildlife and to soak in the hot springs at Hot Springs Camp. To reach the refuge headquarters, continue driving east on Hart Mountain Road for approximately three miles. To reach Hot Springs Camp, drive south on Hart Mountain Road from the refuge headquarters to a fork, where you'll veer right and drive 1.7 miles to another fork. Stay to the right and drive 2.5 miles to a "Hot Springs Camp" sign. Turn right here and you'll find the hot springs sheltered in a not-so-pretty concrete building. If you plan on camping here, be sure to come prepared with mosquito repellant—the mosquitoes are ruthless in this part of the state.

Hike Information

❶ Trail Contacts:
Hart Mountain National Antelope Refuge, Lakeview, OR (541) 947–3315

❶ Schedule:
May through October

❸ Fees/Permits:
None

❷ Local Information:
Lake County Chamber of Commerce, Lakeview, OR 1–877–947–6040 or *www.lakecountychamber.org* · **Lakeview Ranger District,** Lakeview, OR (541) 947–3334

❷ Local Events/Attractions:
Festival of Flight, June 30–July 4, Lakeview, OR 1–877–947–6040

❶ Accommodations:
Hot Springs Camp, Hart Mountain Antelope Refuge, OR—*See the hike description for directions.*

❶ Restaurants:
Tall Town Burgers and Bakery, Lakeview, OR (541) 947–3521

❶ Clubs & Organizations:
The Desert Trail Association, Madras, OR at *www.madras.net/dta/dtainfo.htm*

❶ Hike Tours:
The Desert Trail Association, Madras, OR at *www.madras.net/dta/dtainfo.htm*

❶ Maps:
USGS maps: Campbell Lake, OR

Steens Mountain Trails

Hike Summary

Take a tour through the Wild West in Oregon's southeast desert. The star attraction of your tour is 9,733-foot Steens Mountain, a magnificent geologic wonder located approximately 60 miles southeast of Burns. There are several ways to explore this amazing mountain. You can start your tour in the tiny town of Frenchglen and head up to the summit using Steens Mountain Loop. Along the way you may see wild horses roaming the hills around you. You'll be surrounded by expansive views and pure solitude. At different viewpoints along the route you'll see magnificent glacier-carved gorges, sweeping views of Winter Rim, Summer Lake, Lake Abert, Abert Rim, the Warner Basin, Hart Mountain, and the Alvord Basin.

Hike Specs

Start: All four hikes start on Steens Mountain.

Length:
- **A. Kiger Gorge** Viewpoint: 0.4 miles out-and-back
- **B. East Rim Viewpoint:** 0.1 miles out-and-back
- **C. Steens Summit Trail:** 1.0 mile out-and-back
- **D. Wildhorse Lake Trail:** 3.0 miles out-and-back

Approximate Hiking Time: Varies depending on the trail selected.

Difficulty Rating:
- **A. Kiger Gorge Viewpoint:** Easy
- **B. East Rim Viewpoint:** Easy
- **C. Steens Summit Trail:** Moderate
- **D. Wildhorse Lake Trail:** Moderate

Trail Surface: All trails are dirt paths except for the Steens Summit Trail, which is a rocky doubletrack dirt road.

Elevation Gain: 874 feet

Land Status: National recreation lands

Nearest Town: Frenchglen, OR

Other Trail Users: None

Canine Compatibility: Leashed dog friendly

Getting There

From Frenchglen: Drive south on OR 205 and turn left onto Steens Mountain Loop. Drive three miles to a T-intersection and turn left. (If you turn right here you'll arrive at Page Spring Campground in one mile). Drive 19.2 miles and turn left at the Kiger Gorge Viewpoint and drive 0.5 miles to the parking area. To continue on your tour, drive back to Steens Mountain Road and turn left and drive 2.7 miles to a three-way road junction. Turn left at the junction and drive 0.5 miles to the East Rim Viewpoint. When you're finished enjoying the East Rim, drive back to the junction and take the middle fork of the road where a sign indicates "Wildhorse Lake 2¼ – Steens Summit 2½." Drive two miles to the parking area and trailheads for the Wildhorse Lake Trail and the Steens Summit Trail.

DeLorme: Oregon Atlas & Gazetteer: Page 74 A2

H idden away in the Southeast Oregon desert is the natural wonder of Steens Mountain. This impressive, 9,733-foot fault block mountain rises 5,500 feet from the sagebrush-covered Blitzen and Catlow valleys on its west side and the Alvord Desert on its east side. At over 30 miles wide and 60 miles long, this mountain is a store of startling geologic and ecologic diversity. The mountain's complex evolution began about 25 million years ago when the east side of Steens Mountain surged upward along the Alvord Fault, creating a steep sloping east face and a gentle sloping west face. Roughly 10 million years later, basalt lava flows (known as Steens Basalts) erupted from fissures in the earth, creating almost two thirds of the mountain you see today.

Managed by the Bureau of Land Management, this geologic masterpiece is part of the Burns District, which covers an immense 3.36 million acres of land, stretching over 200 miles from the Oregon/Nevada border northward to the base of the Blue Mountains. This wild and rugged country is the place to be if you're seeking wide-open spaces, sunny blue skies, and solitude.

The plants that live in this open landscape vary from sagebrush, bunch grass, and Western junipers of the valleys and open plains, to the ponderosa pine forests of the Blue Mountains foothills and the aspen groves of Steens Mountain, Trout Creek, and the Pueblo Mountains. The animals that inhabit this area are equally diverse—Rocky Mountain elk, California bighorn sheep, pronghorn antelope, and mule deer are some of the larger game. Also found roaming the lower slopes and valleys in the Steens Mountain area are wild horses. These free-spirited equines are thought to be descendents of horses owned by Native Americans, ranchers, miners, and

early explorers. A variety of raptors claim the skies of the southeast high desert. One of the more impressive raptors is the golden eagle, identified by its dark brown plumage with golden brown highlights. Armed with an impressive wingspan of seven feet and talons designed for gripping and tearing, these magnificent birds soar on the air currents high above the cliffs and slopes of Steens Mountain where they scout their prey: ground jackrabbits, small birds, and other small game.

Your tour of Steens Mountain is along the 66-mile backcountry byway known as Steens Mountain Loop road. You'll hook up with Steens

MilesDirections

A. Kiger Gorge Viewpoint Trail

0.0 START from the Kiger Point Viewpoint Trailhead and turn right on the dirt path.

0.1 Come to a viewpoint and interpretive sign describing how Kiger Gorge was formed. When you're finished reading, continue walking on the faint trail that leads to your right.

0.2 Turn around here.

0.4 Arrive back at the trailhead.

B. East Rim Viewpoint

0.0 START by walking the short trail to the viewpoint and interpretive signs.

0.05 Arrive at the viewpoint. Turn around here.

0.1 Arrive back at the parking area.

C. Wildhorse Lake Trail

0.0 START from the parking area where a wood trail sign indicates the start of the Wildhorse Lake Trail. Be sure to sign in at the trail register.

0.2 Reach a scenic overlook of Wildhorse Lake. Continue down the steep, sometimes slippery path to the lake.

1.5 Reach the lake and turnaround point.

3.0 Arrive back at the parking area.

D. Steens Summit Trail

0.0 START from the parking area where the rocky doubletrack road takes you steeply uphill.

0.2 Pass a viewpoint of Wildhorse Lake on your right.

0.5 Reach the summit of Steens Mountain (9,733 feet). Turn around here.

1.0 Arrive back at the parking area.

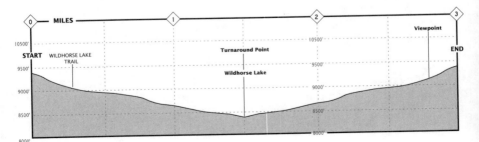

Horse Buyer's Jargon

an angel—*a greenhorn buyer at an auction, who can be depended on to buy unsound horses*

sold to halter—*no guarantee whatsoever*

dizzy—*a dummy; a horse corresponding to a human imbecile*

goosey—*nervous*

Indian—*a horse completely dangerous to handle*

jibber—*a green, untrained horse*

Pilgrim—*a horse once good, now too old*

plug—*a horse of little worth, maybe worn out; no spirit; so poor in conformation that he never was much good*

one bum lamp—*blind in one eye*

smokes his pipe—*lip torn at point where the bit commonly rests*

Source: The Oregon Desert by E.R. Jackman and R.A. Long (pages 394–395)

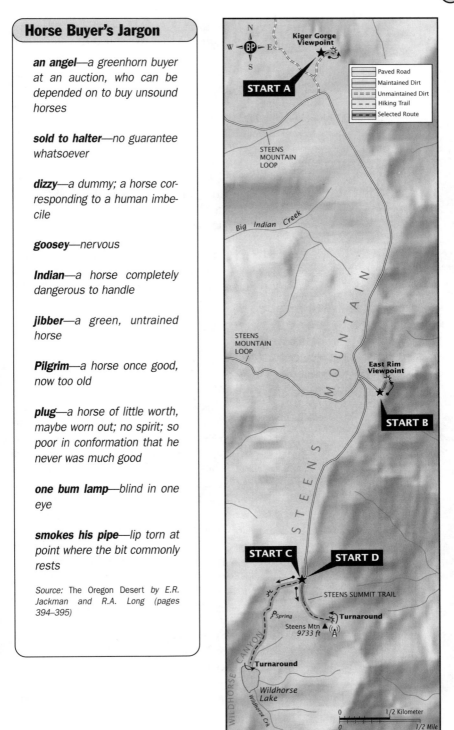

Mountain Loop just outside of the small town of Frenchglen. As you head up to the summit, you'll pass through multiple eco-zones, each with its own unique plants and animals. The historic P Ranch, infamous ranch headquarters of cattle baron Peter French, is along the route, as is the Page Springs Campground. The campground has flush toilets, running water, and hiking trails with interpretive signs. If you camp here, be sure to hike up the trail that parallels the Donner und Blitzen River. There are numerous opportunities to spot deer and other wildlife, and the river affords some excellent fishing.

As you continue on your road tour, approaching elevations of 4,000 to 6,000 feet, you'll pass through the sagebrush-covered Blitzen Valley, dotted with Western juniper and mountain mahogany. Between 6,000 and 8,000 feet the landscape transforms to groves of quaking aspen. These shimmering green trees provide food and shelter for bighorn sheep, pronghorn antelope, and mule deer. Those looking to camp will want to keep their eyes open for Fish Lake and Jackman Park campgrounds. Fish Lake is high moraine lake stocked with brook, rainbow, and native redband trout. Twenty primitive campsites are available here. Jackman Park Campground has six primitive sites.

Your first stop is the Kiger Gorge Viewpoint, on your left. Notice that the landscape on this part of the mountain resembles treeless rocky tundra. From viewpoint you'll be able to see the impressive U-shaped Kiger Gorge. After Kiger Viewpoint continue another 2.7 miles to a three-way junction and turn left to reach the East Rim Viewpoint. This spot rests right on the edge of East Rim, which drops dramatically thousands of feet below you. Here you'll have a commanding view of

> If you'd like to backpack in this area try Little Blitzen Gorge, a unique U-shaped gorge with several waterfalls splashing over the canyon rim. The river can be high in the early season, so be careful crossing. This trail is accessed near South Steens Campground and is about nine miles long. You can find good campsites after hiking about three miles up the gorge. Another backpacking opportunity is the seven-mile Big Indian Gorge trail, also accessed near South Steens Campground. This is a fairly level walk through open meadows and stands of aspen trees. Be careful with the creek crossings, as they can be difficult early in the season.

Mann Lake, an attractive pit stop for migratory waterfowl and a good spot for cutthroat trout. You'll also be able to see the Sheepsheads Mountains, Owyhee Uplands, and one of the oldest settlements in the area, Alvord Ranch, established in 1885. Keep your eye out for bighorn sheep grazing on the ridges below you.

From the East Rim, head back to the three-way junction and take the middle fork toward the Wildhorse Lake Trail where you can descend 1.5 miles to Wildhorse Lake. Nestled in a scenic amphitheater, Wildhorse Lake was carved by a huge ice-age glacier. The lake bottom is rich in pollens from ancient plants. Scientists study these sediments to help determine the region's climatic changes. From the Wildhorse Trailhead parking area, turn right and continue another 0.25 miles to the Steens Summit Trail parking area. You can easily hike 0.5 miles to the 9,733-foot summit of Steens Mountain, where you'll have grand views of Winter Rim, Summer Lake, Lake Abert, Abert Rim, the Warner Basin, Hart Mountain, and the Alvord Basin.

Before you plan a trip to this area, call ahead to verify that Steens Mountain Loop is open. Often it can be closed well into mid July. Also, keep in mind that summit temperatures can be as much as 40 degrees cooler than those in lower elevations. Be sure to wear (or at least carry) warm clothing if you're planning the summit hike, as the summit has a reputation for high winds and intermittent thunderstorms.

Hike Information

🕐 Trail Contacts:
Bureau of Land Management, Burns District Office, Hines, Oregon (541) 573-4400 or *www.or.blm.gov/Burns/index.htm*

🕐 Schedule:
Late July to October. Call ahead to find out if Steens Mountain Loop is open.

💲 Fees/Permits:
None

❓ Local Information:
Harney County Chamber of Commerce, Burns, OR (541) 573-2636 or *www.harneycounty.com/Index.htm*

🎯 Local Events/Attractions:
Malheur National Wildlife Refuge, Burns, OR (541) 493-2612 or *www.r1.fws.gov/malheur/default.htm*

🍴 Accommodations:
Frenchglen Hotel, Frenchglen, OR (541) 493-2825 · **Page Springs Campground,** Frenchglen, OR (541) 473-4400 · **Steens Mountain Resort,** Frenchglen, OR (541) 493-2415

🍴 Restaurants:
Frenchglen Mercantile, Frenchglen, OR (541) 493-2738

🎫 Other Resources:
For online information about Steens Mountain and vicinity visit *www.halcyon.com/rdpayne/smnp-poi.html* · **The Oregon Desert** by E.R. Jackman and R.A. Long, Caxton Printers, Ltd.

🎫 Clubs & Organizations:
The Desert Trail Association, Madras, OR at *www.madras.net/dta/dtainfo.htm*

🥾 Hike Tours:
Visit the Desert Trail Association website to see a calendar of hike tours in this area.

🎫 Local Outdoor Retailers:
Frenchglen Mercantile, Frenchglen, OR (541) 493-2738

🗺 Maps:
USGS maps: French Glen, OR; Page Springs, OR; Tombstone Canyon, OR; Roaring Springs, OR; Fish Lake, OR; McCoy Ridge, OR; Wildhorse Lake, OR

Honorable Mentions

Southeast Oregon

Compiled here is an index of great hikes in Southeast Oregon that didn't make the A-list this time around but deserve recognition. Check them out and let us know what you think. You may decide that one or more of these hikes deserves higher status in future editions or, perhaps, you may have a hike of your own that merits some attention.

58 Hager Mountain

This moderate 3.0-mile out-and-back ascends 7,185-foot Hager Mountain, located on the perimeter of the Fremont National Forest. The trail passes through proud stands of ponderosa pine and mountain hemlock trees to an open ridge crest dotted with bright wildflowers and a fire look-out (in use June through October). From the top you have views of many central Oregon Cascade peaks as well as California's Mount Shasta.

To get there from Silver Lake, take OR 31 to the western part of town and turn south onto CR 4-12 (this road turns into FS 28). Drive nine miles to the intersection with FS 012 where you'll see a sign directing you to the Hager Mountain Trail. Turn left onto FS 012 and drive two miles to Hager Spring and the trailhead. For more information, contact the Fremont National Forest, Silver Lake Ranger District, Silver Lake, OR; (541) 576–2107; *www.fs.fed.us/r6/fremont/welcome.htm*. *DeLorme: Oregon Atlas & Gazetteer:* Page 39 D8

59 Cougar Peak

Located in the Fremont National Forest, this moderate 5.8-mile out-and-back to the summit of 7,919-foot Cougar Peak climbs through open meadows and shimmering stands of aspen.

To get there from Lakeview, drive west on OR 140 for 22.5 miles and turn right on to FS 3870. Follow signs for about 5.8 miles to Cotton Meadow Lake. Once you reach the Cotton Meadow Lake Campground, turn left on to FS 024 and drive 0.7 miles to Cougar Creek Campground. The trailhead begins 0.2 miles from the camping area at the end of the road. For more information, contact the Lakeview Ranger District, Lakeview, OR; (541) 947–3334. *DeLorme: Oregon Atlas & Gazetteer:* Page 72 C2

60 South Harney Lake Hot Springs

While the hike mentioned here is only a short walk from your car to the hot springs, we figured you couldn't pass up a chance to take a hot soak out in the wide-open desert. These hot springs are located on the southeast side of Harney Lake. While you're in the area, be sure to tour Malheur Wildlife Refuge.

To get there from Burns, drive east on OR 78 for two miles. Turn south onto OR 205 and drive 24 miles to the Malheur Wildlife Refuge. Turn right at milepost 24 and drive 8.5 miles on a dusty, rough road to an intersection with a side road. Turn right on the side road and drive 0.25 miles to the hot springs. For more information, contact the Bureau of Land Management (BLM), Burns District Office, Hines, OR; (541) 573–4400; www.or.blm.gov/Burns. *DeLorme: Oregon Atlas & Gazetteer*: Page 77 C8

61 Diamond Craters

This 9.8-mile out-and-back provides an eye-full of lava formations: craters, cinder cones, lava tubes, maars, spatter cones, and much more. The hike is made up of doubletrack roads with short side trails leading to different volcanic formations. Each of the side trails have numbered markers that correspond to an interpretive brochure you can obtain from the BLM office in Burns titled "Self-Guided Tour of Diamond Craters: Oregon's Geologic Gem."

To get there from Burns, drive east on OR 78 for 1.6 miles. Turn right on OR 205 and drive 40 miles south to the Diamond Craters Junction. Turn left on Diamond Grain Camp Road and drive 7.1 miles to the intersection with Lava Beds Road. Turn left on Lava Beds Road and drive 3.4 miles to a cinder pullout on the left side of the road. For more information, contact The BLM, Burns District Office, Hines, OR; (541) 573–4400; www.or.blm.gov/Burns. *DeLorme: Oregon Atlas & Gazetteer*: Page 78 D1

62 Peter French Round Barn

Take a break from the grueling summit hikes to enjoy a short stroll around the historic Peter French Round Barn. The wagon-wheel shaped round barn was built in the 1880s and was used to break horses during the glory days of the Peter French Empire in the Harney Basin.

To get there from Diamond, drive north on Happy Valley Road for about 20 miles. Watch for signs for the round barn. For more information, contact The Oregon Historical Society, Portland, OR 97205; (503) 222–1741; www.ohs.org. *DeLorme: Oregon Atlas & Gazetteer*: Page 78 D2

63 Arizona Creek

This 9.0-mile out-and-back hike takes you on a trek through Oregon's Outback—through Arizona Creek Canyon, past fascinating rocky outcrops, pinnacles, and finally to Stergen Meadows.

To get there from Fields, drive south OR 205 for 9.2 miles to Arizona Creek Road. Follow this dirt road for 0.5 miles to the BLM Wilderness Study Area sign. The hike begins here. Hike along the road for about 1.5 miles to where the road crosses Arizona Creek. Continue straight on the trail (the road goes left at this point) and follow the path for 2.5 miles past spectacular rock spires and cliffs. After about 3.5 miles you'll surface from the canyon, an in about another mile you'll reach Stergen Meadows; this is your turnaround point. For more information, contact the Bureau of Land Management (BLM), Vale District, Vale, OR; (541) 473–3144; *www.or.blm.gov/Vale*. *DeLorme: Oregon Atlas & Gazetteer:* Page 74 D2

64 Wall of Rome

On this short, easy 0.5-mile hike you can view the magnificent basalt tower of The Wall of Rome. If you're lucky, you might also see petroglyphs at the base of this magnificent rock cliff.

To get there from the Burns Junction (located at the intersection of OR 78 and U.S. 95), drive 12.5 miles northeast on U.S. 95 to the intersection with Rome Road. Turn left (north) and drive three miles to the trailhead on the left. For more information, contact the Bureau of Land Management (BLM), Vale District, Vale, OR; (541) 473–3144; *www.or.blm.gov/Vale*. *DeLorme: Oregon Atlas & Gazetteer:* Page 75 A6

65 Jordan Craters

Take a 2.0-mile out-and-back trip to investigate Coffeepot Crater in the Jordan Craters Lava Field. Here you'll have a chance to explore layered lava flows, lava tubes, spatter cones, and lava bombs. Be sure to watch out for rattlesnakes in this area and to bring plenty of water with you.

To get there from the I-84 and U.S. 95 junction in Idaho, travel south on U.S. 95 for approximately 60 miles to Jordan Craters Road. Turn right (west) on to Jordan Craters Road (which eventually becomes Blow Out Reservoir Road) and drive about 35 miles to an unmarked road on your left. Turn left and proceed to the parking area and the trailhead. For more information, contact the Bureau of Land Management (BLM), Vale District, Vale, OR; (541) 473–3144; *www.or.blm.gov/Vale*. *DeLorme: Oregon Atlas & Gazetteer:* Page 79 D7

66 Three Fingers Gulch

This difficult out-and-back hike takes you on a geologic expedition through the unusual formations of the Three Fingers Caldera. The length of this hike varies depending on your motivation. Begin by following a rough jeep track for about 2.5 miles to the bottom of Three Fingers Gulch. Follow the creek bed upstream to explore the multi-colored cliffs, but be sure to watch out for rattlesnakes in the area and bring plenty of water with you.

To get there from Ontario, drive south on U.S. 26/20 for approximately 25 miles to the small town of Adrian. From Adrian, drive about nine miles south on OR 201 to Succor Creek Road. Turn right on Succor Creek Road and drive for about 20 miles to the intersection with Leslie Gulch Road. Turn right and drive 4.2 miles to a saddle in the road between Long Gulch and Three Fingers Creek. For more information, contact the Bureau of Land Management (BLM), Vale District, Vale, OR; (541) 473–3144; *www.or.blm.gov/Vale*. **DeLorme: Oregon Atlas & Gazetteer:** Page 79 C7

(67) Leslie Gulch

This hike takes you on a four- to seven-mile round-trip hike (depending on how ambitious you feel) into the 15.5-million-year-old rocks of Leslie Gulch. The strangely formed lava spires will amaze you.

To get there from Jordan Valley, drive north on U.S. 95 for approximately 18 miles to the intersection with Succor Creek Road. Turn left (west) on to Succor Creek Road and proceed six miles to the intersection with Leslie Gulch Road. Turn left (west) on to Leslie Gulch Road and drive seven miles to a pullout on the left side of the road. You'll hike south into Upper Leslie Gulch Canyon. The trail ends after about a half mile, but you can continue walking cross-country and explore the canyon as far as you desire. Be sure to watch out for rattlesnakes in this area, and bring plenty of water with you. For more information, contact the Bureau of Land Management (BLM), Vale District, Vale, OR; (541) 473–3144; *www.or.blm.gov/Vale*. **DeLorme: Oregon Atlas & Gazetteer:** Page 79 C8

(68) Owyhee Boat Ramp to Echo Rock Hot Spring

This difficult 10.0-mile round-trip takes you to Echo Rock Hot Spring in the Owyhee River Canyon. The hike starts at the Leslie Gulch Boat Ramp. Hike upstream (southwest) and look for a game trail that heads up the canyon. This precipitous route takes you up the steep side of the canyon and around several rocky cliffs before dropping back to river level at Spring Creek (about the 2.0-mile mark). Walk another three miles along the river's edge (the river is high from March through June) until you reach a small side stream with hot water flowing in it. Head up the hill to a primitive soaking pool. Be sure to watch out for rattlesnakes in this area and to bring plenty of water with you.

To get there from the Jordan Valley, drive north on U.S. 95 for 18 miles. Turn left on a road with a sign that reads "Succor Creek State Park." Follow this road for 10 miles and then turn left on a gravel road with a sign reading "Leslie Gulch 15." Follow the road until it ends at a boat ramp on the Owyhee Reservoir. For more information, contact the Bureau of Land Management (BLM), Vale District, Vale, OR; (541) 473–3144; *www.or.blm.gov/Vale*. **DeLorme: Oregon Atlas & Gazetteer:** Page 79 C7

The Art of Hiking

Ethics
Getting Into Shape
Preparedness
First Aid
Navigation
Trip Planning
Equipment
Hiking With Children
Hiking With Your Dog

The Art of Hiking

When standing nose to snout with a grizzly, you're probably not too concerned with the issue of ethical behavior in the wild. No doubt you're just wetting yourself. But let's be honest. How often are you nose to snout with a grizzly? For most of us, a hike into the "wild" means loading up the 4-Runner with everything North Face™ and driving to a toileted trailhead. Sure, you can mourn how civilized we've become—how GPS units have replaced natural instinct and Gortex, true-grit—but the silly gadgets of civilization aside, we have plenty of reason to take pride in how we've matured. With survival now on the back-burner, we've begun to reason—and it's about time—that we have a responsibility to protect, no longer just conquer, our wild places; that *they*, not *we*, are at risk. So please, do what you can. Now, in keeping with our chronic tendency to reduce everything to a list, here are some rules to remember.

Leave no trace. Always leave an area just like you found it—if not better than you found it. Avoid camping in fragile, alpine meadows and along the banks of streams and lakes. Use a camp stove versus building a wood fire. Pack up all of your trash and extra food. Bury human waste at least 100 feet from water sources under six to eight inches of topsoil. Don't bathe with soap in a lake or stream—use prepackaged moistened towels to wipe off sweat and dirt or bathe in the water without soap.

Stay on the trail. It's true, a path anywhere leads nowhere new, but purists will just have to get over it. Paths serve an important purpose; they limit our impact on natural areas. Straying from a designated trail may seem innocent but it can cause damage to sensitive areas—damage that may take years to recover, if it can recover at all. Even simple shortcuts can be destructive. So, please, stay on the trail.

Keep your dog under control. You can buy a flexi-lead that allows your dog to go exploring along the trail, while allowing you the ability to reel him in should another hiker approach or should he decide to chase a rabbit. Always obey leash laws and be sure to bury your dog's waste or pack it in resealable plastic bags.

Yield to horses. When you approach these animals on the trail, always step quietly off the trail and let them pass. If you are wearing a large backpack, it's a good idea to sit down. From a horse's perspective, a hiker wearing a large backpack is a scary trail monster and these sensitive animals can be spooked easily.

GETTING INTO SHAPE

Unless you want to be sore—and possibly have to shorten your trip or vacation—be sure to get in shape before a big hike. If you're terribly out of shape, start a walking program early, preferably eight weeks in advance. Start with a 15-minute walk during your lunch hour or after work and gradually increase your walking time to an hour. You should also increase your elevation gain. Walking briskly up hills really strengthens your leg muscles and gets your heart rate up. If you work in a storied office building, take the stairs instead of the elevator. If you prefer going to a gym, walk the treadmill or use a stair-master. You can further increase your strength and endurance by walking with a loaded backpack. Stationary exercises you might consider are squats, leg lifts, sit-ups, and push-ups. Other good ways to get in shape include biking, running, aerobics, and, of course, short hikes.

PREPAREDNESS

It's been said that failing to plan means planning to fail. So do take the necessary time to plan your trip. Whether going on a short day hike or an extended backpack trip, always prepare for the worst. Simply remembering to pack a copy of the *U.S. Army Survival Manual* is not preparedness. Although it's not a bad idea if you plan on entering truly wild places, it's merely the tourniquet answer to a problem. You need to do your best to prevent the problem from arising in the first place. These days the word "survival" is often replaced with the pathetically feeble term "comfort." In order to remain comfortable (and to survive if you really want to push it), you need to concern yourself with the basics: water, food, and shelter. Don't go on a hike without having these bases covered. And don't go on a hike expecting to find these items in the woods.

Water. Even in frigid conditions, you need at least two quarts of water a day to function efficiently. Add heat and taxing terrain and you can bump that figure up to one gallon. That's simply a base to work from—your metabolism and your level of conditioning can raise or lower that amount. Unless you know your level, assume that you need one gallon of water a day. Now, where do you plan on getting the water?

Preferably not from natural water sources. These sources can be loaded with intestinal disturbers, such as bacteria, viruses, and fertilizers. *Giardia lamblia*, the most common of these disturbers, is a protozoan parasite that lives part of its lifecycle as a cyst in water sources. The parasite spreads when mammals defecate in water sources. Once ingested, Giardia can induce cramping, diarrhea, vomiting, and fatigue within two days to two weeks after ingestion. Giarda is treatable with the prescription drug Flagyl. If you believe you've contracted Giardia, see a doctor immediately.

Treating Water. The best and easiest solution to avoid polluted water is to carry your water with you. Yet, depending on the nature of your hike and the duration, this may not be an option—seeing as one gallon of water weighs 8.5 pounds. In that case, you'll need to look into treating water.

Regardless of which method you choose, you should always carry *some* water with you, in case of an emergency. Save this reserve until you absolutely need it.

There are three methods of treating water: boiling, chemical treatment, and filtering. If you boil water, it's recommended that you do so for 10 to 15 minutes. This is often impractical because you're forced to exhaust a great deal of your fuel supply. You can opt for chemical treatment (e.g. Potable Aqua) which will kill Giardia but will not take care of other chemical pollutants. Another drawback to chemical treatments is the unpleasant taste of the water after it's treated. You can remedy this by adding powdered drink mix to the water. Filters are the preferred method for treating water. Filters remove Giardia, organic and inorganic contaminants, and don't leave an aftertaste. Water filters are far from perfect as they can easily become clogged or leak if a gasket wears out. It's always a good idea to carry a back-up supply of chemical treatment tablets in case your filter decides to quit on you.

Food. If we're talking about "survival," you can go days without food, as long as you have water. But we're talking about "comfort" here. Try to avoid foods that are high in sugar and fat like candy bars and potato chips. These food types are harder to digest and are low in nutritional value. Instead, bring along foods that are easy to pack, nutritious, and high in energy (e.g. bagels, nutrition bars, dehydrated fruit, gorp, and jerky). If you are on an overnight trip, easy-to-fix dinners include rice mixes with dehydrated potatoes, corn pasta with cheese sauce, and soup mixes. For a tasty breakfast, you can fix hot oatmeal with brown sugar and reconstituted milk powder topped off with banana chips. If you like a hot drink in the morning, bring along herbal tea bags or hot chocolate. If you are a coffee junkie, you can purchase coffee that is packaged like tea bags. You can pre-package all of your meals in heavy-duty resealable plastic bags to keep food from spilling in your pack. These bags can be reused to pack out trash.

Shelter. The type of shelter you choose depends less on the conditions than on your tolerance for discomfort. Shelter comes in many forms—tent, tarp, lean to, bivy sack, cabin, cave, etc. If you're camping in the desert, a bivy sack may suffice, but if you're above the treeline and a storm is approaching, a better choice is a three or four season tent. Tents are the logical and most popular choice for most backpackers as they're lightweight and packable—and you can rest assured that you always have shelter from the elements. *[See Equipment: Tents on page 337]* Before you leave on your trip, anticipate what the weather and terrain will be like and plan for the type of shelter that will work best for your comfort level.

The Art of Hiking

Finding a campsite. If there are established campsites, stick to those. If not, start looking for a campsite early—like around 3:30 or 4:00 pm. Stop at the first decent site you see. Depending on the area, it could be a long time before you find another suitable location. Pitch your camp in an area

that's level. Make sure the area is at least 200 feet from fragile areas like lakeshores, meadows, and stream banks. And try to avoid areas thick in under-brush, as they can harbor insects and provide cover for approaching animals.

If you are camping in stormy, rainy weather, look for a rock outcrop or a shelter in the trees to keep the wind from blowing your tent all night. Be sure that you don't camp under trees with dead limbs that might break off on top of you. Also, try to find an area that has an absorbent surface, such as sandy soil or forest duff. This, in addition to camping on a surface with a slight angle, will provide better drainage. By all means, don't dig trenches to provide drainage around your tent—remember you're practicing minimum-impact camping.

If you're in bear country, steer clear of creekbeds or animal paths. If you see any signs of a bear's presence (i.e. scat, footprints), relocate. You'll need to find a campsite near a tall tree where you can hang your food and other items that may attract bears such as deodorant, toothpaste, or soap. Carry a lightweight nylon rope with which to hang your food. As a rule, you should hang your food at least 20 feet from the ground and five feet away from the tree trunk. You can put food and other items in a waterproof stuff sack and tie one end of the rope to the stuff sack. To get the other end of the rope over the tree branch, tie a good size rock to it and gently toss the rock over the tree branch. Pull the stuff sack up until it reaches the top of the branch and tie it off securely. Don't hang your food near your tent! If possible, hang your food at least 100 feet away from your campsite. Alternatives to hang-ing your food are bear-proof plastic tubes and metal bear boxes.

Lastly, think of comfort. Lie down on the ground where you intend to sleep and see if it's a good fit. For morning warmth (and a nice view to wake up to), have your tent face east.

FIRST AID

I know you're tough, but get 10 miles into the woods and develop a blis-ter and you'll wish you had carried that first aid kit. Face it, it's just plain good sense. Many companies produce light-weight, compact first aid kits, just make sure yours contains at least the following:

First Aid

- band aids
- mole skin
- various sterile gauze and dressings
- white surgical tape
- an ace bandage
- an antihistamine
- aspirin
- Betadine® solution
- a First aid book
- Tums®

- tweezers
- scissors
- anti-bacterial wipes
- triple-antibiotic ointment
- plastic gloves
- sterile cotton tip applicators
- syrup of ipecac (to induce vomiting)
- a thermometer
- a wire splint

Here are a few tips to dealing with and hopefully preventing certain ailments.

Sunburn. To avoid sunburn, wear sunscreen (SPF 15 or higher), protective clothing, and a wide-brimmed hat when you are hiking in sunny weather. If you do get sunburn, treat the area with aloe vera gel and protect the area from further sun exposure.

Blisters. Be prepared to take care of these hike-spoilers by carrying moleskin (a lightly padded adhesive), gauze and tape, or Band-Aids. An effective way to apply moleskin is to cut out a circle of moleskin and remove the center—like a donut—and place it over the blistered area. Cutting the center out will reduce the pressure applied to the sensitive skin. Other products that can help you combat blisters are Bodyglide® and Second Skin®. Bodyglide® (1–888–263–9454) is applied to suspicious hot spots before a blister forms to help decrease friction to that area. Second Skin® (made by Spenco) is applied to the blister after it has popped and acts as a "second skin" to help prevent further irritation.

Insect bites and stings. You can treat most insect bites and stings by applying hydrocortisone 1% cream topically and taking a pain medication such as ibuprofen or acetaminophen to reduce swelling. If you forgot to pack these items, a cold compress or a paste of mud and ashes can sometimes assuage the itching and discomfort. Remove any stingers by using tweezers or scraping the area with your fingernail or a knife blade. Don't pinch the area as you'll only spread the venom.

Some hikers are highly sensitive to bites and stings and may have a serious allergic reaction that can be life threatening. Symptoms of a serious allergic reaction can include wheezing, an asthmatic attack, and shock. The treatment for this severe type of reaction is epinephrine (Adrenaline). If you know that you are sensitive to bites and stings, carry a pre-packaged kit of epinephrine (e.g., Anakit®), which can be obtained only by prescription from your doctor.

Ticks. As you well know, ticks can carry disease, such as Rocky Mountain Spotted Fever and Lyme disease. The best defense is, of course, prevention. If you know you're going to be hiking through an area littered with ticks, wear long pants and a long sleeved shirt. You can apply a permethrin repellent to your clothing and a DEET repellent to exposed skin. At the end of your hike, do a spot check for ticks (and insects in general). If you do find a tick, coat the insect with Vaseline® or tree sap to cut off its air supply. The tick should release its hold, but if it doesn't, grab the head of the tick firmly—with a pair of tweezers if you have them—and gently pull it away from the skin with a twisting motion. Sometimes the mouthparts linger, embedded in your skin. If this happens, try to remove them with a disinfected needle. Clean the affected area with an anti-bacterial cleanser and then apply triple antibiotic ointment. Monitor the area for a few days. If irritation persists or a white spot develops, see a doctor for possible infection.

Poison ivy, oak, and sumac. These skin irritants can be found most anywhere in North America and come in the form of a bush or a vine, having leaflets in groups of three, five, seven, or nine. Learn how to spot the plants. The oil they secrete can cause an allergic reaction in the form of blisters, usually

poison ivy

about 12 hours after exposure. The itchy rash can last from ten days to several weeks. The best defense against these irritants is to wear protective clothing and to apply a non-prescription product called IvyBlock® to exposed skin. This lotion is meant to guard against the affects of poison ivy/oak/sumac and can be washed off with soap and water. Taking a hot shower after you return home from your hike will also help to

poison oak

remove any lingering oil from your skin. Should you contract a rash from any of these plants, use Benadryl® or a similar product to reduce the itching. If the rash is localized, create a light Clorox®/water wash to dry up the area. If the rash has spread, either tough it out or see your doctor about getting a dose of Cortisone®

poison sumac

(available both orally and by injection).

Snakebites. First off, snakebites are rare in North America. Unless startled or provoked, the majority of snakes will not bite. If you are wise to their habitats and keep a careful eye on the trail, you should be just fine. Though your chances of being struck are slim, it's wise to know what to do in the event you are.

If a *non-poisonous* snake bites you, allow the wound to bleed a small amount and then cleanse the wounded area with a Betadine® solution (10% povidone iodine). Rinse the wound with clean water (preferably) or fresh urine (it might sound ugly, but it's sterile). Once the area is clean, cover it with triple antibiotic ointment and a clean bandage. Remember, most residual damage from snakebites, poisonous or otherwise, comes from infection, not the snake's venom. Keep the area as clean as possible and get medical attention immediately.

If you are bitten by a *poisonous* snake, remove the toxin with a suctioning device, found in a snakebite kit. If you do not have such a device, squeeze the wound—do NOT use your mouth for suction as the venom will enter your bloodstream through the vessels under the tongue and head straight for your heart. Then, clean the wound just as you would a non-poisonous bite. Tie a clean band of cloth snuggly around the afflicted appendage, about an inch or so above the bite (or the rim of the swelling). This is NOT a tourniquet—you want to simply slow the blood flow, not cut it off. Loosen the band if numbness ensues. Remove the band for a minute and re-apply a little higher every ten minutes

If it is your friend who's been bitten, treat him or her for shock—make him comfortable, have him lie down, elevate the legs, and keep him warm. Avoid applying anything cold to the bite wound. Immobilize the affected area and remove any constricting items such as rings, watches, or restrictive clothing—swelling may occur. Once your friend is stable and relatively calm, hike out to get help. The victim should get treatment within 12 hours, ideally, which usually consists of a tetanus shot, antivenin, and antibiotics.

Now, if you are alone and struck by a poisonous snake, stay calm. Hysteria will only quicken the venom's spread. Follow the procedure above and do your best to reach help. When hiking out, don't run—you'll only increase the flow of blood throughout your system. Instead, walk calmly.

In terms of poisonous snakes, five of the six varieties found in Alabama belong to the pit viper group: the copperhead, cottonmouth, timber rattlesnake, diamondback rattlesnake, and pigmy rattlesnake. These snakes vary in color and marking but are identified by a small "pit" found between the eye and nostril. Be especially careful of where you put your hands and feet with rattlers around since they enjoy sunning themselves on rock ledges and outcroppings. The last poisonous snake found in Alabama is the rarely seen coral snake, characterized by bands of red and black, separated by narrow bands of yellow.

Dehydration. Have you ever hiked in hot weather and had a roaring headache and felt fatigued after only a few miles? More than likely you were dehydrated. Symptoms of dehydration include fatigue, headache, and decreased coordination and judgment. When you are hiking, your body's rate of fluid loss depends on the outside temperature, humidity, altitude, and your activity level. On average, a hiker walking in warm weather will lose four liters of fluid a day. That fluid loss is easily replaced by normal consumption of liquids and food. However, if a hiker is walking briskly in hot, dry weather and hauling a heavy pack, he can lose one to three liters of water an hour. It's important to always carry plenty of water and to stop often and drink fluids regularly, even if you aren't thirsty.

Heat exhaustion is the result of a loss of large amounts of electrolytes and often occurs if a hiker is dehydrated and has been under heavy exertion. Common symptoms of heat exhaustion include cramping, exhaustion, fatigue, lightheadedness, and nausea. You can treat heat exhaustion by getting out of the sun and drinking an electrolyte solution made up of one teaspoon of salt and one tablespoon of sugar dissolved in a liter of water. Drink this solution slowly over a period of one hour. Drinking plenty of fluids (preferably an electrolyte solution like Gatorade®) can prevent heat exhaustion. Avoid hiking during the hottest parts of the day and wear breathable clothing, a wide brimmed hat, and sunglasses.

Hypothermia is one of the biggest dangers in the backcountry—especially for day hikers in the summertime. That may sound strange, but imagine starting out on a hike in mid-summer when it's sunny and 80 degrees out. You're clad in nylon shorts and a cotton T-shirt. About halfway through your hike, the sky begins to cloud up and in the next hour a light drizzle begins to fall and the wind starts to pick up. Before you know it, you are soaking wet and shivering—the perfect recipe for hypothermia. More advanced signs include decreased coordination, slurred speech, and blurred vision. When a victim's temperature falls below 92 degrees Fahrenheit, the blood pressure and pulse plummet, possibly leading to coma and death.

To avoid hypothermia, always bring a windproof/rainproof shell, a fleece jacket, Capilene tights, gloves, and hat when you are hiking in the mountains. Learn to adjust your clothing layers based on the temperature. If you are climbing uphill at a moderate pace you will stay warm, but when you stop for a break you'll become cold quickly, unless you add more layers of clothing.

If a hiker is showing advanced signs of hypothermia, dress him in dry clothes and make sure he is wearing a hat and gloves. Place him in a sleeping bag in a tent or shelter that will protect him from the wind and other elements. Give him warm fluids to drink and keep him awake.

Frostbite. When the mercury dips below 32 degrees Fahrenheit, your extremities begin to chill. If a persistent chill attacks a localized area, say your hands or your toes, the circulatory system reacts by cutting off blood flow to the affected area—the idea being to protect and preserve the body's overall temperature. And so it's death by attrition for the affected area. Ice crystals start to form from the water in the cells of the neglected tissue. Deprived of heat, nourishment, and now water, the tissue literally starves. This is frostbite.

Prevention is your best defense against this situation. Most prone to frostbite are your face, hands, and feet—so protect these areas well. Wool is the material of choice because it provides ample air space for insulation and draws moisture away from the skin. However, synthetic fabrics have recently made great strides in the cold weather clothing market. Do your research. A pair of light silk liners under your regular gloves is a good trick to keeping warm. They afford some additional warmth, but more importantly they'll allow you to remove your mitts for tedious work without exposing the skin.

Now, if your feet or hands start to feel cold or numb due to the elements, warm them as quickly as possible. Place cold hands under your armpits or bury them in your crotch. If your feet are cold, change your socks. If there's plenty of room in your boots, add another pair of socks. Do remember though that constricting your feet in tight boots can restrict blood flow and actually make your feet colder more quickly. Your socks need to have breathing room if they're going to be effective. Dead air provides insulation. If your face is cold, place your warm hands over your face or simply wear a head stocking (called a balaclava).

Should your skin go numb and start to appear white and waxy, chances are you've got or are developing frostbite. Don't try to thaw the area unless you can maintain the warmth. In other words, don't stop to warm up your frostbitten feet only to head back on the trail. You'll do more damage than good. Tests have shown that hikers who walked on thawed feet did more harm, and endured more pain, than hikers who left the affected areas alone. Do your best to get out of the cold entirely and seek medical attention—which usually consists of performing a rapid rewarming in water for 20 to 30 minutes.

The overall objective in preventing both hypothermia and frostbite is to keep the body's core warm. Protect key areas where heat escapes, like the top of the head, and maintain the proper nutrition level. Foods that are high in calories aid the body in producing heat. Never smoke or drink when you're in situations where the cold is threatening. By affecting blood flow, these activities ultimately cool the body's core temperature.

NAVIGATION

Whether you are going on a short hike in a familiar area or planning a weeklong backpack trip, you should always be equipped with the proper navigational equipment—at the very least a detailed map and a sturdy compass.

Maps. There are many different types of maps available to help you find your way on the trail. Easiest to find are Forest Service maps and BLM (Bureau of Land Management) maps. These maps tend to cover large areas, so be sure they are detailed enough for your particular trip. You can also obtain National Park maps as well as high quality maps from private companies and trail groups. These maps can be obtained either from outdoor stores or ranger stations.

U.S. Geological Survey topographic maps are particularly popular with hikers—especially serious backcountry hikers. These maps contain the standard map symbols such as roads, lakes, and rivers, as well as contour lines that show the details of the trail terrain like

courtesy Magellan Systems

Magellan GPS unit.

ridges, valleys, passes, and mountain peaks. The 7.5-minute series (1 inch on the map equals approximately two-fifths of a mile on the ground) provides the closest inspection available. USGS maps are available by mail (U.S. Geological Survey, Map Distribution Branch, PO Box 25286, Denver, Colorado 80225) or you can visit them online at *http://mapping.usgs. gov/esic/to_order.html.*

If you want to check out the high tech world of maps, you can purchase topographic maps on CD-ROM. These software-mapping programs let you select a route on your computer, print it out, and then take it with you on the trail. Some software mapping programs let you insert symbols and labels, download waypoints from a GPS unit, and export the maps to other software programs. Mapping software programs such as DeLorme's TopoUSA™ (*www.delorme.com*) and MAPTECH's Terrain Navigator™ (*www.maptech. com*) let you do all of these things and more.

The art of map reading is a skill that you can develop by first practicing in an area you are familiar with. To begin, orient the map so the map is lined up in the correct direction (i.e. north on the map is lined up with true north). Next, familiarize yourself with the map symbols and try and match them up with terrain features around you such as a high ridge, mountain peak, river, or lake. If you are practicing with an USGS map notice the contour lines. On gentler terrain these contour lines are spaced further apart, and on steeper terrain they are closer together. Pick a short loop trail and stop frequently to check your position on the map. As you practice map reading, you'll learn how to anticipate a steep section on the trail or a good place to take a rest break, etc.

The Compass. First off, the sun is not a substitute for a compass. So, what kind of compass should you have? Here are some characteristics you should look for: a rectangular base with detailed scales, a liquid-filled housing, protective housing, a sighting line on the mirror, luminous alignment and back-bearing arrows, a luminous north-seeking arrow, and a well-defined bezel ring.

You can learn compass basics by reading the detailed instructions included with your compass. If you want to fine-tune your compass skills, sign up for an orienteering class or purchase a book on compass reading. Once you've learned the basic skills on using a compass, remember to practice these skills before you head into the backcountry.

If you are a klutz at using a compass, you may be interested in checking out the technical wizardry of the **GPS (Global Positioning System)** device. The GPS was developed by the Pentagon and works off 24 NAVSTAR satellites, which were designed to guide missiles to their targets. A GPS device is a handheld unit that calculates your latitude and longitude with the easy press of a button. However, the crafty defense department doesn't want civilians (or spies) to have the same pinpoint accuracy, so they have purposefully mixed the signals a bit so a GPS unit's accuracy is generally within 100 meters or 328 feet.

There are many different types of GPS units available and they range in price from $100 to $400. In general, all GPS units have a display screen and keypad where you input information. In addition to acting as a compass, the unit allows you to plot your route, easily retrace your path, track your travelling speed, find the mileage between waypoints, and calculate the total mileage of your route.

Before you purchase a GPS unit, keep in mind that these devices don't pick up signals indoors, in heavily wooded areas, on mountain peaks, or in deep valleys.

A **pedometer** is a handy device that can track your mileage as you hike. This device is a small, clip-on unit with a digital display that calculates your hiking distance in miles or kilometers based on your walking stride. Some units also calculate the calories you burn and your total hiking time. Pedometers are available at most large outdoor stores and range in price from $20 to $40.

TRIP PLANNING

Planning your hiking adventure begins with letting a friend or relative know your trip itinerary so they can call for help if you don't return at your scheduled time. Your next task is to make sure you are outfitted to experience the risks and rewards of the trail. This section highlights gear and clothing you may want to take with you to get the most out of your hike.

Day Hikes	
• camera/film	• matches in waterproof container and fire starter
• compass/GPS unit	
• pedometer	• polar fleece jacket
• daypack	• raingear
• First Aid kit	• space blanket
• food	• sunglasses
• guidebook	• sunscreen
• headlamp/flashlight with extra batteries and bulbs	• swim suit
	• watch
• hat	• water
• insect repellant	• water bottles/water hydration system
• knife/multi-purpose tool	
• map	

EQUIPMENT

With the outdoor market currently flooded with products, many of which are pure gimmickry, it seems impossible to both differentiate and choose. Do I really need a tropical-fish-lined collapsible shower? (No, you don't.) The only defense against the maddening quantity of items thrust in your face is to think practically—and to do so *before* you go shopping. The worst buys are impulsive buys. Since most of your name brands will differ only slightly in quality, it's best to know what you're looking for in terms of function. Buy only what you need. You will, don't forget, be carrying what you've bought on your back. Here are some things to keep in mind before you go shopping.

Overnight Trips

- backpack and waterproof rain cover
- backpacker's trowel
- bandanna
- bear repellant spray
- bear bell
- biodegradable soap
- pot scrubber
- collapsible water container (2-3 gallon capacity)
- clothing—extra wool socks, shirt and shorts
- cook set/utensils
- ditty bags to store gear
- extra plastic resealable bags
- gaiters
- garbage bag
- ground cloth
- journal/pen
- nylon rope to hang food
- long underwear
- permit (if required)
- rain jacket and pants
- sandals to wear around camp and to ford streams
- sleeping bag
- waterproof stuff sack
- sleeping pad
- small bath towel
- stove and fuel
- tent
- toiletry items
- water filter
- whistle

Clothes. Clothing is your armor against Mother Nature's little surprises. Although Alabama's weather isn't generally severe, even in the winter months, buying clothing that can be worn in layers is always a good strategy. In the winter months the first layer you'll want to wear is a "wicking" layer of long underwear that keeps perspiration away from your skin. Wearing long underwear made from synthetic fibers such as Capilene, Coolmax, or Thermax is an excellent choice. These fabrics wick moisture away from the skin and draw it toward the next layer of clothing where it then evaporates. Avoid wearing long underwear made of cotton as it is slow to dry and keeps moisture next to your skin.

The second layer you'll wear is the "insulating" layer. Aside from keeping you warm, this layer needs to "breathe" so you stay dry while hiking. A fabric that provides insulation and dries quickly is fleece. It's interesting to note that this one-of-a-kind fabric is made out of recycled plastic. Purchasing a zip-up jacket made of this material is highly recommended.

The last line of layering defense is the "shell" layer. You'll need some type of waterproof, windproof, breathable jacket that'll fit over all of your other layers. It should have a large hood that fits over a hat. You'll also need a good pair of rain pants made from a similar waterproof, breathable fabric. A fabric that easily fits the bill is GORE-TEX®. However, while a quality GOR-TEX jacket can range in price from $100 to $450, you should know that there are more affordable fabrics out there that work just as well.

Now that you've learned the basics of layering, you can't forget to protect your hands and face. In cold, windy, or rainy weather you'll need a hat made of wool or fleece and insulated, waterproof gloves that will keep your hands warm and toasty. As mentioned earlier, buying an additional pair of light silk liners to wear under your regular gloves is a good idea. They'll allow you to remove your outer-gloves for tedious work without exposing the skin.

Footwear. If you have any extra money to spend on your trip, put that money into boots or trail shoes. Poor shoes will bring a hike to a halt faster than anything else. To avoid this annoyance, buy shoes that provide support and are lightweight and flexible. A lightweight hiking boot is better than a heavy, leather mountaineering boot for most day hikes and backpacking. Trail running shoes provide a little extra cushion and are made in a high-top style that many people wear for hiking. These running shoes are lighter, more flexible, and more breathable than hiking boots. If you know you'll be hiking in wet weather often, purchase boots or shoes with a GORE-TEX® liner, which will help keep your feet dry.

When buying your boots, be sure to wear the same type of socks you'll be wearing on the trail. If the boots you're buying are for cold weather hiking, try the boots on while wearing two pairs of socks. Speaking of socks, a good cold weather sock combination is to wear a thinner sock made of wool or polypropylene covered by a heavier outer sock made of wool. The inner sock protects the foot from the rubbing effects of the outer sock and prevents blisters.

Once you've purchased your footwear, be sure to break them in before you hit the trail. New footwear is often stiff and needs to be stretched and molded to your foot.

Backpacks. No matter what type of hiking you do you'll need a pack of some sort to carry the basic trail essentials. There are a variety of backpacks on the market, but let's first discuss what you intend to use it for. Day hikes or overnight trips?

If you plan on doing a day hike, a daypack should have some of the following characteristics: a padded hip belt that's at least two inches in diameter (avoid packs with only a small nylon piece of webbing for a hip belt); a chest strap (the chest strap helps stabilize the pack against your body); external pockets to carry water and other items that you want easy access to; an internal pocket to hold keys, a knife, a wallet, and other miscellaneous items; an external lashing system to hold a jacket; and a hydration pocket for carrying a hydration system (which consists of a water bladder with an attachable drinking hose).

For short hikes, some hikers like to use a fanny pack to store just a camera, food, a compass, a map, and other trail essentials. Most fanny packs have pockets for two water bottles and a padded hip belt.

If you intend to do an extended, overnight trip, there are multiple considerations. First off, you need to decide what kind of framed pack you want. There are two backpack types for backpacking: the internal frame and the external frame. An internal frame pack rests closer to your body, making it more stable and easier to balance when hiking over rough terrain. An external frame pack is just that, an aluminum frame attached to the exterior of the pack. An external frame pack is better for long backpack trips because it distributes the pack weight better and you can carry heavier loads. It's easier to pack, and your gear is more accessible. It also offers better back ventilation in hot weather.

The most critical measurement for fitting a pack is torso length. The pack needs to rest evenly on your hips without sagging. A good pack will come in two or three sizes and have straps and hip belts that are adjustable according to your body size and characteristics.

When you purchase a backpack, go to an outdoor store with salespeople who are knowledgeable in how to properly fit a pack. Once the pack is fitted for you, load the pack with the amount of weight you plan on taking on the trail. The weight of the pack should be distributed evenly and you should be able to swing your arms and walk briskly without feeling out of balance. Another good technique for evaluating a pack is to walk up and down stairs and make quick turns to the right and to the left to be sure the pack doesn't feel out of balance.

Other features that are nice to have on a backpack include a removable day pack or fanny pack, external pockets for extra water, and extra lash points to attach a jacket or other items.

Sleeping bags and pads. Sleeping bags are rated by temperature. You can purchase a bag made of synthetic fiber such as Polarguard® HV or DuPont Hollofil® II, or you can buy a goose down bag. Goose down bags are more expensive, but they have a higher insulating capacity by weight and will keep their loft longer. You'll want to purchase a bag with a temperature rating that fits the time of year and conditions you are most likely to camp in. One caveat: the techno-standard for temperature ratings is far from perfect. Ratings vary from manufacturer to manufacturer, so to protect yourself you should purchase a bag rated 10 to 15 degrees below the temperature you expect to be camping in. Synthetic bags are more resistant to water than down bags, but many down bags are now made with a GORE-TEX® shell that helps to repel water. Down bags are also more compressible than synthetic bags and take up less room in your pack, which is an important consideration if you are planning a multi-day backpack trip. Features to look for in a sleeping bag include: a mummy style bag, a hood you can cinch down around your head in cold weather, and draft tubes along the zippers that help keep heat in and drafts out.

You'll also want a sleeping pad to provide insulation and padding from the cold ground. There are different types of sleeping pads available, from the more expensive self-inflating air mattresses to the less expensive closed-cell foam pads (e.g., Ridge Rest®). Self-inflating air mattresses are usually heavier than closed-cell foam mattresses and are prone to punctures.

Tents. The tent is your home away from home while on the trail. It provides protection from wind, snow, rain, and insects. A three-season tent is a good choice for backpacking and can range in price from $100 to $500. These lightweight and versatile tents provide protection in all types of weather, except heavy snowstorms or high winds, and range in weight from four to eight pounds. Look for a tent that's easy to set up and will easily fit two people with gear. Dome type tents usually offer more headroom and places to store gear. Other tent designs include a vestibule where you can store wet boots and backpacks. Some nice-to-have items in a tent include interior pockets to store small items and lashing points to hang a clothesline. Most three-season tents also come with stakes so you can secure the tent in high winds. Before you purchase a tent, set it up and take it down a few times to be sure it is easy to handle. Also, sit inside the tent and make sure it has enough room for you and your gear.

HIKING WITH CHILDREN

Hiking with children isn't a matter of how many miles you can cover or how much elevation gain you make in a day, it's about seeing and experiencing nature through their eyes.

Kids like to explore and have fun. They like to stop and point out bugs and plants, look under rocks, jump in puddles, and throw sticks. If you're taking a toddler or young child on a hike, start with a trail that you're familiar with. Trails that have interesting things for kids, like piles of leaves to play in or a small stream to wade through during the summer, will make the hike much more enjoyable for them and will keep them from getting bored.

You can keep your child's attention if you have a strategy before starting on the trail. Using games is not only an effective way to keep a child's attention, it's also a great way to teach him or her about nature. Play hide and seek, where your child is the mouse and you are the hawk. Quiz children on the names of plants and animals. If your children are old enough, let them carry their own daypack filled with snacks and water. So that you are sure to go at their pace and not yours, let them lead the way. Playing follow the leader works particularly well when you have a group of children. Have each child take a turn at being the leader.

With children, a lot of clothing is key. The only thing predictable about weather is that it will change. Even in Alabama the weather can sometimes be unpredictable, so you always want to bring extra clothing for your children no matter what the season. In the winter, have your children wear wool socks, and warm layers such as long underwear, a polar fleece jacket and hat, wool mittens, and good rain gear. It's not a bad idea to have these along in late fall and early spring as well. Good footwear is also important. A sturdy pair of high top tennis shoes or lightweight hiking boots are the best bet for little ones. If you're hiking in the summer near a lake or stream, bring along a pair of old sneakers that your child can put on when he wants to go exploring in the water. Remember when you're near any type of water, always watch your child at all times. Also, keep a close eye on teething toddlers who may decide a rock or leaf of poison oak is an interesting item to put in their mouth.

From spring through fall, you'll want your kids to wear a wide brimmed hat to keep their face, head, and ears protected from the hot sun. Also, make sure your children wear sunscreen at all times. Choose a brand without Paba—children have sensitive skin and may have an allergic reaction to sunscreen that contains Paba. If you are hiking with a child younger than six months, don't use sunscreen or insect repellant. Instead, be sure that their head, face, neck, and ears are protected from the sun with a wide brimmed hat, and that all other skin exposed to the sun is protected with the appropriate clothing.

Remember that food is fun. Kids like snacks so it's important to bring a lot of munchies for the trail. Stopping often for snack breaks is a fun way to keep the trail interesting. Raisins, apples, granola bars, crackers and cheese, Cheerios, and trail mix all make great snacks. If your child is old enough to carry his/her own backpack, fill it with treats before you leave. If your kids don't like drinking water, you can bring boxes of fruit juice.

Avoid poorly designed child-carrying packs—you don't want to break your back carrying your child. Most child-carrying backpacks designed to hold a 40-pound child will contain a large carrying pocket to hold diapers and other items. Some have an optional rain/sun hood. Tough Traveler® (1–800–GO–TOUGH or *www.toughtraveler.com*) is a company that specializes in making backpacks for carrying children and other outdoor gear for children.

HIKING WITH YOUR DOG

Bringing your furry friend with you is always more fun than leaving him behind. Our canine pals make great trail buddies because they never complain and always make good company. Hiking with your dog can be a rewarding experience, especially if you plan ahead.

Getting your dog in shape. Before you plan outdoor adventures with your dog, make sure he's in shape for the trail. Getting your dog into shape takes the same discipline as getting yourself into shape, but luckily, your dog can get in shape with you. Take your dog with you on your daily runs or walks. If there is a park near your house, hit a tennis ball or play Frisbee with your dog.

Swimming is also an excellent way to get your dog into shape. If there is a lake or river near where you live and your dog likes the water, have him retrieve a tennis ball or stick. Gradually build your dog's stamina up over a two to three month period. A good rule of thumb is to assume that your dog will travel twice as far as you will on the trail. If you plan on doing a five-mile hike, be sure your dog is in shape for a ten-mile hike.

Training your dog for the trail. Before you go on your first hiking adventure with your dog, be sure he has a firm grasp on the basics of canine etiquette and behavior. Make sure he can sit, lay down, stay, and come. One of the most important commands you can teach your canine pal is to "come" under any situation. It's easy for your friend's nose to lead him astray or possibly get lost. Another helpful command is the "get behind" command. When you're on a hiking trail that's narrow, you can have your dog follow behind you when other trail users approach. Nothing is more bothersome than an enthusiastic dog that runs back and forth on the trail and disrupts the peace of the trail for others. When you see other trail users approaching you on the trail, give them the right of way by quietly stepping off the trail and making your dog lie down and stay until they pass.

Equipment. The most critical pieces of equipment you can invest in for your dog are proper identification and a sturdy leash. Flexi-leads work well for hiking because they give your dog more freedom to explore but still leave you in control. Make sure your dog has identification that includes your name and address and a number for your veterinarian. Other forms of identification for your dog include a tattoo or a microchip. You should consult your veterinarian for more information on these last two options.

The next piece of equipment you'll want to consider is a pack for your dog. By no means should you hold all of your dog's essentials in your pack—let him carry his own gear! Dogs that are in good shape can carry up to 30 percent to 40 percent of their own weight.

Companies that make good quality packs include RuffWear™ (1–888–RUFF–WEAR; *www.ruffwear.com*) and Wolf Packs® (1–541–482–7669; *www.wolfpacks.com*). Most packs are fitted by a dog's weight and girth measurement. Companies that make dog packs generally include guidelines to help you pick out the size that's right for your dog. Some characteristics to look for when purchasing a pack for your dog include: a harness that contains two padded girth straps, a padded chest strap, leash attachments, removable saddle bags, internal water bladders, and external gear cords.

You can introduce your dog to the pack by first placing the empty pack on his back and letting him wear it around the yard. Keep an eye on him during this first introduction. He may decide to chew through the straps if you aren't watching him closely. Once he learns to treat the pack as an object of fun and not a foreign enemy, fill the pack evenly on both sides with a few ounces of dog food in resealable plastic bags. Have your dog wear his pack on your daily walks for a period of two to three weeks. Each week add a little more weight to the pack until your dog will accept carrying the maximum amount of weight he can carry.

You can also purchase collapsible water and dog food bowls for your dog. These bowls are lightweight and can easily be stashed into your pack or your dog's. If you are hiking on rocky terrain or in the snow, you can purchase footwear for your dog that will protect his feet from cuts and bruises. All of these products can be purchased from RuffWear™ (1–888–RUFF–WEAR; www.ruffwear.com).

The following is a checklist of items to bring when you take your dog hiking: collapsible water bowls, a comb, a collar and a leash, dog food, a dog pack, flea/tick powder, paw protection, water, and a First Aid kit that contains eye ointment, tweezers, scissors, stretchy foot wrap, gauze, anti-bacterial wash, sterile cotton tip applicators, antibiotic ointment, and cotton wrap.

First aid for your dog. Your dog is just as prone—if not more prone—to getting in trouble on the trail as you are, so be prepared. Here's a run down of the more likely misfortunes that might befall your little friend.

Bees and wasps. If a bee or wasp stings your dog, remove the stinger with a pair of tweezers and place a mudpack or a cloth dipped in cold water over the affected area.

Heat stroke. Avoid hiking with your dog in really hot weather. Dogs with heat stroke will pant excessively, lie down and refuse to get up, and become lethargic and disoriented. If your dog shows any of these signs on the trail, have him lie down in the shade. If you are near a stream, pour cool water over your dog's entire body to help bring his body temperature back to normal.

Heartworm. Dogs get heartworms from mosquitoes which carry the disease in the prime mosquito months of July and August. Giving your dog a monthly pill prescribed by your veterinarian easily prevents this condition.

Plant pitfalls. One of the biggest plant hazards for dogs on the trail are fox-tails. Foxtails are pointed grass seed heads that bury themselves in your friend's fur, between his toes, and even get in his ear canal. If left unattended, these nasty seeds can work their way under the skin and cause abscesses and other problems. If you have a longhaired dog, consider trimming the hair between his toes and giving him a summer haircut to help prevent fox-tails from attaching to his fur. After every hike, always look over your dog for these seeds—especially between his toes and his ears.

Other plant hazards include burrs, thorns, thistles, and poison oak. If you find any burrs or thistles on your dog, remove them as soon as possible before they become an unmanageable mat. Thorns can pierce a dog's foot and cause a great deal of pain. If you see that your dog is lame, stop and check his feet for thorns. Dogs are immune to poison oak but they can pick up the sticky, oily substance from the plant and transfer it to you.

Protect those paws. Be sure to keep your dog's nails trimmed so he avoids getting soft tissue or joint injuries. If your dog slows and refuses to go on, check to see that his paws aren't torn or worn. You can protect your dog's paws from trail hazards such as sharp gravel, foxtails, lava scree, and thorns by purchasing dog boots.

Sunburn. If your dog has light skin he is an easy target for sunburn on his nose and other exposed skin areas. You can apply a non-toxic sunscreen to exposed skin areas that will help protect him from over-exposure to the sun.

Ticks and fleas. Ticks can easily give your dog Lyme disease, as well as other diseases. Before you hit the trail, treat your dog with a flea and tick spray or powder. You can also ask your veterinarian about a once-a-month pour-on treatment that repels fleas and ticks.

When you are finally ready to hit the trail with your dog, keep in mind that National Parks and many wilderness areas do not allow dogs on trails. Your best bet is to hike in National forests, BLM lands, and state parks. Always call ahead to see what the restrictions are.

Adventure Directory

Outside America's Guide to Outdoor Adventure

If you're anything like us, one sport just won't do it. To give you an idea of what else is out there in the way of outdoor recreation, we at Outside America have created the Adventure Directory, your one-stop adventure-guide catalogue. Since your hiking boots can't take you everywhere you'll want to go (they're virtually worthless on water), check out one of these guide companies and experience, under the direction of a local pro, the many facets of Oregon's great outdoors.

Bicycling

The Adventure Center. Ashland, OR 1-800-444-2819 or (541) 488-2819. Guided mountain bike tours around Mt. Ashland and the Mountain Lakes.

Backroads. Berkeley, CA. 1-800-462-2848 or (510) 527-1555. Guided road bike tours of the Oregon Coast.

Bicycle Adventures. Olympia, WA 1-800-443-6060 or (360) 786-0989. International bicycle tours; concentration on Pacific Northwest.

Blackwater Bikes.
Davis, WV (304) 259-5286

Elk River Touring Center.
Slatyfork, WV (304) 572-3771

Hells Canyon Bicycle Tours.
Joseph, OR (541) 432-2453

Oregon Ridge & River Excursions. Glide, OR 1-888-454-9696 or (541) 496-3333. Mountain biking trips in the Umpqua National Forest.

Pacific Crest Mountain Bike Tours. 1-800-849-6589 or (541) 593-5058. Guided mountain bike tours.

Roads Less Traveled.
Longmont, CO (303) 678-8750

Timberline Bicycle Tours.
Denver, CO (303) 759-3804

Trails Unlimited, Inc.
Nashville, IN (812) 988-6232

Vermont Bicycling Touring.
Bristol, VT 1-800-245-3868

Mountain Biking at Ski Resorts

Mount Bachelor Resort. Bend, OR (541) 382-2242. Many trails open for mountain biking; lift service available.

Mount Hood Ski Bowl. Government Camp, OR (503) 272-3206. Many trails open for mountain biking; lift service available.

Winter Sports

Adventure Out. Hood River, OR (541) 387-4626. Guided one-day and overnight backcountry ski trips.

Fantastic Adventures. Bend, OR (541) 389-5640. Guided snowmobile trips.

The Adventure Center. Ashland, OR 1-800-444-2819 or (541) 488-2819. Guided cross-country and telemark trips; lessons available.

Steens Mountain Packers. Frenchglen, OR 1-800-977-3995 or (541) 495-2315. Cross-country and heli-skiing trips in the Steens Mountain area.

Horseback Riding

Bandon Beach Riding Stables. Bandon, OR (541) 347-3423. Guided rides along the beach.

Black Butte Ranch Stables. 7 miles west of Sisters, OR (541) 595-2061. Guided horseback rides.

C Bow Arrow Ranch. Coburg, OR (541) 345-5643. Guided rides through the Coburg foothills.

C&M Stables. Florence, OR (541) 997-7540. Guided beach, dune, or mountain rides.

Crazy Cayuse Ranch & Pack Station. Union Creek, OR (541) 779-9121. Guided horseback rides.

Eagle Crest Equestrian Center. Redmond, OR (541) 923-2072. Guided one and two-hour horseback rides.

Hawk's Rest Ranch. Gold Beach, OR (541) 247-6423. Guided one and two-hour ranch and beach rides.

Indian Creek Trail Rides. Gold Beach, OR (541) 247-7704. Guided one and two-hour rides on a working cattle ranch.

Mountain Gate Stables. Ashland, OR (541) 482-8873. Guided trips into the hills outside of Ashland; instruction available.

Mountain Shadow Ranch. Cascade Locks, OR (541) 374-8592. Guided day rides into the Columbia River Gorge National Scenic Area.

Rock Springs Guest Ranch. Bend, OR 1-800-225-3833 or (541) 382-1957. Guided horseback rides; hiking and backpacking; lodging.

Pruitt Equestrian Centre. Lowell, OR (541) 937-3265. Guided horseback rides.

Steens Mountain Packers. Frenchglen, OR 1-800-977-3995 or (541) 495-2315. Guided horseback riding and horsepack trips; cattle drives.

Saddleback Stables. Sunriver, OR (541) 593-6995. Guided one to eight-hour rides; instruction available.

Llama Trecking

Oregon Llamas. Camp Sherman, OR 1-800-722-5262 or (541) 595-2088. Packstock trips into the central Oregon Cascades.

Mountaineering & Climbing

Adventure Out. Hood River, OR (541) 387-4626. Year-round rock climbing opportunities.

Adventure Smith Guides. Portland, OR (503) 293-6727. Outdoor, rock-climbing classes.

First Ascent Climbing & Guide Service. (541) 548-5137. Climbing instruction at Smith Rock.

Portland Community College. Portland, OR (503) 977-4933. Outdoor, rock-climbing classes.

Rainier Mountaineering Inc. Tacoma, WA (253) 627-6242 in winter or (360) 569-2227 in summer. Guided trips up Mount Rainier; instruction available.

Timberline Mountain Guides. Government Camp, OR 1-800-464-7704 or (503) 272-3699. Leads summit climbs on Mt. Hood; instruction available for snow, ice, and rock-climbing.

Valhalla Adventures. Seattle, WA (206) 782-3767. Guided mountaineering and climbing trips into the Cascades, the Olympics, and Canadian mountains.

Vertical Ventures. (541) 389-7937. Climbing instruction at Smith Rock.

Hiking & Backpacking

Adventure Trails Northwest. Seattle, WA (206) 671-5711. Custom hiking trips.

Destination Wilderness. Sisters, OR 1-888-423-8868 or (541) 383-1900. Guided hiking/backpacking trips; outdoor skills training.

Oregon Ridge & River Excursions. Glide, OR 1-888-454-9696 or (541) 496-3333. Hiking trips in the Umpqua National Forest.

Rogue Wilderness, Inc. Merlin, OR 1-800-336-1647 or (541) 479-9554. Half to 4-day hiking trips in the Rogue River region.

Windsurfing

Adventure Out. Hood River, OR (541) 387-4626. Windsurfing trips.

Hood River Windsurfing. Hood River, OR (541) 386-5787. Windsurfing instruction, beginner to advanced.

Rhonda Smith Windsurfing Center. Hood River, OR (541) 386-9463. Windsurfing instruction, beginner to advanced; windsurfing vacations.

Sail World. Hood River Hood River, OR (541) 386-9400. Windsurfing instruction, beginner to advanced.

Rafting

Allrivers Adventures. (Wenatchee Whitewater & Co) Cashmere, WA 1-800-743-5628 or (509) 782-2254. One to 3-day, guided rafting trips in OR and WA; instruction.

All Star Rafting & Kayaking. 1-800-909-7238 or (503) 235-3663. Rafting trips; instruction and equipment available.

Arrowhead River Adventures. Eagle Point, OR 1-800-227-7741 or (541) 830-3388. Guided rafting trips.

Bend Whitewater Supply. Bend, OR (541) 389-7191. Guided rafting trips.

C&J Lodge Whitewater Rafting. Maupin, OR 1-800-395-3903 or (541) 395-2404. Guided rafting trips down the Deschutes John Day, and Grande Ronde rivers; lodging.

Cooley River Expeditions, Inc. Albany, OR (541) 926-7252. Guided rafting trips.

Dave Helfrich River Outfitter, Inc. Vida, OR (541) 896-3786. One to 6-day combination rafting, inflatable-kayaking, and fishing trips; single sport trips available.

Deschutes Whitewater Services. Maupin, OR (541) 395-2232 or (541) 395-2639. Guided rafting trips down the Deschutes River.

Destination Wilderness. Sisters, OR 1-888-423-8868 or (541) 383-1900. Guided raft and cataraft trips; instruction available.

DMJ Consulting/Guide. Scappoose, OR (503) 543-5119. Guided raft and cataraft trips; instruction available.

Ewings' Whitewater. Maupin, OR 1-800-538-7238 or (541) 395-2697. Combination trips: mountain biking along the Gorge; rafting down the Deschutes.

Fantastic Adventures. Bend, OR (541) 389-5640. Guided rafting trips.

Ferron's Fun Trips. Merlin, OR 1-800-404-2201 or (541) 474-2201. Guided rafting, inflatable-kayaking, and fishing trips; on a smaller, more intimate scale.

Fishawk River Company. Brookings, OR (541) 469-2422. Guided rafting trips; interpretive trips.

Galice Resorts. Merlin, OR (541) 476-3818. Half-day and day trips down the Rogue River; lodging.

Helfrich River Outfitters. Eugene, OR (541) 741-1905. Guided rafting trips down the Rogue, Salmon, and McKenzie rivers.

Hells Canyon Adventures, Inc. Oxbow, OR 1-800-422-3568 or (541) 785-3352. Guided rafting trips down the Snake River of Hells Canyon; interpretive trips.

Inn of the Seventh Mountain. Bend, OR (541) 382-8711, ext. 601. Rafting trips down the Big Eddy run; lodging.

Jim's Oregon Whitewater. McKenzie Bridge, OR 1-800-254-5467 or (541) 822-6003. One to 5-day, guided rafting trips.

Lone Wolf Expeditions. Beaverton, OR 1-800-515-9653 or (503) 643-8469. Guided rafting trips; instruction available.

McKenzie River Rafting Company. Eugene, OR (541) 726-6078. Guided rafting trips.

Noah's River Adventure Float Trips. Ashland, OR 1-800-858-2811 or (541) 488-2811. Guided half-day to 3-day rafting trips in the Rogue River Canyon.

Orange Torpedo Trips. Grants Pass, OR 1-800-635-2925 or (541) 479-5061. Guided raft and inflatable kayak trips; national and international.

Oregon Ridge & River Excursions. Glide, OR 1-888-454-9696 or (541) 496-3333. Rafting trips in the Umpqua National Forest.

Oregon River Expeditions. Lake Oswego, OR. 1-800-827-1358 or (503) 697-8133. Guided raft and cataraft trips; interpretive trips; instruction available.

Oregon Whitewater Adventures. Eugene, OR 1-800-820-7238. Guided rafting trips.

Ouzel Outfitters. Bend, OR. 1-800-788-7238 or (541) 385-5947. Guided rafting trips; interpretive trips; instruction available.

Rapid River Rafters. 1-800-962-3327 or (541) 382-1514. Guided rafting trips.

River Trips Unlimited. Medford, OR 1-800-460-3865 or (541) 779-3798. Guided rafting trips down the Rogue River.

Rogue River Outfitters. Gold Beach, OR 1-888-420-6585 or (541) 247-2684. Guided rafting trips down the Rogue River.

Rogue River Raft Trips. Merlin, OR 1-800-826-1963 or (541) 476-3825. Three and 4-day, guided rafting trips down the Rogue River.

Rogue Wilderness, Inc. Merlin, OR 1-800-336-1647 or (541) 479-9554. Half to 4-day rafting trips down the Rogue River.

Rogue/Klamath River Adventures. 1-800-231-0769 or (541) 779-3708. Guided rafting trips down the Rogue and Klamath rivers.

Siskiyou Adventures, Inc. Ashland, OR 1-800-250-4602 or (541) 488-1632. Guided rafting trips down the Rogue and Applegate rivers.

Steens Mountain Packers. Frenchglen, OR 1-800-977-3995 or (541) 495-2315. Guided rafting trips.

Sun Country Tours/Cascade River Adventures. Bend, OR 1-800-770-2161 or (541) 382-6277. Guided rafting trips down the Deschutes River.

Sundance Kayak School & Rafting Expeditions. Merlin, OR (541) 479-8508. Guided rafting trips.

The Adventure Center. Ashland, OR 1-800-444-2819 or (541) 488-2819. Guided rafting trips down 9 different rivers.

Whitewater Warehouse. Corvallis, OR 1-800-214-0579 or (541) 758-3150. Guided rafting trips, primarily down the Rogue River.

Wilderness River Outfitters. Springfield, OR (541) 726-9471. One to 5-day, guided rafting trips in Oregon and Idaho; also a moonlight float.

Wy-East Expeditions. Mount Hood, OR (541) 352-6457. Guided rafting trips down the Deschutes River.

Whale Watching

Bay Front Charters (Newport Sportfishing). Newport, OR 1-800-828-8777 or (541) 265-7558. Chartered whale-watching trips out of Yaquina Bay.

Garibaldi/D&D Charters. Garibaldi, OR 1-800-900-4665 or (503) 322-0007. Chartered whale-watching trips out of Tillamook Bay.

Dockside Charters. Depoe Bay, OR 1-800-733-8915 or (541) 765-2545. Chartered whale-watching trips out of Depoe Bay.

Marine Discovery Tours. Newport, OR 1-800-903-2628 or (541) 265-6200. Marine life and estuary tours out of Yaquina Bay.

Tradewinds. Depoe Bay, OR 1-800-445-8730 or (541) 765-2345. Marine life and estuary tours out of Depoe Bay.

Troller Charters. Garibaldi, OR 1-800-546-3666 or (503) 322-3666. Chartered whale-watching trips out of Tillamook Bay.

Diving

Doug's Diving. Garibaldi, OR (503) 322-2200. Guided diving trips out of Tillamook Bay; instruction and equipment available.

Emerald Seas Dive Center. San Juan, WA (360) 378-2772. Dive boat charters; instruction and equipment available.

Garibaldi Aqua Sports. Garibaldi, OR (503) 322-0113. Dive instruction; can arrange charters.

Newport Waters Sports. Newport, OR (541) 867-3742. Dive boat charters; instruction and equipment available.

Kayaking & Canoeing

Allrivers Adventures (Wenatchee Whitewater & Co). Cashmere, WA 1-800-743-5628 or (509) 782-2254. Guided kayaking and tubing trips in OR and WA; instruction.

All Star Rafting & Kayaking. 1-800-909-7238 or (503) 235-3663. Guided kayaking trips; instruction and equipment available.

Arrowhead River Adventures. Eagle Point, OR 1-800-227-7741 or (541) 830-3388. Guided kayaking trips.

Bend Whitewater Supply. Bend, OR (541) 389-7191. Guided canoe and kayak trips; kayaking instruction.

C&J Lodge Whitewater Rafting. Maupin, OR 1-800-395-3903 or (541) 395-2404. Guided kayaking trips down the Deschutes John Day, and Grande Ronde rivers; lodging.

Destination Wilderness. Sisters, OR 1-888-423-8868 or (541) 383-1900. Guided kayaking trips.

Hood River Outfitters. Hood River, OR (541) 386-6202. Kayaking and canoeing instruction.

Lone Wolf Expeditions. Beaverton, OR 1-800-515-9653 or (503) 643-8469. Guided canoeing trips; instruction available.

Nehalem Bay Kayak Company. Wheeler, OR (503) 368-6055. Guided kayaking trips along Oregon's north coast.

Orange Torpedo Trips. Grants Pass, OR 1-800-635-2925 or (541) 479-5061. Guided raft and inflatable kayak trips; national and international.

Oregon Ridge & River Excursions. Glide, OR 1-888-454-9696 or (541) 496-3333. Guided lake kayaking and canoeing trips in the Umpqua National Forest.

Siskiyou Adventures. Ashland, OR 1-800-250-4602 or (541) 488-1632. Guided kayaking trips on the Rogue and Applegate rivers.

Siskiyou Kayak School. 1-800-571-3311 or (541) 772-9743. Kayaking instruction and tours.

Solitude River Trips. Merlin, OR 1-800-396-1776 or (541) 476-1876. Guided kayaking trips on Idaho's Middle Fork of the Salmon River; instruction available.

Sundance Kayak School & Rafting Expeditions. Merlin, OR (541) 479-8508. Kayaking instruction, beginner to advanced; trips available.

Whitewater Warehouse. Corvallis, OR 1-800-214-0579. Kayaking instruction, beginner to advanced; trips available.

Wy-East Expeditions. Mount Hood, OR (541) 352-6457. Guided canoeing trips.

Boating

Fishawk River Company. Brookings, OR (541) 469-2422. Jet boat tours; interpretive trips.

Jerry's Rogue Jet Boat Tours. Gold Beach, OR 1-800-451-3645 or (541) 247-4571. Eco tours on the Rogue River; lodging.

Jot's Resort. Gold Beach, OR (541) 247-6676. Jet boat tours up the Rogue River; lodging.

McKenzie Pontoon Trips (Helfrich River Outfitters). Eugene, OR (541) 741-1905. Pontoon trips down the McKenzie River.

Fishing

Allrivers Adventures (Wenatchee Whitewater & Co). Cashmere, WA 1-800-743-5628 or (509) 782-2254. Guided fishing trips in OR and WA.

Arrowhead River Adventures. Eagle Point, OR 1-800-227-7741 or (541) 830-3388. Guided fishing trips.

Bay Front Charters (Newport Sportfishing). Newport, OR 1-800-828-8777 or (541) 265-7558. Charter boat, deep-sea fishing out of Yaquina Bay.

Betty Kay Charters. Charleston, OR 1-800-752-6303 or (541) 888-9021. Charter boat, deep-sea fishing out of Coos Bay.

Bob Brown's Guided Sport Fishing. Tillamook, OR (503) 842-9696. Guided bay and coastal river fishing trips.

Bob's Sport Fishing. Charleston, OR 1-800-628-9633 or (541) 888-4241. Charter boat, deep-sea fishing out of Coos Bay.

Dave Helfrich River Outfitter, Inc. Vida, OR (541) 896-3786. One to 6-day guided fishing trips on various local rivers; combination rafting trips available.

DMJ Consulting/Guide. Scappoose, OR (503) 543-5119. Guided fishing trips; instruction available.

Dockside Charters. Depoe Bay, OR 1-800-733-8915 or (541) 765-2545. Charter boat, deep-sea fishing out of Depoe Bay.

Doug's Diving. Garibaldi, OR (503) 322-2200. Spear-fishing and crabbing in Tillamook Bay; instruction and equipment available.

Ferron's Fun Trips. Merlin, OR 1-800-404-2201 or (541) 474-2201. Rafting, inflatable-kayaking, and fishing trips; on a smaller, more intimate scale.

Garibaldi/D&D Charters. Garibaldi, OR 1-800-900-4665 or (503) 322-0007. Charter boat, deep-sea fishing out of Tillamook Bay.

Geoff's Guide Service. (541) 474-0602. Guided fishing trips on the Rogue River.

Glenn Summers Outfitters. (541) 296-5949. Guided fishing trips.

Gorge Fly Shop. Hood River, OR 1-800-685-7309, pin# 1019 or (541) 386-6977. One to 5-day, guided fishing trips on local rivers; scenic tours, full-service shop.

Harvey Young Fishing (Fishawk River Company). Brookings, OR (541) 469-2422. Guided fishing trips.

Helfrich River Outfitters. Eugene, OR (541) 741-1905. Guided fishing trips on various local rivers, including the Rogue, Salmon, and McKenzie rivers.

Hells Canyon Adventures, Inc. Oxbow, OR 1-800-422-3568 or (541) 785-3352. Guided fishing trips on the Snake River of Hells Canyon; interpretive trips.

High Desert Drifters Guides & Outfitters, Inc. Bend, OR 1-800-685-3474 or (541) 389-0607. Guided fishing trips on the Deschutes River; instruction and equipment.

Jerry Q. Phelps. (541) 672-8324. Guided fishing trips on the North Umpqua River.

Jim's Oregon Whitewater. McKenzie Bridge, OR 1-800-254-5467 or (541) 822-6003. Guided fishing trips on the McKenzie and Deschutes rivers.

John Garrison Guide Service. Sun River, OR (541) 593-8394. Guided spin and fly-fishing trips on local lakes and rivers.

Jot's Resort. Gold Beach, OR (541) 247-6676. Guided fishing trips on the Rogue River; boat rentals and supplies; lodging.

Larry Levine's River Wolf Guide Service. (541) 496-0326. Guided fishing trips on the North Umpqua River.

Lone Wolf Expeditions. Beaverton, OR 1-800-515-9653 or (503) 643-8469. Guided fishing trips.

Mike's Guide Service. Cascade Locks, OR (541) 374-2228. Guided fishing trips.

Noah's River Adventure Float Trips. Ashland, OR 1-800-858-2811 or (541) 488-2811. Guided fishing trips in the Rogue River Canyon.

Northwest Guide Service. Skamania, WA (509) 427-4625. Guided fishing trips on the Columbia River; some lake fishing.

Rippling Brook Flies. (503) 362-0624. Guided fly-fishing trips.

River Trips Unlimited. Medford, OR 1-800-460-3865 or (541) 779-3798. Guided fishing trips on the Rogue River.

Rogue River Outfitters. Gold Beach, OR 1-888-420-6585 or (541) 247-2684. Guided fishing trips; drift fishing on the Rogue River.

Rogue River Raft Trips. Merlin, OR 1-800-826-1963 or (541) 476-3825. Guided fishing trips on the Rogue River.

Rogue Wilderness, Inc. Merlin, OR 1-800-336-1647 or (541) 479-9554. Half to 4-day fishing trips on the Rogue River.

Shamrock Charters (out of Jot's Resort). Gold Beach, OR (541) 247-6676. Charter boat, deep-sea fishing.

Siggi-G Ocean Charters. Garibaldi, OR (503) 322-3285. Charter boat, deep-sea fishing out of Tillamook Bay.

Solitude River Trips. Merlin, OR 1-800-396-1776 or (541) 476-1876. Guided fishing trips on Idaho's Middle Fork of the Salmon River; instruction available.

Steve Beyerlin's Southern Oregon River Tours. Gold Beach, OR 1-800-348-4138 or (541) 247-4138. Guided fishing trips on the Rogue, Elk, Chetco, and Sixes rivers.

Summer Run Guide Service. Roseburg, OR (541) 496-3037. Guided fly-fishing trips on the North Umpqua River.

Sunriver Outfitters. Sunriver, OR (541) 593-8814. Guided fly-fishing trips on nearby lakes and streams; rentals and instruction available.

The Adventure Center. Ashland, OR 1-800-444-2819 or (541) 488-2819. Guided fishing trips in Southern Oregon.

The Caddis Fly Angling Shop. Eugene, OR (541) 342-7005. Guided fly-fishing trips on nearby lakes and streams; rentals and instruction available.

The Fly Box. Bend, OR (541) 388-3330. Guided fly-fishing trips on nearby lakes and streams; rentals and instruction available.

The Fly Fishing Shop. Welches, OR (503) 622-4607. Guided fishing trips on various local rivers and lakes, including the Sandy and Deschutes rivers; full-service shop.

The Patient Angler Fly Shop. Bend, OR (541) 389-6208. Guided fly-fishing trips on nearby lakes and streams; 1- 7-day excursions; rentals and instruction available.

Todd Hannah Charters. Winchester Bay, OR 1-800-428-8585 or (541) 584-2277. Charter boat, deep-sea fishing out of Winchester Bay.

Tradewinds. Depoe Bay, OR 1-800-445-8730 or (541) 765-2345. Charter fishing and crabbing trips out of Depoe Bay.

Troller Charters. Garibaldi, OR 1-800-546-3666 or (503) 322-3666. Charter boat, deep-sea fishing out of Tillamook Bay.

Wilderness River Outfitters. Springfield, OR (541) 726-9471. One to 5-day, guided fishing trips.

Wy-East Expeditions. Mount Hood, OR (541) 352-6457. Guided fishing trips.

Young's Fishing Service. The Dalles, OR 1-800-270-7962 or (541) 296-5371. Guided fishing trips, mostly on the Columbia River; jet boat or drift.

Thrills by Air

Aero West Aviation. Troutdale, OR (503) 661-4940. Charter flights over Mt. St. Helens, the Columbia Gorge, the coast, etc.

Multi-Sport Adventures

High Desert Outfitters, Inc. Adel, OR (541) 947-5526. Horsepack trips, hunting, fishing, cross-country skiing, and hiking trips in southeastern Oregon.

Hood River Trails. Hood River, OR 1-800-979-4453 or (541) 387-2000. Week-long, 6-sport, multi-adventure trips; custom trips also available.

Inn of the Seventh Mountain. Bend, OR (541) 382-8711, ext. 601. Rafting, hiking, mountain biking, canoeing, and horseback riding trips at the inn.

A

B

C

356

L

M

T

U

V

W

Meet the Author

Lizann Dunegan has spent the last 10 years hiking the trails of Oregon's diverse landscapes. Lizann was introduced to hiking by her partner Ken Skeen and went on to fine-tune her outdoor skills when she completed a basic mountaineering course given by Mazamas, a Portland based mountaineering club, in 1990. Since that time, Lizann has climbed Mount St. Helens, Mount Hood, Three Fingered Jack, South Sister, Middle Sister, and many other Oregon peaks and has explored hundreds of trails throughout the state. For the past nine years, Lizann has worked as a free-lance writer and photographer and has published several outdoor- and agricultural-related articles and stories for *Weekend Sports Magazine*, *Oregon Cycling*, *The Oregonian*, *Sheep! Magazine*, and *The Ranch Dog Trainer*. In 1998 she published her first guidebook, *Mountain Bike America: Oregon*. For the past five years, Lizann has also worked as a technical writer for a Beaverton-based software company. Lizann also enjoys mountain biking, trail running, and cross-country skiing and is often accompanied by her two fun-loving Border collies, Levi and Sage, and her trail partner Ken Skeen. When she isn't out of town exploring Oregon's scenic trails, she enjoys reading, playing the cello, and spinning and dyeing wool.